Truth Matters

A Verse-by Verse Explanation of
Romans for Serious Bible Students

JIM ANDREWS

Truth Matters

A Verse-by-Verse Explanation of Romans for Serious Bible Students

JIM ANDREWS

Studio of Books LLC
5900 Balcones Drive Suite 100
Austin, Texas 78731
www.studioofbooks.org
Hotline: (254) 800-1183

Ordering Information:
Special discounts are available on quantity purchases by corporations, associations, and others. For details, contact the publisher at the address above.

Printed in the United States of America.

ISBN-13:   Softcover   978-1-968491-89-5
              eBook   978-1-968491-90-1

Table of Contents

Dedication

To Olsie, my wife of now sixty-five years, who loves Christ and the Scriptures more than just about anyone I know. She has long insisted that I finally publish my Romans classroom notes for the benefit of others when we are gone. Our marriage has endured so long because I learned ages ago to say, "Yes, dear."

Preface

In my classics program at the University of Colorado (Boulder), I was once taking a Latin course reading the Roman poet, Horace. In one session, our professor was lyricizing Horace when he offered that if he were consigned to a lonely island somewhere and could only have one book to take with him, that book would be the *Odes and Epodes of Horace.*

On Horace, I myself was not that sanguine. In that same circumstance, my own choice would be starkly different. Of the vast array of tomes available to modern man, none can compare with the Bible as the ultimate resource for true knowledge and divine wisdom. Were my choices limited, however, to only one biblical document, hands down, it would be Paul's *Epistle to the Romans*.

Not because it is more inspired than the other sixty-five books in the biblical corpus, but simply because, of all the books in the Bible, it is, to my mind, at least, the most *fundamental* to our Christian faith. By that assessment, I mean that in it, the apostle brilliantly expounds in its fullest sense the gospel in its indicatives (what God has done for us in Christ) and imperatives (and what we should do in response for Christ). So engaging (to me) is its tightly logical literary structure and a litany of issues that still resonant today with a plethora of timeless principles of Christian theology and practice that I consider, as do many, Romans the crown jewel of biblical literature and revelation.

As much as I admire the work of (sound) Christian theologians, ancient and modern, I personally would not trade all of them put together for the Gospel of John, the Epistle to the Romans, and the Epistle to the Hebrews, but of these three, if I had to choose just one, I would take Romans as my pick of "the litter," so to speak.

Because I so resonate with this great document, I naturally have studied it more intensely than any other biblical document over the course of my ministry. Also, I have had a sentimental attachment to it since right out of seminary in my first pastorate; Romans was the first book I attempted to expound. Seven years later, when I accepted a teaching position at (then) Western Bible College (Denver), one of my assigned courses (providentially) was teaching Romans. Thereafter, every fall for my ten-year tenure there, I taught Romans to approximately seventy to eighty students total between two sections that met at 7 a.m. and 8 a.m., respectively.

Despite the early hours, I think most students looked forward to their Romans class. To my recollection, the only student I ever recall dozing off a bit was a poor guy who worked nights and had the misfortune to be signed up for this early challenge. To this day, I still occasionally hear from students who have transforming memories of that class.

Whatever their take, I myself thoroughly enjoyed my expeditions through this monument of Pauline theology. It shaped my own theology, as well it should. I loved the challenge of tracking Paul's nuanced thought, always trying to fine-tune my grasp on his concepts and his argument. Others may have done it better, but nobody ever enjoyed it more.

As I did so, over the years, an unintended "commentary" gradually took shape until, finally, it was expanded to the tune of maybe 600 pages. For years, the manuscript (like certain others) has been lying around unmolested in my office, begging for love and attention while I spent my time studying and writing other things. Ashamed of my neglect of my love, I decided recently that the next thing I must do before my meter expires is round this manuscript into shape as a formal commentary.

On my shelves, as you might expect, are many, many commentaries and more on the epistle to the Romans than any other. Some are very scholarly (and technical), and some are better suited to the lay student than the professional academic. All are useful, depending upon the need. In my sights, however, are not stuffy academics but serious Bible students who just want a more knowledgeable teacher to lead them verse by verse through Romans, carefully tracing out the argument (where there is polemic) and elucidating and apply the text. I myself think this commentary does that very well, but you, the user, will have to judge that for yourself.

It had been years since I last looked at my manuscript, so not everything was still fresh in my mind. So, when I started editing, something surprised me. As I told my wife, "Honey, this is weird. Believe it or not, my own commentary is enlightening me and opening up the epistle afresh!" She laughed.

Maybe that was because I am older and possibly losing a few of my marbles, but I would prefer to think that effect was because the Spirit really had helped me understand this epistle better and deeper than I realized at the time. Anyway, it occurred to me that if, after all the years I spent teaching this book and writing this commentary, it still enlightens *me*, then surely its contents ought to be helpful to many less experienced students of Romans.

I would hope so because, as I have always said, anybody who gets a good grip on the theology of Romans has a firm grip on apostolic Christianity, both in terms of what we ought to believe and how we ought to behave. Of those perspectives, this epistle is the epicenter.

A word about features of the commentary. I am a teacher, and good teachers, I have found, are often deliberately redundant. There used to be (maybe still is) an old saying in the advertising world, "Six and it sticks." Romans, in its first 11 chapters, is largely a polemic. In his argumentation, Paul is quite logical, but the turns in his logic can be subtle at times or elliptical (depending on the reader to supply the unstated but rather obvious) in context.

I am all about accuracy (and relevancy) in interpretation and clarity in exposition. Thus, I try very hard in this commentary (as does Paul in his treatise) to keep the reader on the train before it leaves the station, maybe overly so. Because so much gets skewed when we miss his point (e.g., in Romans 7), I bend over backward in my exposition to help the reader track.

If you are a quick study, I apologize in advance. As a teacher, however, my sights are not focused on the top ten percent but the ordinary serious-minded reader who probably needs more of a helping (repetitive) hand.

If this commentary proves valuable to you, all my labor is well worth it. And if it doesn't, there is a wealth of alternative resources that might serve you better.

Introduction

The Author
Paul the Apostle, a.k.a. Saul, a Jew of the Pharisee sect and a former persecutor of the Church and enemy of Christ.

The Date and Occasion of Writing
From Romans 15:25, we are able to place the time of writing toward the end of Paul's third missionary journey. It was apparently composed at the port of Cenchrea, near Corinth, as Paul prepared to evacuate Greece en route to Jerusalem.

Using information in Acts 18 and the dates of the consulship of Gallio as a reference point (AD 53–54), we can fix the time of writing around AD 57.

The Purpose of the Epistle
One must infer it from the contents since it is not explicitly stated.

It is clear that Paul had long aspired to minister in the Capitol itself. He felt a sense of obligation to proclaim the gospel there also. Hindered so far in his plans to come to Rome, Paul seized the moment to proclaim in writing the gospel that, so far, he had been unable to preach in person.

At this time, the main opposition to the gospel emanated from the Jewish community. His purpose seems to have been mainly apologetic, that is, to explain the gospel in such a way as to neutralize what were, by now, familiar objections of the Jewish opponents of his messages. At the same time, he hoped to firm up the faith of Christians under siege and encourage them to live in a manner consistent with the mercies and character of God.

Alongside his passion for the gospel was a profound concern for unbelieving Israel and a desire on his part to exonerate the faithlessness of God from any inference that He had defaulted on His promises to Israel (if Paul's preaching was true).

The Theme of the Epistle

It is stated fully in Romans 1:16–17. The gospel is the power of God for salvation for all who believe it because in it is revealed the righteousness of God, which is based on faith.

Outline of the Epistle to the Romans

I. The Divine Plan of Salvation (1:1–8:39)
  A. Introduction (1:1–15)
  B. The Power of the Gospel for Salvation (1:16–17)
  C. The Universal Need of the Gospel (1:18–3:20)
  D. The Divine Provision for Justification [i.e., for the penalty of sin] (3:21–5:21)
  E. The Divine Provision for Sanctification [i.e., for the power of sin] (6:1–8:39)

II. The Divine Plan for Israel (9:1–11:36)
  A. The Tragedy of Israel's Unbelief Lamented (9:1–5)
  B. The Faithfulness of Israel's God Defended (9:6–29)
  C. Israel's Guilt Exposed (9:30–10:21)
  D. The Eventual Recovery of Israel Anticipated (11:1–33)
  E. Praise of God's Wisdom (11:33–36)

III. The Divine Prescription for Christian Living (12:1–15:13)
  A. Exhortations concerning Devotion to Service (12:1–2)
  B. Exhortations concerning Spiritual Gifts (12:3–8)
  C. Exhortations concerning Social Relations (12:9–21)
  D. Exhortations concerning Civil Authority (13:1–7)
  E. Exhortations concerning the Duty of Love (13:8–10)
  F. Exhortations concerning the Armor of Light (13:11–14)
  G. Exhortations concerning Conflicting Consciences (14:1–15:4)
  H. Exhortations concerning Christian Unity (15:5–13)

IV. Personal Words to the Roman Church (15:14–16:27)
  A. His Apostolic Agenda (15:14–22)
  B. His Personal Plans (15:23–29)
  C. His Prayer Requests (15:30–33)
  D. His Commendation of a Fellow Worker (16:1–2)
  E. His Greetings to Fellow Christians in Rome (16:3–16)

Romans Chapter 1

Salutation

In this opening section, verses 1–7 constitute a salutation or greeting. The format is a creative variation of the conventional format of the time.

Whereas a modern letter might begin with the greeting, "Dear John," in Greco-Roman times, the customary format was a terse "Philogus to Demetrius" greeting. (Compare Acts 23:26: "Claudius Lysias unto the most excellent governor Felix, greetings.")

Paul's salutation here and elsewhere in the NT follows that pattern in its essentials—for example, the sender's identity, the recipients' name, and a greeting—but typically expands all three.

His habit is noteworthy. Paul typically uses his greetings to get a jump start on his pastoral burdens. These amplified greetings are by no means an exercise in pious verbosity. Every phrase is calculated... every word counts. Nothing is filler... every thought has a good reason for being there. Somehow, each idea serves a purpose relevant to his apostolic focus.

Embedded in his salutations often are keynotes of his epistles. Almost immediately, in germinal form, he starts pulling the chains that ring his bells. It's as if he can't wait to start scratching where his heart itches.

In this instance, for example, every expansion beyond the conventional component of his greeting carries theological freight, which serves his purpose. Note, for instance, how (in a compressed way) his greeting affirms the validity of his mission and message to the Gentiles. In tight verbal strokes, he offers his credentials (i.e., his right to be heard), affirms the integrity of his message (i.e., his right to be believed), highlights its great theme (Jesus Christ), elaborates the majesty and mandate of his Master, and celebrates the great dignity his Gentile readers share with him and other saints while hailing the pervasive report of their firmness in the faith.

Let's consider some of the specific features of his greeting that are especially significant and striking.

(1:1) *Paul, a bond-servant of Christ Jesus, called as an apostle, set apart for the gospel of God...*

Initially, he presents his apostolic credentials. He identifies himself as "a bondservant (slave) of Christ Jesus." That self-description testifies to his total voluntary submission to our Lord. It serves double duty to underscore his sense of accountability to Christ as His apostolic representative in the Church.

Two features of his credentials call for comment—its format and its position.

1) The format corresponds to the way OT prophets were identified. The analogy is undoubtedly intentional. The apostle meant by this device to align himself and his message with the OT prophets.[1] Yet note how instead of "servant of the Lord," he writes "servant of Christ Jesus." By this subtle substitution, he implies the interchangeability of the two names.[2] Jesus Christ *is* Yahweh of the OT incarnate (revealed historically in union of real humanity).

2) In tendering the fact of his awesome accountability ahead of his apostolic authority, he underscores a personal perspective that restrained in the apostle the undertow of corruption so regularly evident in the exercise of unfettered power.

But let us not misunderstand his unabashed revelry in his bondage to Christ. The apostle is not a religious masochist. "Slave," it has been noted, does not define the *spirit* of his service to Christ; rather, it defines the scope of his joyous, voluntary self-surrender to His master—in all times and in every way, he is a voluntary slave of Jesus Christ. What a model for us all! His is not a cheerless bondage to God but an unreserved, happy submission to His will. The magnitude—plus the magnanimity of his Master—lends honor to all His servants; call it, if you will, *guilt* by association. The tighter the bond between servant and Master, the greater the glory of the servant.

You see, the onerousness of a life of servitude does not lie in having a master as such. What makes servitude slavery in the bad sense is the humiliation and burden of being forced to serve and grovel before another human being no better than oneself, perhaps not even as capable nor as virtuous. But one should feel no shame nor be considered a fool who is wise enough to humbly and voluntarily surrender his being to One infinitely superior who also happens to be immeasurably loving and gracious.

Inherent in that proud surrender is the resignation of self. As a slave of Christ Jesus, one is obliged to have no will but His, to pursue no goals but Christ's, and to covet no honor but the Savior's. A slave will not upstage His Lord but is content in the shadows to advance His interests. Once, an enormously wealthy businessman in another state confessed to me over the phone, "Jimmy, I don't know what I am in the world for." A week and a half later, another businessman in my church told me in my office that he was having trouble figuring out just what it was God wanted of him. Well, he wants you and me to give ourselves unconditionally to Him, to be what He has called us to be (disciples), to do what He wants us to do (be light in the world), and to go where He wants us to go (wherever the Spirit leads us).

If the apostle is accountable to God, he also has authority from God. His authority resides in His divine commission. He is "*a called apostle.*" "Called" here means "divinely commissioned,"[3] not self-appointed. Many in all ages have gone out ostensibly in the name of Christ, but God has not called them. They ran, but He did not send them (Jer. 23:21). They had their own agenda, not His. And so it is to this day and ever shall be until the Lord returns and sorts it all out. Though Paul is related to Christ as a servant, he is a servant vested with official power.[4][5] As such, he has been set apart for the task of heralding the gospel (good news), originating with God Himself.

In describing himself as a messenger handpicked by God Himself and entrusted with a divine message, His message admits of no modification. The options are belief or disbelief. It's of God, or it isn't. Paul leaves no middle ground. Either he and his message are divinely accredited, or he is an impostor and his message a fraud.

Of interest in connection with his apostolic calling to the gospel ministry is the word "set apart for..." (verse 1). The perfect tense of the Greek participle here implies Paul was reserved by God for this labor long before his actual commission transpired. (See also Jer. 1:5: "Before I formed you in the womb I knew you, and before you were born I consecrated you.")

How strange that today, some find it quaint to propose that God still raises up special people, specially equipped, for special tasks! And what work would be more special to His divine heart than the redemption of His elect? Why would God abolish a pattern of selectivity so evident throughout the history of revelation?[6]

(1:2) *Which He promised beforehand through His prophets in the holy Scriptures...*

Now, his salutatory focus shifts from the messenger and his credentials to the message and its critical center. The apostle has a special concern. He and his Jewish opponents occupied shared ground where the OT was concerned. The OT, all agreed, was the repository of divine revelation in objective, propositional form. Any deviation from that standard was, by definition, exposed as false. So, it was crucial to Paul to stress the continuity and consistency of his message with the OT revelation. Hence, right up front, he begins to counter this anticipated objection. This "gospel or good news of God" is, contrary to what his Jewish opponents alleged, no sectarian aberration. The gospel of Jesus Christ, far from any deviation from the older revelation, is but the climax of prophetic revelation. His message is no religious novelty but actually the fulfillment of a salvation long ago predicted by the OT prophets in the sacred writings. So, the gospel represents a climax and closure, not a departure.

The OT prophecies the apostle had in mind no doubt included those anticipating the New Covenant (Jer. 31:31–34; 32:40; Ezek. 37:26ff) as well as Messianic prophecies like Isaiah 53.

Note the focal point of the gospel. "His Son" (verse 3) stands out like a beacon in the night. Paul reaches into the heart of his message and puts his finger on the critical center—the *sine qua non* ("without which nothing") of his proclamation.

The gospel does not concern a new ethical system, though a new ethical system should be a by-product of it. The gospel is not concerned with the establishment of a new religion or philosophy, though religion and philosophy both take new directions in response to it. In the final analysis, the gospel concerns *His Son.*[7] It is not, first of all, about ethics or religion but about a person. His worth, His work, and His will all have ramifications in matters ethical and religious. The two go together. A commitment to the latter (Christian ethics) without faith in the former (Christ Jesus our Lord and Savior) will be as useless and non-viable as a tree severed from its roots.

(1:3) *Concerning His Son, who was born of the seed of David according to the flesh...*

Having focalized "His Son" as the critical core of the gospel message, Paul now amplifies upon the mystery and magnitude of this One whose Person and Work are the foundations of the good news.

This One whom he has identified as the Son of God is further described by a well-known and critical Messianic qualification, that is, one "who was born (lit., "became" = *genomai)* of the seed (descendants) of David."[8]

Worth noting is the verb "became" in this context. While it is sometimes used of being born, it is not the expected verb. Here it may be employed in conjunction with the previous mention of His Sonship to suggest that He was God's Son before He became David's.

The modifying phrase "according to the flesh" stands in contrast to its parallel in verse 4, "according to the Spirit of holiness." The former phrase is obviously intended to qualify in some manner the assertion that "His Son... became (or was made or born) of the seed of David." David refers to ancient King David. Davidic descendancy was a crucial credential for the Messiah or Savior predicted by the prophets. In making this point early, Paul shows his interest in this epistle to establish the continuity of revelation, the harmony between the testimony of the OT prophets and that of the Apostles.

As Hodge remarks, the phrase "according to the flesh"—whatever its precise meaning—certainly implies that "His Son" was more than human[9] (cf. John 1:1, 14; Col. 2:9). Otherwise, its addition would have been superfluous. In what way His exalted Being transcends his distinguished pedigree as a royal descendant of King David is elaborated in verse 4.

"According to the flesh" is ambiguous by itself, but in this context, "according to his human nature," makes the best sense, in my opinion.[10] If so, then its counterpart in verse 4, "according to the Spirit of holiness," would most likely refer to that higher aspect of his being, which transcended the merely human.[11]

(1:4) *Who was declared with power to be the Son of God by the resurrection from the dead, according to the Spirit of holiness, Jesus Christ our Lord...*

Verse 4 brings out His cosmic transcendence. Our Lord Jesus Christ was a man but more than a man. He is the very Son of God.

The interpretive issues in this verse are four: 1) the meaning of the verb translated in the NASB "declared," 2) whether the prepositional phrase "with power" modifies the verb or the predicate "Son of God," 3) the meaning of "Spirit of holiness," and 4) the import of the prepositional phrase "by the resurrection from the dead."

The Greek verb here translated "declared" is *horizo.* The word means to mark out, to limit, appoint, or determine. Then it comes to have a secondary sense of "define," as in "define" a word.[12] Does the verb here mean "appoint," or can it mean "determine" or "mark out" in the sense of "show to be"? Some, like Cranfield,[13] think the latter is improbable.

Others, however, have favored the second sense. One reason is because the former might imply adoptionism (the theory that Jesus was a mere man whom God adopted as His son; hence, not His son in essence, but by decree), a form of Christology totally at variance with Paul's (and NT) theology. Bruce and Cranfield would reject any adoptionist implication, but they still prefer "appoint"[14] or "invest"[15].

Sanday and Headlam, however, make an important point in deciding the issue:

> It is usual to propose for this word an alternative (i) "proved to be," "marked out as being"... and (ii) "appointed," "instituted," "installed,"... [Noting that this latter sense is adopted by most modern commentators, they add:] The word itself does not determine the meaning either way: it must be determined by context. But here the particular context is also neutral; so that we must look to the wider context of Paul's teaching generally (brackets mine).[16]

They (as I) prefer "designated" in the sense that by virtue of the resurrection, the Father has affirmed loudly and clearly a pre-existing reality, that Jesus Christ is His only begotten Son. This rendering seems to me to best satisfy the context. Additionally, it is, I believe, more consistent with Paul's appeal to the resurrection as the ultimate apologetic on behalf of the claims of Christ.

Thus, our Lord was "declared" in the sense of "marked out," "defined," or "designated" as uniquely the Son of God. On this understanding of the verb, "with power" is better construed adverbially (i.e., with the verb rather than the title).

So, our Lord (with respect to His Spirit or higher nature irradiated with impeccable holiness) was marked out with power (i.e., powerfully) by means of the resurrection as the Son of God. Bottom line: by means of the resurrection, the Father powerfully announces the true identity of Christ and confirms Jesus's own testimony ("I and the Father are One").

This construction seems to tally well with the context and be more straightforward than the alternative, namely, understanding the text to mean that Christ was vested *with power* as the Son of God after the resurrection mediated through the Holy Spirit.

This view, in my judgment, puts an unnatural strain upon the last two prepositional phrases and disallows (for no compelling reason) "declare" or "show to be" (in the sense of mark out or define). Besides, it breaks down the obvious contrast between the flesh and the Spirit of holiness.

(1:5) *Through whom we have received grace and apostleship to bring about the obedience of faith among all the Gentiles, for His name's sake...*

"Grace" is that unmerited favor by which we and the apostle have been saved and now he is enabled in Christ's behalf to exercise his apostolic office. He is not a free agent or religious entrepreneur. He is a man under divine orders and endowed with whatever grace (or provisions of God's gratuitous favor) is necessary to execute His will.

"To bring about the obedience of faith..." Paul means "that obedience which consists in faith."[17] This reminds us of John 6:28–29:

"They said therefore to Him, 'What shall we do, that we may work the works of God?' Jesus answered and said to them, 'This is the work of God, that you believe in Him whom He has sent.'"

Believing Christ is the core and capstone of obedience. It is the starting point, the middle, and the end. Every act of righteousness is an outburst of a conviction of the faithfulness of the Word of God revealed in Christ. Faith operates through love (Gal. 5:6), and love operates in righteousness. (1 John 5:1–3). The tap root of all godly works is inward faith. Our obedience is faith-driven, not law-driven. We are not trying to earn our salvation by law-keeping but we show gratitude for the grace of God by keeping His commandments.

"Among all the Gentiles...," the special province of the apostle by divine appointment (15:16).

"For His name's sake"... lit., on behalf of His name (i.e., glory). His ministry was not institutionalized so that its excuse was its own preservation or promotion. This was not an ego trip. He was out to make a name for Christ, not for himself. He never forgot Who he was serving. Nor should we. His name encompasses all that He is.

(1:6) *Among whom you also are the called of Jesus Christ.*

"Among whom...," that is, the Gentiles, by which phraseology he undoubtedly means that they, too, are Gentiles (as opposed to Jews living among them).

"Also the called of Jesus Christ..." We did not choose Him, Jesus reminded His disciples, but He chose us (John 15:16). Our salvation is the result of divine initiative, because of which we belong, through the grace of God, to a privileged class, to a cosmic aristocracy.

(1:7) *To all who are beloved of God in Rome, called as saints: Grace to you and peace from God our Father and the Lord Jesus Christ.*

"Beloved of God"—the ultimate asset, which eventually neutralizes every deficit, and brings victory out of every defeat. No believer can ever complain of a deficit of love, for the love of God far surpasses the love of any person or class toward us.

"Called (as) saints," that is, they were "saints by divine vocation".[18] Just as Paul enjoys the distinction of being an apostle who was *kletos* (i.e., called), so they (and we) enjoy the shared honor of being *kletos* saints... that is, those called to a life of separation to God. *Holiness is our calling.* It's that simple. We are not called to conform to the world but to separate from it—not socially but morally (Rom. 12:1–2). Separation is not the same as isolation. *Our business is not to blend in but to stand apart and stick out like a rose in a garbage bin.* For those in this position, Paul can confidently pray.

"Grace... peace" is a creative combination of conventional Greek[19] and Hebrew forms of greeting. "Grace" invites the unmerited favor of God, and "peace" begs for them the well-being and security that God gives those in Christ. Together these words "express the sum of evangelical blessings."[20] This is more than a wish; it is a blessing (the antithesis of a curse) for which they are eligible in Christ. And a blessing bestowed on the impulse of the Spirit is a form of prophecy and certain, therefore, in its fulfillment to all who are worthy (in the relative sense).

The combination of these two forms of greeting wherever they occur probably implies a mixed ethnic consistency (cf. 1 Cor. 1:3; 2 Cor. 1:2; Gal. 1:3; Eph. 1:2; Phil. 1:2; Philem. 3; 2 Thess. 1:2; Titus 1:4). Grace is the Gentile word; peace or "shalom" is the Hebrew form of blessing.

1:8–15

2. His Interest in the Roman Saints

After an expansive salutation in which he strikes some key theological notes in his preaching of the gospel, the apostle moves forward to express his deep interest in the Roman church and his long-standing desire to preach the gospel in Rome itself.[21]

There is a tendency to pass over these personalized sections on the assumption that the contents are so historicized (or particularized) that they have little relevance to any beyond the original audience. That assumption is mistaken. Passages like these (and this one is no exception) often exemplify practices, principles, and perspectives beneficial or detrimental to the life and health of a church and its individual members.

In verse 8, for instance, take note of the apostle's healthy value system (as compared to that by which a modern church gains celebrity in the eyes of contemporary Christian leaders). What moves the apostle to thanksgiving is the continual report around the Graeco-Roman world of their faith in Christ Jesus. Whether this report testifies to the *fact* of their faith or the *strength* of it is not clear—although the implication seems to be the latter. For faith to be published abroad, it must somehow flag its own existence.

The "success" of the mission Paul himself measured in strictly spiritual and moral categories. Any attributes or achievements of the churches short of its spiritual objectives would not have impressed the apostle.[22]

> (1:8) *First of all, I thank my God through Jesus Christ for you all, because your faith is being proclaimed throughout the world.*

"First of all..." The apostle occasionally anticipates a sequence of enumerated ideas, which, in the course of expansion, get reformatted in a manner different than he initially planned. (See Eph. 3:1, where he breaks off and picks up the thread again in verse 14.)

Note, too, the apostle's example in intercessory prayer. He is his own best example of the practice, which he enjoins upon all believers in Ephesians 6:18:

"With all prayer and petition pray at all times in the Spirit and with this in view, be on the alert with all perseverance and petition for all the saints..."

Why is intercession for others so important tactically in the divine scheme of things? For two reasons, at least.

1) It broadens the base of opportunity of God to enrich and enlarge our faith through petitions answered in the case of others.

2) There is something about praying for others that a) breaks down our natural self-centeredness and b) cooperates with the Holy Spirit in heightening our sensitivity toward and concern for the well-being of others.

In short, intercessory prayer is a divinely prescribed antidote for a stagnant faith and narrow self-centered life.

"Through Jesus Christ..." The apostle never loses sight of the fact—nor will he let his readers overlook it—that all benefits that accrue to the saints are *in and through Jesus Christ. Christ is the redemptive imperative.* It is because of His work that the believer is now qualified—yes, invited—to "come boldly to the throne of grace to find grace and mercy to help in time of need" (Heb. 4:12).

(1:9) *For God, whom I serve in my spirit in the preaching of the gospel of His Son, is my witness as to how unceasingly I make mention of you...*

"For God... is my witness..." This sentence underlines the sincerity of his interest in them. In case of any suspicion that his "thanksgiving" is merely *pro forma*, the apostle invokes God as witness to his heart and its relentless intercession in their behalf.[23]

Whom I serve in my spirit in the preaching of the gospel...

"Serve" here translates the Greek verb *latreuo*. *Latreuo*, a worship term, means "to discharge religious obligations, especially of a cultic (i.e., formally prescribed) nature."[24] It is more than a little significant, I judge, that the apostle uses this worship-related term of his preaching. Its usage in that context contradicts by implication those who would dichotomize worship and preaching as if two were dissimilar acts. Paul had a concept of worship (or *latreuo*) that not only *allowed* preaching as a legitimate expression of it but, in fact, *demanded* it.

And the reason is not hard to come by. For proclamation underlies all forms of veneration and is the catalyst of all our responses to God. Without proclamation, there is no adoration nor any thanksgiving nor any other responses appropriate to the greatness and goodness of our God.

Just as a car with a dead alternator can run well (albeit briefly) on energy reserves in its battery, so also a church with a moribund pulpit can appear to function normally for a while. Eventually, its worship will break down because the catalyst the Spirit uses (the proclamation of the Word) to replenish its expressions before it is depleted.

How unceasingly I make mention of you... (Cf. 1 Thess. 5:17: "Pray without ceasing.")

The Greek word for "unceasingly" is *adialeiptos*. It means "constantly" or "unceasingly."[25] Either of those meanings is relative, however, to whatever pattern a speaker or writer has in view at the time. For example, "I constantly watch classified ads for good buys" doesn't mean twenty-four hours a day without interruption but rather that "I regularly watch each day's paper for good buys."[26]

The point is important because some have inferred from this word an impossible habit, which has placed an intolerable burden on the introspective believer. "Unceasingly" does not mean an uninterrupted pattern of twenty-four-hour prayer marathons 365 days a year. To attempt to moderate this demand in the direction of reality by calling instead for a constant "attitude of prayer" is nonsense.

One is either praying or not praying, just as one is talking or not talking. There is no such thing as an attitude of prayer any more than there is an attitude of talking. All the apostle meant was that he prayed consistently for the Roman believers. They were regularly upheld before the throne of grace in his apostolic petitions.

(1:10) *if perhaps now at last by the will of God I may succeed in coming to you...*

Divine priorities had been setting his agenda. Man proposes, as the saying goes, but God disposes.

Calvin: "We may take this to mean that the Lord employed him in more urgent business, which he could not have neglected without damage to the Church."

(1:11–12) *For I long to see you in order that I may impart some spiritual gift to you, that you may be established; that is, that I may be encouraged together with you while among you, each of us by the other's faith, both yours and mine.*

How noteworthy that his desire to visit the Christians in Rome was motivated by a sense of *mutual* dependency. Though an apostle, Paul needed the stimulation of his fellow saints as much as they needed his. That perspective is wholly consistent with the metaphor of the physical body and its members (1 Cor. 12; Eph. 4:1–16) in their interdependency.

It is this attribute of body life, which lends significance to admonitions like Hebrews 10:25, "not to forsake the assembling of yourselves together, as the manner of some is." Community with other believers is a vital feature of the divine blueprint for stabilizing and enriching our faith.

John Wesley somewhere once said something like this:

"Christianity is a social religion. Whenever you make it solitary, you destroy it."[27]

You kill it because you cut its members off from that vital mutual supply necessary to maintain their spiritual health (Eph. 4:16).

The "lone ranger" believer who feels so spiritually independent that he or she can thrive spiritually without the fellowship of the body is one whose arrogance is only exceeded by his ignorance. If one no less than the Apostle felt that fellowship with the Roman church would be a boon to his own spiritual life, who are we to pretend to be so self-sufficient? Such self-sufficiency is a notorious hallmark of great spiritual deficiency.

impart some spiritual gift to you...

The reference here is not to some so-called "second work of grace," as though Paul hoped to impart some fundamental spiritual endowment which, as yet they were still wanting. For verse 12 indicates that what he had in mind was that edification is the expected and normal result of shared faith operating in love and according to the unique gifts in each believer.

(1:13) *And I do not want you to be unaware, brethren, that often I have planned to come to you (and have been prevented thus far) in order that I might obtain some fruit among you also, even as among the rest of the Gentiles.*

This note reminds us that the tendency of people to take offense and misunderstand even the best of intentions is as ancient as society itself. Satan loves to leverage that natural tendency to sow seeds of discord among brethren. The wise pastor must try to understand human nature and anticipate the breeding grounds of trouble. Paul did not want any in Rome to feel slighted by his failure to visit there. It had not been for lack of personal desire, he assures them, but rather because of precluding circumstances. Those include one principle driving his missionary agenda mentioned in 15:20, 22:

"I aspired to preach the gospel, not where Christ was already named, that I might not build upon another man's foundation...

For this reason I have often been hindered from coming to you."

Even as among the rest of the Gentiles...

This clause, along with verse 5, makes it fairly conclusive that Paul regards the Roman church as a Gentile entity, whatever the extent of its Jewish constituency.

> (1:14) *I am under obligation both to the Greeks and to the Barbarians, both to the wise and to the unwise."*

"Under obligation"—lit. "am a debtor."

Note that the apostle is obliged to these, not because of anything they have done to put him in their debt, but rather because of what God has done. God has commissioned him to carry the gospel to the Gentiles. Because God has decided to proclaim the good news to the Gentiles through Paul, in a sense, the message is something that already belongs to them (whether they claim its benefits or not). So, vested with Paul is a God-granted benefit that he "owes" to the Gentiles of every tribe. The only way he can discharge his obligation is proclamation.

Although there are various theories about the intended scope of these two divisions of mankind distinguished by Paul (see Cranfield), the naturalness of Sanday and Headlam's view is appealing. They interpret these divisions as breaking down the class of "the nations" (i.e., Gentiles) into two subsets distinguishing respectively Greek-speaking Gentiles from non-Greek-speaking nations and cultured Gentiles from non-cultured ones.[28]

> (1:15) *Thus, for my part, I am eager to preach the gospel to you also who are in Rome.*

"For my part"—that is, insofar as the decision rests with me (which personal readiness to this point has been overruled by divine direction).

To preach the gospel to you also who are in Rome...

"You" is obviously the church in Rome among whom he hopes to impart some spiritual gift (verse 11) and obtain some fruit (verse 13).

The fact that he wants to "preach the gospel to you also" is significant in two ways:

1) It indicates the error of that modern bifurcation between preaching and teaching in which the former has *unbelievers* for its proper context and the latter, *believers.*

Obviously, Paul has no intention of limiting his preaching to the believers in Rome. Certainly, his mission there as everywhere would target the unbelieving while including the believing.

2) It suggests since the preaching of the gospel is a form of nurture continually mandatory among believers, that by "gospel," Paul means all that revelation in Christ which is germane to our salvation in the past, present, and future tenses.

In other words, the gospel properly includes the whole revelation of God in Christ. As such, it embraces not only its *indicatives*, that is, all that Christ has done to accomplish our redemption, but also its *imperatives*, that is, all that we are summoned to do in response to His glory and grace. Understood in that broader Pauline perspective, it is no surprise that Paul would see the proclamation of the gospel as a matter of continuing relevance to believers as well as unbelievers.

1:16–17

The Theme of the Epistle

(1:16) *For I am not ashamed of the gospel, for it is the power of God for salvation to everyone who believes, to the Jew first and also to the Greek.*

For I am not ashamed of the gospel...
"For" introduces a conviction which accounts for his eagerness to carry the gospel to the heart of the Empire.

"I am not ashamed of the gospel..." Some see this as an example of literary *litotes* (li-to-tez), that is, a form of understatement where the positive is put in the form of a negative, as in "Not a bad job!"

19

But the form of the sentence reflects something deeper. Nor is it a touch of defensiveness in the face of detractors.

Cranfield is highly insightful at this point:

> [This statement reflects] Paul's sober recognition of the fact that the gospel is something of which, by the very nature of the case, Christians will in the world constantly be tempted to be ashamed... Paul knows full well the inevitability of the temptation to be ashamed of the gospel in view of the continuing hostility of the world to God, on the one hand, and, on the other, the nature of the gospel itself, its unimpressiveness over against the impressiveness of the world, the fact that God (because He desires to leave men room to make a free personal decision of faith rather than compel them) has intervened in history for the salvation of men not in obvious might and majesty but in a veiled way which was bound to look to the world like abject weakness and foolishness.[29]

For it is the power of God unto salvation...

Herein lies the explanation of his holy boldness in the face of hostility and contempt. He understands what he is dealing with. The gospel is more than a collection of words coherently expounding a common religious theme... more than a message of hope. It is that, but much, much more.

The gospel is a specialized form of divine energy that is all alone sufficient for salvation. It is a verbal proclamation so energized by the Spirit that it is able at His sovereign discretion to quicken dead hearts and stir into existence the very faith that it requires. As it goes forth, refracted through human agencies and means, it strikes human hearts with whatever effect God intended to produce (compare Isaiah 55:6–11 and Hebrews 4:12).

Sandy and Headlam:

> "We shall not do wrong if we think of the Gospel as a 'force' in the same kind of sense as that in which science has revealed to us the great 'forces' of nature. It is a principle operating on a

vast and continually enlarging scale, and taking effect in a countless number of individuals."[30]

The gospel is like dry yeast. It appears impotent and inert. Yet its effect on its proper object is transforming.

In a chapel message at Western Bible College, the late Alan Redpath said of Paul with a touch of British understatement, "He was quite convinced of the adequacy of his message."[31]

That conviction is what sets men like Paul apart. How does a man come by such an exalted vision of the true nature of the gospel so that he refuses to be put on the defensive and accommodate the mockery of scoffers without a single blush?

Conviction doesn't come by theological indoctrination alone. What is required in addition is experiential input. The key is a connection drawn by Jesus in John 8:31–32. In that context, Jesus greets the newly professed (but doubtful) faith of some of his recent enemies with this word of caution:

> If you continue in my word [that is, in trusting conformity to my Word], then you are truly my disciples [that is, you will prove that you really are what you claim to be, that you actually possess what you profess] and [as a consequence] you will know the truth [that is, possess inner assurance of the truth with which you have aligned yourself] and the truth will make you free [that is, from the enslaving power of sin] (brackets my amplifications for clarity).

Moral conformity is the handmaid of spiritual certainty. It is those who walk in the truth who come to see it most clearly, those who walk in the will of God who develop the keenest sense of the presence and power of God. Paul was one of those. *The strongest conviction of the truth is born of obedience, not apologetics. The latter is useful; the former is most essential.*

The gospel had transformed Paul's life. He had followed out its implications and accepted all the temporal risks and liabilities of following Christ his Lord. The result was that he experienced firsthand the life-changing power of the gospel. And in preaching the message to others, he broadened his experiential base, witnessing firsthand its radically transforming power.

Convictions born of arguments wilt in the face of ridicule. Conviction of the truth reinforced by experience of the truth can easily face down hollow mockery.

For salvation...

"Salvation" in the broadest sense of delivering a person from all the liabilities of his sinfulness. This includes not only those aspects of our redemption in Christ already accomplished, once and for all, such as regeneration and justification, but also what is in process in the present, that is, the work of sanctification, climaxing in the future in our glorification. In reality, the work of salvation is best conceived as an on-going *program* rather than a one-time *event,* though it is initiated and guaranteed by an event, namely, our justification.

So, this concept (of salvation) means far more than the simple fact that we have been rescued from the wrath of God (as foundational as that is). It includes all those benefits involved in our transformation into the likeness of Christ and our final perfection and eventual admission into His glorious presence.

To everyone who believes...

The gospel is effectual for salvation for one class of men and without exception—for everyone who believes. Right up front, the apostle strikes his keynote. The condition of salvation is not circumcision (the sign of those belonging to the old covenant and its promises), not the righteousness of the law, but faith—more specifically contingent on faith in God, now manifested by faith in His Son, Christ Jesus. The power of the gospel takes effect in a context of faith.

To the Jew first...

Theoretically, this could mean that in the preaching of the gospel, the Jew 1) enjoyed divine preference or 2) had historical priority in the sense of "privilege of first refusal." Of the two options, only the latter is consistent with Paul's theology. God is no respecter of persons, but He has the right to give to that nation He chose as His channel of revelation the privilege of being the first beneficiary of His salvation. Their claim on His grace is first, but by no means exclusive, just as their exposure to His judgment in the case of unbelief is first (compare 2:9–11).

> (1:17) *For in it the righteousness of God is revealed from faith to faith; as it is written: "But the righteous one will live by faith."*

"For in it..." Here in summary form is an explanation of the redemptive core of the gospel message. The gospel is a *power* efficient for salvation in the case of believers because it contains (and conveys into the human heart with quickening power) a revelation of God essential to our acceptance before God. That revelation concerns something every human being natively lacks, a gift which God freely confers upon the believing... and withholds from the unbelieving.

The righteousness of God is [being] revealed...

What the preachers of the gospel are making known on God's behalf is the availability of a covering for our moral and spiritual bankruptcy. The cosmic scandal is that in Adam, we were ruined and now stand before a holy God, morally naked. We are defiled with both inherited sin and our own love of it. As such, we are unacceptable in His holy presence. Our sin cries out for judgment before the bar of His justice.

That's the bad news. The gospel heralds the amazing, good news that God, in His grace and mercy, has made a way to confer upon sinners the status of righteousness. How? He legally imputes to us through faith in Christ the very righteousness of God. Apart from that, we stand condemned.[32]

"From faith to faith..."[33] This phraseology is highly compressed and standing alone, capable of being understood in a variety of ways. Its meaning must be settled by the logic of the context.

What is Paul's overriding interest in this epistle? Clearly, to establish the fact that all men, Jew and Gentile alike, gain a righteous standing before God on the basis of faith in Christ, not on the basis of human merit or keeping the law of God. In light of that emphasis and keeping in mind that these two verses are the keynote for his whole discourse, the "right" interpretation must be one that serves that interest.

Hence, I prefer the interpretation (of the first prepositional phrase) that understands the apostle to be saying that this righteousness of God, which is now being revealed, flows strictly from faith rather than from any works in which they may pride themselves.

"To faith..." This phrase, I take it, adds the thought that the righteousness that is revealed as flowing from faith or coming to us by way of faith is discerned or manifest only where there is a believing heart toward God. In other words, it's those who believe God in whose hearts God has implanted a living faith who hear the message... who recognize it for what it is... the Word of God... and embrace it as such.

> *Even as it is written, "But the righteous (person) shall live by faith."* (parenthesis mine)

Ever conscious of the need to show that what he preaches squares up the OT (for God will not contradict Himself), Paul cites in confirmation of the gospel message the words of the prophet Habakkuk (2:4). God has not changed His mind about the terms on which men are acceptable to Him. Paul wants it understood that the OT confirms that God accepts those whom He regards as righteous, as having a righteous standing before Him, enjoy that status, not because of their personal merit, but strictly on the basis of their faith. The quotation from the ancient prophet verifies the presence of that (faith) principle of justification in the older revelation.

In its historical context, the prophecy of Habakkuk anticipates a visitation of the judgment of God upon Israel. It will come in the form of the savage onslaught of the haughty Babylonians. This prospect does not strike the prophet as just. He remonstrates with God. Though acknowledging the need for divine retribution upon his own disobedient nation, it confuses the prophet that God's plan is to punish a wicked nation by a worse one.

The Lord answers that in due time, He will rectify that situation. It won't happen right away, however. Those Israelites loyal to Him must exercise believing patience and wait for what they will not immediately see come to pass. In the immediate future, their nation will be exposed to severe suffering and Babylonian brutality. The proud and wicked Babylonians, the epitome of the haughty souls that God always brings into judgment, will come in all their rapacity and wreak havoc. The situation will test their loyalty to God. But the comfort of God to the prophet and his faithful kind is a promise and principle rolled into one.

The promise is that those who enjoy a righteous status with God, that is, the people who are truly loyal to Him, will come through all this and live. They will survive not by their own merit but will experience the merciful favor of God on the same basis that Abraham and everyone else have always found the favor of God—on the basis of their faith. So, keep on believing.

Paul picks up this promise and lays it down as an OT confirmation of his principle. Those who are righteous before God enjoy that justified standing based on faith (rather than works of law or any other kind). He means faith in the word of God, not some kind of vague optimism.

To get on the same horizon with the author, remember the common theological ground shared by Apostle Paul and his first-century adversaries (i.e., his Jewish countrymen). Both parties understood that 1) God was a righteous Judge who would ultimately bring the wicked to account and 2) that one must have a righteous standing before God to be accepted by Him.

The bone of contention between them was the basis of the righteousness that God would accept. Was it an *earned* righteousness, that is, based on legal merit (i.e., meticulous performance of the external righteousness of the law), or was it an *imputed* righteousness conferred on the basis of faith alone, that is, conferred on those who acknowledged and embraced Jesus Christ as the promised Messiah? The Jews affirmed the former. Paul argues the latter.

PARAPHRASE OF THE THOUGHT IN 1:16–17

The gospel does not embarrass me. It is a specialized form of divine energy, efficient for salvation of all men—that is, effective for whoever will embrace it by faith.

It reveals God's free gift of righteousness—something we all lack but must have if we are to stand before God. This righteousness is conferred on the basis of faith alone to the believing, not on the basis of human merit. That a righteous standing with God is and always has been based on the faith principle is confirmed even by the prophet Habakkuk (Hab 2:4).

PREVIEW OF THE GENERAL ARGUMENT FROM 1:16–3:20

(1:16–17)–The gospel makes provision for a righteous standing before God for all men on the basis of faith exclusively.

(1:18–32)–The need for it is urgent because the unrighteous are exposed to the wrath of God.

(2:1–3:7)–You, my fellow Jews (or whoever you are), are surely included among the unrighteous because you do the same old sinful things as the rest.

(3:8–20)–Therefore, you, too, stand condemned and exposed to the wrath of God and require the same remedy.

Calvin: "Paul shows that the whole world is deserving of eternal death."[34]

THE LOGIC BRIDGE BETWEEN 1:16–17 AND 1:18FF[35]

Hodge: [To show that righteousness is by faith alone] "it was necessary to show that men in themselves are exposed to condemnation and are destitute of any righteousness which can satisfy the demands of God. His argument is, God is just; he is determined to punish sin, and as all men are sinners, all are exposed to punishment... Men must be justified by faith, for the wrath of God is revealed."[36]

I like Bruce's statement of the connection:

He shows why it is so urgently necessary that the way to get right with God should be known. As things are [right now], men are "in the wrong" with God, and His wrath is revealed against them. There is a moral law in life that men are left to the consequences of their own freely chosen course of action, and unless this tendency is reversed by divine grace, their situation will go from bad to worse.[37]

PREVIEW OF THE ARGUMENT IN 1:18–32

The need for the gospel is urgent. For alongside the gospel revelation of the faith-righteousness of God is another ongoing revelation—one far more ominous and manifest on planet Earth every single day in a thousand painful ways in the subtle displays and outworking of the wrath of God against the unrighteous who persist in ignoring the light God has given them (verse 18).

Paul then proceeds to demonstrate that the wrath of God against the unrighteous is well deserved. The objects of His anger don't have a leg to stand on. God has seen to it that they are without excuse (verses 19–23).

Their inexcusability is confirmed by three facts:

1) God has given them generous access to sufficient natural revelation to test their willingness to know Him (verses 19–20).

2) But they had rejected the light they enjoyed (verse 21).

3) Worse yet, they had perverted the knowledge they had no excuse for being ignorant of (verses 22–23).

Now let us examine some of the content of this section in more detail.

(1:18) *For the wrath of God is revealed from heaven against all ungodliness and unrighteousness of men, who suppress the truth in unrighteousness...*

Is revealed...

Note the present tense of "is revealed." This implies an ongoing, right-up-to-this-very-minute exhibition. The outpouring of the wrath of God is a *contemporaneous* event with an eschatological (end times) crescendo. Bruce cites Schiller: "The history of the world is the judgment of the world."[38] Bingo!

History is a museum of the reality of divine wrath... God allowing fallen man to follow the bent of his moral tree and sow the seeds of sin and reap a whirlwind of wickedness in wars, rumors of wars, man's inhumanity to man, unspeakable savagery every hour all around the globe in hot spots like Bosnia, Somalia, Cambodia, Columbia, Peru, Italy, the Middle East, Iraq, Afghanistan, Ukraine, Russia, North Korea, Israel, Gaza, Lebanon, South and Central America, and American inner cities.

The wrath of God...

The wrath of God is not an irrational outburst of passion but a settled, holy indignation against evil. Cranfield's response to Dodd's rejection[39] of the literalism of this phraseology is apropos:

[Dodd] is begging the question by assuming that anger is always an irrational passion. Certainly it sometimes is; but there is also anger which is thoroughly rational... But a consideration of what Dodd calls "the highest human ideals of personality" might well lead us to question whether God could be the good and loving God, if He did not react to our evil with wrath. For *indignation against wickedness is surely an essential element of human goodness in a world in which moral evil is always present*[40] (emphasis mine).

From heaven...

The phrase is not redundant. It adds a solemnizing effect. It reinforces the cosmic ramifications of unrighteousness. Wrath *from heaven* answers the wickedness *on earth.* This phrase reminds us, if necessary, that what the unrighteous must be concerned about is more than "nature taking its course." It is heaven taking steps.

Against all ungodliness and unrighteousness of men...

The two terms are probably not intended to denote two discrete kinds of evil. They are most likely two terms for the same concept to bring out two aspects of evil in a way that neither could do as well alone.[41] Ungodliness *(asebeia)* suggests implicitly that all sin is an affront to God's majesty, while unrighteousness *(adikia)* calls attention to its violation of God's laws (or standards of right and wrong written in the conscience).

Who suppress the truth in unrighteousness...

"Suppress" is a so-called conative present, a present of attempt. The force of it equals "attempting to suppress" the truth of God. "The truth" refers to the knowledge of God available in natural revelation. They actively resist the light they have, lest their conscience inhibit their freedom to follow their natural inclinations.

In unrighteousness...

The "in" may be 1) instrumental in the sense of "through unrighteousness or 2) environmental in the sense of "in the course of." Either makes good sense (and probably both are true to the facts of the matter). The question is, which sense was intended here? I lean toward the former because it tends to heighten the guilt, which is harmonious with the author's intent here. So, they acquiesce in whatever lies and vices are sufficient to blunt the influence of natural revelation.

(1:19) *Because that which is known about God is evident within them; for God made it evident to them.*

Because...

This thought may be intended to explain either 1) the justice of the wrath of God or 2) why they are accused of suppressing the truth. Either connection makes good sense, but the latter is more likely[42], given the tendency to make logical linkages with the more proximate ideas.

That which is known about God...

He means "what is known" without the help of what we call "special or biblical revelation." Theologians distinguish between natural and special revelation. The repository of the former is creation. The Bible is the repository of special revelation.

Godet says:

> "God is not known like an ordinary object; when He is known, it is He who gives himself to be known."[43]

Contextually, the apostle implies that the scope of natural revelation is limited.

The word *gnostos* means "known" in the sense of "common knowledge."[44] In the sense of "knowable" (unless this is the lone exception), the term does not appear in the NT. Natural revelation is "community property," a public domain knowledge that requires no tutor.

Is evident within them.

"Within them" rather than "among them,"[45] as the Greek (*en autois*) could also be rendered. Most commentators, I believe rightly, prefer the first, primarily because it appears from verse 20 ("being understood through what has been made") that the external "light" of natural creation is internalized in its import.

This phrase is not a tautologism[46] (needless repetition of an idea in different terms) but merely confirms that knowledge belongs to the public domain, that is, human common sense, and is more than externally accessible but is, in fact, "*evident within them.*" *Phaneros* (= evident) means "open to sight," "manifest," "conspicuous."[47] There is nothing obscure about it. It is light, and it is clear.

Nor is it merely external. In some manner, it is *in* them, and it is conspicuous. "In" (*en autois*) should not be rendered "among them" to avoid the paradox of their blindness (verse 21). This light is not only among them in some external form but somehow ignored by them; it is also plainly *in* them. Note verse 20: "clearly seen, being understood." This is an intellectual enlightenment based upon natural revelation. The next clause supports this interpretation.

"For God made it evident to them."

Calvin's comment is colorfully to the point:

"He means that man was formed to be a spectator of the created world, and that he was endowed with eyes for the purpose of his being led to God Himself, the Author of the World, by contemplating so magnificent an image."[48]

"God personally made it clear to them." But what is the foundation of this "public domain" revelation that is so evident to men—whether they acknowledge it or not?

(1:20) *For since the creation of the world His invisible attributes, His eternal power and divine nature, have been clearly perceived, being understood by what has been made, so that they are without excuse.*

For since the creation of the world...
The *"gar"* (for) explains specifically 19b, but in a more general way, explains the affirmation of a clear universal knowledge of God "since (or dating from) the creation of the world." This clause marks the inception of natural revelation. The beacon has been in existence from that point.

His invisible attributes, His eternal power and divine nature...
Lit. "The invisible things of Him..."

"Aidios dunamis" ("eternal power") points to that attribute most obvious in nature, while "eternal" sets that "power" in a class apart. It is not a secondary power which has some greater power for its Cause. Because He is eternal, God is, by definition, the Uncaused Cause of all things. That is the intuitive lesson of natural revelation... public domain knowledge. Liddon: "The first impression which nature yields as to its Author is His power."[49] Aren't our latest telescopic probes deep into space accentuating this point?

"It is clearly seen to be *eternal*, because by it all things temporal were created."[50]

"Theiotes" ("divine nature") means divine nature and its properties[51], "a summary term for those attributes which constitute Divinity."[52] That is, they mark God off clearly from the things He has created and which (we shall hear) men have come to worship

instead of their Creator. The reason Paul uses this language is to show that the paganism contemporary to him in its worship of grotesque idols and human gods had reduced God to something way beneath the light the pagan world possessed.

Note the paradox—the invisible is seen through the visible. Obviously, the "sight" is mental rather than physical; the physical phenomena are the eyeglasses through which the mind reads the unseen attributes of God.

Have been clearly seen (lit., *are being* clearly seen.)

Note the intensive verb accentuates the conspicuousness of this revelation.

Being understood through what has been made...

Again, the participle implies that, in some way, this natural light persists however the pagan spirit has tried to suppress it.

The vehicle of this revelation is nature itself. God has so programmed the human consciousness that it "reads" (without prompting) the implications of nature. The means by which the mind grasps in physical creation the intended notion of its Author, Gifford describes, as a "spontaneous act of reason."[53]

The passage does not precisely define the content of nature revelation. It only makes it abundantly clear that the knowledge of God revealed in that source is sufficient to condemn those who reject God as nature so eloquently declares He is. That light would not, however, be adequate to save. Yet that does not excuse any, for the light they have is sufficient to test in advance their response to any more light they (potentially) might receive.[54]

Bruce cites B. Gartner:

> "Both the verbs... describe how, on contemplating God's works, man can grasp enough of His nature to prevent him from the error of identifying any of the created things with the Creator, enabling him to keep his conception of the Deity free from idolatry."[55]

"So *that they are without excuse.*"

The Greek construction could mean "in order that" (purpose) or less likely "so that" (result). The former is most natural grammatically and is perfectly suitable theologically, but I feel the difference is more nuanced than substantial. In the end, it all comes down about the same way.

"The first aim of the Creator was to make Himself known to His creature. But if, through his own fault, man came to turn away from this light, he should not be able to accuse God of the darkness into which he plunged himself."[56]

The next verse elaborates on their accountability. He describes more graphically how they (the unbelieving Gentiles, especially blatant pagans are sharply in view) have refused to act upon the light God gave them.

(1:21) *For even though they knew God, they did not honor Him as God, or give thanks; but they became futile in their speculations, and their foolish heart was darkened.*

Knew God...[57]
Our translations can mislead us here if we assume that this implies that the intuitive knowledge of God once present is now generally obliterated. All he really intends here is to trace contemporary paganism back to its roots, showing first how paganism rejected natural light and then, in the false pretense of wisdom, perverted the light God had given.

Noteworthy also in connection with this present/past tense issue (and especially in reference to this last solution) is the fact that in verse 30, the author reverts to the present tense with respect to man's consciousness of the ordinance of God. Surely this awareness implies that to whatever extent "their foolish heart was darkened" (verse 21), that darkening did not in fact obliterate all previous knowledge.

They did not honor Him as God...

Calvin catalogs eloquently the implications reverberating throughout creation, which the pagan has refused to acknowledge:

No conception of God can be formed without including his eternity, power, wisdom, goodness, truth, righteousness, and mercy. His eternity is evidenced by the fact that He holds all things in His hand and makes all things consist in Himself. His wisdom is seen, because He has arranged all things in perfect order; His goodness, because there is no other cause for His creation of all things, nor can any other reason than His goodness itself induce Him to preserve them. His justice is evident in His governing of the world, because He punishes the guilty and defends the innocent; His mercy, because He bears the perversity of men with so much patience; and His truth, because He is unchangeable.[58]

Or give thanks...

"As God's creature, man was bound to render glory and thanksgiving to his Creator; this means not merely to acknowledge his existence, and to employ the words and rites of religion, but to recognize his lordship and live in grateful obedience..." [59]

In all of Paul's writings, a great deal of emphasis is placed on the duty of thanksgiving. Francis Schaeffer was probably not overstating the case when he observed a correlation between gratitude and religious attitude, that all apostasy begins with an ungrateful heart. Besides honoring God, thanksgiving is a stimulus to faith.

But they became foolish in their speculations, and their foolish heart was darkened.

That is, they became vain in their reasonings. Out of touch with ultimate reality, their intentions miscarry. In the words of Barrett, one is not capable of "truly rational thought" apart from a right relation with God.[60] Surely there is a sense in which the whole unbelieving world is befogged in a cloud of insanity, out of touch with the truth (reality) about God.

The language reflects perhaps a paradox extant in the minds of pagans, that is, a seeming contradiction that is best explained, I think, in terms of the conscious and subconscious mind. No matter how hard people try to suppress that intuitive apprehension of God revealed in nature from their conscious mind, there remains in the *subconscious*[61] of every individual an indelible imprint of it.

In other words, perverted reason suppresses this natural knowledge of God and eventually succeeds in pushing it into the background of its consciousness. It is indeed curious how this instinctual awareness of God often leaks around the edges and bolts past the watch posts of surprised and unguarded reason and betrays its hidden presence.

(1:22) *Professing to be wise, they became fools...*

The apostle is not speaking of philosophers merely, but as Gifford says, "the conceit of wisdom which is necessarily connected with a departure from divine truth..." [62] Intellectual pride always makes a fool of its professor. (cf. 1 Cor. 1:18–31.)

(1:23) *And exchanged the glory of the incorruptible God for an image in the form of corruptible man and of birds and four-footed animals and crawling creatures.*

Their obtuseness is manifest in their idolatrous contradiction of the light of natural revelation. (Compare the apocryphal writing, *The Wisdom of Solomon*, 13:1–19 on idol-worship as contrary to reason and common sense).

It was G. K. Chesterton, I believe, who once observed that when men cease to believe in God, they do not believe in nothing; they believe in anything. The same can be said for their worship. When they cease to worship the true God, they do not worship nothing; they will worship anything.

The reason is that repressed intuition of God... an instinct as undeniable as a baby's cry, however layered over with unenlightened reasonings. Man doesn't want God as God... he wants to be self-governing... independent... unaccountable. So, he reduces God to manageable dimensions. That way, he tries to salvage something that his heart cries for, yet does not have to deal with it on terms he doesn't want to. It's the old principle of trying to have one's cake and eat it too.

Even those who don't serve idols in their crasser forms turn out to be idolators. It may be the State, the Cause, the Party, the Ideology, Wealth, Power, Status, and so on, but men always bow to something that they enshrine as their authority, even if it is some worm like themselves.

In closing our commentary on this section, though I have already touched on it above, I feel it is an "elephant in the room" that needs to be treated more at length.

A bit of a conundrum emerges here as to Paul's teaching regarding the present status of natural light. To take a step back, observe that Paul, who speaks of the experience of the inner light of natural revelation as though it were universally contemporary in every human breast, now refers to it in the past tense ("knew"). The possibility of having stifled this natural light gains plausibility in the next sentence, where the apostle adds that because of their unresponsiveness to it, "they became futile in their speculations, and their foolish heart was darkened."

What are we to make of this? Has that "knowledge" once clearly possessed now been lost? If so, how does one account for the present tenses in verses 19 and 20, which seem to imply the continuity of intuitive enlightenment?

Or conversely, if one takes the position that the import of natural revelation persists universally in human consciousness, how does one account for the past tenses in verse 21, which seem to imply cessation of it?

There seem (to me) to be four possible solutions to this difficulty, and I opt for the fourth:

1) The position (Barrett and Cranfield), namely, that natural revelation is universal in the objective sense only ("knowable" and

"among them"), not in the subjective ("known" and "in them") sense.

Thus, this view attempts to circumvent the difficulty by making the present tenses apply to the continuity of natural revelation *in its objective or external form*. Crucial to this interpretation is construing "that which is known" to mean "that which is knowable" and rendering "evident within them" as "among them."

However appealing, this view falters on improbabilities. 1) It takes "known" in the unlikely sense of "knowable" (it has that meaning nowhere else in the NT), and 2) it does not seem (to me at least) to give due weight to verse 19b (for God made it evident *to* them); to verse 20d ("being understood through what has been made") and to verses 20e and 21a ("so that they are without excuse, for even though they knew God...) and to verse 30 ("they know the ordinance of God. . .," all of which evidences imply *an internalized* enlightenment, which they are held guilty for *suppressing*. Their delinquency seems to be deeper than ignoring clear *external* signposts to an invisible reality. The imprint of this external evidence seems somehow to have been branded by divine action upon the internal consciousness.

2) The universal light of natural revelation, though once clearly implanted in the racial consciousness, has been effaced by suppression.[63]

The chief deficiency of this view is, in my opinion, its inability to explain in any satisfactory manner (so far as I am aware) the present tenses of verses 19, 20, and 30. If one adopts this solution, it is hard to explain why the apostle didn't employ the past tense in those verses as well. It would have made much better sense that way.

3) The light of natural revelation existing early on in all individuals is regularly suppressed so that the knowing and darkening are cyclical.[64]

This answer, even if true to reality to some extent, evades the issue. While this solution might explain how two conditions (knowing God and darkened understanding of natural revelation) might coexist in a given time frame or reappear from generation to generation, it does not explain how persons who are described as "knowing" something can also be characterized as *having known* that same object. In other words, it does not reconcile the apparent contradiction inherent in the present and past tenses and in the conditions of present knowledge and intellectual darkness.

4) I, therefore, think we must conclude that the eclipse referred to there is *relative* and *partial,* not *total.* If that conclusion is correct, it greatly alleviates, in my opinion, the seeming discrepancy between the present and the past tenses in these verses. It's still there, but its clarity often suppressed and then obscured by stiff resistance, a stroke of concurrent wrath. It's still in there, but it is way down there in the mental basement. "You want to get Me out of your consciousness; you got it!" (compare verse 28)

This interpretation ties in nicely with what follows:
Having proved the culpability of contemporary paganism, the apostle now proceeds to the judicial consequences (1:24–32).

In the very first sentence of this section, the apostle avers that *even now,* God is revealing His indignation toward unbelievers. What fuels His wrath is their persistent habit of suppressing the truth about Himself in blatant sacrilege and unrighteous behaviors—both of which are forms of denial or suppression of a better light within their hearts.

In just what way or ways does God, *on a day-to-day* basis, manifest His holy indignation against such offenses? How do we know heaven is aboil? What are the signs?

In its regular form, the present-time revelation of the wrath of God consists in letting men hoist themselves on the petard of their own perversions, as it were, thereby imprisoning them in the consequences of their rejection of God and their degenerate desires. In short, we make ourselves a bed of thorns in suppressing the truth; God just sees that we must lie in it.

Those who reject God, says C. S. Lewis, "enjoy the horrible freedom they have demanded, and are therefore self-enslaved."[65]

"Though the mills of God grind slowly, yet they grind exceeding small; Though with patience He stands waiting, with exactness grinds He all."[66]

So, divine retribution upon those who reject him takes the form of shutting up sinners to the consequences of their own corruption. Human beings sow to the wind, and God sees that they reap the whirlwind (Hosea 8:7; 10:13). Divine judgment is presently afoot as we see sin is visited by all its evil relatives, dragging behind it as with cords all its unreckoned punishments (Prov. 5:22).

Note the highly stylized structure of this description. This section oscillates thematically between the judicial sentence and the charges that support it. There are three sections, each marked by a repetition of the verdict: "God... gave them up..." (verses 24, 26, 28). Each is preceded by a bill of particulars accounting for the judgment.

We see a literary progression (and a religious regression) in this section. Observe a perverse movement from 1) rejection of the knowledge of God, followed by 2) perversion of the glory of God, resulting in 3) sexual perversion, moral confusion, and social degeneration. Nygren puts the consequences well: "sin itself disgraces man (vv. 24–27) and disturbs human society" (vv. 28–31). All around our world, for anyone with eyes to see are the harbingers of terrible judgment to come in the efflorescence of the right-here and right-now painful consequences of human sin. As much as the world feels the pain and frantically ponders how to numb it, people rarely connect the dots but persist in "remedies" that only aggravate the conditions. It's called purblind.

In this section, the apostle confirms what the history of idolatry suggests, namely, that idolatry represents not a step forward in man's presumed evolution to higher religious conceptions but rather a deadly devolution to baser ones. At the same time, he observes the inevitable link between idolatry and immorality. A lower view of

Deity always leads to the degradation of humanity. Where is there an exception in the history of the human race?

This historical linkage between idolatry and immorality is striking. Bad religion and bad morals tend to go together.[67] The only reason individuals and cultures never become as bad as they could be is the restraining influence of the common grace of God (2 Thess. 2:7). Otherwise, that evil "gravity" prevails.

(1:24) *Therefore God gave them over in the lusts of their hearts to impurity, that their bodies would be dishonored among them.*

Therefore God gave them over...

This verb "gave over" represents the Greek verb *paradidomi,* which often has the sense of *surrendering* or *turning over*[68] a prisoner to authorities for judgment or incarceration. (cf. Mark 4:12; 17:22; Acts 12:4; 27:1; and many other places.)

This phraseology, however, does not necessarily indicate a final judgment upon the offenders, final meaning that they are sealed forever in this condition. The penalties spoken of here are simply interim warning signals of God's holy outrage. Heaven's message to earth is that God is indignant. Therefore, He is allowing sin to take its natural course in working out all its debasing, dehumanizing, and corrupting tendencies. He is punishing pagans with the harvest of their wickedness, reaping what they sow, punishing sin with more devastating sin.

That there may indeed be room for mercy and grace for those who, in God's mercy, awaken and are warned toward repentance, see 1 Corinthians 6:9–11, especially verse 11, "And such were some of you..."

In the lusts of their hearts to impurity in order to dishonor their bodies among themselves.

"In the lusts of their hearts"—Notice what I think is perhaps a metaphor. God, in His wrath, in effect, takes his rejectors into custody unawares. The invisible chains in which he turns them over to the jailer (uncleanness) are their "lusts." Their lusts (i.e., lawless desires) are the chains that bind (or enslave) them. Thus, they are delivered or turned over to (*eis*) uncleanness in all its perverse variety. Uncleanness is a condition antecedent to divine judgment; God's retribution just imprisons them in this corrupt condition they have chosen for themselves. "This is what you wanted; this is what you've got... and all that goes with it. Have a good day!" —God. Isn't that what we are seeing in our time with sin brewing like a savage, demon-driven storm on every front?

Lust (*epithumia*) is a broad term, which simply means "desire" in either a good (e.g., Luke 22:15; 1 Tim. 3:1) or bad (Rom. 7:7; 13:14) sense. [69] Context, obviously, is the deciding factor. In the latter instance, it refers to the unlawful or over-the-top desires springing from what the Bible calls "the flesh."

Here "hearts" is a verbal stand-in for the *flesh*, sometimes a biblical synonym for the physical nature of man; sometimes it is a broader concept that refers to all that is in our present life that is transitory, mortal, weak, and dying. This aspect of our being is the seat or throne room of the active sin principle (or drive) that animates the life of the natural man. In short, the heart or flesh is *ruled* by this sin principle. It is through the avenue of the fleshly desires that Satan expertly plies us with temptations... the lusts stemming from the bodily appetites, the lusts stemming from that which appeals to the eye, and the things in life which appeal to human pride (i.e., the lusts of the flesh, lusts of the eye, and the pride of life, 1 John 2:16).

Unbelievers (or natural or unregenerate men) walk after the flesh. This is their defining moral characteristic. The sin principle ("the law of sin" – Rom. 7:23; 8:2) is their master. It resides in that aspect of our being the Bible calls *the flesh.* By contrast, believers walk after the Spirit of God, who occupies (Rom. 8.11) the regenerated human spirit.

Like unbelievers, we are still *in* the flesh. However, we are no longer *of* it. We can be influenced by its presence; we can, in weakness, yield to its clamors, but regenerated persons are no longer *slaves* of sin, that is, sold into bondage to sin (Rom. 7:14), helpless to do anything but follow the desires of the flesh. In short, the sin principle still resides in us, but it no longer, like a slave master, reigns over us. Yet daily, it clamors for gratification like the incessant cry of an unhappy child.

It should be noted that what modern counselors speak of as "needs" correspond in many instances to what the Bible calls "desires." Some so-called "felt needs" are neither real needs nor valid desires. It is crucial that those who serve as spiritual and emotional advisers carefully distinguish these and not assume that every "need" that modern society or psychology canonizes is legitimate.[70] The "need" for higher self-esteem can fit into this category. Some people would benefit from lower self-esteem. The "need" for self-fulfillment can be an expression of self-absorption.

"Of their hearts" —in biblical nomenclature, "the heart" is simply a code word for our "flesh" or inner life where our thoughts, will, and affections are formed and hardened into shape. From these headwaters, under the dominion of the flesh, issue carnal "desires."

"To dishonor their bodies among themselves." It is a form of poetic justice. A consequence of their dishonoring God is the disgrace of their own bodies.

Idolatry, let me reiterate, has always been a stimulant and hotbed of immorality. ("For the idea of making idols was the beginning of fornication."[71].) All immorality is defiling and degrading. It robs humanity of something precious—a vital sense of cleanness. Immorality always steals something from one's self-respect.[72] Paganism in its various iterations down through history has been a spawning ground of every kind of moral vice. Where in the history of man has it ever had an elevating and ennobling influence? Just the opposite. Just one reading of Greek and Roman history should confirm that in a heartbeat.

People tend to follow the logic of their beliefs just as, in driving, our vehicle tends to follow our eyes. If wrong ideas about God take hold on the mind, then wrong behaviors will follow in their wake. That is why the Church must take its doctrine seriously. Our American anti-intellectual pragmatism in its contempt of theology is perilously myopic. In fact, the corruption of the American church in particular bears eloquent testimony to our premise.

(1:25) *"For they (who are such as) exchanged the truth of God for a (the) lie and worshiped and served the creation rather than the Creator, who is blessed forever. Amen"* (parentheses mine).

This verse reiterates (with some elaboration) the reason for which the heathen, in His great displeasure, God has "turned over to uncleanness to dishonor their bodies among themselves." The repetition is for emphasis and clarification.

The miscarriage of light-rejecting reason is seen in the blind way in which they have missed the point. To honor creation rather than the Creator is like worshiping the art in the Sistine Chapel and disdaining its creator, Michelangelo, as of no relevance or account.[73]

"Exchanged," more literally, changed or altered the truth of God into a lie. The history of comparative religions views religion as a product of evolution. According to this thinking, religion evolved from simpler and cruder forms to more sophisticated beliefs and practices. Thus, instead of a step back (according to Paul), polytheistic paganism would represent a step up from more primitive forms of religion. The reality is, however, that all false religion represents *devolution*, not evolution; not an earnest effort to find God but a serious effort to suppress the truth embedded in their consciousness mediated through natural light.

"The truth of God" refers to right conceptions about God in accordance with the light of nature. Paganism honors many "gods," but none of its worship is consistent with the realities imprinted upon its intuitions through natural revelation. It is all reductionistic and intended to accommodate the carnal desires of the worshipper.

"The lie"—literally. Here is an echo of the OT prophets who referred to idols as a lie (Isa. 44:20; Jer. 10:14; 13:25), so called because they falsify the nature of God, radically diminish His glory (i.e., the sum of His divine perfections), and misdirect the faith and practice of their worshipers. Idols are religious impostors... gross and misleading counterfeits of what God is like. More generally, an idol is anyone or anything that is or becomes more important to us than the living God in terms of serving or worshipping.

"Blessed forever"—or, as Hodge has it, ever-blessed.[74] That is, the Creator, who is ever worthy of our honor. Critique here gives way to spontaneous praise, which is never far from his heart and lips. To worship any other is outrageous, a crime of cosmic proportions.

"Amen" is a word of Hebrew origin, which crowns His praise with the exclamation, "so be it!" or "it is true!"

> (1:26–27) *For this reason God gave them over to degrading passions; for their women exchanged natural function for that which is unnatural, and in the same way also the men abandoned natural function of the woman and burned in their desire toward one another, men with men committing indecent acts and receiving in their own persons the due penalty of their error.*

For this reason God gave them over to degrading passions...

The second refrain—God gave them over. Because they dishonored God in their preference for darkness, God allowed the darkness they preferred to overwhelm their instinctual and moral senses so that shameful passions ruled them. The "passions of disgrace" (*pathe atimias*) the apostle had in mind are illustrated in the remainder of verses 26–27. Darkened reason succumbs to the rule of corrupt passions.

> *For their women exchanged [metellexan ten physiken chesin] the natural function for that which is unnatural [ten para physin], and in the same way also the men abandoned the natural use of the woman and burned in their desire [orexsei] towards one another, men with men committing indecent acts and receiving in their own persons the due penalty of their error. (brackets mine)*

This passage clearly[75] identifies the practice of homosexuality as one shocking evidence of divine judgment. Though merely *one* form of perversion to which God has surrendered those who dishonored

Him, it is highlighted because of its *unnatural* grossness and self-condemning character.[76]

Women, no doubt, are mentioned first because their complicity in this species of vile conduct shocks the sensibilities even more than that of men, who are no strangers to degeneracy. Note the Greek particle (ignored in the NASV) emphasizes this—"for *even* their women..." This is a picture of what Murray terms "moral squalor."[77]

The apostle in his portrait of divine judgment upon a God-rejecting paganism does not mean that all pagans are guilty of these sins. Rather, his picture is an immoral mosaic representative of the kinds of excesses and corruptions to which their rejection of God has led. Just look around and one will see it all in living color all over the Western world in our day, if not elsewhere. What has changed except the technology? Certainly not the profusion of immorality. Those not guilty of this particular evil certainly could be indicted for many of those listed in the catalog of 1:30ff.

> "The implication is that however grievous is fornication or adultery the desecration involved in homosexuality is on a lower plane of degeneracy; it is unnatural and therefore evinces a perversion still more basic" [78]

Exchanged the natural function for that which is against nature...

This language implies a divinely constituted order in sexual arrangements, which is transgressed and perverted. When people abandon God, they eventually lose their sense of moral direction. God's laws give way to traditional values, and traditional values, without any anchor, dissolve into nothing but moral anarchy on one hand and, on the other, the ever-shifting and hollow standards of political correctness arbitrarily imposed by the most influential sectors of society. [79]

"Against nature... "This same Greek phrase (*para physin*) is employed by Philo of homosexuality.[80]

"Burning...," an intensive metaphor of unbridled lust.

"Producing (the) shamefulness (*ten aschemosynen*)..." that is, that form of moral disgrace alluded to previously in the case of women.

The article has an identifying force.

"Receiving... the due penalty of their error." The penal effect of their rejection of the knowledge of God is enslavement in such unnatural vice. That anyone could be so blind as to "misread" the message embedded in human anatomy and reproduction is testimony to the power of human self-deception.

Years ago (1980s), a Sacramento pastor and author who has spent tons of time in San Francisco reaching out to gays, often successfully (as his church constituency bore witness), told me that in his experience, the highest barrier his group faced in trying to bring gay people to Christ was this desperate feeling—enslavement to it. And that feeling, by the way, along with the guilt, explains why the reaction of gay people to evangelism is often shrill to the point of near hysteria. Despite the onerous weight of guilt, they perversely love their unnatural sin anyway and cannot imagine even the power of God is great enough to separate them from it, hence, their hateful, red-in-the-claw reaction to those who would condemn that lifestyle. This is the due penalty of their error unless God mercifully intervenes to break the chains of their slavery.

"Error..." The Greek word (*planes*) implies more than a mistake; it connotes at bottom "wandering," or "roaming."[81] Rejecting the knowledge of God, in darkness and self-delusion, they go far afield in moral adventuresomeness.

"Due..." It was fitting in the eyes of God that men who so degraded God should find what one might call divine retribution in them degrading their own bodies.

Abandonment: The High Price of Uncomfortable Knowledge

(1:28) *And just as they did not see fit to acknowledge God any longer, God gave them over to a depraved mind, to do those things that are not proper...*

"And even as they did not approve to have God in (their) knowledge..."

This is a literal translation of the Greek text.

This is the fundamental indictment from which God's abandonment to moral vertigo stems. They simply did not cherish the light they had; it was not at all something that they valued. It was "uncomfortable" knowledge.

So again, he repeats the refrain for the third time—God abandoned them.

"To an unqualified or reprobate (*adokimos*) mind..." *Adokimos* means "not passing the test," "unqualified," "unfit," "worthless."[82] Notice how poetic God's judgments are. They tested and disapproved the knowledge they had of God; God, in turn, left their intellects to the inevitable effects of the light they despised. Without the light of God, moral judgment operates in the dark; it is like a hunter in a pitch-black forest without a compass, bumping around from tree to tree. The outcome is moral vertigo (in a fog, not knowing up from down) and a mind, which, in our state of fallenness, gravitates to evil choices.

Does not all this sound eerily contemporary?

In the words of Calvin, the godless are "blind at noonday."[83]

To do the things which are not proper (kathekonta)...

God's judicial abandonment to the moral outcomes of religious defection is now seen in all its kaleidoscopic varieties of evil behaviors. Homosexuality may be the ultimate in unnaturalness, but it is by no means the only symptom of judicial abandonment. As stark as this sin may be in its unnaturalness and twistedness, let no one think its stands alone in hatefulness to God. No, but it stands out in its unnaturalness. It just shows the insane places rejection of God can take fallen man.

> (1:29–31) *having been filled with all unrighteousness, wickedness, greed, and malice; full of envy, murder, strife, deceit, and malice; they are gossips, slanderers, haters of God, insolent, arrogant, boastful, inventors of evil, disobedient to parents, without understanding, untrustworthy, unfeeling, and unmerciful...*

Now begins an ugly catalog of diabolical corruptions, which signal the drumbeat wrath of God already reverberating in our world.

Being filled with all (every kind of) unrighteousness...

The verb is in the perfect tense, implying that a moral condition occurring in the past still stands and stirs. The verb itself suggests an intensification of moral degradation in society so that it cannibalizes itself with a host of evil inclinations.

(1:32) *And although they know the ordinance of God, that those who practice such things are worthy of death, they not only do the same, but also approve of those who practice them.*

"Who knowing (very well) the requirement of God, that those who are practicing such things are worthy of death, not only do them, but also approve of those who are doing them." [my translation of the Nestle Greek text]

The present tense reaffirms that, despite their every effort to suppress the knowledge of God, it persists against their will. The participle (*epignotes* = knowing) in many contexts has an intensive force, which implies more than a faint or vague knowledge. The point is that they clearly know better than their conduct. They sin against clear light. They intuitively understand that they deserve the sentence of death, whatever they may say otherwise.

What compounds their guilt is their approval of such wickedness. That is a clear sign of a society or individual under the wrath of God —they approve what they inherently know God disapproves. Not only do they practice sin, but they also enlist others to follow suit. They mock righteousness and purity and promote outrageousness as the best thing since apple pie.

That phenomenon one sees unfolding all over the degrading face of the Western world, where, for example, in the arts and entertainment industries, the perennial rage is "to push the envelope" as much and as far as possible in the direction of libertinism in the name of liberty. The only freedom in that is the God-given liberty, as a punitive measure, to lose our moral minds.

[1] cf. Jos. 1:1,7; 24:29; Jer. 29:19; Isa. 42:1; Psa. 105:6, 25, 42; 2 Sam. 7:5,8; Isa. 37:35; 20:3; Amos 3:7; Zech. 1:6; Deut. 34:5

[2] "It is noticeable how quietly St. Paul steps into the place of the prophets and leaders of the Old Covenant, and how quietly he substitutes the name of His own master in a connection hitherto reserved for that of Jehovah." Sanday and Headlam, *ICC: Romans,* 3.

[3] Vine, *Expository Dictionary of New Testament Words,* 163.

[4] There is no contradiction between a servant spirit and the exercise of authority. A servant of God is obliged to serve the will of God. To some God gives special authority to carry out His will. The two are incompatible only when a purported servant of God prostitutes his biblical authority to serve his own agenda rather than God's.

It is also worth noting that our servitude is to God pre-eminently and to man only derivatively. That secondary obligation has an inherent limit. The parameters for what constitute "serving one another" are set by biblical norms. To please people at the expense of God's will never qualifies as a servant spirit.

That point is important, because unfortunately a servant spirit is too often confused with wishy-washy spirit of compliance that goes along to get along. A servant of God, like a parent, will sometimes find it necessary to refuse the will of men in order to serve the will of God. Moreover, we should not be surprised in such cases when some confuse their desires with God's and accuse us of lacking a "servant spirit" for balking at their agenda.

[5] An apostle in the *official* (versus a merely *functional* sense as, e.g. in 2 Cor. 8:3) is one immediately "selected and commissioned by Christ Himself to deliver in His name the message of Salvation." Hodge, *Epistle to the Romans*, 15. An official apostle must also have been a first-hand witness of the resurrection and immediate knowledge of His doctrine. Cf. John 15.27; Acts 1:21; 1 Cor. 9:1; Acts 10:39; 26:16 and Gal. 1:12

[6] Compare 1 Thessalonians 2:4 where Paul declares that "we have been approved (or *dedokimasmetha*) with the connotation of checked out and accepted after examination as approved or worthy) by (*hypo*) God to be entrusted with the Gospel. It is noteworthy that Paul implies that God holds the work of carrying the Gospel message far too sacred to be entrusted to just any "free agent" who happens to be willing. Paul indicates that not only was he hand-picked, but intimates that the holy character of the message causes God to select appropriate messengers.

Incidentally passages like this expose a current theological fallacy. It is fashionable among many in these egalitarian times to scoff at the notion of a special (or pastoral) calling. Opponents of this idea delight in pointing out that the word "call" (from the Greek *verb kaleo* and its relatives) are used in the NT only of the general calling of believers to Christ and His service, never of a special calling to preach the Gospel (though this premise is not totally accurate [compare Hebrews 5:4.)

However, this argument presupposes that the concept (of calling) and fact (of calling) cannot exist apart from the use of that specific word. Following that logic, we could not derive the doctrine of the Trinity from the Scriptures because the Bible does not anywhere use that specific word, even though it indicates a trinitarian concept of God in many places.

The reality is that the concept of selectivity for divine service, including a calling to proclaim the Word of God, runs through the Scriptures like a stream. The fact that the specific word "call" or one of its cognates is not regularly employed to describe the situation is quite irrelevant. The real issues are whether or not the Bible describes and teaches explicitly or implicitly that God handpicks and specially equips servants for sacred tasks and whether or not that selectivity appears to extend also to those who preach the Word. If so, then the burden of proof lies with those who challenge it to show why that same divine practice is no longer in force.

[7] Surely it is alarmingly ironic that more and more evangelical (the very word refers to the gospel and its proclamation of the Person and Work of Christ) preaching in this era speaks less and less about Christ. It perhaps would not be too strong to say that most evangelical sermons preached in American pulpits on any given Sunday require virtually no appeal (for their foundations) to the incarnation, example, atonement, resurrection, or ascension of our Lord. As churches have become progressively secularized, therapeutic Sunday preaching has pandered more and more to popular themes and sunk to shallow moralizing and pop counseling concerned with little more than helping people cope with their glitches and salve their itches. Preaching today has largely lost its Christo-centricity. And in doing so it has lost its power and elevation.

[8] Cf. 2 Sam. 7:12-16; Psalm 89:3; 132:11; Isa. 9:6ff; 11:1; and Luke 1:32 for significance of this as a Messianic credential.

[9] Hodge, *Epistle to the Romans*, 18.

[10] So, Hodge, Cranfield, although Bruce prefers to see the two parallel clauses as contrasting the two states of humiliation and exaltation.

[11] Cf. Cranfield, pp. 63-64 for other interpretations. Some, including Cranfield and Bruce, see this as a reference to the Holy Spirit—an interpretation which accords well with the interpretation of verse 4, which sees the resurrection not as declaring His Sonship, but as marking out His exaltation in power.

The humanity of Christ is crucial to our Christology in that 1) our redemption requires a *real* atonement (while a Docetic view of Christ [which denies the reality of his humanity] would reduce it to a mirage and 2) our redemption requires a *sympathetic* high priestly intercessor who has shared the weakness (sans fallenness) of our human condition.

[12] Abbott-Smith, *Greek Lexicon of the New Testament*, 323.

[13] Cranfield, *ICC: Romans Vol 1*, 61.

[14] Bruce, *The Epistle of Paul to the Romans*, 72.

[15] Cranfield, *ICC: Romans Vol 1*, 61.

[16] Sanday and Headlam, *ICC: Romans*, 7.

[17] Hodge, *Epistle to the Romans*, 21.

[18] Bruce, *The Epistle of Paul to the Romans*, 74.

[19] Except that the Greek infinitive *charein* (greeting) is replaced by the Greek noun *charis* (grace) to Christianize the conventional format.

[20] Cranfield, *ICC: Romans Vol. 1*, 72.

[21] See Cranfield, *ICC: Romans Vol. 1,* 73 on the conventional form of this section, yet far from formal in character and content. "The first sentence (after protocol) of an ancient Greek letter was very often of a pious nature, informing the recipient of the writer's prayer to the gods on his behalf. The prayer was sometimes a thanksgiving, but more often a petition: it was usually concerned with the recipient's health. Thus, formally, the beginning of Romans follows contemporary convention. But the character and content of Paul's thanksgiving are very far from being conventional. The subject of it is not the health or outward prosperity of those to whom he is writing, but the fact that their faith is everywhere reported." An interesting illustration here of the way Christians adapt the conventions, structures and forms of culture to Christian usages.

[22] Surely Paul would have despised and condemned our traditional benchmarks of effective ministry—burgeoning attendance inflated by half-washed pagans enticed by a half-baked 'gospel' (the be-happy-think-positive-God-loves-you-and-accepts-you-just-as-you-are-and-makes-no-demands-upon-you version, for instance), sprawling church plants, round-the-clock programming, holiday musicals and entertainment extravaganzas, corporate staffs, seven or eight figure budgets, and an impressive inventory of far-flung missionary supportees (many of whom are "carrying a lamp to Malaysia which never burnt at home." –the late Jess Moody

[23] If this is considered a form of oath (and that may be questioned) it does not fall within the spirit of that which Jesus (Matt. 5:33-37) and James (5:12) forbade. Ancients used oaths for the purpose of *incurring* obligation for performance. Hence what Jesus and James denounced was the notion that an oath *contracted* a duty to fulfill a promise or to tell the truth. Any use of oaths in that spirit was forbidden. Instead, one's word ought to be one's performance bond. And thought to be as secure as any oath could make it.

This prohibition did not address situations where one's word or promise might be genuinely susceptible to doubt (as, for example, in court cases). To reassure doubters of one's sincerity or truthfulness is not necessarily included in Jesus' injunction. For there is a fundamental difference whether one uses an oath merely as a concession to the misgivings of another or invokes one as a personal pledge or bond of performance. In the former case, one is simply attempting to convince another by the most solemn means of what he already knows to be true or intended. In the latter he is intending to obligate himself to be true and faithful to his word, a commitment which should take no form of oath to impose.

[24] Arndt & Gingrich, *Greek-English Lexicon of the New Testament*, 468.

[25] Arndt & Gingrich, *Greek-English Lexicon of the New Testament*, 17.

[26] For example, "We always observe Christmas," is relative to the pattern one has in mind. In this case it is annually. So we are saying that every year we celebrate Christmas in its season.

[27] https://www.ccel.org/ccel/wesley/sermons.v.xxiv.html, accessed 10/21/2023.

[28] Paul's egalitarianism in his preaching vision is striking. He stands apart from the 'vision' of those who prefer to major in evangelizing people of stature and influence. Such elitism was foreign to the spirit of the Apostle, himself evidently the scion of a wealthy and doubtless influential Jewish family from Cilicia.

Today there is a kind of 'yuppie' evangelical who makes a special target of people of influence, the uptown crowd—so-called business and political movers and shakers, the wealthy and the beautiful, the educated and the privileged—not, I suspect, all because they yearn for their salvation (which they may indeed) but partially also because they aspire (in a subliminal way) to be identified with their class. Such elitism would be repugnant to the Apostle who valued every man, not by a worldly standard, but by the immeasurable price Christ paid for his redemption.

[29] Cranfield, *ICC: Romans Vol 1*, 86-87.

[30] Sanday and Headlam, *ICC: Romans*, 23.

[31] Alan Redpath, chapel address, Western Bible College c. 1975.

[32] Grammatically, the righteousness of God could mean 1) the righteous character or activity of God [that is, the righteousness that belongs to God] is displayed in the gospel {subjective genitive} or 2) the righteousness that originates or comes from God [that is, the righteousness that God gives, or graciously imputes [to those who believe] {genitive of origin}.

As a matter of fact, the gospel manifests the righteousness of God in both senses. The question here is which aspect does the context demand.

As for the first sense, in Romans 3:25-26 it is clear that the gospel message confirms the perfect righteousness (in the sense of justice) of our holy God in that He never winks at sin in any generation but deals with it justly in Christ. Christ was our substitute at the cross. He became sin for us, so to speak. He bore our sins as if they were His own. Sin was justly atoned for in the precious blood of One unblemished and of infinite worth.

On the other hand, the whole epistle resounds with the theme that the moral righteousness of God is legally imputed or freely conferred on believers as a free gift. The believer is identified legally with Christ in His death for sin and thus before God is now treated as though he personally suffered for sin instead of Christ. Because of that legal identification with our Savior, our sins are summarily dismissed and the righteousness of Christ by legal decree is conferred upon us. This legal transaction is known as "justification." It is more than the subtraction of our sin and guilt (forgiveness); it includes the addition (by legal imputation) of the personal righteousness of Jesus Christ. This way of salvation is the major chord of the Epistle to the Romans.

In my view, the second jibes best with the context, especially when the two prepositional phrases are taken into consideration as well as the citation from the prophet Habakkuk.

[33] Other interpretations have been proposed, many far out and quite aside from the point. More viable is the view that understands Paul to be saying that faith is not only the ground of this righteousness, but also the goal for which it is so proclaimed. I find this view tempting, but the one adopted, which understands it to refer to that audience which alone recognizes it and welcomes it (those who believe God), seems most natural to the context. Cranfield's preference for the view that sees the two phrases combined as a kind of rhetorical device to simply emphasize *ex pisteos* or literally, from faith (thus the equivalent of sola fide—by faith alone) simplifies the meaning and is indeed consistent with the Apostle's main interest. However, this seems to discount the force of *eis pistin* (i.e. to faith) without explaining his right to do so. Is there any grammatical analogy for this? Until a clear one is adduced, it seems too convenient to me.

[34] Calvin, *The Epistles of Paul to the Romans and Thessalonians*, 30.

[35] Other proposals:

Barth: He views the 'for' in verse 18 as providing a second reason why Paul is not ashamed of the Gospel.

Barrett: He views the revelation of wrath as a proof put forth that the righteousness of God (viewed as an attribute rather than a gift) is being revealed. For discussion and rebuttal, refer to Cranfield, pages 107-8.

[36] Hodge, *Epistle to the Romans*, 35 (brackets mine).

[37] Bruce, *The Epistle of Paul to the Romans*, 81 (brackets mine).

[38] Bruce, *The Epistle of Paul to the Romans*, 83.

[39] On grounds that 'we cannot think with full consistency of God in terms of the highest human ideals of personality and yet attribute to Him the irrational passion of anger.' Dodd prefers therefore to understand this language impersonally, i.e., an inevitable process or cause and effect in the realm of objective facts,' 'an inevitable process of cause and effect in a moral universe'. [cited by Cranfield, p. 108]

[40] Cranfield makes three further points about the wrath of God which bear noting:

1) in analogizing between the human and divine expressions of wrath, we must compare the latter only to the higher, not the lower forms of human passion (such as indignation against injustice, cruelty and corruption).

2) even in its highest form, human wrath is a distorted expression of the purity of divine anger, for it is always compromised in sinful human nature by residual

pollutions.

3) that there is nothing irrational, unjust or perverse about the wrath of God is evident from its manifestation in this passage.

[41] Cranfield, *ICC: Romans Vol* 1, 112.

[42] So Hodge and Cranfield. Sanday and Headlam evade the question as do Bruce, Calvin. However, the problem is not terribly consequential logically.

[43] Godet, *Epistle to the Romans,* 103.

[44] Arndt & Gingrich, *Greek-English Lexicon of the New Testament*, 163.

[45] This view is preferred by Barrett and Cranfield because in their view the ensuing context implies natural revelation is only objectively present *among* men, not universally existing *in* them.

[46] As Cranfield argues

[47] Abbott-Smith, *Greek Lexicon of the New Testament,* 464

[48] Calvin, The *Epistles of Paul to the Romans and Thessalonians*, 31.

[49] Liddon, *Explanatory Analysis of Romans*, 26.

[50] Gifford, *Romans*, 63.

[51] Abbott-Smith, *Manual Greek Lexicon of the New Testament*, 204.

[52] Sanday and Headlam, *ICC: Romans*, 43.

[53] Gifford, *Romans*, 63. See also Acts 14:17 and 17:24 for other Pauline comments on natural revelation.

[54] One would need only a small sliver of liver to find out if a starving man would accept that food for relief of his hunger. That amount would not save him unless supplemented, but its rejection would be adequate to refuse him any more — even if liver were the only food capable of sustaining his life.

[55] Bruce, *The Epistle of Paul to the Romans*, 84.

[56] Godet, *Epistle to the Romans*, 104.

[57] Here we have an aorist active participle *gnontes* (from *ginosko*=I know). "The participle, as a verbal adjective, is timeless. The tenses of the participle express only continuance, simple occurrence, and completion with permanent result. Whether the action expressed by the participle is antecedent, coincident, or subsequent to that of the leading verb (in any tense) depends on the context." Herbert Weir Smyth, *Greek Grammar*, Harvard, p. 419.

[58] Calvin, *The Epistles of Paul to the Romans and Thessalonians*, 32.

[59] Barrett, *The Epistle to the Romans*, 36.

[60] Ibid, 37.

[61] That which is repressed tends to break out in indirect ways and betray itself. I think one symptom of this phenomenon is the way people use the name of God in profanity as in "Oh, my God!" Underlying this, I suspect, is a deep-seated God-consciousness.

[62] Gifford, *Romans*, 64.

[63] Charles Hodge seems to take this view though he does not elaborate nor discuss the problem as such. Cf. his *Commentary on the Epistle to the Romans,* p. 39.

[64] I am not aware of anyone who actually takes this position, but it is a viewpoint I can imagine being put forward.

[65] Lewis, *The Problem of Pain*, 115.

[66] Von Logau [trans. H.W. Longfellow], *Oxford Dictionary of Quotations.*

[67] The late false prophet, cult leader David Koresh, was an infamous example of religion gone bad. Bad religion lies even at the root of the immorality we see today in churches and church leaders. First, people turn their backs on the light they have and then they turn their backs on the laws of God.

[68] Abbott-Smith, *Greek Lexicon of the New Testament*, 339.

[69] Ibid, 170.

[70] E.g., 'Freedom' is a virtual sacred in our society. Anything that impinges on personal freedom, like authority, is looked upon as undesirable. Actually, the Bible does not sanctify the idea of freedom except in the sense of liberation from the power of sin. Much of our freedom-lust has its roots in the natural human desire for complete moral autonomy—in short, to do our thing without having to account to anyone else.

[71] *Wisdom of Solomon* 14:12, *The Apocrypha* NRSV, 51.

[72] The comfort that people find in the sheer numbers of fellow moral offenders is no more enduring or sustaining than that found on a skid row in the company drunks and derelicts. One may rationalize and bluster with self-righteous bravado, but the posturing is hollow. The very appearances of those who live outside moral boundaries mutely betray most of them eventually. Don't we all notice that people who live hard usually start looking hard? When one dishonors the body, generally the erosive effects reverberate throughout the whole being.

Nor is the impact self-contained. One of our modern myths is that people ought to be able to do any immoral thing they mutually consent to because they supposedly aren't hurting anyone but themselves, if they are hurting anyone at all. The reality of human nature is, the immorality of one always weakens the will of others to resist it, if it doesn't already debase another as an accomplice in it. Every lie makes it easier for others to lie; every robbery makes the thought of robbery less heinous to others and every act of infidelity or fornication has the effect of making the unthinkable more thinkable.

[73] Secular humanism partakes of this folly in putting man and his worth at the center of the universe.

[74] Hodge, *Epistle to the Romans*, 41.

[75] Homosexual advocates have tried to explain away the plain meaning of this passage. For a discussion of the ways in which they have attempted to circumvent this indictment of their perversion, see James B. DeYoung, *Journal of the Evangelical Theological Society*, Vol. 31, No. 4, December 1988, p. 429.

[76] It is nonsense for homosexuals to attempt to evade this condemnation of their perverse practice on grounds that it merely reflects an ancient and unenlightened bias. The truth is, homosexuality may have enjoyed greater approval among ancient Greeks and Romans than it does today in decadent Western cultures.
Consider this citation from Cranfield:
"The fact that ancient Greek and Roman society not only regarded pederasty with indulgence but was inclined to glorify it as actually superior to heterosexual love is too well known to need to be dwelt upon here. References in classical literature are frequent and widespread. Few indeed were the voices raised in protest from within Graeco-Roman society, but there were some. It is only fair to remember that Greece and Rome had no monopoly in homosexuality: it was common also in the Semitic world. To the Jews it was an abomination (see, e.g., Gen 19.1-28; Lev 18.22; Deut. 23,17f; I Kgs 14.24; 2 Kgs 23.7; Isa I.9; 3.9; Lam 4.6; Wisd. 14.26; Test. Levi 17.11; Or. Sib. 2.73; 3.59ff; Philo, *Spec. Leg.* 3.39, etc.), and Paul clearly shared his fellow-countrymen's abhorrence of it. In the NT compare I Cor 6.9; 1 Tim 1.10; 2 Pet 2.6ff; Jude 7 and also—for dominical words which must not be overlooked in this connection—Mt 10.14f; 11.23f." [*ICC: Romans Vol. 1*, 127.]

[77] Murray, *NICNT: Epistle to the Romans Vol. 1*, 48.

[78] Ibid, 47.

[79] Before the so-called sexual revolution in the 60's, Christians who rebuked sexual misconduct and spoke out against sources and instruments of sexual titillation, were often accused of being "obsessed" with sex. It should by now be apparent that this was a classic instance of that psychological device known as "projection" on the part of our accusers. Who has ever seen a society so preoccupied with sex (e.g., the TV talk shows). Where homosexuals are concerned, their whole life is built around the gratification of unnatural sexual appetite. Their preoccupation with sex, the way it controls their lives, would in the case of heterosexuals be considered pathological in and of itself.

[80] Cranfield, *ICC: Romans Vol 1*, 126 fn. 1. Citing Philo, *Spec. Leg. 3.39*.

[81] Abbott-Smith, *Greek Lexicon of the New Testament*, 363.

[82] Ibid, 10.

[83] Calvin, *The Epistles of Paul to the Romans and Thessalonians*, 37.

Romans Chapter 2

The gospel makes provision for a righteous standing or justification before God for all men on the basis of faith exclusively (1:16–17).

The need for it is urgent because the unrighteous are exposed to the wrath of God (1:18–32).

You (whoever you are) surely are included in the unrighteous, for you, in principle, do the same things (2:1–3:7).

Therefore, all individuals, Gentile or Jew, stand condemned and exposed to the wrath of God (3:8–20).

THE LOGIC BRIDGE FROM 1:18–32 TO 2:1ff

Nygren[84]: The Jews could agree immediately and entirely with all that Paul has thus far said against the Gentiles, with their idolatry and unrighteousness. The Gentiles are without excuse in their ungodliness and moral transgression. The wrath of God overtakes them justly. But now Paul directs the same charge against the Jews themselves.[85] The very fact that the Jew agrees so entirely with Paul's charge against the Gentile shows that he himself is without excuse and subject to the wrath of God.

His strategy now is to blow away the cover of false (self-righteous) security with which contemporary Judaism had surrounded its religious consciousness.

> (2:1) *Therefore you are without excuse, every man of you who passes judgment, for in that you judge another, you condemn yourself; for you who judge practice the same things...*

Therefore, you are without excuse, O man, whoever who condemns [them]. . .

"Therefore" reflects an inference drawn from two facts yet to be stated:

1) that the Jews do the very same things, and

2) that they condemn all those things they themselves do.

If they practice the sins of the Gentiles yet condemn them, they are religious hypocrites without a leg to stand on before God.

"Without excuse" is the same word used of the judicial status of the pagans in 1:20 (*anapologetos*). The point is that their standing before God is as indefensible as that of the Gentiles.

O man, whoever [literally, everyone who] is condemning. . .

From the ensuing section, it appears that the apostle has primarily in mind a prototypical religious Jew. The religious Jews felt themselves morally superior to Gentiles. With great disdain, they looked down on them in every way that matters. Considering themselves chosen of God, they felt securely in His divine favor. Never did it occur to most of them that they, too, might be in the same jeopardy as the godless Gentiles whom they despised.[86]

For. . .

Here, an explanation of their mutual inexcusability now follows.

Wherein you pass judgment on the other [man], you are condemning yourself.

This is a case of the pot calling the kettle black. You, Paul declares, are in the final analysis as guilty as they are.[87]

"Are practicing the same things..." This doesn't mean that every Jew practiced exactly the same vices as every pagan. The point is that all dishonor God, all suppress the truth in various forms of unrighteousness of the kind previously described, some being more disposed to one kind of sin than another, but all are deeply involved in these sorts of excesses. Besides, there is, as Cranfield notes, more than one way of committing the same sin[88] (like idolatry, this commentator would add).

"Another" (lit., "the other [man]")—the Greek word *heteron* (versus *allon*) frequently suggests one of a different kind as opposed to one of the same kind. Its use here perhaps indicates Paul's recognition that those in view in this section tend to set themselves above those in chapter 1 and write them off as a degenerate class all unto themselves.

(2:2) *And we know that the judgment of God rightly (kata alatheian) falls upon those who practice such things.*

"We know..."[89] An argument from shared ground. A pious Jew would concede that God's judgment would be *"according to truth"* (*kata alatheian*).

In other words, let no one who imitates such sin entertain false assumptions about the principle upon which the judgment of God works. Abandon any illusion that the judgment of God is based on different principles for different people, allowing Jews, for instance, to escape accountability for practices that Gentiles are condemned for.

Note two major accents here:

1) God's verdict is *against* the unrighteous.

"Against those who practice such things" (*ta toiauta prassontas*), wording which appears also in verse 3, the exact Greek phrase in 1:32. It links, therefore, these self-secure sinners with the indulgent sinners whose hateful vices were cataloged in that section.

2) God's verdict corresponds or conforms to ethical reality (*kata aletheian*), is according to truth; God will not "cook the books" to make allowance for racial identity or any other presumed basis of personal merit.[90] He does not grade on a curve.

(2:3) *And do you suppose this, O man, when you pass judgment upon those who practice such things and do the same yourself, that you will escape the judgment of God?*

"You" in the Greek (*su*) is emphatic. "That *you* (one such as you) shall escape..."

"There is abundant illustration of the view current among the Jews that the Israelite was secure simply as such by virtue of his descent from Abraham and of his possession of the Law: cf. Matt iii. 8,9 'Think not to say within yourselves, We have Abraham to our Father'; Jo. viii.33;..."[91]

Sanday and Headlam acknowledge the possibility of a strong element of popular misunderstanding since "we know that [the rabbis] insisted strenuously on the performance of the precepts of the Law, moral as well as ceremonial. But in any case, there must have been a strong tendency to rest on supposed religious privileges apart from any attempt to make practice conform to them."[92]

> *(2:4–5) Or do you think lightly (kataphroneo = treat with contempt) of the riches of His kindness and forbearance (anoches = holding back) and patience (makrothumia = long-temperedness), not knowing that the kindness of God is leading you to repentance, but because of your stubbornness (sklerotes = hardness) and unrepentant heart, you are storing up (thesaurizo) for yourself wrath in the day of wrath and revelation of the righteous judgment of God? (parentheses my insertions)*

Let no one who lives in disobedience to God misinterpret the meaning of the patience of God, that is, that forbearance of God, which withholds the full measure of His holy indignatio. His restraint in judgment should not be misconstrued as a signal of His indulgence or partiality. On the contrary, it is simply the "bait" of divine kindness coaxing one to repentance—a mercy, which, if scorned, will only aggravate the eventual intensity of His wrath.

"*Leads*" (*agei*) is a so-called conative present, that is, in the sense of "endeavors to lead." God's designs are always successful within the scope of His own intentions. In this case, His agenda intends to give their rebellious hearts incentive for repentance. When His mercy is refused, its rejection seals and intensifies the severity of their condemnation. God prods the impenitent to turn by displaying His kindness in the form of wonderous restraint. What the sinner should infer from His holding back is the conclusion that if God is so merciful when we are His enemies, imagine the kindness of God if we were to repent of our sins and become His servants.

In the day of wrath and revelation of the righteous judgment of God...

The wrath of God, which is presently evident in the form described in 1:24–32, will climax in the Day of the Lord, the time of the outpouring of the judgment of God upon evil. That judgment, characterized as just (righteous) in its execution, is impelled by indignation against those who, even at their best in the common grace of God, ultimately oppose Him who is the Source of all good.

(2:6) *Who will render to every man according to his deeds...*

This language may startle. We aren't saved by works, are we? Does not Paul himself emphatically teach that "by grace we have been saved through faith?" (Eph. 2:8) Does not he himself declare our salvation is "not by works, lest anyone should boast" (Eph. 2:8–9). Does this relative clause contradict his own words? No, not at all. If one is hung up there, it is because one is missing something important.

The apostle does not aver that God will *save* every man according to his deeds. Rather, he declares God will judge (i.e., render to) every man according to his deeds. Big difference. It is totally true that we have been saved (or justified) by God's grace through faith in Christ alone. Whether or not we actually possess the justification we profess will, at the end of the day, be confirmed (or exposed) by our fruits. No fruit, no root. No sanctification is proof positive that there has been no justification. We are not saved by faith plus works. Ah, no. We are saved by a faith that works or is operating through love (Gal. 5:6; James 2:26). That is why, when Christ returns, He will take measure of our walk, not merely our talk (Matt. 7:21–23).

So, the apostle offers no comfort to anyone who walks on the dark side, whether Jew or Gentile, to imagine God will fudge that principle in their case. It is what it is. There is no favoritism in His principle of judgment for anyone, and that includes Jews (and godless Baptists and whoever) who, in hope of heaven, assented with their mouth to a creedal statement but proceeded thereafter with their feet to agree with Hell. That will not happen.

Let no one ever imagine that there is any extenuating circumstance or compensatory merit that will overturn this impartial principle: God will render impartially to each person—Jew or Gentile—in a manner consistent with one's behavior. That principle of judgment is inviolate, so let us all sober up and be more diligent to make our calling and election sure (2 Pet. 1:10).

To be specific about this "deeds" business, our apostle teaches us the way God's judgment will play out—every single time:

> (2:7–10) *To those who by perseverance in doing good seek for glory and honor and immortality, eternal life; but to those who are selfishly ambitious and do not obey the truth, but obey unrighteousness, wrath and indignation. There will be tribulation and distress for every soul of man who does evil, of the Jew first and also of the Greek, but glory and peace to every man who does good, to the Jew first and also to the Greek.*

The phrase implies faith since "perseverance" (*hypomonen*) is in biblical nomenclature a steadfastness in the face of affliction and apparent contradiction of God's Word. This perseverance is driven by steadfast confidence in the ultimate fulfillment of God's promises in and through Christ; this perseverance and the walk that springs from it has, by implication, an underpinning in faith. But now is not Paul's time to unfold all that but here to simply establish the way the judgment of God will play out, lest any imagine God is a respecter of persons.

See the linkage between faith and perseverance (as its accompaniment) indicated in Romans 5:3–4; 1 Thessalonians 1:3 and 2 Thessalonians 1:4; Hebrews 10:36; 12:1; and James 1:4; 5:11, where Greek original *hypomone* is in the NASB often translated "endurance." It is the same word used in 2:7.

And do not obey the truth…

The phraseology implies unbelief. See 1:5 and 2 Thessalonians 2:12 and John 6:29. Faith (with all that it implies) expresses the essence of obedience to the truth, the "truth" referring to the revelation of God. Not "obeying the truth" is not responding to the revelation of God because of unbelief.

Before proceeding, I must acknowledge what the reader will very shortly observe independently. In the commentary notes (and footnotes) following, one will find a good deal of redundancy in exposition. Normally, I would hate that. However, in teaching, both as an instructor and as a student, when traversing often misunderstood and controverted terrain, I found pedagogical crisscrossing and backtracking sometimes helpful. For, occasionally, when I didn't quite get it (or get it across) I found sometimes coming at it a different way or expressing it perhaps another way, the lights came on. To the reader, I say, if you got it clearly the first time, no harm in moving on. But if this passage is not all that transparent to you, as it was not to me when I started expounding Romans in my first church out of seminary, then this variegated repetitiousness will be, I hope, beneficial.

So again, in red letters, Paul is not contradicting his principle of justification by faith alone apart from works; the fact is, he has not gotten around to that doctrine yet. Right now, he is not showing how men are *saved*; his present purpose is to show how men will be *judged*. In short, those who look like *this*, Jew or Gentile, will inherit eternal life, whereas those who look like *that* will meet with wrath and indignation—no matter who.

The principle of judgment stated in 2:6 is accepted by most commentators[93] as a universal principle applicable to believers and unbelievers alike. Obviously, I concur with this position.[94]

The relationship of faith to works is like that of life to a pulse. A pulse (or its absence) is a sign of life (or death).

The question has been asked, how the declaration that God will render to every man, whether Jew or Gentile, according to his works—to the good, eternal life, to the wicked, indignation and wrath—is to be reconciled with the apostle's doctrine, that no man is justified by works, that righteousness and life are not by works, but by faith, and through grace... to be borne in mind [is]... that notwithstanding the doctrine of gratuitous justification, and in perfect consistency with it, the apostle still teaches that the retributions of eternity are according to our works. The good only are saved, and the wicked only are condemned.[95]

"According to his deeds..." Imagine some local hosts preparing to throw a lavish party at an elegant, borrowed estate for a visiting popular celebrity. The trouble is that his admirers cut across social lines. Some are highly cultivated people who will respect the borrowed property, show good manners, and will not embarrass the hosts. The other set is a rowdy and disorderly bunch who are apt to turn up drunk and, in a mood, to tear up the place.

They sit down to try to figure out whom to let in and whom to turn away at the gate. They decide that one can judge a book by its cover. So, they look for some sort of litmus test as a fairly reliable indicator of both decorous and disorderly guests. After some reflection, they agree that in their past experience, appearance is a fairly reliable barometer of the two types. The orderly kind is invariably neatly groomed and well-dressed; the disorderly always show up looking disheveled and distinctly grunge.

They then agree that for purposes of admission to this event, they will judge would-be guests "according to their appearance."

Note that guests were not admitted *on account of* or *because of* their appearance but *according to* their appearance. They were admitted on account of their presumed decorum. Their appearance was merely an outward sign of an inward condition. Their appearance merely verifies that they represent a certain kind of person.

The bottom line (and this is consistent with the testimony of Scripture elsewhere, OT and NT) is that those whose lives are characterized (in God's terms) by goodness will be saved, and those who are bad (as God defines them) will be lost (cf. John 5:29; Heb. 12:14). We may as well come to terms with that outcome.[96] No sanctification says no justification.

At this point, Paul's burden is not to explain who and how some people qualify in God's sight as "good" and the rest as "unrighteous." His concern here was simply to shake out the popular Jewish misconceptions about the judgment of God and disabuse them of any notion that somehow unrighteous Jews would make the cut because they were Jews with all the privileges appertaining thereto.[97]

Good people do not *earn* justification for their goodness; but the ranks of the justified include only good people. At this junction, Paul is not saying how they became good people. That is beyond the scope of his present argument. He is just making it crystal clear that the judgment of God corresponds to reality, that in the end, God renders to each person a judgment that is consistent with their character. If modern professors of Christ ever really came to terms with this reality, it would blow a hole in the massive spiritual presumption that pervades our pews as it once did the tribes and clans of Israel.

(12:11) *For there is no partiality with God.*

Let no one be under any illusion that when it comes to salvation, the terms are the same for all—by grace through faith alone, be it Jew or Gentile, male or female, rich or poor, or whoever. The Jews, in particular, must not think that their favored standing as members of the chosen people through Abraham put the basis of their salvation on a different footing that allows them to be saved apart from the same faith as Abraham.

Review

Unless one stays in close touch with the flow of the argument in this section, it will confuse those who know very well that one is saved by grace through faith alone. And some commentators, in fact, do misconstrue Paul's point badly, especially 2:6.

The argument, I remind you, from 1:18 to 3:20, is to prove that the whole world—not only pagan Greeks (Gentiles), but the Jews too—stands in urgent need of salvation. So far, the author has shown that the pagans are without excuse before God and deserve condemnation.

Now in chapter 2, his burden is to awaken the unbelieving Jews to their own peril. Contrary to their religious delusions, they, he shows, are in the crosshairs of divine judgment, the same as the Gentiles whom they despise and condemn. They are, therefore, totally exposed to the same condemnation. What a shock!

On this point, the author's Jewish contemporaries were not up to speed. As for the wretched Gentiles, they had no trouble understanding why they deserved the indignant wrath of a holy God. They needed no one to tell them that the Gentiles were religiously deformed and morally degraded. What they never suspected, however, is that in God's eyes, they were in the same boat. Did they think God graded mankind on a curve?

As descendants of Abraham with whom God had established a covenant of blessing (circumcision being the outward sign of that promise), and by virtue of their privileged position as the custodians of the divine revelation and the law of God, well, to them that said it all. They were good to go. Their presumption is not greatly dissimilar to that so evident in our day in the case of nominal "Christians" who are smugly secure in their embrace of creedal orthodoxy but largely indifferent to the orthopraxy that should spring reflexively from genuine faith.

All such people, that day or this, need a wakeup call. Paul sets out to enlighten that kind about the principles of divine judgment. Here it is important to clearly understand his limited objective at this point in his argument.

How one gets right with God is a question still to be answered. Right now, his overriding objective is to persuade Christ-rejecting Jews that they are just as in need of redemption as those awful Gentiles to whom they felt so superior.

Again, his angle at this juncture is not to show them how to be saved but to alert them that they are not saved.

His approach is to confront them with their lifestyle, to confront them with the fact that they don't honor the law of God that they take so much pride in being the custodians of. The fact is, they are as fundamentally lawless as the Greeks (or Gentiles) whom they condemn. Thus, let them be aware that when they face God in the end, they are in for a rude discovery. The principles of divine judgment are absolutely impartial and conform in every case to moral reality. The truth is, unrighteous people (as all humans are in the flesh) never inherit the kingdom of God. If they are depending on some other overriding point of merit, they need to face facts. In this way, he attempts to loosen the bolts on their presumptuousness. Whether they know it or not, they are in trouble.

Totally apart from the question of how people are saved, Paul, in red letters, let all men know, and for all time, how God judges everybody without exception, Jew or Gentile, male or female, red, yellow, black, or white: God will measure profession against practice and will without respect of persons, judge everyone "according to his (or her) works." At the end of the day, the apostle teaches those to pass the test and inherit eternal life, glory and honor, and immortality will, in each and every case, fit the profile of 2:7 and 2:10. And those who don't pass muster will, in each and every case, be condemned because their profile matches 2:8 and 2:9. And it so happens that those characterizations (before God) describe unbelieving Jews (as well as the better kind of Gentiles) to a T. So let them take warning.[98]

Do not misunderstand. There is no implication that our salvation is in any way based upon our works. If Paul teaches anything, it is that salvation is by grace through faith alone. That is his central message. Again, I must stress: he is not *here* talking about how men are *saved*. So far his argument has to do with how people are *judged* in the end. The cold fact is, the lawless, whoever they happen to be—Jew, moralistic Gentile, or professing "Christian" CHINOs (Christians in name only) —won't wind up in God's Heaven. Only the godly do.

Though Paul doesn't overtly make these connections in this section, he will later make it clear that those who are saved (through grace by faith alone) can be judged or recognized by their fruit or works. You see, the faith that saves is never alone. Faith is known (verified) by its godly works. A godly lifestyle is a litmus test of a living faith just as the presence of physical life is verified by a pulse. It is no surprise that in the end, God will attest the genuineness of our professed faith by possessing the fruit of the Spirit in our lives (2

Cor. 5:10). Our godly works are, in effect, a kind of spiritual pulse that confirms that our faith is alive and not dead (James 2:26; 1 John 3:4–10).

For the moment, however, I repeat, the crucial business for Paul is simply to disabuse the very religious but lawless and unrighteous Jews (or anyone else who pretends to be "good enough") that they don't have the future they imagine. They are as lost as the deeply paganized Gentiles. The author understands that one cannot be saved until one comes to terms with the fact that one is lost.

Paul wants everybody to understand that when we stand before God, *who* you are will be established by *what* you are. Many yet today, in their antinomianism, fail to understand that. When God renders His verdict, let everyone understand that He will cook the books for no one. There will be no fudging. The verdict will be in strict accordance with moral reality. He will not cut Jews (nor church people) any slack. His judgment will be without partiality. So, it is time to find out if your life is in alignment with God and if the faith we profess has any roots or is just a religious tumbleweed.

Paul now proceeds to expand upon this principle that "there is no partiality with God" in terms of His judgment.

> (2:12) *For all who have sinned without the Law will also perish without the Law; and all who have sinned under the Law will be judged by the Law...*

There is no place for any sinner—be he Gentile or Jew—to hide from the strict justice of a holy God. Here are two classes of transgressors—those without knowledge of God's law (in its codified [Mosaic] form) and those in possession of His objectively revealed law. Neither category will escape the searching eye of an all-knowing God. Each will be held accountable to the light he has—and both have light to a degree sufficient to condemn them.

"All who have sinned..." that is, who have missed the mark in the ways described in the preceding verses. "Have sinned" gathers up all those forms and instances of sin as if they were a unit, that is, all textures of a solitary fabric of defiance and sinful self-will. [99] So, "sinned" looks back collectively to verses 8 and 9 to all the rebellion against God that is involved in the phrases "disobedient to the truth" (*apeithousi te aletheia*) and "producing that which is evil" (*katergazoumenou to kakon*).[100]

without the Law (*anomos*). . . *under the Law* (*en nomo*)

"Law" in this context appears to refer to formal or codified law objectively revealed by God (as opposed to that inscribed intuitively on the human conscience (cf. 2:15).[101]

The bottom line is this: all who have missed God's mark—whether in the case of propositionally revealed law or in the case of the internally revealed law of conscience—will find themselves condemned by whichever standard they have failed to live up to. In the words of Hodge, "God is impartial, for he will judge men according to the light which they have enjoyed."[102] He suggests that our Lord lays down the same principle in Luke 12:47–48.

Without the Law... will be condemned.

The Gentiles, on the other hand, have no exemption from accountability in their lack of special revelation in the form of a legal code. They will be judged—and condemned—by the light they do possess, that is, by the moral imperatives of that law inscribed on their consciences. He will develop this thought later.

Of those two categories of humanity, Paul first puts in his crosshairs the Jews who felt superior and condemnation-immune because they, after all, were divine custodians of the written revelation of God. Being stewards of the Law in the absence of obedience means little. In that, there is no refuge from condemnation. Here's why:

(2:13) *For it is not the hearers of the Law who are just (righteous) before God, but the doers of the Law will be justified... (parenthesis mine)*

"Hearers" (as opposed to readers) reflects the Jewish synagogue practice of listening to the reading the Law in services.

His Jewish kinsmen took great pride in their role as God's chosen custodians of the Law and congratulated themselves on their traditional attentiveness to it. Hence, they felt vastly more righteous than the Gentiles on both counts. Some of their teachers[103] did indeed emphasize the importance of practice, but it appears that in the main, the Jews, like many church attenders today, were more comfortable with the trappings of formal religiosity than attentive to practical righteousness as an expression of faithfulness. So, Paul warns that any sense of security derived from their faithful attendance to the reading of God's law at synagogue services was unfounded.

"Will be justified..."[104] that is, declared righteous by God at the final judgment. In every case, he warns, those approved by God will turn out to be those who were *doers* of the Law and not mere hearers. Again, I must re-emphasize the apostle is not teaching that anybody is justified by obedience to God; the point is that God's true people are verified at the end of the day not by who they are (i.e., Jews) but by *what* they are. By their walk, not their talk and privileges.

As Murray indicates, the simple point is that conformity, not custody of the law of God—obedience, not attendance—is the basis of judgment (evaluation). Where the ability to keep the requirement of the Law comes from (see Rom. 8:1–4) is a question not even in view at this point. Right now, Paul is concerned only with establishing that pedigree and privilege don't justify anybody and will shortly make the point that Gentiles who do obey God will be accepted by God before Jews who don't. That is just the bottom line.

Justification is spoken of in a forensic or legal sense, an act of God, whereby He declares a sinner (as we all natively are) righteous in His eyes. The author does not, at this point, explain how justification works (that comes in chapter 3), but here merely informs us that those persons (Jew or Gentile) whom God justifies will, in every instance, prove to be those who walk the walk, not those who just talk the talk. God's people are all players; none is a religious pretender.

So the apostle is, by implication, telling all within earshot, "Get real." The proof of what you are is in the practice, not in your profession, your privileges, or your pedigree. So, look in the mirror.

Don't get all puffed up by who you are; get sobered up by what you are. That tells the story, and God will not fudge His verdict for anyone.

This phraseology should not surprise us. Jesus said to some Jews who had ostensibly believed in Him that the proof was in the pudding: "If you continue in My word (i.e., My teaching), you are truly My disciples..." (John 8:31). Our Lord wasn't talking about merely giving nodding assent to what He taught (orthodoxy). By that language, He also meant abiding faithfully in it (orthopraxy). He also taught us that the badge of discipleship is that "you love one another as I have loved you" and that "by this all men will know that you are My disciples, if you have love for one another" (John 13:34–35). Moreover, Jesus and Paul both stress the point that the sum and substance of obedience to the Law is love for God and our neighbor (Matt. 22:36–40; Rom. 13:10). If there is life, there will be a pulse. If there is a root (faith), we can expect fruit appropriate to the root.

Now Paul turns to enlarge on his premise about the Gentiles being judged without the Law.

How can those without the Law, one might inquire, be judged guilty of transgressions they never knew existed? Well, each, Paul will explain, has a form of light sufficient to condemn his sinful ways. For, E. H. Gifford aptly notes, "the want of greater light gives no impunity to the abuse of the less."[105] To the implicit question, Paul responds:

(2:14) *For when the Gentiles who do not have the Law do instinctively (physei = instrumental dative) the things of the Law, these, not having the Law, are a law unto themselves. (parenthesis mine)*

The presence of such an internal code is verified when Gentiles measure and regulate their behavior by that unwritten code within (intuitive). Its existence is further confirmed as they wage moral debate within themselves, their private thoughts alternately accusing and defending their personal actions. That is the giveaway. Again, there is no place to hide once a person begins moralizing—and everybody does it.

The point is this: God has not left anybody without a witness of His will (though that testimony doesn't exist in the same form or fullness in all cases). Nevertheless, the Gentiles have deviated from their own intuitive standard as badly as the Jews have missed the other. Their mutual condemnation will be revealed on that day when God, in accordance with the truth revealed in the gospel, confronts men and exposes the secrets of their hearts.

Now, here, we face an interpretative problem: What is the logical connection of this verse with the previous discussion from verse 12? The usual views of the transitional logic are these:

1) Some say this verse harks back verse 13b ("For not the hearers of the law are righteous before God, but the doers of the law shall be justified.") but the logic is seen differently:

   a) It says: "That strict principle applies also to the Gentiles, since they too have a certain kind of law to which they may be held to account."

Though that sense is good, verse 13 is talking not about law as a principle but the codified law of God. This connection would break his systematic two-step exposition of the principle of verse 12. That seems to be what Paul is doing here, dealing first with the Jewish side, then the Gentile.

   b) Others think it says: "For if it were otherwise, some Gentiles might have as good or better claim to justification as the Jews, since they also give evidence of possessing law in another form and even practice the morality that your law requires."

The problem with this take on it is Paul's supposed coup de grace would not carry much weight. The very point of the popular Jewish false security (rooted somewhat in custodianship of the Law) was that God had spoken to them in a special way, in a way that he had not revealed Himself to any other nation. Therein lay one big source of their religious presumption. The internal law the Gentiles possessed, even if conceded, did not in the Jewish mind compare to what they had in the OT. So, to argue that the Gentiles had a form of natural law and that some of them obeyed natural law, the standards of written law would not prove too much to the Jew. Apples and oranges!

 c) Others take it this way: "Gentiles who respect God's law will be justified just the same as obedient Jews."

But this slant is beside the point. Paul's burden at this juncture, I remind, is not to show the means of justification but the basis of judgment. True, he has just mentioned justification, but only to indicate that, contrary to popular Jewish assumptions, mere possession of the Law is not sufficient for a favorable verdict for anyone who presumes to approach God on a legal basis. The emphasis, therefore, is not on a method of justification but on the strict consistency of divine judgment in rewarding men—Jew or Gentile—according to their works.

2) Others say this verse comes back logically to pick up and expand upon the declaration in the first clause of verse 12 ("For as many as have sinned without the law, shall be judged without the law..."). It amplifies the ground of Gentile accountability and shows how Gentiles living outside the pale of revealed religion can be justly held accountable for light (i.e., the law of Moses) they didn't possess.

Paul says (extending into verse 15): in effect, the Gentiles will be judged without the law, *for* they have another form of law, of which they give evidence in numerous ways, and that law will convict them on that day in which (in accordance with the gospel that I preach) they stand before God and will be judged by Jesus Christ, and every secret of their heart is laid open.

Thus, *verse 14 intends to show that while the Jews have no shelter in the possession of the written Law, the Gentiles have no refuge in its absence.* For the fact is, they do possess another standard by which they may be judged. It would then be answering the natural question, as Murray puts it, "'If the Gentiles are without the law, how can they be regarded as having sinned?' The answer is that although the Gentiles are 'without the law' and 'have not the law' in the sense of specially revealed law, nevertheless they are not entirely without law; the law is made known to them and is brought to bear upon them in another way."[106]

This view of the logic serves the argument better since it is much closer to the point at hand.

"Do by nature the things of the Law."

On the face of it:

1) Fulfill the moral demands of the Law (absolutely).

2) Walk uprightly in relative moral consistency (i.e., a Christian walk).

3) Conform in some respects to the moral directives of the written Law in the sense of "doing from time to time of things which are in accordance with the law." [107]

As always, when language is so elastic that it is capable of more than one sense, the context must decide. By "context," we mean that the best interpretation will be the sense that is more agreeable to the immediate context and the larger biblical context—the one that explains the most and leaves us with the fewest problems.

The first is impossible (cf. 3:20). It would fly in the face of his whole argument and NT theology. No one has ever fulfilled the demands of the Law absolutely—except Jesus.

The second possibility is impertinent to his argument. His argument requires him to show that Gentiles, as well as Jews, may be fairly condemned, the Jews on the basis of the written code they possess but don't practice, and the Gentiles on the basis of another kind of law which their practices prove that they do possess.

Thus, the third option harmonizes far better with the apostle's logic.

By nature... (physei. . . poiosin).

"What is done 'by nature' is done by native instinct or propension, by spontaneous impulse as distinguished from what is induced by forces extraneous to ourselves."[108]

Are a law unto themselves... (*heautois eisin nomos*).

Paul intimates by this expression that the Gentiles betray by certain behaviors (about to be mentioned) that phenomenon we call "conscience," upon the tables of which one finds imprinted a kind of code resembling His objectively revealed moral law.

"They have in their own nature a rule of duty; a knowledge of what is right, and a sense of obligation."[109]

Murray[110] says this involves three realities: 1) the law of God confronts them and registers itself in their consciousness by reason of what they natively and constitutionally are; 2) they do things which this law prescribes; and 3) this doing is not by extraneous constraint but by natural impulse.

One proof of its existence is its derivatives: human law codes and behaviors which are consistent with divine law (in external terms).[111]

(2:15) *In that they show the work of the Law written in their hearts, their conscience bearing witness, and their thoughts alternately accusing or else defending themselves...*

Another testimony to its existence is the conscience quarrelling with itself (or other consciences) in the battle of moral choices.

Show the work of the Law...

"It is not a different law that confronts the Gentiles who are without the Law [in codified form] but the same law brought to bear upon them by a different method of revelation." [112]

The work of the Law, as Murray indicates, simply means the "things required and stipulated by the law"[113] are etched into their consciousness as moral imperatives.

"Their conscience bearing witness together..." i.e., with their moral behavior. Unlike brutes, human behavior is morally selective. The very fact of conforming to the Law of God in response to natural intuitions is a reflection of the image of God in man (as opposed to mere animals) and the existence of His Law in the conscience.

"Alternately accusing or else defending..." This language depicts the conscience monitoring moral options and policing choices according to whether they are good or bad. The fact that the human conscience is not universal at all points, and seemingly non-existent in some, merely reflects how the fall wreaked havoc upon man's conscience and how susceptible it is to cultural conditioning apart from the knowledge of God. Yet its persistence and pervasiveness at so many points indicate the presence of a divine imprint that can be suppressed only by the "dumbing down" of sinful influence.

In the end, guilt trips and moral defensiveness tell the tale. The Gentiles as well as the Jews know better than they live. We have no excuse. There is no place to hide. God's law is, to some degree, accessible to all, and the final test will be whether people honored it or whether they didn't. People who reject Christ reject God, and those who reject God inevitably dishonor His law. The converse is true as well. However, this connection of things comes later. Right now, the point is simply to get across the idea that no place is safe for the person who lives a life disobedient to God.

(2:16) *On the day when, according to my gospel [i.e., the good news with which I am divinely entrusted], God will judge the secrets of men through Jesus Christ. [brackets mine]*

What is the referent here? What does "on the day when…" refer to? One would naturally look for that referent in verse 15 or, if not there, close behind it. The trouble is, verse 15 is citing a present-time phenomenon (the activity of conscience in quarrelling with itself) as an evidence of an intuitive imprint of the law of God upon the human consciousness, thereby rendering sinners without formally revealed law accountable and condemnable, whereas verse 16, without warning, transitions the action (whatever it is) to the future "when God shall judge the secrets of men by Jesus Christ."

Logically, it makes little sense to speak of Gentile sinners as "showing the work of the Law written in their hearts, their conscience bearing witness, and their thoughts alternately accusing or else defending themselves, on the day when… God will judge…" How can a phenomenon described as a present-time activity and produced by the author as contemporary evidence of guilt suddenly (and without any clue or warning) be relocated to an end-time phenomenon? That's the problem.

So, verse 15, grammatically speaking, almost begs for a close connection, but logically, every alternative seems strained. So, many commentators (most, I think) have looked elsewhere for a more feasible one. Logically, the most satisfying is verse 12 (all will be judged... on the day when... God will judge the secrets of men..."). Hence, they have concluded that verses 13–15 are, in effect, a parenthetical expansion upon verse 12 and that verse 16 just picks up verse 12, where the author broke off to follow another trail.

As natural a sense as this proposal yields, it still leaves us, I think, with a forbidding problem. People just don't write that way. Nobody —at least I have yet to see an instance of it—interposes that much material plus a significant argument at that—between the main sentence and a dangling dependent clause. Psychologically and compositionally, it simply isn't natural, and I, for one, can't imagine anyone, including the apostle, deferring such a thought for so long.

Of course, someone, especially Paul, may (and does) sometimes break off an idea, go into a parenthetical mode, and then come back and pick up the thread again. He clearly does this between Ephesians 3:1 and 14. However, in that instance, he does the natural thing: he reformats his original thought and starts over with a whole new sentence. That's what one would expect (at least I would) here in verse 16, where our author is coming back to finish the thought of verse 12. The fact that he doesn't is, in my opinion, a rather compelling argument against that view.

So, we are left with a dilemma—to choose between an interpretation that seems logically nonsensible, one that is grammatically unsound and compositionally improbable.

Again, the soundest choice is the alternative that explains the most in total context and leaves the interpreter with the fewest difficulties. In this case, that may be a toss-up.

Calvin prefers the connection with verse 15. In his view, it emphasizes that the present activity of conscience will also be operative when mankind has its rendezvous with God. Still, it is an awkward way of expressing the thought.

Consider the present tense as a usage that Smyth[114] describes as a "present of general truth," that is, "the present is used to express an action that is true for all time," as, for example, in the expression, "Time brings the truth to light."

Taken that way, we read verse 15 as a timeless activity of conscience and one that will reach a loud crescendo and be fully exposed to plain view in all its self-excusing and self-condemning cacophony on that day when sinners are confronted with the searching eye of an all-knowing God who will condemn them with their secrets.[115]

When God shall judge the secrets of men...

"He informs those who willfully conceal themselves in the hideaways of their moral insensibility that those innermost thoughts, which are at present entirely hidden in the depths of their hearts [but nevertheless there] will then be brought to light."[116]

"According to my Gospel through Christ Jesus."

Part and parcel of the gospel message is the announcement of the Day of the Lord and the righteous judgment of God. That impending event was not news to the Jews. What would, however, disturb their minds was the proclamation that God would judge in the person of Jesus Christ (in the Greek text it is <u>Christ</u> [Messiah] Jesus). Him they had shamefully rejected and crucified with the assistance of the Gentiles (represented in Roman authority). If Jesus was the Messiah and He was going to be the Judge, any further question about the final outcome was moot. They were colossal sinners with no place to run.

2:17–24

Let not the Jew take refuge in his Jewish pedigree or religious privileges if he is a transgressor, which, in fact, he is.

(2:17) *But if you bear the name 'Jew', and rely upon the Law and boast in God...*

"But if you bear the name 'Jew'. . ." a name that his countrymen wore like a badge of honor. They boasted in their Jewishness as

Abraham's physical descendants through Isaac and Jacob. They considered themselves as certified heirs (so they thought) of God's covenant promises to his seed.

The trouble is, they misunderstood the qualifications for heirship to God's promises to Abraham. To be his physical descendants through Israel (Jacob), duly circumcised (properly cleansed), and observing the religious rituals prescribed by the law, they fulfilled (so they thought) all the essential conditions for divine approval and inheritance of the kingdom of God.

"And rely (*epanapauei*) upon the Law..." The Greek verb (in the present tense) means to rest, find rest or comfort in (something). The present tense implies a habit or custom in this case.

Jewish reliance on the law took two forms:

1) The complacent and self-indulgent kind who took false security in the mere fact that God had privileged them to be the repositories of His revelation, implying, they thought their favored status as Jews.

2) Those who were scrupulous about the external forms of the Law and prided themselves on their rigorous conformity to its external requirements, both ritual and moral. These viewed themselves as law-keepers, deserving of salvation on the basis of their legal conformity to God's requirements, when, in fact, they missed the spirit of the law by miles. They even learned how to twist the Law to justify the very things God's law disallowed. Jesus excoriated their moral and legal hypocrisy (see Matt. 15:1–8; 23:1–33).

Cranfield comments:

> The Jew is absolutely right to be seriously concerned with God's law, to follow after it (cf. 9.31) with the utmost diligence, and to rely on it as God's true and righteous word. But the trouble is that he follows after it (out of works) instead of (out of faith) (cf. 9.32) and relies on it in the sense of thinking to fulfill it in such a way as to put God in his debt or imagining complacently

that the mere fact of possessing it gives him security against God's judgment.[117]

And boast in God...

How tragically ironic, for, as Murray notes, "glorying in God was in itself the epitome of true worship (cf. 45:25; Jer. 9:24; 1 Cor. 1:31)." Yet, he continues, this implied rejection of their "worship" reminds us "how close lies the grossest vice to the service of the worst."[118]

This implicit indictment reminds us of the folly of the persistent myth that all religion leads in the same direction (pluralism[119]) merely by a different path and that sincerity is a pass key to the kingdom that God will never fail to honor.

The Jew claimed Yahweh as his God, the true and only God (Deut. 6:4). The problem was that the average Jew did not know the character of the God they worshiped by that name. As Paul said, "I bear them witness that they have a zeal for God, but not in accordance with knowledge" (10:2). The God they worshiped under the name of Yahweh was less the God of biblical revelation than it was a construct of their imagination. "Yahweh" in the mind of unbelieving Israel was a God who favored Israel for Israel's sake, a legalistic God who was content with formal, ritualistic righteousness (at least in Israel's case).

The clinching proof that Israel had no true conception of Yahweh was her failure at last to recognize Yahweh in Jesus. Instead, they opposed Him. They slandered Him as a blasphemer and an imposter. Finally, the nation demanded His death, and in His cruel crucifixion, it stood by and mocked Him. In its religious zeal, unbelieving Israel worshiped God by the right name, but had the wrong person in mind. It was a case of mistaken identity.

The fact is, wrong-headed religious "sincerity," whatever doctrines it espouses, is never anything more than the fruit of self-delusion stemming from underlying human desires to shape one's religion in a fashion agreeable to our carnal appetites. The common denominator of all false religion lies right there: what is false in it, one will always find, is curiously agreeable to the flesh.

On the other hand, everything about true religion is distasteful and unnatural to our fleshly (I did not say "human") cravings.

(2:18) *And know His will and approve the things that are essential, being instructed out of the law...*

That is, as the custodians of His revelation, they have been taught the requirements of God's law (at least in its formal or external sense). They know His will in that they possess cognitive knowledge of the law of God revealed in Scripture, much as some professing Christians, well-schooled in Bible knowledge, might pride themselves on their knowledge of God's Word and His revealed will.

"Instructed" (*katecheo*) connotes the mere possession of information conveyed from another. Thus, the head may hold information the spirit of which the heart has not yet discerned in its deeper implications.

"Approve" (*dokimazo*) often implies approval after testing. So, the Jews prided themselves on rejecting Gentile traditions and adopting as their standard morally superior "biblical values," as we would say. They boasted in their superior moral sensibilities and patted themselves on the back for the discernment to recognize the excellence of God's law in comparison to the low standards of the Gentiles. Better that they should rather have praised the mercy of God for letting them in on the secret rather than credit themselves for their intrinsic virtuosity.

(2:19–20) *and are confident (pepoithas) that you yourself are a guide to the blind, a light to those in darkness, a corrector of the foolish, a teacher of the immature, having in the Law the embodiment (i.e., the form = (morphosin) of knowledge and of the truth in the law. (parentheses mine)*

The perfect tense reflects the foundational assumptions about their role in the world. These are antecedent to and concurrent with their sense of moral superiority—a sense of superiority founded primarily on who they were and a knowledge that they possessed (rather than actually conformed to) it.

In a sense, Israel's self-perception of its place in the scheme of things was true. Her role was indeed to function as a conduit of light to those in darkness, to mediate the truth of God. God meant for Israel to act as a priest to the nations. "Now then, if you will indeed obey My voice and keep My covenant, then you shall be My own possession among all the peoples, for all the earth is Mine; and you shall be to Me a kingdom of priests and a holy nation" (Exod. 19:5–6). Where it all fell apart was that Israel 1) failed to walk in the truth she possessed and 2) glorified the letter of the Law, failing miserably to understand its inner spirit. This failure is what Jesus highlights in Matthew 5:17ff, where He rejects the superficial "righteousness" of the scribes and Pharisees and expounds the fuller scope and intent of the Law.

This was then her appointed vocation, but in that career, the nation as a whole badly disappointed her job description.

> (2:21–23) *You therefore, who teach another, do you not teach yourself? You who preach that one should not steal, do you steal? You who say that one should not commit adultery, do you commit adultery? You who abhor idols, do you rob temples? You who boast in the Law, through your breaking the Law, do you dishonor God?*

Verse 17 began with the protasis of a conditional sentence, that is, a string of (implicit) "if" clauses containing traditional Jewish assumptions and professions. Now comes the apodosis (i.e., the main or concluding part of a conditional sentence). In the form of rhetorical questions that expect (from the Jewish conscience) an affirmative answer, the apostle exposes their moral hypocrisy. The simple fact is that they typically don't walk their talk; they don't practice what they preach.

Traditionally, the nation flaunted the very law it regularly flouted. Jesus had indicted the Pharisees, the epitome of the "best" of Jewish religiosity, for its flagrant hypocrisy and casuistic evasions of the plain intent of divine law (see again Matt. 15:1–8; 23:1ff).

"Do you rob temples…" I am uncertain exactly what form this took. Formal idolatry of the kind that exposed Israel to the Babylonian captivity had disappeared in Israel. I can only speculate that in its contempt for paganism (but still with an idolatrous love of the gold and other precious metals and stones), the Jews may have rationalized "heists" and thefts of valuable artifacts from the sacred places of the Gentiles, either serving as "fences" for others or taking these items themselves. In any case, the habit the apostle condemns is a form of back-door idolatry, one expression of covetousness. They loved material wealth more than they loved God and didn't mind plundering even pagan sanctuaries to obtain it, directly or indirectly.

(2:24) For "the name of God is blasphemed among the Gentiles because of you," just as it is written.

In summary fashion, the apostle goes all the way back to the prophet Isaiah for a citation confirming Israel's long-standing tradition of moral hypocrisy and the reproach that cupidity (52:5) had brought down on the name of Yahweh among the Gentiles. Whether that reproach took the form of reviling and belittling Israel's God for failing to stand up for her when Yahweh found it necessary to punish His covenant people for their sins or in making themselves (and in the process) their religion odious among the nations because of their excesses and vices, doesn't matter. The effect was all the same. God was dishonored. That, at bottom, is the offense of idolatry in a left-handed form..

(2:25–26) Circumcision is of value…

Circumcision is the surgical abscission of the foreskin of the male private part. It was a physical procedure with religious significance performed on all Jewish male infants on the eighth day after birth.

It functioned as a seal. It marked each Jewish male and his family as a descendant of Abraham and signified that they (supposedly) shared the same faith of Father Abraham and were therefore heirs of all the promises that God made to him and his (true spiritual) seed.

A Jew was not considered "holy" or "clean" until his pedigree was ratified by the sign of circumcision.

Circumcision, when (and only when) it truly signifies what it was supposed to mean, that is, true faith and holiness or cleanness in the sight of God, was an honorable thing in the sight of God. That condition existed when and only when it was accompanied by the kind of obedience to God that is born of faith, the kind of obedient faith that God found in Abraham and upon the basis of which justified the patriarch.

"Of value" doesn't mean that circumcision in itself was a ground of merit before God, but that it meant something when backed up by the faith and holiness for which it stood. It is like saying that a dollar has value when backed up by gold reserves but is worthless paper without it.

Somewhere along the line, as often happens with religious rituals and symbols, the original significance of the rite got lost in the shuffle. After that, it in itself came to be viewed as imparting of itself "holiness" or "cleanness" and therefore rendering a Jew (or proselyte) acceptable to God.

What got lost along the way, as we shall see in chapter 4, was the fact that circumcision per se was never a *source* of holiness but merely a badge and *reminder* of Abraham's faith (on the basis of which God, in His mercy, saw fit to freely justify him and make him (and all those who walked in his same steps of faith toward God) an heir of great and precious promises of salvation.

The rite of physical circumcision was, in reality, a spiritual pointer to all Abraham's descendants. It marked the path that Abraham walked... the path of obedient faith. When Abraham embarked on that path, God graciously counted his faith for righteousness. Then, as his earthly reward, not on the basis of works, but on the ground of grace, God bestowed on Abraham and all his descendants who would walk in his same footsteps of faith, many great and precious promises. Unfortunately, most of his biological descendants missed that contingency—Abraham's true descendants were those who walked in the faith of their father, Abraham. And it is precisely the point embedded in Paul's later assertion (9:6): "for they are not all Israel who are descended from Israel (Jacob)."

So, physical circumcision was meant to be a kind of Jewish beacon to beckon all of Abraham's seed (through Isacc and Jacob) to emulate his same obedient faith. So, the acid test of faith—of which circumcision is merely an outward sign of affirmation—is *faith-full* obedience to God. That had blown right by unbelieving Israel.

Paul's point is that circumcision without faith is hollow... that it is as meaningless and worthless as baptism without faith, as a wedding band without marital fidelity. It means nothing to God. God hates symbols unsupported by substance. He hates religious rites without righteousness. Obedience is the *sine qua non* ("without which nothing") of biblical religion. Real faith produces love and cheerful obedience, and nothing counts a plug nickel without it. It is not faith plus works we are talking about: it is faith that works in response (James 2:14–26).

"Circumcision is nothing, and uncircumcision is nothing, but what matters is the keeping of the commandments of God" (1 Cor. 7:19), which is simply to say, "doing what God directs us to do." Grace is not without demands, as some antinomian types think. But the demands of grace are not legal (as in earning God's favor) but are moral (if we trust Him and love Him, please Him, and do this or that).

"For in Christ Jesus neither circumcision nor uncircumcision means anything, but faith working through love" (Gal. 5:6). It is not about performing rites but doing faith-driven righteousness for the love of Christ).

(2:25) But if you are a transgressor of the law, your circumcision has become (amounts to) uncircumcision. (parenthesis mine)

Put another way, if you are lawless, you, in effect, make yourself a Gentile, a pagan; your vaunted, self-professed "holiness" or "cleanness" becomes nothing more than "uncleanness," and one is unacceptable to God.

Circumcision as a badge of Abrahamic faith is null and void in that the faith it is supposed to signify is contradicted by lawlessness. As

James makes quite clear, "Just as the body without the spirit is dead, so also faith without works is dead" (2:26). Faith, Paul teaches in Galatians 5:6, *works* or operates (*energomene* = a present participial form of the verb from which we get our English word "energy"). It is not a static state. It cannot fail to express itself any more than a living body can fail to breathe. It works or *operates* through love. And love is the peg on which hangs all the law and the commandments of God (Matt. 22:40). Without righteousness, there is no religious reality, and circumcision is emptied of all its meaning. The unbelieving Jew may as well be a pagan Gentile for all the good his circumcision will do him.[120]

A man would a million times over rather be married to a faithful wife who never wore his ring as married to one who did and played him false. So it is with God, Paul informs the unbelieving Jews who trample in their faithlessness upon God's law while they flaunt their circumcision as a badge of religious security.

> (2:26) *If therefore the uncircumcised man (the Gentile person) keeps the righteousness of the Law, will not his uncircumcision be reckoned for circumcision?*

The question implies "Yes!" for an answer. Gentiles who respond to God in obedient faith (rather than a lip-service faith that is dead and without root) will be accepted by God and treated as "holy." They will be considered spiritual seed of Abraham, for they emulate him in faith-driven obedience. The absence of physical circumcision will in no way prejudice the case against them, for their holiness or circumcision is in the heart, where it really matters. Obviously, unbelieving Israel has placed inordinate weight on physical circumcision as a passport to the kingdom of God. That is not a ticket that will gain them passage.

That is what Peter learned and reported in Acts 10:35:

> "In every nation the man who fears Him and does what is right, is welcome to Him" (compare Isa. 56:6–7).

(2:27) *And will not he who is physically uncircumcised, if he keeps the Law, will he not judge you (by example) who though having the letter of the Law and circumcision are a transgressor of the Law? (parenthesis mine)*

If he keeps the Law...

This phraseology does not refer to absolute moral perfection any more than it does in 2:13 or 8:4. It refers to that obedient spirit that springs from Abraham-like faith, which includes acknowledgment of personal sin and appropriation of God's covenantal provisions for forgiveness.

"Will he not judge you. . ." "does not mean that they will sit in judgment but refers to the judgment of comparison or contrast (cf. Matt. 12:41, 42)."[121]

Those who have responded in obedient faith to the Word of God outside the flock of Israel will, in effect, show up and condemn by contrast those who have been born into the nation's religious privilege (meaning born into a heritage of biblical revelation and God's gracious invitation to Abraham's descendants to share the promises bequeathed to him by faith). When others enthusiastically embrace and respond to privileges that Israel despises and squanders, it exposes the nation to greater judgment for its contempt of its privileges.[122]

(2:28) *For he is not a Jew who is one outwardly; neither is circumcision (holiness) that which outward in the flesh... (parenthesis mine)*

Lost on the average Jew was the fact that physical descent from Abraham was not the essence of Jewishness, that is, not the essence of belonging to Abrahamic descendancy or being an heir of the Abrahamic covenant. Nor was the circumcision that really matters a physical abscission of flesh but putting off an unclean heart.

True holiness is interior, not exterior. It was not affected through surgery performed by human hands, nor is true holiness accomplished by keeping the superficial letter of the Law[123] but exists in a transformation of heart wrought by the Spirit of God, who inscribes God's will upon the desires of the human heart.

(2:29) *But he is a Jew who is one inwardly; and circumcision is that which is of the heart, by the Spirit, not by the letter; and his praise is not from men, but from God.*

The true Jew enjoys the approval of God, whereas surface Jews follow a form of religion that is based on personal merit and seeks and finds human approval—which is totally irrelevant. True Jewishness is measured by circumcision of the heart, not the flesh.

---

[84] Nygren, *Commentary on Romans*, 113.

[85] I would agree with Bruce and others that, while the Apostle has the Jew preeminently in view, he also wishes his indictment to embrace also the 'better' (moralistic) type of Gentile who also might want to distance himself from the pagan extremities that Paul has just arraigned. Bruce illustrates this type well with the case of Seneca, the Stoic moralist and tutor of the infamous Emperor Nero:
". . . Seneca could write so effectively on the good life that Christian writers of later days were prone to call him 'our own Seneca'. Not only did he exalt the great moral virtues; he exposed hypocrisy, he preached the equality of all men, he acknowledged the pervasive character of evil ('all vices exist in all men, though all vices do not stand out prominently in each man'), he practiced and inculcated daily self-examination, he ridiculed vulgar idolatry, he assumed the role of a moral guide. But too often he tolerated in himself vices not so different from those which he condemned in others —the most flagrant instance being his connivance at Nero's murder of his mother Agrippina." (Bruce, *The Epistle of Paul to the Romans*, 87)

[86] It is possible however that Paul may have "neutered" his language at this point to widen the embrace of his statement to also include any high-minded Gentiles who condescendingly frowned upon the pagan excesses of their own kind.

[87] The argument put more formally is thus:
All who denounce in others sins that they also practice condemn themselves.
All who condemn the pagan wickedness described in 1:18-32 are guilty of the same offences.
Therefore, everyone who condemns them condemns himself.
Therefore you, like them, are also without excuse before God.

Because you too know the ordinance of God against those who practice such evils.

Because you condemn those who engage in them.

[88] Cranfield, *ICC: Romans, Vol. 1*, 142.

[89] Barrett (following Dodd perhaps) views this as a response from a Jewish objector whom Paul rebuts in 2:3. But this interpretation does not meet with general favor. That is not impossible, but it is simpler and makes better sense to take this sentiment as an argument from common ground.

[90] The fact is, in the end good people enter into life and bad people are sentenced to death. The former, not because they are good, but because through faith they experience the work of salvation, which entails more than a decree of justification, but also an inner work of sanctification as well.

Redemption means that those who are at first declared righteous are at last made righteous. . . that eventually their practice conforms to their righteous position. They are justified by faith and faith alone. However, the work of salvation never leaves the justified with justification and justification alone. God's redemptive work is more than an *event*; it is more properly a *transforming program* initiated with once-for-all works of regeneration and justification. However, it never stops with its beginnings. Every justified person also experiences the purifying work of sanctification so that in every case justified people turn out to be *on balance* good and righteous people, people with eyes to see, ears to hear and hearts ready to obey, people with hearts that seek after God and long to please him. (Jere. 24:7; 32:38-40; Ezek. 36:24-28) Those without that work of sanctification will not see God. (Heb. 12:14)

[91] Sanday and Headlam, *ICC: Romans*, 55.

[92] Ibid, 55.

[93] See Hodge, Godet, Meyer, Stifler, Liddon, Murray, Sanday and Headlam, Cranfield, Nygren, Bruce, Philippi, Calvin

[94] Some Bible teachers take this passage *in a hypothetical way* (as if Paul were saying, "He will render to every man according to his deeds *who chooses to approach him on a legal footing).*

This viewpoint does not see this principle as applicable to those who have been justified by faith but sees it as a statement of what standard of judgment *would* be operative if one dared to approach God in his own rags of 'righteousness'. It is held by R. Haldane and W.G.T. Shedd.

Those who hold this view do so because they feel the principle as it stands (i.e., unqualified) is in conflict with the principle of justification by faith alone. If that is true, then certainly their objection is valid. But it is significant, I think, that most of the better commentators, including those of the Reformed persuasion, think otherwise.

One major misunderstanding underlying the *hypothetical* view (in my opinion and others) is the assumption that verse 6 means that "he shall render to every man *on account of* his works" or that "he shall render to every man *as his works deserve.*" To say that reward shall correspond to conduct is saying something different than reward shall be on account of conduct. To say, for example, that taxation shall correspond to income is not saying the same thing as taxation is on account of income. To say that scholarship grants shall correspond to relative need is not saying that the grants are on account of relative need.

[95] Hodge, *Epistle to the Romans*, 49.

[96] But this principle of judgement does not in any way imply that people earn their justification by good works. One is justified solely upon the grounds of faith. When one is united to Christ by faith (as Paul will later show), one is regenerated, and the process of sanctification is initiated. Moral transformation begins, working from the inside out so that first in motive and then in manner the believer who was declared righteous (legally) becomes righteous actually in his attitudes and lifestyle.

Where that redemptive sequence fails to occur, it can only mean one thing: the 'believer' was stillborn. The root is dead. A saving faith was non-existent.

So, in the final analysis the judgment of God according to works is really a test of the reality of faith. Faith is known by its works. ". . . faith without works is dead," James reminds us (Jas. 2:26). If faith had existed in the first place, its works would have been in evidence in the last place.

It is impossible for a living faith to exist and not manifest itself in works appropriate to it. In fact, that is the point James makes in 2:18: ". . . show me your faith without the works, and I will show you my faith by my works." He issues a challenge. "Show me, if you can, the existence of your faith without the activity that corresponds to that faith you allege." The fact is faith is known by its works.

[97] The force of his argument is equally apropos to unrighteous church members who profess a faith they do not walk and imagine that their bankrupt profession, their merely verbal allegiance to Christ is ample guarantee of their passing the bar of God's judgment. Those who trust in Christ by faith alone will be justified, but the justified will all be sanctified. The judgment of God will correspond to the presence or absence of sanctification. Sanctification is not 'optional equipment' in His program of redemption.

[98] Paul's teaching ought to sober any man or woman who walks after the flesh and imagines that he or she is a temple of the Spirit of God, a child of God, who follows the world and yet feels secure as a disciple of Christ, who serves self and imagines that he or she belongs to the Savior, who lives like Hell and presumes to have a home in Heaven. This chapter, I repeat, is a wake-up call for the religiously presumptuous.

[99] Cf. Cranfield, *ICC: Romans, Vol. 1*, 153 fn. 2.

[100] "The aorist. . . **sinned**, transports us to the point of time when the result of human life appears as a completed fact, the hour of judgment." (Godet, *Epistle to the Romans*, 121.) The whole course of life viewed in retrospect is summed up in one word: sinned.

[101] So also, Hodge, *Epistle to the Romans*, 53. He calls attention to 1 Cor. 9:21 where the heathen is called *anomoi* (without law) as distinguished from the Jews, who were *hypo nomon* (under the law).

[102] Hodge, *Epistle to the Romans*, 53.

[103] In a footnote Cranfield cites "words ascribed to Rabban Simeon, the son of Rabban Gamaliel I (Paul's own teacher) in Aboth 1.17: 'not the expounding [of the Law] is the chief thing but the doing [of it];. . ." *ICC: Romans, Vol. 1*, 154.

[104] ". . . the verb 'to justify' is employed [by Paul] as the divine verdict that means the opposite of divine condemnation in judgment (Rom. 2:12, 13; cf. Rom. 5:16,18) and "the just before [i.e., in the judgment of God] can be spoken of (Rom. 2:13) in contrast with 'sinners' (understood in the forensic sense; Rom. 5:19)" Ridderbos, *Paul: An Outline of His Theology*, 163 *[first brackets mine]*.

So also Cranfield, *ICC: Romans Vol. 1*, 154: "*dikaioun* is here used with reference to the ultimate eschatological verdict."

Cranfield also adds (p. 155): "In this context in Romans this sentence can hardly be intended to imply that there are some who are doers of the law in the sense that they so fulfill it as to earn God's justification. Rather Paul is thinking of that beginning of grateful obedience to be found in those who believe in Christ, which though very weak and faltering and in no way deserving God's favor, is, as the expression of humble trust in God, well-pleasing in His sight."

I prefer this interpretation to that of Hodge who sees this verse as a statement of the legal standard for those who would presume to earn their salvation by works. That is not impossible, of course, but in a context where he has already made it clear that the good will be saved and the bad will be condemned, that there are in fact those who are good (through grace) and those who are bad, it is simpler to see his point as reminding the Jews that custody of the Law won't cut it. He will make the point shortly that they aren't keeping it. But he will also make the point that there are some who do honor the Law in practice (in which cases grace is the implied or stated basis of empowerment, cf. 2:26-27 and 8:4). There is one who in the sight of God "keeps the Law" in a relative sense that is pleasing to God. This practical righteousness is legally insufficient to merit salvation, but it is always a barometer of the presence of grace and the enablement of the Spirit of God; it is the hallmark of those whom God in His mercy has graciously forgiven and received into His family.

[105] Gifford, *Romans*, 75.

[106] Murray, *NICNT: Epistle to the Romans, Vol. 1*, 75.

[107] An interpretation cited by Cranfield, *ICC: Romans, Vol. 1*, 155 fn. 4

[108] Murray, *NICNT: Epistle to the Romans, Vol. 1*, 73.

[109] Hodge, *Epistle to the Romans*, 55.

[110] Murray, *NICNT: Epistle to the Romans, Vol. 1*, 74.

[111] Compare C.S. Lewis, *Mere Christianity*, pp. 18-20, esp. p. 19 and *Abolition of Man*, p. 95ff.

"I know that some people say the idea of a Law of Nature or decent behavior known to all men is unsound, because different civilizations and different ages have had quite different moralities.

"But this is not true. There have been differences between their moralities, but these have never amounted to anything like a total difference. If anyone will take the trouble to compare the moral teachings of, say, the ancient Egyptians, Babylonians, Hindus, Chinese, Greeks and Romans, what will really strike him will be how very like they are to each other and to our own...

"But the most remarkable thing is this. Whenever you find a man who says he does not believe in a real Right and Wrong, you will find the same man going back on this a moment later. He may break his promise to you, but if you try breaking one to him he will be complaining "It's not fair: before you can say Jack Robinson." (p. 19-20, *Mere Christianity*)

[112] Murray, *NICNT: Epistle to the Romans, Vol. 1*, 74.

[113] Ibid, 75.

[114] Smyth, *Greek Grammar*, 421.

[115] See Matthew 7:21-22 and 24:31ff. for an example of terrified consciences still trying to excuse themselves before the Judge Himself.

[116] Calvin, *The Epistles of Paul to the Romans and Thessalonians*, 29.

[117] Cranfield, *ICC: Romans Vol. 1*, 164.

[118] Murray, *NICNT: Epistle to the Romans, Vol. 1*, 82.

[119] Andrews, *The Finality of Christ: Exploring the Many Roads to God Myth*.

[120] The sense of false security ancient Jews drew from their circumcision and its presumed guarantee of their inheritance of the Abrahamic promises is similar to what many church people find in their baptism and the presumption that their participation in this ritual guarantees them a place in the Kingdom of Heaven. But baptism, like circumcision, is intended to symbolize faith. If the two are disconnected (and a lifestyle of transgression would indeed indicate they are), then baptism is as meaningless for a professing Christian as circumcision was for a professing descendant of Abraham.

[121] Murray, *NICNT: Epistle to the Romans, Vol. 1*, 87.

[122] In a similar way, for example, people in Russia, Africa, Latin America, long deprived of any great exposure to God's Word and the Gospel, expose the American church and Americans in general to double indemnity for their disdain of our extraordinary privilege of hearing the Word of God. When in other parts of the world poor people will sometimes walk for miles and miles, weather the elements only to hear the Word under uncomfortable conditions, think how that will condemn by example church people who can barely drag themselves out of bed to worship.

"How striking is the picture which Moffat draws of an Africaner, the fierce South African chieftain, when first brought under the power of the Gospel! 'Often have I seen him,' he says, 'under the shadow of a great rock nearly the live-long day, eagerly perusing the pages of the Bible.'—How touching is the expression of a poor converted Negro, speaking of the Bible! He said, 'It is never old and never cold.'—How affecting was the language of another old negro, when some would have dissuaded him from learning to read, because of his great age. 'No!' he said, 'I will never give it up till I die. It is worth all the labour to be able to read that one verse, 'God so loved the world, that he gave his only begotten Son, that whosoever believeth in him should not perish, but have eternal life.'" (J.C. Ryle, *Practical Religion*, p. 123)

[123] E.g., the prohibition against murder is not fulfilled in a hateful heart nor can the prohibition against adultery be fulfilled in a lustful heart nor the prohibition against idolatry honored as long as there is anyone or anything that comes before God. Biblical obedience covers the spirit as well as the letter in its pursuit of holiness.

Romans Chapter 3

In the last chapter, our author set out to demonstrate to the non-believing Jews that their dependence on the seal of circumcision as a warranty of God's favor and that their immunity from condemnation was a false hope. In fact, he pointed out that Gentiles who were circumcised in heart (code for having been cleansed by God) and honored the law of God would be accepted by God, whereas those who were circumcised in the flesh but trampled on His will would not. This blew away the iron-clad assumptions of his unbelieving Jewish contemporaries and excited their hostilities to his message no end.

By the time Paul wrote this epistle to the Roman church (with the hope that it would enrich their own understanding of the gospel and would be used as a doctrinal and polemical resource in reaching lost Jews), some of their favorite "dodges" were now very familiar. Here, at the beginning of chapter 3, the apostle anticipates and rebuts some of their all too familiar objections to his warnings. We can be sure he had heard and refuted his opponents many times before in the course of his missionary endeavors.

Here is one tactic they took:

(3:1) *Then what is the advantage of the Jew? Or what is the benefit of (the rite) of circumcision? (parenthesis mine)*

The question restated: Your argument puts Jew and Gentile on precisely the same footing before the judgment of God. That can't be right. We Jews are God's chosen people... a holy nation... heirs of the promises of the Abrahamic covenant. If what you're saying is true, namely, our seal of circumcision doesn't mean squat. Do you actually mean that an uncircumcised, law-keeping Gentile will enter the kingdom of God long before a disobedient but duly circumcised Jew? In that event, the Jew has no advantage over the Gentile! Where is the benefit of Jewishness?

That objection the apostle now addresses.

(3:2) *Great in every respect...*

He concedes the correctness of the assumptions underlying the indignant question. Indeed, the benefits of Jewishness are considerable, but at this particular point, Paul defers a definitive answer except for the chief advantage. Later, in 9:4, he will enumerate a number of squandered privileges belonging to their national heritage that should have given the Jews a great jump start in coming to know God and enjoying His special blessings... advantages which they, in their unbelief, have largely forfeited.

For now, he simply specifies the main advantage of the Jew.

"First of all..." This adverb *proton* may signify the first item in a list ("first") or just the main thing ("chiefly").[124] If he intended the former, he simply broke away (not uncommon in his passionate style) from his first intention and contented himself with identifying the key advantage. Then again, he may have intended the latter sense. It matters little.

(3:2) "[The Jews enjoy a great advantage] because (*oti*) they [not the Gentiles] God first entrusted with His oracles." (author's paraphrase, brackets mine)

God "oracles"[125] are a unique and immeasurable treasure trove. The term encompasses the OT, that is, the totality of the special revelation of which God made the Jews his chosen custodian. That revelation, denominated *logia* (oracles), imparts at least three special advantages: 1) unprecedented access to divine revelation through the prophetic tradition, 2) the blessing of divine guidance, and 3) prophetic promises bequeathed to the descendants of Abraham.[126]

Of course, this answer raises a natural and inevitable question: what good are God's promises, if, as Paul preaches, their disbelief about Christ has left them outside looking in on God's promises to their nation? If their unbelief canceled out the benefit, it was a *false* advantage. If God is unable to deliver on what He promised, then He is not faithful to His own word to Abraham, Isaac, and Jacob. Something has got to be wrong with that.

To which Paul responds, "Not so fast!" Do you happen to think that just because your unbelief wrote you out as heirs of God's covenant promises, He is unable to deliver and make good on His Word? You are quite wrong!

> (3:3) *What then? [So what] if some did not believe, their unbelief will not nullify the faithfulness of God, will it?"* (brackets mine)

Just because you (the Messiah-rejecting Jews) don't believe the Word of God in no way means God cannot fulfill His Word. He is not impeded by your rejection of His Son in performing what He has promised and bestowing upon the Jews every benefit He promised to our patriarchs.

"If some did not believe..." that is, if some did not trust (*epistesan*) the oracles God entrusted (*episteuthesan*) to them for their benefit, their lack of trust (*apistia*) will not nullify (*katargesei*) the trustworthiness *(pistin)* of God, will it (*me*)?

What line of argument the apostle here anticipates is a second familiar objection.[127] His question doesn't formally pose the objection, but the force of it is clearly implicit in it. Their logic was approximately this:

Scripture teaches that God keeps His promises.

God made some unconditional promises to the descendants of Abraham.

You say some in Israel have disbelieved God's oracles.

Therefore, they have forfeited their inheritance in the kingdom.

You know what that means, don't you?

It means God cannot deliver on His unconditional promises to those in Israel who are guilty of disbelieving His oracles.

And the upshot of that is that God would then be going back on His Word.

And in that case, God would be unfaithful.

So, your premise must be wrong.

That is the line of logic implicit in the rhetorical question(s) above.

The form (the particle *me*) of the question in the Greek implies a negative answer to his question.

Paul's response is emphatic:

(3:4) *May it never be! (equivalent to "God forbid!") (i.e., the very idea that God will default on His promises to His chosen people!)* (parentheses mine)

Paul rejects any logic that would render God a liar.

Though the majority (*tines* puts it with painful delicacy) has forfeited its birthright through unbelief, nobody should infer that this squandering of privilege has put God in an unplanned and impossible situation, where he is unable to perform His promises to Abraham and his descendants. Even if they persist in national unbelief and let their opportunity to inherit the kingdom of God slip through their unbelieving fingers, let no one think for a minute that God's hands are tied and He has no choice but go back on His Word.

Your disqualification, Paul is protesting, will in no way prevent God from doing what He promised for Abraham and his seed. Let anyone who would presume by such logic to infer that God is unable to perform on His promises be regarded as a liar. Amplified, here is retort of the apostle:

Amplification: "Rather (than rush to judgment with such premature conclusions), let us (as a matter of principle whenever any line of logic or presumed evidence calls the fidelity of God into question) let God be found true (a priori—before the fact), even if it means that we have to stand up in the face of world opinion and declare every man who presumes to contradict His Word or His ability to perform it, a liar."

Calvin calls this "the primary axiom of all Christian philosophy." [128] No matter how bad it looks for the Word of God, no matter how wrong the Word appears to be, when all is said and done, God will be right, and men will turn out to be wrong. God will do exactly what He promised despite every indication that He couldn't or wouldn't. That is the theological rebar that must, at all times, fix the

Christian mind in place against all the storms of skepticism that rail against it.

> "The Lord, in spite of the lies of men, which otherwise are hindrances to His truth, will still find a way for it when there is no way, that He may emerge victorious..."[129]

To his point, Paul cites a repentant king David:

> "*So that You are justified when You speak, and blameless when You judge.*" (Ps. 51:4)

Let us in all such cases, Paul insists, take the stance of David, who, in the face of divine discipline for his enormous sin in the case of Bathsheba and her husband, Uriah, confessed:

Amplification: "I acknowledge that you are a faithful and righteous God and that anything you might say or do is right; I acknowledge it that no one might ever be so presumptuous as to contradict when you issue your verdict. God is right. God is faithful, period. Any discussion of God and His ways must work from that premise. Let our minds always be tightly linked to that immutable anchor."

In the words of David, anytime it is a question of perfidy and an issue of contradiction between the Word of God and the word of man, don't even go to court; just take it for granted that man is the liar and God is faithful.

Now, here comes a third familiar (to Paul) Jewish objection:

> (3:5) *But if our unrighteousness demonstrates (sunistesin = brings out) the righteousness of God, what shall we say (about that)? The God who inflicts wrath is not unrighteous, is He? (I am speaking in human terms.) (first two parentheses mine, third one in the original)*

Paul now takes on a clever but absurd twist in logic of the kind Jewish teachers had no compunction about putting forward. Their intent, we can assume, was not to make a serious case, as if they themselves bought into it, but merely to pose a logical conundrum calculated to confuse and baffle simple Christians. That is not to say that some then and now may not seriously believe such principles. But, at this point, all Paul's opponents were doing was simply trying to find a way to defeat him polemically.

Calvin puts the objection this way:

> "If God looks only for the glorification of men (he means from them), why does He punish them when they offend, since by their offence they glorify Him? He has certainly no reason to be offended, if the cause of His displeasure is derived from the means of His glorification." [130]

I myself, less succinctly and in a cruder form, would express the Jewish objection like this:

> "Well, if God can pull a rabbit out of the hat and find a way to fulfill His promises to the Jews when the Jews have rejected this alleged Messiah, then the Jews deserve some kind of bonus for making Him look so good. In a left-handed way, we have actually caused Him to be glorified. For if our unrighteousness serves as a foil for His faithfulness and throws it into bolder relief through our unbelief, you must admit that we have contributed to the glory of God, right? Well, then, it would be downright unjust for God, in that case, not to reward our good work, wouldn't you say? Would he damn us who have been instruments of his glorification?"

(3:6) *May it never be (so considered)! For otherwise how shall God judge the world? (parenthesis mine)*

Rebuttal: "You're reaching," Paul responds. This is a really specious objection, totally devoid of merit. Your argument proves more than you want it to. That reasoning would exempt the Gentiles from divine condemnation. That conclusion you would never stand still for. If God is obliged to exonerate anyone who in some manner has indirectly contributed to his glorification, then the Gentiles also must be exempted from the wrath of God. The Day of the Lord would never happen. The Gentiles would walk.

For in that case, any sinner, putting the case in a form that fits the lips of a Gentile sinner, could plead:

> (3:7) *But (de = now) if through my lie (a "lie" is sometimes a biblical code word for idolatry) the truth of God abounded to His glory (i.e., if I created lying images and conceptions of God, which He showed up and magnified His glory in so doing), why am I also still being judged as a sinner (a common Jewish code word for Gentiles and other reprobates).* (parentheses mine for clarity)

Here, Paul shows how a Gentile could turn that same argument to his own advantage. If it spares the Jew, it spares the Gentile. The argument that works for the goose would also work for the gander.

> (3:8) *And why not (if this is your reasoning, just extend it to its logical conclusion and come out baldly and) say (by the way, we are slanderously reported and some (of you falsely) affirm that we say—and you imply the enormity of it—), "Let us do evil that good may come"? Their condemnation is just (who would propose such a godless principle)"*[131] (parentheses mine for clarity).

Now Paul puts his finger on another monstrous fallacy lurking in the shadows of that clever piece of Jewish sophistry.

Followed out to its logical conclusion, it would lead one to the notion that it's okay to do evil whenever we persuade ourselves that good may come of it.

Paul's paraphrased retort is this: "I know very well you won't accept that premise. In fact, many of you have slandered the doctrine of justification-by-faith by telling people that I go around teaching that it's okay to sin so that the grace of God might be magnified. You profess to deplore such a moral perversion, and I join with you in condemning any line of reasoning to that effect. But that is exactly where your argument leads, and any who follow it richly deserve the damnation they will receive."

Knowing now where it logically leads, do you want to stick with that line of argument? I didn't think so.

(3:9) What then? Are we better than they? Not at all, for we have already charged that both Jews and Greeks are all under sin...

The conclusion of the matter is that Jews are no better off than Gentiles where guilt and judgment are concerned. Both are equally guilty and accountable before God.

"What then?"[132] is the logical equivalent of "So, where do matters stand?" or "So, what is the conclusion of the matter?"

"Are we better than they?" That is, do we Jews have the right (in light of what has been said) to make ourselves out to better than they (Gentiles)?[133]

"Not at all" (*ou pantos*). Again, the translation is problematic. The construction of the phrase would suggest "Not entirely." Cranfield is right when he finds this agreeable to the context. After all, Paul has established one point at which the Jews had a leg up on the Gentiles (3:2). But, assuming that his question relates to moral superiority, we must agree with Sanday and Headlam[134] and take it as the NASB translators do (and most others).

For we have already charged that both Jews and Greeks are all under sin...

A summary statement of his general thrust.

"Already charged" (*proeitiasametha*), that is, made an accusation beforehand, referring to the indictment from 1:18 through 2:29.

"Under sin" is a phrase by which Paul depicts his conception of the sin problem. Note that he does not say, "under sins." The problem is deeper than infractions of God's law. Actually, behind incidents of sin is something more ominous... the power of sin. Sin is master; man is the slave. He is *under* sin as a slave is under the power of a despot. Sin is in charge.

(3:10–19) Now through this catena of sometimes loosely quoted OT texts, drawn mainly from the Psalms,[135] Paul portrays the sway of sin on the human race, including the Jew.

The Law (which addresses first and foremost those under the Law -v. 19) confirms the bankruptcy of the Jew as well as the Gentile in order to force every man to acknowledge his guilt before God.

C. Hodge rightly notes the structure of the collated chain as beginning with a general description of the spiritual obtuseness and moral bankruptcy of man followed by a litany of the kinds of wickedness symptomatic of that condition[136] (vv. 10–12; 13–18).

(3:10) *There is none righteous, not even one.*

An emphatic affirmation of the universality of sin and guilt and the impossibility of a righteousness-by-works. God finds nobody on the planet righteous in his natural condition unrenewed by the grace of God and without the influence of the Spirit.

(3:11) *There is none who understands, there is none who seeks after God.*

"Understands..." refers to spiritual discernment or right apprehension of the true nature of God.

"Seeks after God...," the natural sequel of rightly knowing God. To know Him, to understand Him is to look at Him, to seek after Him, to long to please Him, and to trust in Him. In the natural man, this is wholly absent.

The citation reflects the meaning the Psalmist implied, not his precise words. The Lord from heaven, as it were, conducted a "field test" to see if any could be found who understood, whose hearts sought after God. The result was negative. Rather:

(3:12) *All have turned aside (ekklino is the lexical form), together they have become useless (achreioo is the lexical form); there is none who does good, there is not even one. (parentheses mine)*

Some people do seek God, but the point is that none initiates that quest on his own. Left to himself, man always turns his back on God. The sequence here is instructive and one observed in Romans 1:18ff. First, one turns from God, then one becomes useless in the sense of corrupted, depraved in mind, and morally worthless. When one abandons God, God abandons man to the whips inherent in his sin. Nature takes over.

The only circumstance that ameliorates this situation... that keeps people from sinking as low as they might... is the common grace of God in the restraining influence of the Holy Spirit (2 Thess. 2:7), which keeps things in check as the purposes of God are being worked out in accordance with His eternal plan.

(3:13) *Their throat is an open grave, with their tongues they keep deceiving. The poison of asps is under their lips.*

"Throat" is a metonym for effects of a malicious mouth. When the wicked open their mouths, the social effect of what they disgorge is to foster death. Our modern media, for instance, is the cultural equivalent of our social throat. The cumulative folly that daily emits from that odiferous source is sufficiently toxic to destroy and bury our culture. It is a moral killing field.

"Keep deceiving..." The world of the natural man is built around lies, for natural men serve the father of lies, the devil. They go on and on, deceiving and being deceived... deceiving themselves about God... about death and accountability (read J.C Ryle)... about judgment... about wealth... about right and wrong. You name it.

The poison of an asp is painful as well as deadly (cf. James 3:8).

(3:14–17) *Whose mouth is full of cursing and bitterness; Destruction and misery are in their paths, and the path of peace they have not known.*

"Full of cursing and bitterness..." The idea is a mouth that boils over like an overfull septic tank with vile malignity... hatefulness. Their spirits are toxic. Cursing does not refer to profanity per se, but invectives of hate accompanied by a wish for harm and destruction to befall those whom one detests for one's selfish reasons.

"The path of peace..." that is, the way that produces true *shalom* (Heb.), welfare, safety, and reconciliation among men is foreign to them.

(3:18) *"There is no fear of God before their eyes."*

Here is the problem at its core... no fear of God. He (I believe it was A.W. Tozer) was right who said that the most predictive factor that can be known about a man is his view of God. So also with a society.

(3:19) *Now we know that whatever the Law says, it speaks to those who are under the Law...*

"The Law says..." refers to the OT per se. The citations were all from the Psalter and Isaiah, not from the Pentateuch (or Torah).

"Under the Law. . ." Literally, the Greek says, "in the law," that is, in that sphere where the revealed Word of God is in force, where obedience to the written Law of God is the standard by which one will be judged (2:12). He is referring to the situation of the Jews as opposed to the Gentiles, who have only an intuitive echo of it inscribed on their conscience.

The point is that the moral portrait of man etched in the scrolls of the OT applies to those who may be described as belonging to the sphere of the Law first and foremost. The Jews are given to understand, "this means you."

That every mouth may be closed (phrage), and all the world become accountable (hypodikos) to God. (parenthesis mine)

The function of the Law is to arouse a sense of guilt... to unmask religious hypocrisy... to show us how far short we fall from the moral perfections demanded by a holy God. It was intended to arrest the self-righteous prattle of the Jews and raise their consciousness of their own sinfulness and eventual accountability for their sins... in fact, to bring the whole world of mankind under a sense of indictment as the law of God was broadcast throughout the world.

(3:20) *Because by the deeds of the law shall no flesh be justified in his sight...*

No one will earn a passing grade if the standard is measuring up to the demands of the Law. Let no one be deceived. No one can keep God's law in a way that will earn their justification.

For through the Law comes the knowledge of sin.

To think otherwise is to misconstrue the intended function of the Law. For the function of the Law was never to set a target that people should aim for as a way of earning their approval with God. Rather, the function of the Law is to awaken a consciousness of personal sin. It was not intended as an instrument for imparting righteousness but as an instrument to reveal its absence.

Are you under the impression that you yourself are a pretty good person... that God, if He is fair and just, would not condemn a person like you?

Have you ever said about somebody you know... or heard someone comment about a person of their acquaintance... that so and so is really a wonderful person with such a good heart... that there is really nothing wrong with them... that they are a better person than most Christians... that all they need is Christ? Wrong!

You've seen the surface... the socialized surface which may be refined, but you've never plumbed the secrets of the heart where the eye of God is able to investigate. God says all is not what it appears to be... that there is a lot more crud down there than you would ever suspect. All the horrors of human fallenness are visible from there.

Have you ever thought, or do you know anyone who thinks, that if a person will just follow the Golden Rule or observe the Ten Commandments, they will come out alright? What more can God ask? More than any mortal can give! Moral perfection.

Have you ever picked up your newspapers, turned on your TV, or jumped on your social media platforms, and asked yourself, what on earth is wrong with the world? Genocide, homicide, violence, child abuse, drug and alcohol abuse, rape, gang banging, sexual promiscuity and perversion, unwed mothers, irresponsible fathers, drunk drivers, robbery, housebreaking, kidnapping, extortion, injustice, lying, slander, breaking of contracts, satanism... you name it. The media, on any given day, is full of it.

Are you a person who thinks that people are fundamentally good... that the difference between them is primarily a function of nurture rather than nature... that people go bad primarily because of environmental factors in their upbringing? That is the fundamental and most dangerous premise of the political liberal... dangerous because it is contrary to reality... and that means it verges on insanity, depending on how far from reality it drifts.

"The Roman poet Horace, laying down some line of guidance for writers of tragedies in his day, criticizes those who resort too readily to the device of a *deus ex machina* to solve the knotty problems which have developed in the course of the plot.

'Do not bring a god on to the stage,' he says, 'unless the problem is one that deserves a god to solve it.'"[137]

"Luther took up these words," Bruce continues, "and applied them to the forgiveness of sins: here, he [Luther] said, is a problem which needs God to solve it... True, for sinful man cannot solve it, though he desperately needs a solution to it; it is his problem; it is he who has to be forgiven. And what Paul tells us here is that the problem has been worthily solved by the grace of God, who has set forth Christ as the solution, the means of forgiveness, the guarantor of our acceptance. All that is required of sinful man is that he should embrace by faith what God's grace has provided."[138]

> (3:21) *But now apart from the Law the righteousness of God has been manifested, being witnessed by the Law and the Prophets...*

"But now..." marks a new stage in the progress of divine revelation. A way of justification apart from legal obedience (the standard of justification by works) is now clearly manifested.

The adverb "now" does not imply that previously 1) a legal means of justification was revealed (it existed only in the minds of the Jews, cf. 3:20 and 9:31) or 2) that this non-legal means of justification was previously unheard of. For, in this same sentence, the apostle acknowledges that the OT bears witness to the principle of justification by faith.

What he, therefore, means to say is that with the atoning death and resurrection of Christ, the whole divine scheme of justification is now laid bare in all its wonderful particulars. What is now manifest is not merely the fact that God justifies people on the basis of faith but that the means whereby He accomplishes this wondrous feat in perfect love and justice.

"The righteousness of God has been manifested..." The subject matter of this new revelation is the righteousness of God. This can refer to either 1) the revelation of the perfect righteousness that distinguishes God's moral being or 2) the revelation concerning a righteousness of which God is the author and not human effort. Verse 22 makes it clear that the second sense is intended.[139]

Charles Hodge defines it as "the righteousness of which God is the author, which comes from him, which he gives, and which consequently is acceptable in his sight."[140]

God's law demands righteousness; God Himself confers what sinners need—when they accept it on the basis of faith and acknowledge the futility of fashioning their own legal righteousness through legal obedience. Trying in the flesh to measure up to the standards of God's law: an impossible feat for natural man.

"Being witnessed by the Law and the Prophets..." The OT, as he has already shown in his citation of the prophet Habakkuk (2:4) in 1:17 (and will more fully demonstrate in chapter 4 and 9–10), confirms that it is through faith, not legal conformity, that God justifies sinners.

> (3:22) *Even the righteousness of God through faith in Jesus Christ for all those who believe; for there is no distinction.*

"Even..." defines more precisely what he means by the manifestation of "the righteousness of God."

What he is talking about is:

1) A righteousness that has God for its author, not human effort ("the righteousness *of God*").

2) A righteousness that is conferred on the basis of faith, which has the person and work of Jesus Christ as its object, not obedience to the requirements of the Law ("through faith in Jesus Christ").

3) A righteousness that is accessible to *all* who will believe, whether Jew or Gentile, male or female, rich or poor, learned or unlearned,

red, yellow, black or white ("for *all* those who believe").

"Through faith..." Through *faith*, not *through legal works*, that is, not through conforming to the Ten Commandments, not through performing the religious rites and observances and maintaining ceremonial holiness as prescribed by the law of Moses for the Israelites. Although God Himself ordained these through Moses, they were never intended to be the means of achieving personal righteousness and acceptance with a holy God. The Law was intended to show us our shortfalls, and the rituals and observances of Israel were ceremonies that were intended to point to Israel's need and the promise of God's saving provision based on grace.

"For all those who believe..." There is no redundancy here with the previous phrase, for the accent now falls on the adjective *all* (as the next clause shows). This righteousness of God, which is conferred on sinners by faith, is not merely for the Jews or any particular class of men but for all who believe without respect of persons. Our God is an equal opportunity Savior. Those who believe will be saved.

Saving belief or faith, in biblical theology, involves more than mere intellectual assent to the premise that Jesus represents the promised Messiah (Christ) but also entails a trusting surrender to Him.[141]

"For there is no distinction," that is, as to the need or opportunity of the Jew or Gentiles. Their footing before God is the same.

(3:23) *For all have sinned and fall short of the glory of God...*

This statement reaffirms the argument of 1:18–3:20.

The offer of justification by faith extends to all, for all share the same need. The fact is all have sinned. This is an example of what Smyth labels a "complexive" or "concentrative" aorist (*hemarton*) "because [it] is used to survey at a glance the course of past action from beginning to end," or put another way, "it concentrates the entire course of an action to a single point."[142]

As in 2:12, "sinned" gathers up a lifetime of rebellion, pride, and self-will as though it were a single act. Sin is the defining act of a life of unbelief. It permeates everything and defiles even the noblest deeds of the wicked.

"Fall short of the glory of God..." As a result of a life characterized by sin, man is constantly coming up short (*usterountai*) of "the glory of God." Does this mean that he 1) fails to fulfill the purpose of glorifying God for which he was created (Bruce) or 2) falls short of the approval of God (Hodge) or 3) misses out on the glory God promises the righteous or 4) fails to measure up to the image of God in us? Usually, when commentators struggle with the text, the justification is self-evident to me. In this instance, I fail to see the problem.

The glory of God is the sum of His perfections, the centerpiece of which is His moral goodness (see Exod. 33:18–19, where the glory of God is correlated with His goodness). To "fall short of the glory of God" defines from one point of view the very essence of sin; it is failing to measure up to the standard. The moral goodness of God is that standard. God is love. His own character defines it.

Men in their natural state consistently (*usterountai*) fall short of that mark. In some way, men always fall short and fail to emulate the goodness of God. Outwardly, at times, their behavior is laudable and appears consistent with the divine standard. Even in those instances, however, the motives behind the actions are indictable in some respects. The bottom line is that the character and behavior of men, Jew or Gentile, just doesn't come up to code, and that code is expressed in the moral goodness of God. The target is beyond human moral reach.

(3:24) *being justified as a gift by His grace though the redemption which is in Christ Jesus...*

This participial clause obviously modifies a previous idea by way of explanation or amplification. The question is which one. At first blush, it does not seem to expand upon the immediately preceding statement, "for all have sinned and fall short of the glory of God." Hence, treat the material from 3:22b as parenthetical and see this verse as further amplifying 3:22a. It makes good sense.

However, on second thought, it also makes equally good sense to connect it with 3:23.

Taken that way, this clause reiterates the *only* way guilty sinners can be accepted by a holy God. They are not justified on the basis of personal merit or scrupulously conforming to some list of rules or meticulous observance of the legal requirements of the OT law. Rather their acceptance with God depends on "being justified gratis (by His grace through the redemption which (applies) in (union with) Jesus Christ."

Embedded in this verse is a mouthful of redemptive theology:

1) Justification is a free gift to us.

2) Justification is *by His grace*, not by our works.

3) Justification is purchased at a great cost—through the redemption which is in Jesus Christ.

4) Justification entails a buying out of the claims of justice and death upon our lives.

5) Redemption from the penalty of sin is bound up in the sacrificial death of Jesus Christ.

"Justified..." To be justified means more than to be treated by God just as if I had never sinned. That is simple forgiveness. Justification includes that, but its benefit goes well beyond mere forgiveness.

Justification is that act of God whereby on the basis of faith He legally imputes to the believing sinner the very righteousness of Christ Himself and declares for all time that we are righteous in His sight.

It means that God credits to my account the totality of the righteousness of Christ Himself. It means that not only is my sin covered (i.e., pardoned) so that, in terms of the penalty of sin, it will never again sever me from God and condemn me to death, but it means that I am clothed, as it were, with the very righteousness of God Himself. I am seen forevermore *in Christ,* much like a nesting doll or a coin in a purse. My sin is out of view in terms of my position with God; I am legally, not figuratively, *in Him,* and His righteousness becomes *by imputation* my very own.

In reality, I am still encumbered with the flesh; I am still a man very much prone to carnal temptations and subject to sin. Yet, in terms of my legal position before God, my standing is perfectly and indisputably righteous before God. My position is unassailable. Christ's merit is my merit—not earned, but freely conferred upon those who believe by a gracious God.

"As a gift" underscores the fact that justification is a status freely conferred by a gracious God, not a standing earned and granted by an indebted God.

"By His grace"—God is gracious. That means He is a God who freely gives us blessings we don't deserve. The ultimate blessing is our salvation. From God's side, our justification is *by His grace*; from our side, it is *through personal faith*.

"Through the redemption..." God's grace may be free to us, but it was costly to our heavenly Father and His Son. We have been purchased from the slave market of sin at the price of blood... the precious blood of the Lamb of God... our Savior Jesus Christ. Jesus was not a martyr; He was a voluntary offering for us. He came to earth by the foreordination of the Father (Acts 2:23) to be a sacrifice for the sins of the world so that whoever believed in Him might not perish but have everlasting life. He came to bear the penalty of sin for us and set us free from it. It was an act of cosmic redemption. His sacrifice, as other good men have remarked before me, is *sufficient* for all the world, but it is *efficient* only for those who receive it by faith.

> (3:25–26) *Whom God displayed publicly as a propitiation (i.e., as an atoning sacrifice) in His blood through faith. This was to demonstrate His righteousness, because in the forbearance of God He passed over the sins previously committed; for the demonstration, I say, of His righteousness at the present time, that He might be just and the justifier of the one who has faith in Jesus. (parenthesis mine)*

Whom God displayed publicly as a propitiation in His blood through faith.

This clause is added to more fully explain the divine intention behind the death of Christ. Behind the bloody hand of human wickedness was the sovereign hand of a gracious God working out His saving purpose and serving historical notice of His unfailing justice in dealing with sin.

The death of Jesus served two functions:

1) It was a public propitiation for the penalty of sin and

2) A public vindication of the righteousness of God in terms of satisfying the demands of His justice.

In past eras, God had, in effect, passed over human sin (Acts 17:30) in the sense that He had not visited mankind with the full measure of judgment our sins called for. Even now, God is patient, restraining the full fury of His offended justice as the human race goes on thumbing its nose at its Creator and sowing wickedness with seeming impunity.

Well, God has served notice that no one should infer from His great mercy any wrong ideas about His justice. The day Christ died, that was a cosmic statement that sin will be accounted for, that God is just, and all accounts will be squared in the end.

The cross is a historic skywriter that says to all generations that you have a choice: The wages of sin is death. Accept the death of Jesus Christ as the just settlement for your own sin or pay for them yourself. One way or another, justice will be served.

Long before Jesus appeared to die for our sins, God was forgiving people in the OT period. Abraham was justified by faith. How? One might ask the question: if God could forgive people in the OT before Christ appeared, why can't He forgive sin now apart from Christ? Why was it even necessary for Him to die if sin can be pardoned without His death (as appeared to be the case with OT saints)?

At the cross, God set the record straight. There, He made a thundering statement that nobody is pardoned on the cheap. The sin problem is never satisfied without justice. When Christ died on the cross, it was demonstrated that no sin accounts are settled at any price less than perfect justice. The day Christ died for our sins, it vindicated God for passing over the sins of OT saints in previous ages. He had justified them by faith—*but on credit, as it were,* in the prospect of a perfect sacrifice to be made later. At the same time, he vindicated His justice in forgiving our sins in this present era. God winked at nothing. He never discounted the price of sin. All were paid in full.

"Propitiation" is something that expiates guilt, atones for it, that which represents a satisfaction for wrong done. The Romans, with the consent of the Jews, executed Jesus out of malice and imagined state interest. Their malice was the unwitting tool of the sovereign God to cause the perfect Lamb of God, the Lord Jesus Christ, to take our place before the bar of divine justice, to bear on the cross the judgment for sin that we ourselves deserved (2 Cor. 5:21). His blood (a metonym for His atoning death) pays the price of the sins of all who embrace Jesus by faith. It satisfied the claims of divine justice against us. It expiates our guilt, and His blood washes it away in the floodtide of God's abundant forgiveness. Inasmuch as His worth (as the Son of God) is infinite, His blood is more than sufficient atonement for the sins of all who will trust in Him.

That is a reminder to all sinners that there is no end run around the justice of God. Sin will be paid for—and in full. Either we allow Jesus to stand in for us and accept His death on our behalf, or we will pay the price in our own persons.

The death of Christ then enabled God the Father, on the one hand, to confirm and establish His absolute justice in past times and on the other to be the justifier of sinners now who cast themselves on the cross and claim Christ as their propitiation.

(3:27) *Where then is boasting? It is excluded. By what kind of law? Of works? No, but a law of faith.*

The apostle now draws out the implications of justification by faith.

Does God's plan of salvation leave any room for human pride in the form of boasting of moral merit or religious achievement? Obviously not. It is ruled out by this "by grace through faith" principle. The initiative is all God's. The work is all God's. Our salvation is full and free. Nothing is left for us to add in order to accomplish our acceptance. Nothing for us to do to earn it; rather, our part is simply to believe it and in faith take God up on His offer. Justification then is not based on the principle (or law) of works. It is based strictly upon the law (or principle) of faith.

(3:28) *For we maintain that a man is justified by faith apart from the works of the Law.*

Reiterating the grounds of his assertion that human boasting is preempted by grace, and that abounding grace allows us sinners to be justified strictly on the basis of faith.

(3:29–30) *Or is God the God of the Jews only? Is He not also the God of the Gentiles also? Yes, of the Gentiles also—if indeed God is one—and He will justify the circumcised by faith and the uncircumcised through faith.*

"Does this justification by faith principle extend also to the Gentiles?" is the underlying question. A similar question is faced in 4:10, where the apostle anticipates the possible objection that even if God justifies on the basis of faith, the benefit would extend to the Jews only—not the Gentiles.

Answer: If there is one God (every Jew would stoutly affirm that), then there is one plan. The God of the Jews is God of the Gentiles, and He has one plan of salvation. Unless they want to insist that He is their God and theirs alone and that His rule and sovereignty does not extend to the Gentiles, then they must concede that He will save the Gentiles on the same basis that He will save the Jew.

"Circumcised by faith" emphasizes that it is not the Jewish rite of circumcision that is the vehicle of their justification, but faith.

"Uncircumcised through faith" attests the fact that the absence of Jewishness and the seal of circumcision is no bar to the Gentile who comes to God in faith.

Another way of marking the distinction Paul makes (by and through) is to understand the point thusly: the Jew whose circumcision is supposed to signify that he shares the faith of His father Abraham is confirmed or certified as such *by* faith, whereas the Gentile who has no such outward seal will nevertheless be qualified for salvation *through* inward faith.

(3:31) *Do we nullify the Law through faith? May it never be! On the contrary, we establish the Law.*

Is this teaching contrary to the doctrine of the OT? (If so, then Paul is obviously mistaken, for God cannot contradict Himself.) Emphatically not. In fact, this doctrine of justification by faith is in complete harmony with what one finds there.

---

[124] Arndt & Gingrich, *Greek-English Lexicon of the New Testament*, 732-733.

[125] In the Septuagint, the Greek version of the OT, the singular form (logion) is used extensively in Psalm 119 to refer to the "word" of God. (see Hatch/Redpath, *Concordance to the Septuagint*, Vols. II-III, p. 881)

[126] Of course, what they haven't caught up with yet is the fact that unbelief excludes them as true seed, for that relation involves spiritual as well as physical lineage.

[127] Interpreters have disagreed about the connective logic of this verse as well as about the grammatical structure of the sentence itself, (i.e., whether in the original it represents one question or two—the Greek allows either; the issue has to be decided contextually). Does the question arise from his answer in verse two or from his general premise that the unbelief of his contemporary Jewish countrymen has excluded them from salvation, implying the loss of the covenant blessings promised to the descendants of Abraham? The latter connection seems to me to square better with the general context. As mentioned at the top, Paul appears to be rebutting a familiar series of specious objections.

If one construes the question to connect with the question in 3:2, then the logic (amplified) appears to be approximately this:

Objection: But according to your preaching, virtually the entire nation has missed the train in unbelief. According to your preaching, all God's promises to the Jews are bound up in this Jesus whom you allege to be the promised Messiah. If that's the case, then everything God promised the Jews is now null and void through national unbelief. So, the privilege of being the recipients of God's oracles or promises turns out to be pretty hollow. In the end there is nothing to show for them. Everything God promised is down the drink. God is unable to deliver on what He promised, and the faithfulness of God appears to be unfaithful. Surely there is something wrong with that supposition.

This makes good sense in context. The main weakness I find with this interpretation, however, is that it implies that the privilege the Jews enjoyed in mere access to the Word was pretty hollow in and of itself. That is not the case.

The door of salvation was always open through the revelation of God provided the Jew used the privilege God had given. They could reclaim their birthright through faith. That, it seems, to me would have been the point to follow with, had this been the angle of the question.

[128] Calvin, *The Epistles of Paul to the Romans and Thessalonians*, 60.

[129] Ibid, 60.

[130] Ibid, 62.

[131] This heresy has always hung around in the churches, especially in those circles tinged with antinomianism (also known as "easy believism" or "cheap grace") where grace is virtually viewed as a license to sin. Some in that mode will actually cross God's boundaries just to show that under grace sin has no consequences and that sinning can enlarge the outpouring of God's grace and thereby honor God. I have personally known such folks. This view is, as Paul suggests, an abominable heresy and those who pass it around are worthy of condemnation. I was acquainted with an immoral Southern California counselor (supposedly a Christian) who bought into and pushed that very viewpoint. You know what Paul would think of him. Unfortunately, there are way too many who go there these days.

[132] *ti oun (eroumen* is probably implied); see 6:1; 6:15; 7:7; 8:31; 9:14; 9:30.

[133] The translation of *proechometha* is problematic and commentators disagree about the meaning of the word in this context. The problem starts with the fact that the word is used this one time in the NT, so we have no "history" of Pauline usage to compare for a benchmark. In classical Greek the intransitive form of the verb means to jut out, project (like headlands, towers, hills, etc.), then in reference to running, to be the first, have the start, then in reference to rank, to be superior, to be eminent, and finally comes to bear the sense, to surpass, excel.

The question here is whether the word is middle voice or passive. In the latter case it might be translated, "Are we surpassed or excelled (by the Gentiles)?" Is the bottom line, according to you (Paul) that the Gentiles are better off, after all? This would make little sense in light of his answer in 3:2

Take it in the middle voice and the verb might be translated, "Do we make ourselves out to be superior? (says Paul, perhaps taking his place as a descendant of Abraham).

What we know for sure from the surrounding context is the force of the question: whether either an unbelieving Jew or Gentile is any better off before God than the other. The answer is a resounding, No!

It seems to me that many commentators stumble more than necessary over this verb because they are hung up on its transitive sense, "to hold before." Here it is used intransitively. That is the meaning one should work from, it seems to me, in resolving this little conundrum. (see *An Intermediate Greek Lexicon*, Oxford Press, p. 676)

[134] "Strictly speaking *ou* should qualify *pantos*, 'not altogether,' 'not entirely,' as in 1 Cor. v. 10 *ou pantos pornios tou kosmou toutou:* but in some cases, as here, *pantos* qualifies *ou*, 'altogether not,' 'entirely not,' i.e. 'not at all'..." (Sanday and Headlam, *ICC: Romans*, 77.)

[135] Compare 3:10-12 with Psa. 14:1-3; 53.1-3; verse 13 with Psa. 5:9; 140:3; verse 14 with Psa. 10:7 and verses 15-17 with Isa. 59:7-8 and Prov. 1:16; verse 18 with 36.1.

[136] Hodge, *Epistle to the Romans*, 78.

[137] *Ars Poetica*, 191f, cited by Bruce, *The Epistle of Paul to the Romans*, 101.

[138] Ibid.

[139] It should be noted, however, that the Gospel, as is plain in verse 25, reveals not only the free gift of God's righteousness conferred upon believing sinners, but also manifests His uncompromising righteousness in dealing justly with sin and sinners. There is no fudging. The penalty of sin must be paid—and was paid—in full in the atoning death of Jesus.

In verse 22 the righteousness of God is set over against that pursuit of justification alluded to in verse 20 as *by the works of the law* (*ex ergon nomou*). The same contrast reflected in different language is in view in Romans 9:30-32 ("a righteousness which is by faith" differentiated from "a law of righteousness," i.e. a law based personal righteousness). We see the opposing principles again in 10:3 where Israel's mistake is described in terms of ignorance and self-will: "not knowing about God's righteousness, and seeking to establish their own, they did not subject themselves to the righteousness of God." In 10:4-5 Paul speaks of Israel's approach to justification in terms of "the law for righteousness," that is, a legal approach and "the man who practices the righteousness which is based on the law." That is differentiated in 10:6 from "the righteousness which is based on faith."

[140] Hodge, *Epistle to the Romans*, 88.

[141] Cf. Benjamin Warfield, *Biblical and Theological Studies*, "Faith," p. 404-444.

[142] Smyth, *Greek Grammar*, 430-431.

Romans Chapter 4

Now in chapter 4, the apostle sets out to establish the truth of what he has just affirmed.

Logic Bridge:

All people need the forgiveness of God.

All people can be forgiven by God.

That forgiveness is not obtained by any form of human merit.

Rather, it is freely conferred upon all who receive Christ by faith.

Natural Question: Is this way of salvation—this principle of justification by faith (rather than by law keeping)—consistent with the OT revelation? If not, it was heresy, and Paul was a false prophet, for God would not contradict Himself, pointing men to one way of salvation in the OT economy and then denying it in the NT era.

Chapter 4 sets out to confirm that what he is proclaiming is thoroughly consistent with the witness of the OT with respect to the patriarch Abraham and the great King David.

In doing so, the apostle goes on to answer tangential questions, explicit or implied. Not only is justification by faith clear in the OT, but that even there is it abundantly clear that this gracious benefit applies to Gentiles as well as Jews. Moreover, he proceeds to show that justification by faith is not merely a theological fact of the older revelation, but that it is a very *essential* condition. For if justification was based upon law-keeping rather than faith, the result would be to render all the promises of God null and void.

Why? For the simple reason that men in the flesh cannot keep the Law and, therefore, cannot meet the condition of blessing. That is why, the apostle explains, that God designed a plan of salvation for sinners based upon justification by faith rather by works, so that the believer might be secure in His favor and God's promise might be guaranteed.

That is only possible where the ground of our acceptance is based on a righteousness that He freely confers rather than a righteousness that we earn by conforming to His Law—something impossible for men in the flesh. Following that, he goes further to hold up Abraham's faith, the patriarch of the Jews, as a model for any who want to be justified. He shows that contemporary believers are asked to emulate the faith of Abraham, that is, trust in the same God in the same way. Those who do so inherit the assurance of the same result.

Overview of 4:1–8

He refers to two of the most illustrious figures in the annals of Israel's storied history in support of his premise that justification by faith is the means of salvation, even in the OT.

1) He shows that the Scripture expressly says that Abraham was justified by faith and shows how the very language is the language of grace, not the rhetoric of indebtedness.

2) He shows that King David in the Psalms exults about his own standing with God in terms descriptive of one justified by faith, thus proving that David was not only aware of this principle but included himself among its beneficiaries.

(4:1) *What then shall we say that Abraham, our forefather according to the flesh, has found?*

The question harks back to 3:31 and offers Abraham as a case in point. He was a good starting point. After all, he was the physical father[143] of the nation. Nobody would question his standing with God. So, the method of his justification is highly germane. So then, Paul asks rhetorically, what did Abraham discover with respect to the issue of justification with God?

(4:2) *For if Abraham was justified by works, he has something to boast about; but [the fact is, he does] not before God. [brackets mine)*

Paul is just sharpening the issue here. If Abraham was justified on the basis of human merit, then, obviously, he would have some basis of boasting before God of his own religious and moral accomplishments. So, if we find a form of justification that evokes a basis of human boasting, then, obviously, that is not justification by faith, which precludes it (3:27).

But (as a matter of fact) what we see in Abraham's case is a divine announcement of his justification that by its very language excludes any basis of human self-congratulation.

The next verse adduces proof of that. Paul cites the passage where the Lord declares the justification of Abraham. The phrase "justification by faith" is not there, but the terms of the declaration are clearly indicative of that principle.

(4:3) *For what does the Scripture say? [It says] "And Abraham believed God, and it was reckoned to him as righteousness." (brackets mine)*

Paul says, in effect, let's go to the text and see for ourselves. He cites Genesis 15:6. In that context, God reassures childless Abraham, who, along with his wife, Sarah, were well-advanced in years and past prime time in terms of human reproduction, that God would still provide him a son as his heir. Moreover, God promised him that his descendants would be as numerous as "the stars of the heavens." Look at the heavens, God invited Abraham. Count the stars, if you can. So shall your descendants be, an incredible promise for a man and his wife whose reproductive powers were biologically dead. "Then he believed in the Lord; and He reckoned it to Him as righteousness."[144]

Abraham did nothing more than believe that God was God. Unlimited in His power, faithful to His promises. God rewarded that trust with far more than it deserved. He imputed or reckoned to Abraham something he did not possess or earn... righteousness, that is, a righteous standing with God, a righteousness of God and from God.

(4:4) *Now to the one who works, his wage is not reckoned as a favor, but as what is due.*

Paul draws out the implications of the OT testimony that God *reckoned* or *counted* the faith of Abraham to him for righteousness. The language implies that Abraham received grace, that is, an unearned blessing, not a repayment of a debt that God owed him. What is *owed* is not reckoned or imputed as something else.

If one attempts to earn his or her justification, then the wage one receives will be what is earned or owed. There will be no talk of "reckoning" or "counting" this thing for that thing, as is the case here.

(4:5) *But to the one who does not work [i.e., for his justification] but believes in Him who justifies the ungodly, his faith is reckoned as righteousness. (brackets mine)*

But whenever a person approaches God, as Abraham did, not attempting to earn their justification on the basis of personal merit, but simply trusting in God who graciously confers the free gift of righteousness upon trustful sinners, then in those cases, faith is counted as righteousness. That is what we have in the case of Abraham.

The language, Paul argues, speaks of a person who wasn't attempting to earn his salvation by merit badges.

(4:6) *Just as David also speaks of the blessing upon the man to whom God reckons righteousness apart from works...*

"Just as..." The witness of David is consistent with the principle of justification by faith. David speaks of the *blessing* of justification in such terms that it is apparent that David is describing justification based on faith and not on works.

(4:7–8) *Blessed are those whose lawless deeds have been forgiven, and whose sins have been covered. Blessed is the man whose sin the Lord will not take into account.*

This quotation comes from Psalm 32:1–2, where David celebrates the joy and assurance of a right standing with God. He speaks of the misery of guilt and unconfessed sin, of heartful repentance and the renewal of a sense of cleansing and acceptance with God—and acceptance and forgiveness and clearing of accounts that would not be possible if men were justified on the basis of merit rather than on the ground of grace.

Note two important features about this description of the benefits of justification by faith. First, blanket forgiveness of sins committed ("whose lawless deeds [past guilt] have been forgiven, and whose sins have been covered"); second, blanket immunity to legal sanctions ("whose sin [note the singular] the Lord will not take into account"). David speaks of a durable, not a probationary, justification.

> (4:9) *Is this blessing then upon the circumcised, or upon the uncircumcised also? For we say, "Faith was reckoned to Abraham as righteousness."*

A possible Jewish objection to Paul's teaching about justification by faith might be this: even if one finds (conceded for the sake of argument) justification by faith in the case of Abraham, the patriarch of the Jewish nation, is it not a leap of logic to assume that God extends that blessing to non-Jews? Abraham was a Jew in a covenant relationship with God, sealed by the sign of circumcision. Hence, the Jews are known as "the circumcision," signifying their (presumed) inheritance of the promises attached to the Abrahamic covenant.

Paul's rebuttal of this objection is simple and effective. The key, he notes, is in the timing of the divine proclamation of Abraham's justification. Actually, it *preceded*, as Paul's rhetorical question anticipates, the divine institution of the seal of circumcision.

> (4:10) *How (i.e., under what circumstances) was it (i.e., faith) reckoned [to Abraham] as righteousness? Not while circumcised, but while uncircumcised... (parenthesis and brackets mine)*

As a matter of fact, the patriarch Abraham was uncircumcised at that time. That is, when justified Abraham was not yet circumcised. That came later. So, technically speaking, when God pronounced Abraham a justified person, he was still a Gentile! At that point the seal of membership in the covenant, that defining sign of a Jewish male, was missing. Lacking that signature, one was not considered an heir of the covenant promises. So, to repeat, technically Abraham was not even a Jew (by the prevailing standard of Jewishness) at the time God declared him justified! Did God mess up? Hardly.

That timing was providential and critical and contained an important message for all time. Let the Jew take note. Justification by faith, therefore, is not for Jews only.

(4:11–12) *And he received the sign of circumcision, [which is] a seal of the righteousness of the faith which he had while uncircumcised, that he might be the father (i.e., the spiritual head) of all who believe without being circumcised (i.e., of believing Gentiles), that righteousness might be reckoned to them [too] and the father of circumcision to those who not only are of the circumcision, but who also follow in the steps of the faith of our father Abraham which he had while uncircumcised"* (parentheses and brackets mine for clarity).

Circumcision didn't—and was never intended—to impart a right standing with God. Rather, when later God commanded Abraham to be circumcised, the function or import of that ritual was threefold:

1) It was a symbol of an accomplished fact, that God had graciously imparted to Abraham a righteous standing based solely upon his faith.

In other words, circumcision in the case of Abraham is not to be misconstrued as a seal having any merit of its own but was merely a divinely authorized statement and seal after the fact that Abraham was graciously declared righteous on the ground of his faith.

2) It held him up as the spiritual father of all who emulate his faith, even though they may be non-Jews, that is, uncircumcised (for religious purposes). In effect, it testifies to the fact that lack of circumcision is no bar to the believing Gentile.

3) It restricted his spiritual headship strictly to that class of Jews who followed in the footsteps of his faith.

Though Abraham is the physical father of the Jewish nation, only those can claim spiritual descent who emulate his same faith toward God. Circumcision is a flashing beacon to remind the Jews of the faith Abraham manifested toward God and a tacit reminder that those who are his *true* sons and daughters must walk in his same faith. Otherwise, their physical circumcision is null and void as a ticket into His kingdom.

The bottom line is that faith is everything for everybody. It is the highway to God. It looks directly to Jesus and goes by way of the cross. There is no other way for any human being. Never believe the pernicious myth that all religions lead the same place by many different roads.

The way of salvation is open to all nations, all tribes, all races, and all conditions of life on exactly the same gracious terms. A loving and merciful God has made a way for everyone who is willing to come to Him on His terms to enjoy His eternal acceptance.

But that way is through faith, and faith understands and believes this word of Jesus: "I am the way, the truth and the life; no man comes to the Father, except by Me" (John 14:6). Faith bows to the revelation that "neither is there any other name under heaven whereby we must be saved," speaking of the name of Jesus, through whom alone we are justified (Acts 4:12; Rom. 3:21–25).

(4:13) *For the promise to Abraham or to his descendants that he would be heir of the world was not through the Law, but through the righteousness of faith.*

"For the promise..." implies a misunderstanding of the historical situation that needs to be clarified.

In Genesis 17:1–8, God reaffirmed the original covenant He made with Abraham when he was still in Mesopotamia (before He migrated by divine command to the land God promised Him [hence, the promised land], the land of Canaan, later to become known as the land of Israel or Palestine). That covenant essentially promised to make Abraham and his descendants ascendant in the affairs of the earth. Eventually, they would inherit the world. That pledge was not explicit but implicit in the words, "I will bless those who bless you, and the one who curses you I will curse. And in you all the families of the earth shall be blessed" (Gen. 12:3). The notion of ascendancy was also inferred from God's promise to "make you (Abraham) the father of a multitude of nations... I will make nations of you, and kings shall come forth from you" (17:5–6.)

Now two things were commonly misunderstood by the (unbelieving) Jews about the Abrahamic covenant:

1) They defined the descendants of Abraham in terms of physical descendant and legal prerequisites (under the seal of circumcision), whereas the true Jewish descendants of Abraham shared the faith of Abraham, something most of Paul's Jewish contemporaries did not (Gal. 3:7). The Israel of God (Gal. 6:16) was circumcised in the inner man (Rom. 2:28–29), not merely in the flesh.

2) They linked the inheritance of those promises with "keeping the covenant," which the average Jew defined (Gen. 17:10) (at best) in terms of the observance of the rite of circumcision and outward observance of the moral letter and ceremonies of the Law.

This background explains Paul's attempt here to disabuse his unbelieving countrymen of the illusion that God's promises to Abraham and his descendants was based on legal performance. God's promises where not linked to legal righteousness (i.e., "through conformity to the Law") but based upon "the righteousness of faith."

He now proceeds to explain why it could have been no other way.

(4:14) *For if those who are of the Law are heirs, faith is made void and the promise is nullified.*

"For if those who are of the Law..." A code phrase designating those who were living under the terms and conditions of the Old Covenant and expecting to merit favor with God on strictly legal grounds.

If God's promises were based on legal stipulations, then faith, as the condition of justification, is obviously ruled out by definition. Now the implication of that is this: when faith as the basis of justification is ruled out, the expectation of the fulfillment of God's promises is also nullified. He now proceeds to explain the inevitable loss of promise.

(4:15) *For the Law brings about wrath, but where there is no law, neither is there violation.*

As he explained earlier (3:19–20), people, including the Jews, don't keep the Law. They inevitably transgress God's commandments. Lawlessness is sin (1 John 3:4), and the wages of sin is death (6:23). The promises, if based upon law-keeping, go right down the drink, and instead of inheriting the world, what they inherit is wrath.

Now he explains why the inheritance of God's promises was deliberately and wisely placed by a merciful God on the footing of faith instead of law-keeping. God, in His grace, wanted to provide His people and their promises with built-in security... with a fail-safe salvation.

(4:16) *For this reason, it is by faith, that it might be in accordance with grace, in order that the promise may be certain to all the descendants, not only those who are of the Law, but also those who are of the faith of Abraham, who is the father of us all...*

For salvation to be fail-safe, for our inheritance to be inviolably secure, it had to rest on some foundation other than our works. So, God based inheritance for the spiritual descendants of Abraham on the opposite principle of grace and enabled believing sinners to be justified simply on the basis of faith. Only in that way can possession of the promises be by grace (or unmerited favor).

It is so important to observe that the whole plan of salvation is intentionally aimed at the security of the believer. Any form of salvation doctrine that leaves the believer and God's promises to him insecure is faulty and imports legalism in some form back into the equation... a kind of teaching that Paul denounces in Galatians 1.

(4:17) *(As it is written, "A FATHER OF MANY NATIONS HAVE I MADE YOU") in the sight of Him whom He believed [or trusted], even God, who gives life to the dead and calls into being that which does not exist"* (brackets mine, parenthesis in the original).

Paul had just described Abraham as the spiritual "father of us *all,"* meaning not only of believing Jews but also of believing Gentiles as well.

"As it is written..."—a parenthetical confirmation of that fact drawn from the OT. In reconfirming His original covenant with Abram, God literally changed Abram's name ("exalted father") to "Abraham" (meaning "father of a multitude"). The reason for changing it was to signify God's explicit promise to make Abraham the father or head of a multitude of nations. Note the plural. It implies the extension of the honor of headship beyond the confines of the Jewish people.

All who trust in God in His character as One "who gives life to the dead [i.e., in His resurrection power] and calls[145] into being that which does not exist" [i.e., who creates] can rightly—and exclusively —claim descent from Abraham. This phraseology defines those who are the true descendants of Abraham (brackets mine). Those who are physical descendants qualify only if they also share this credential. Those who are not physical descendants qualify just because they share it.

This is in accord with what Paul says in Galatians 3:6–9:

> "Even so Abraham believed God, and it was reckoned to him as righteousness. Therefore, be sure that it is those who are of faith that are the sons of Abraham. And the Scriptures, foreseeing that God would justify the Gentiles by faith, preached the gospel beforehand to Abraham, saying, "All the nations shall be blessed in you. So then those who are of faith are blessed (inherit salvation) with Abraham the believer."

Also, Galatians 3:29: "And if you belong to Christ, then you are Abraham's offspring, heirs according to the promise."

Also, Romans 2:28–29: "For he is not a Jew who is one outwardly; neither is circumcision that which is outward in the flesh; but he is a Jew who is one inwardly; and circumcision is that which is of the heart, by the Spirit, not by the letter; and his praise is not from men, but from God."

Thus, the circumcised without faith have no claim before God as the posterity of Abraham, no claim on the Abrahamic promises; uncircumcised Gentiles with faith have every claim before God as the true seed of Abraham and to consider themselves heirs of the covenant.

Paul now proceeds to set Abraham's faith up as a model or benchmark of saving faith... the kind of faith that God calls for and through which, by His grace, all sinners are justified and set free from the penalty of sin.

> **(4:18)** *In hope against hope he believed, in order that he might become a father of many nations, according to that which had been spoken, "So shall your descendants be."*

Abraham's faith in God's power to perform His promises did not falter in the face of what men regard as impossible. Even when, humanly speaking, there was no real hope that a centenarian man and his ninety-year-old wife could produce a child when their reproductive capacities were already biologically dead and when there was little prospect after so late a start that that child would produce a multitude of nations, Abraham waxed strong in his confidence that God would fulfill His promise. Not because he was gullible... he fully appreciated the impossibility of the situation, humanly considered, but because he knew the character and attributes of God. He knew God was faithful to His promises and also understood that God the Creator, who had in His hands the control of the issues of life and death, was able to bring into existence what does not exist. His faith drove its stakes in the integrity, sovereign authority, and power of the living God.

> (4:19–21) And without becoming weak in faith he contemplated his own body, now as good as dead since he was about a hundred years old, and the deadness (infertility) of Sarah's womb; yet, with respect to the promise of God, he did not waver (diekritha *= hesitate, doubt) in unbelief but grew strong in faith, giving glory to God and being*

fully assured that what He promised, He is able also to perform. (parenthesis mine)

He looked reality squarely in the eye *(katenoasen* = considered)—the so-called laws of nature (which merely describe God's regular ways of sustaining His creation)—and never blinked ("did not doubt but grew strong") in His confidence. He was steadfast in his conviction that what God had promised He was able to deliver. He believed that God is not a slave to the laws of nature, as if they were a higher power. Rather, he was confident God was their Creator and Sustainer and that He can alter them when and where He pleases; he believed that whatever is an insurmountable obstacle for the mind and power of puny men is no challenge for an all-knowing and all-powerful God.

"Giving glory to God..." That is, by his actions, Abraham honored God by magnifying Him. He responded to the promise of God by treating God *as God*, by not confining His ability to the small box of human preconceptions of possibility. He treated God as One of unimpeachable veracity and unlimited ability.[146]

Note the bottom line of a biblical faith in its ideal form: *When the Word of God speaks, the man of faith takes hold of that Word, being fully assured that what he promised, he is able also to do.* Not all faith is so strong as Abraham's, but saving faith is no less real. Biblical faith may, at times, wrestle with doubt more than did Abraham on this occasion, but in the end, faith rises above its surrounding doubts and overcomes them.

Abraham was asked to believe something that would stagger the credulity of any thoughtful person. He was challenged to believe, in effect, that God could (and would) raise the dead, that is, restore the long-dead powers of reproduction to him and Sarah. He demands that we believe He raised Jesus from the dead (with all that particular act of resurrection implies).

(4:22) *Therefore also "IT WAS RECKONED TO HIM AS RIGHTEOUSNESS."*

God greeted his faith with the blessing of justification. The reason God announced Abraham's justification in conjunction with this heroic act of faith was for more reason than a historical marker to celebrate Abraham. God intended it for future believers.

(4:23–24) *Now not for his sake only was it written, that "IT WAS RECKONED TO HIM," but for our sake also, to whom it will be reckoned, as those who believe in Him who raised Jesus our Lord from the dead...*

Paul tells us that this record is something more than a historical footnote. What God did for Abraham has a bearing on what God will do for us. It is a signal to all mankind. Abraham's justification heralds the fact that God will likewise justify anyone else who follows in the footsteps of Abraham's kind of faith.

We, like Abraham, are confronted with the Word of God, which affirms the impossible. We, too, are challenged to believe it. In our case, as well as that of Abraham, the challenge is to believe in the veracity of God's testimony and His ability to raise the dead (in this case, Jesus) and His power to command and control and bring about entities and circumstances that don't even yet exist. Same song, different verse, in other words.

God's Word testifies that God raised the crucified Jesus from the dead. Implicit in that affirmation is the whole gospel. For His death was not an isolated event in history. It was integrally connected with His claims as Lord, with His mission as Savior, and with the proof of our justification. In short, the resurrection is the lynchpin of the whole mission of redemption, and without it, the whole scheme falls apart. That is why Paul draws the analogy between the saving faith of Abraham and the kind of faith that saves us at the point of the resurrection.

(4:25) *Him who was delivered up because of our transgressions, and was raised because of our justification.*

What we believe in is not simply the event of the resurrection, but we trust in the meaning of it. Paul here links the event with its meaning as part of the package, which faith embraces.

The person who, in faith, embraces the resurrection of Jesus acknowledges that His death was intended by God as a sacrificial offering to atone for our transgressions.

The person who embraces the resurrection of Jesus recognizes the Lordship of Christ, for the resurrection stands as a divine verification of His claims that 1) Jesus came from God, 2) He spoke for the Father and 3) we owe to Him our undivided loyalty and allegiance as Lord and Savior.

The person who embraces the resurrection in real faith rejoices in it as the receipt of the cancelation of the penalty of sin, the essential prerequisite for our justification. The resurrection is our admission ticket to justification, for it is, in effect, a canceled check, which shows our sin debt to be "paid in full."

---

[143] Does "according to the flesh" modify "our forefather" or the verb "has found" (*heurekenai*)? Its grammatical position favors the former. That makes good sense also, since it was appropriate to Paul to limit mutuality of the "fatherhood" of Abraham among the Jews to physical descendancy. He was not the spiritual father of unbelieving Jews (4:12; 2:29 and Gal. 3:7)

The difference would be that in connecting it with the verb the question would be, "What did Abraham discover with respect to his own natural efforts?" whereas construing it with the noun it would be, "What did Abraham, our physical forefather, discover about justification?" The former question is less natural, in my view, since the issue that evokes the question is whether or not justification by faith is consistent with OT revelation. Now the question is, what did Abraham, for example, discover about the way of justification.

[144] It is unnecessary to think that it was upon this occasion of demonstrated faith that God initially justified Abraham. Abraham had previously exercised faith in God, as in the case of leaving his homeland (Gen. 12). Probably his justification is deliberately highlighted in this particular demonstration of faith because 1) it is connected with the coming of the Messiah and 2) represented faith in his ability to believe in the power of God to raise the dead. Thus, in this instance especially the faith of Abraham is *typological* and therefore providentially convenient to connect with justification by faith.

[145] We follow Hodge who takes "call" here in the sense of commanding or controlling (see analogous uses in Psalm 1:1, Isaiah 40:26). "God is described as controlling with equal ease things which are not, and those which are. The actual and the possible are equally subject to His command. All things are present to his view, and all are under his control." (Hodge, *Epistle to the Romans,* 124.)

When we talk about the omnipotence of God, one should exclude from that concept any affirmation of the kind of silly potentialities in the sorts of irrelevant questions intellectual pretenders sometimes propose to "stump" the Christian. For example, "Can God make a rock he can't lift" or "Can God create something that exists and doesn't exist at the same time?"

The postulate of the almightiness of God does not include logical impossibilities (A cannot be non-A at the same time and under the same circumstances). In other words, that proposition does not include in its reference nonsensical things, (what we cannot even think or conceive). We can frame them in words, but we cannot even imagine logical contradictions. If you can, draw one. . . describe one! That's what we mean.

Romans Chapter 5

(5:1) *Therefore having been justified by faith, we have[147] peace with God through our Lord Jesus Christ...*

"Peace" refers to a change of status effected through our justification. Whereas once we were enemies of God (by virtue of our transgressions of His law and our rebellious self-will)... were under condemnation and objects of His wrath (1:18), now having been justified by faith, we are reconciled to God... the death sentence has been lifted... we are no longer at war with God... peace has been declared. Christ, the mediator between God and man, has intervened. He offered himself a ransom for all men to appease the justice of a holy God. He became sin for us... He bore the whole brunt of the wrath of God against sin... on Him, God, in His mercy, laid the whole weight of the penalty of sin... Jesus paid the price in His own blood. To as many as receive Him, God gives the right to become the children of God... adopts them into the divine family with all the rights and privileges pertaining thereto. Peace with God replaces the penalty of sin. The natural consequence of *peace with God* for all who grasp the impact of the transaction is a subjective filling of *the peace of God.*

Both benefits hang on the peg of justification by faith. And the benefit of justification by faith, no less than reconciliation to God that flows from it is "through our Lord Jesus Christ." There is nothing arbitrary about God's work of redemption. God is impeccably just. Our reconciliation required a just atonement for our sins. Only Christ could satisfy the requirement for a substitute at once perfectly righteous and of infinite worth.

(5:2) *Through whom also we have obtained our introduction by faith into this grace in which we stand; and we exult in the hope of the glory of God.*

"Through whom..." That is, Christ. Justification by faith places us in organic union with the living Christ. His spirit dwells in us. In Christ, we have enjoyed from the first minute[148] of that relationship access (*prosagoge*) to grace.

In a generic way, "grace" speaks of the unmerited favor of God. However, depending on the context, "grace" often has reference to some specific manifestation of God's favor or blessing. The key point to remember, however, any time we see the word "grace" in the Bible is that it accentuates that the favor of God, whatever form it takes, is wholly gratuitous, unmerited, and undeserved.

"Introduction..." (*prosagoge*) also means "approach" or "access." Sometimes, in extra-biblical Koine Greek, the word referred to a "landing stage."[149] Thus, Paul could have in mind a nautical metaphor in which "grace" is a *haven* to which we are conducted through Christ... that is, Christ is the "approach" or point of "access" to this grace by which we stand.

"This grace..." refers to our justification and all the gratuitous benefits bound up in it which God confers upon believers.

"In which we stand *(hestekamen)*..." The perfect implies a state of firm fixity having been established at some point in past time and continuing to the present moment. The expression conjures up an image of immunity to the withering blast of the holy wrath of God, which was poured out on Christ in our stead. We stand (rather than fall) through Christ who provides us shelter in the haven of God's grace from the stormy blast of divine indignation. In short, Christ mediates our acceptance with God, and through His grace, we stand.

"And we exult in the hope of the glory of God..." Another outcome of justification by faith and the sheltering grace of God is the well-founded and joyful (rather than fearful) expectation[150] of the (coming manifestation of the) glory of God. This is not something we have to dread but an event to which, now, because of grace, we can await with confident expectation and exultant assurance. That day will mark our debut, not our ruin... our coming out as the children of God... not our going down to destruction as sinners and rebels.

We exult in the revelation of the glory of God because, if we are now children of God, then we are "heirs also, heirs of God and fellow heirs with Christ, if indeed we suffer with Him in order that we may be glorified with Him. For I consider not the sufferings of this present time to be worthy to be compared with the glory that is to be revealed to us" (8:17–18; cf. also 2 Cor. 4:17–18).

The logic of justification by faith, the logic of grace, reorients our lives from a pattern of temporal preoccupation to preoccupation with the future advent of the glory of God. This world is no longer the center of our hopes and dreams... we have written this world off as a loss... all our "money" is invested in the future. The more mature our faith, the better its grasp of the logic of revealed reality, the more centered we are on the future, and the less wed we are to this present temporal order.

(5:3) *And not only this, but we also exult in our tribulations; knowing that tribulation brings about perseverance...*

"And not only this..." that is, not only do we exult in the expectation of the revelation of the glory of God, but something else, quite unexpected and ironic, we also take pride in, namely, our tribulations.

Christians are not masochists who enjoy adversity for adversity's sake; we do not rejoice in pain and suffering per se, but we exult in the fact that these experiences of adversity are sovereignly managed and directed to produce effects that finish and polish God's redemptive purposes in our lives. They introduce into our lives a chain reaction of beneficial effects that nothing else will accomplish; in the end, they intensify (rather than diminish) the strength of our hope and buoy our hearts with a greater sense of the love of God for us.

The reason Paul injects this ironic point here is that, to some eyes, the tribulations that Christians endure in this world might appear to contradict their claims to enjoy the favor of God. You know the cynical logic... if that's grace, then who needs it! You remember the ad line from years back: "If you're so smart, how come you're not rich?" Well, the Jewish cynic might respond to Paul's Christian exuberance about the blessings of justification by faith: "If you're in such good standing with God, how come you Christians are not better off? How come you are getting pounded on so much? Give me a break!"

Paul anticipates and pre-empts this empty but understandable objection by showing that even our tribulations in the mysteries of God's inscrutable designs express in a left-handed way His gracious intentions.

Knowing that tribulation brings about perseverance...

"Knowing..." The poise of faith amid tribulation is rooted in spiritual understanding. That is a relationship one must bear in mind. Faith does not draw its strength from thin air... it does not move in a vacuum... it soars on the wings of revelation understood and appropriated. Faith comes by hearing, not by feeling. The Word of God quickens faith... causes it to germinate and bear fruit. Show me faith, and behind it is always that word "knowing." People can hear and not believe the truth, but they can never believe what they do not know. That is why, in our worship, hearing the Word of God is central. Without "knowing," there is no faith, no obedience, no praise, no joy, no ministry, no evangelism. Without knowing, there is only brain-dead religion.

What we know (i.e., what mature faith understands) is a series of cause-and-effect relationships that are vital to God's redemptive work and the preservation of our faith. In the constitution of the spiritual order, there is a spiritual law corresponding to the sense in which we speak of a natural law. According to this law, spiritual vitality is not strengthened by the absence of adversity but by the presence of it.

"Tribulation..." (*thlipsesin*). Tribulation for the Christian is a normative part of the spiritual package. In Acts 14:22, Paul encourages some of his first converts to hang tough, reminding them that "Through many tribulations we must enter into the kingdom of God." Those words were reminiscent of Jesus's warning to His disciples upon the eve of His crucifixion: "In the world you shall have tribulation" (John 16:33). Tribulation follows Christians like trouble follows an alien.

Thlipsis, in its root idea, connotes pressure. It refers to anything that presses upon or burdens the spirit.[151] Thus, "tribulation" refers to all those stresses, heavy burdens, and pressures, physical or mental, with which Satan (remember Job!) encumbers our lives to hinder our faith and render our walk with God so burdensome and tiresome that we will give up our faith, abandon our walk with God, and turn away into apostasy.

So why does God allow Satan's interference and his attempts to interdict our obedience to God? Because the same experiences through which Satan designs to upset our faith and destroy our relationship to God and discredit the gospel are the very same pressures and tensions necessary to improve our spiritual fitness and give muscle tone to our faith.

That relationship between tribulation and spiritual fitness should not surprise us, for there is often an analogy between the spiritual and natural worlds. What body becomes strong without tension, without resistance; what becomes of muscles that aren't exercised, that are never exposed to burden bearing? Atrophy and weakness are the inevitable result. So it is with faith and the development of Christian character. Heaviness strengthens it; heat refines it.

The first result of tribulation in the cause-and-effect chain is perseverance (*hypomonen*). "Perseverance" comes from a combination of two Greek words (the preposition *hypo* + the verb form *meno*), which (in the verbal form) means *to remain under.* Although, in biblical usage, not all Greek words remain in touch with their root etymology, this one does. "Perseverance" contains the idea of "remaining under" the burden, of enduring it and not prematurely shedding it before God's purpose is accomplished, but patiently staying in harness, so to speak, in the heat of the day and allowing our sovereign God to finish His work in us.

"Perseverance" is a spiritual attribute that implies faith for its base and fuel. One endures tribulation because one believes the promises of God. That is why in some NT passages (like Matt. 10:22; 24:13, where we have Jesus saying that "He who endures to the end shall be saved."), one finds "endures" where one might have expected "believes" or "continues in faith." Or note Luke 21:19, where Jesus says: "By your *perseverance* you will win your souls." Did Jesus mean there were two ways of salvation, one by faith and another by perseverance. Of course not. Perseverance, like obedience, is just the flip side of Christian faith. They go together inseparably. Perseverance confirms the reality of faith; it is a vital sign of it. In Revelation 14:12, we find the expression, "Here is the *perseverance* of the saints who keep the commandments of God and their faith in Jesus." Paraphrased, that means, "Here is the *confident inspiration* of the perseverance of the saints..." As we mentioned earlier, this insight is the clue that unlocks Romans 2:7, where "perseverance in good works" refers to the life of faith, not legal righteousness or do-goodism.

Now the question emerges: How does tribulation produce (*katergazetai*) perseverance? It is obvious that in many cases, it certainly does not. Many professing Christians, when they no longer can take the heat, proceed to vacate the "kitchen." Apostasy abounds.

The tacit assumption in the context is a base of genuine faith. The NT teaches that adversity separates the men from the boys, the real from the false, the silver from the dross (Matt. 13:21; 1 Pet. 1:6–7; James 1:12). Where genuine faith exists, tribulation produces perseverance, not apostasy (James 1:3).

Those who wait upon the Lord, those who do not prematurely bail out on the promises and assurances of God, these inevitably experience the "outcome of the Lord's dealing, that the Lord is full of compassion and is merciful" (James 5:11). Each time one stays in the harness of affliction and, in the end, is visited with kindness of God, the willingness and the strength to endure is increased. Such monuments fortify our capacity for endurance by strengthening our confidence in God's promises.

For example, if one suffered and prayed for years about some affliction and then at last sees the intervention of God, one will have a second wind the next time around. We likely won't "hit the wall" so easily on the next occasion.

(5:4) *And perseverance, proven character; and proven character, hope...*

"Proven character..." (*dokimen*). The original word conveys the idea of something "proved by testing," hence, "approved." Sometimes in usage, the emphasis is upon the process; at other times, on the outcome. Here, it is the latter. Perseverance produces in its turn a spiritual character that bears the mark of approval before God. The bottom line is that heat and heaviness produce spiritual refinement and strength of Christian character.

James's conception of the impact of tribulation upon Christian faith corresponds to Paul's:

> *"Consider it all joy, my brethren, when you encounter various trials; knowing that the testing of your faith produces endurance (hypomonen or perseverance). And let endurance have its perfect result, that you may be perfect (i.e., mature) and complete, lacking in nothing (i.e., any Christlike grace that God wants to reproduce in your character)"* (James 1:2–4 parentheses mine).

"*Proven character, hope*"— Godly character in its turn results in an intensification of that futuristic aspect of faith the Bible calls "hope." Faith is the broader term, which speaks of our confidence in God's character and word in any respect, whereas hope is that narrower aspect of faith, which relates to the final outcome of our redemption.

Hope is our confident expectation of the consummation of our salvation in which our redemption is completed, and we come into our full inheritance as heirs of God and joint heirs of Christ and share in the glory of our God.[152]

Hope, like faith, admits to growth. The question is: How does sanctification (growth in Christian character) trigger or effect an increase in the measure of our hope? I believe we see the correlation of the two implied in Jesus's Beatitudes (Matt. 5:8):

Blessed are the pure in heart, for they shall see God.

This promise includes, but is not limited to, the idea of entering, at the end, the presence of God in the physical kingdom. But the promise contains, I believe, a spiritual realization in the form of something akin to a beatific vision of God; that is, we shall see God in the sense of coming into a richer and more intimate knowledge of God. The more one becomes like Christ, the more one becomes attuned to God, the better one understands the mind and heart of God. Knowing the heart of God, "seeing" God for the believer enlivens, excites, and stirs up our hope, for then the believer begins to understand better the ways of God, to be more fully assured that God honors those who honor Him, that He is true to His Word, and that what He has promised, He will perform.

(5:5) *And hope does not disappoint; because the love of God has been poured out within our hearts through the Holy Spirit who was given to us.*

"And hope does not disappoint..." That is, our hope, even though our lives are often swallowed up by affliction instead of elevated in glory and bliss, even though Christ has not yet returned as He promised... our hope does not embarrass us before a doubting world... our hope does not make us blush in the face of smirking cynics.

Because the love of God has been poured out within our hearts through the Holy Spirit who was given to us.

Why is our hope so bold and shameless in the face of external contradictions? Because of an internal witness that overpowers all the external objections to it.

Throughout this chain of effects introduced by tribulation, there is an anchoring confidence fed by the Spirit of God. What the Spirit of God does amid affliction, as we respond in faith and endure with steadfastness, is nourish our hope with an outpouring of a sense of the love of God in the inner man.

"Is poured out..." (*ekkechutai*). The perfect tense again implies that the Spirit sustains an original conviction. He started "pouring out" in our hearts a conviction of the love of God for us,[153] and the flow continues.

Through the Holy Spirit who was given to us.

Paul does not develop this reality here but picks it up later. This is the razor's edge, so to speak. Here is one of the great differences between the person under law and under grace. This is the victory secret whereby God has bestowed upon us "everything necessary for life and godliness" (2 Pet. 1:3).

"Within our hearts. . . " There is a confirmation of reality that is purely subjective and out of reach of empirical demonstration or historical verification. We are not left with feelings for our sole basis of assurance, however, as Paul proceeds to show. The love of God for His own has been confirmed historically in the sacrifice of Christ our Savior.

But this proof is personalized by the Spirit of God in the case of individual children of God and doubly reinforced in their hearts.

So how does one know what impressions are of the Spirit and which arise from some other source? The Bible seems to teach that the godly heart has error filters, so to speak; John 10:4, 5, 14, 16, 27; 8:47; 1 John 4:6; and 1 Corinthians 2:12–16, for example. We know what we know. Our hearts hear the witness of the Spirit and are confirmed.

What plumblines can we use to confirm the voice of the Spirit?

The revealed Word will always be consistent with the "heart" word. The Spirit does not contradict Himself. God will never call upon us to act or speak contrary to His character.

Always remember where the subjective testimony of the Spirit is involved, that it is our heart that is on trial. Bad hearts have bad ears. They tend to hear what they want to hear, and that is their judgment... to be convinced of a lie (2 Thess. 2:11–12). Just because the truth is subjectively revealed does not make it any less truth or the evidence any less compelling; it only means that it is less accessible to those who might wish to evaluate our claims. But then we must remember that the unbeliever is hopelessly blind (barring divine intervention) even in assessing objective evidence of our truth claims (1 Cor. 2:14–15). They can't understand even what they see and hear with their own eyes and ears; their unbelief in the face of the miracles and presence of Jesus is proof of that. Water seeks its own level. The things of God can only be penetrated by those with spiritual minds. That is the key ingredient... spirituality. With the Spirit, one form of evidence is as compelling as another.

(5:6) *For while we were still helpless, at the right time Christ died for the ungodly.*

Our confidence in the love[154] of God rests on two pillars, one subjective and the other objective:

1) The internal witness of the Holy Spirit is confirmed and augmented by

2) The logic of Christ's death in our behalf as revealed in the Word of God. That confirmatory effect is the import of the conjunction "for" (*gar*).

With respect to the latter, Paul proceeds to draw out its implicit logic that adds force to the premise 1) that God loves us and 2) that we are secure in His love and acceptance.

The timing as well as the objects of Christ's self-sacrifice are significant in this regard.

Note first *when* he laid down his life for them—*when* they were helpless. In other words, we had nothing to offer him... when we lacked any moral capacity to please Him, to win any credit with Him. "Weakness" in this context amounts essentially to our expression "good for nothing."

Note secondly the objects for whom He died... not for upright people, not persons who deserved something... (none fit into those categories before God we have learned) but He gave Himself for those wholly without inherent merit—namely, the ungodly. This word (where we might have expected simply "us" to answer "we"), as Hodge observes, is inserted to accentuate the gratuitousness of God's love... nothing in us elicited or invited it.[155]

"At the right time" (*kata kairon*)—a phrase which speaks of a planned and deliberate action on Christ's part... not an accidental circumstance, which took Him by surprise. Rather, He was "delivered up by the predetermined plan and foreknowledge of God... ." (Acts 2:23). I am more grateful to the man who put himself deliberately and with forethought into the path of a bullet intended for me than to one who simply caught it by accident.

Jesus said: *I am the good shepherd; the good shepherd lay down His life for the sheep... I lay down My life that I may take it again. No one has taken it away from Me, but I lay it down on My own initiative. I have the authority to lay it down, and I have authority to take it up again* (John 10:11, 17–18).

(5:7) *For one will hardly die for a righteous man; though perhaps for the good man someone would dare even to die.*

How stupendous is the love of God? It is to be measured by the extremity of the suffering God endured over against the worthlessness of the object for whom He suffered.

That Christ, the Son of God, would allow himself to be humiliated at the hands of, and by the mouths of, sinful men and submit himself to the unspeakable agonies of the cross is amazing in itself. But to endure all that—not for good and deserving people—but all for the sake of the certified godless—that begs explanation.

It is not easy to find someone who will die for a very deserving and upright person. Very few of us will lay it on the line for even a very good person.[156] ('Good' as we human beings morally weigh one another.)

(5:8) *But God demonstrates His own love toward us, in that while we were yet sinners, Christ died for us.*

What makes the death of Christ so astounding... so unique... is the people He died for. The objects of it were unworthy of His sacrifice. He knew it in advance, yet He did it anyway without blinking. Who knows anything about love like that?

(5:9) *Much more then, having now been justified by His blood, we shall be saved from the wrath of God through Him.*

Here is an argument from the greater to the less... if God would do the greater thing, then surely, He would not stop at the lesser. Specifically, if God would go so far to justify us when we were

143

ungodly, then He will stop at nothing to glorify us now that we are His children.

> (5:10) *For if while we were enemies, we were reconciled to God through the death of His Son, much more, having been reconciled, we shall be saved*[157] *by His life.*

The hard part was to reconcile us when we were enemies. The easy part is to bring us as adopted children into His glory.

It is more of a feat to reconcile enemies to God through the death of His Son than to finish the salvation of God's friends through the power of Jesus's life. If power of the death of Christ can accomplish so much in the case of God's enemies, imagine what the power of Christ's life can achieve in the case of God's friends.

Paul's point is that the hardest thing imaginable was to make God's enemies, God's friends... to reconcile hostiles to God. After that, it is, comparatively speaking, a small thing for God to finish His redemptive work in the lives of His friends through the power of the living Christ.

What God has already done, then, is logical proof of His great love and of His determination and power to finish what He has started in our lives. He has gone this far. Nothing will stop Him now. He has loved us this much when we were godless enemies. Will He ever love us less now that we are His true friends?

No wonder he says:

> (5:11) *And not only this, but we also exult in God through our Lord Jesus Christ, through whom we have now received the reconciliation.*

"And not only this..." This exact expression occurred at 5:3, where the apostle was cataloguing the benefits that flow from our justification by faith. One is tempted to see this as a resumption of that enumeration, which he broke off at 5:5 to defend the integrity of our Christian hope. However, it is psychologically unrealistic, it seems to me, to refer "this" all the way back to the ironic blessing of tribulation, as if a long "parenthesis" had never broken the thought.

The referent has left commentators in a quandary. Most likely, it is "we shall be saved." The thought, then, is this: "We shall be saved (God shall *finish* our salvation and bring us into the promised glory) in union with the power of His life." But don't let anyone think that we are just hanging on gritting our teeth, hanging on our fingernails, and sweating it out until God intervenes and terminates our miseries. No, no! The truth is, for all our tribulations... for all our pain... for all our desire for our hope to be consummated and for this mortal to put on immortality and for death to be swallowed up in victory, our hearts are in no way barren of the voice of joy and triumph.

No way! Right now, every day, we live in the presence of the living God. His Spirit inhabits our being. The power of the living God dwells within. His love sustains us. We are rejoicing enroute to the consummation of our redemption in the presence and communion of the living God. We exult in what God is... not just what He does for us. We rejoice not simply in God's heaven but above all, in heaven's God... not simply in the salvation of God, but in the God of salvation.

There is the mark of Christian maturity... there is the beginning of true worship... when we come to the point that we see God for what He is, and love Him for what He is, and not just for what He has done for us.

In showing the outcomes of justification by faith, a major emphasis with Paul is to elucidate the idea of imputation and the inherent security of the scheme. He now imports an analogy to reinforce that point.

He shows that the status of men before God hinges on their relationship either to Adam or to Christ... that whether we live or die has to do with the action of another.

> (5:12) *"Therefore, just as through one man sin entered into the world, and death [entered into the world] through sin, and so death spread to all men, because all sinned—" [brackets mine]*

"Therefore..." Commentators have struggled with the contextual connection. *Dia touto* indicates an inference, but from what thought? From a specific idea in the immediate context or an inference from the larger context, such as 5:1–11? The answer can best be determined by catching what his overriding interest is in his contrastive analogy between the ill-effects of Adam on those related to him and the good effects of Christ on those related to Him and then figuring out what big idea in the preceding context suggests this turn and emphasis.

As I see it, Paul has a major interest in magnifying not only the blessings attendant to justification by faith but also showing the inviolable security of this scheme of salvation. We saw him strike this chord strongly in 4:16 and are familiar with his way of coming back to develop such thoughts in a fuller way later.

This motif he seems to return to, but with particular force in 5:5–11. There his interest seems to be not only assuring us of the great love of God but of our security in His redemptive program as we await the outcome of our salvation. That this theme is of major interest to Him as "a selling point," if you please, is clear from its reiteration in 8:31ff.

So, I see this analogy as a historical-theological perspective designed to show that just as surely as those in Adam perish, so those in Christ live—and not because of their own works, but because of the acts of another. The analogy has the effect of pulling together and illustrating his major drumbeats with respects of justification by faith—that we are righteous, not on our own account, but on account of another, that we live, not because of our own behavior but because of our relationship to Christ and that our security in those effects derives from our identity with Him.

Viewed this way, this analogy amounts to a kind of summation of the situation in the form of an illustration that puts the human predicament and experience into cosmic and historic perspective. All of a sudden, we have an account of life, an account of death, a distillation of the foundational issues, and a predictor of outcomes. It is an analogy that serves his purpose and transcends it; it goes to the bone of history and reality and provides a sweeping explanation of life on this planet.

Through one man (i.e., Adam [see verse 14])

"Sin entered into the world" That is, entered the "world" in the sense of the human community, not the physical universe. "Sin" can refer to 1) a specific act of disobedience or non-conformity to God's law, 2) the corruption or depravity of human nature owing to a predilection to transgression, or 3) guiltiness arising therefrom. In the case of Adam, this "one man," all three are inextricably bound up together... a specific act of disobedience corrupted his and our natures resulting in guilt as an effect.

"And death by sin..." Death, in the words of Hodge, follows sin like a shadow. "Death" like "sin" is a more complex idea than is usually contained in the popular conception. "Death" in popular terms is associated with the separation of the soul from the body. That, however, is a secondary symptom; its profounder meaning is the separation of the soul from God... the separation of the human spirit from communion with the Spirit of God... the separation of chemical life from spiritual life.

When God prohibited Adam from partaking of the fruit of the tree on pain of death, the sanction (death) was imposed immediately, though it didn't appear to be. That is because death, in its primary sense, entails separation from God and encumbrance of all the penal miseries of sin. The secondary effect is the separation of the soul from the body. There's the confusion, if any.

Death, then, is a penal aberration of God's created order. It was no original part of the constitutional nature of creation. God imposed it as a judgment on a race corrupted in Adam.

Because (eph' o)[158] *all sinned*—"Because" in the sense of "on the ground that."

Death passed to all (it is implied) rather than confining itself to Adam because it is the penalty of sin, and in some sense, God holds all—not just Adam—to have sinned.

The crucial theological question is: In what sense is sin said to be universal? How did *all* sin? Various views are advanced to the effect that:

1) In some way, the whole race was literally in Adam when he sinned, acted in concert with him in some manner understood only

in the mind of God, and thus shares in his culpability.[159] His sin was not merely ours representatively, but actually.

2) The sin of Adam corrupted human nature and, in that way, predetermined the inevitability of our own rebellion, resulting in a divine write-off, so to speak, of the whole race. In an anticipatory way, we are conceded to be sinners before the fact and written off as such in advance because the outcome was inevitable.[160]

3) There was no necessary cause and effect relationship; it is just a statement that the rest of the race has imitated the sin of Adam. "Death has passed on all men, because all have actually sinned personally."[161]

This Pelagian view is almost universally rejected by the Church. "It would make the apostle teach, that as all men die because they personally sin, so all men live because they are personally and inherently righteous," thus negating the whole analogy between Adam and Christ and is beside the point.[162]

4) Adam stood in the mind and purpose of God as the representative of the whole human race, and his sin was our sin by imputation. In effect, when Adam "voted" with Satan and consented to rebel against the one law that God had established, that is he acted as our divinely appointed representative, and we are held accountable for his actions in a sense similar to the way we hold those who voted for President Clinton responsible for his actions.

If someone should balk at this "injustice" and respond with the disclaimer that they didn't elect or appoint Adam to stand in their place and shouldn't be held accountable for his behavior, two valid questions follow: 1) why do they, then, persist in imitating his rebellion, and 2) why do they persist on keeping him as their representative when they have an alternative (Christ) in whom they may find refuge from the ill consequences of their relationship to Adam?

They are born *in Adam*; by the grace of God, they can opt out. They can elect to be *in Christ*; that would set them free. Their refusal to accept the grace of God and their imitation of the sin of Adam justifies the mystery of divine wisdom, which made Adam their spiritual head and representative.

We "sinned" in Adam in precisely the same way that 2 Corinthians 5:14 says, "all died." "The death of Christ was legally and effectively our death; and the sin of Adam was legally and effectively our sin."[163]

> (5:13–14) *For until the Law, sin was in the world but sin is not imputed when there is no law (legal standard). Nevertheless death reigned from Adam until Moses, even over those who had not sinned in the likeness of Adam's offense, who is a type of Him who was to come. (parenthesis mine)*

Here, Paul temporarily breaks off his analogy between Adam and Christ to explain something that begged for elaboration and confirmation. That was his affirmation that death extended from Adam to all mankind because, in some sense, God held all men responsible for what Adam did. In short, men don't die because they break the law (although they regularly and willfully do), but because they are in Adam and are subject to the curse inflicted on the race because of Adam's sin.

That point is too crucial to leave to chance because he is about to show that we die because of our connection with Adam, and we live because of our connection with Christ. If we miss that, we miss the point. So, he goes out of his way to make sure the foundation of his premise is secured.

Crucial to his analogy is establishing the point that we die because we are in Adam and that we die in Adam because his sin is imputed to us. This relationship highlights *an analogy in contrast.* In Adam, we are written off as sinners; in Christ, we are written up as righteous. In Adam, we are linked to death in all its manifold curses and terrors; in Christ, we joined to life in all its blessings and joys. In Adam, death is assured; in Christ, life is secure. In both cases, their outcomes owe nothing to our own conduct but to our relationship with another, either Adam or Christ.

It is true that in Adam, our conduct is imitative or Adamic and worthy of damnation, but we were written off as sinners long before we did anything because Adam was our representative—one we all have proved we deserved. It may be true that in Christ, our conduct becomes more and more imitative or Christlike, but our life in Christ is not based on our imitation but on the fact that God, in His grace, allowed us to opt out of Adam and choose Christ, the new Adam, as our new representative, as the Head of our race, and His righteousness becomes our righteousness by imputation, and His life extends to us in the same way that Adam's death extended to us.

The logic flow of 5:12–14 paraphrased:

Death is the penalty for sin, that is, the transgression of the law of God.

No external law code existed between the time of Adam and Moses.

People are not subjected to the death penalty for violating a law that does not exist.

Yet, people suffered the death penalty in that interval.

Therefore, they must have transgressed the law of God in some specific form.

The non-existent law of Moses could not have been the law that they transgressed.

Hence, the death penalty imposed upon them must go back to the curse imposed on the race because of Adam's transgression of the law of God.

Therefore, the sin of Adam is clearly imputed to his posterity.

"But sin is not imputed when there is no law." That is, sin is not charged, a death warrant is not issued, so to speak, in the absence of an objective law to define transgression.[164]

This statement is not inconsistent with Paul's earlier affirmation of the presence of a form of natural law inscribed on the conscience of men (2:15) or with his statement that pagans who spurn the will of God imprinted on the conscience stand self-condemned and perceive that their actions warrant the death penalty (1:32). Nor does it contradict the fact (2:16) that God will bring to light the "inner voice" that they deny, their defiance of it, and will hold them accountable for their lawlessness.

His point is that the sentence of death did not wait (or need to wait) to discover them sinners. God pronounced them sinners when Adam failed as their representative. The final judgment of God will simply confirm the righteousness of the original verdict in finding them also sinners by choice and will visit upon those who elect to stay with Adam, the just wrath of a holy God whose law they despised.

The curse following Adam's fall illustrates the point. The penal sufferings inflicted on mankind in consequence of the fall are precisely that—in consequence of Adam's failure. He tangled us all up in the web of his sin. Every day we pay... and pay... and pay. Men still earn their bread by the sweat of their brow... survival is a struggle... visit a maternity ward and listen to a mother's cry... watch men tyrannize and dominate women... watch women try to rule men by manipulation, seduction, or subversion... visit the mortuaries and cemeteries each day... watch the mourners and see the caskets. We are encumbered with our own sins, but we are paying the price of Adam's default. But I repeat, we can't find fault with that judgment if 1) we keep aligning ourselves with Adam's sin by choice, and 2) we refuse to realign ourselves with Christ. Case closed.

Now the apostle returns to his analogy but in a different manner than he started. This analogy is between the ill-effects of Adam's sin on those connected with Adam and the good effects of those connected with Christ. What he highlights in these three verses is the *transcendence* on the side of Christ. What happened in Christ for those in Christ is greatly superior in the direction of good than anything that happened in Adam in the direction of evil. In short, the upsides accruing to those in Christ greatly exceed by comparison the downsides to those in Adam.

> (5:15) *But the free gift is not like the transgression. For if by the transgression of the one the many died, much more by the grace of God and the gift by the grace of the one Man, Jesus Christ, abounded to many.*

"Much more..." looks at the disposition of the merciful heart of God. If in the justice of God, that by the transgression of one, many died, then much more so the heart of God abounded with grace toward sinners and lavished joyfully the gracious gift of righteousness (justification) on all those who would, by faith, identify with Christ.

God is not a have-it-your-way God who, as it were, just lays out the two options, shrugs His shoulders, and says it is all the same to Him. God takes no delight in the death of sinners. The heart of God delights in showing mercy (Luke 6:36; 2 Pet. 3:9; 1 Tim. 2:4). The heart of God is freer and richer with grace than the sentence of death.

> (5:16) *And the gift is not like that which came through the one who sinned; for on the one hand the judgment arose from one transgression resulting in condemnation, but on the other hand the free gift arose from many transgressions resulting in justification.*

If the justice of God was unbending in passing sentence upon us (representatively) for Adam's single transgression, the grace of God in Christ is almost unending in lifting the sentence in covering many transgressions.

> (5:17) *For if by the transgression of the one, death reigned through the one, much more those who receive the abundance of grace and of the gift of righteousness will reign in life through the One, Jesus Christ.*

In 5:18–19, Paul picks up the thread of the analogy he dropped at the end of verse 12 and summarizes the analogy. The idea is this:

The Man in Adam	The Man in Christ
Adam's disobedience imputed to him	Christ's obedience imputed to him
Condemnation is the result	Justification is the result
Death is inevitable	Life is assured

This scheme spells absolute spiritual security[165] in Christ.

If mankind is under the sentence of death because of its relationship to Adam... if people die because of their relationship to Adam and live because of their relationship to Christ, what is the function of the law of Moses, if it accounts for neither life nor death?

(5:20–21) *The law came in that the transgression might increase. But where sin increased, grace increased all the more, that, as sin reigned in death, even so grace might reign through righteousness to eternal life through Jesus Christ our Lord.*

God revealed the Law for the purpose of raising our consciousness to our sin problem. The patient has to know that he has a disease... that his case is terminal in order to apply for the remedy. Without law to define sin, there is no *legal* transgression, even though one possesses the heart of a transgressor.

For instance, if there is no legal speed limit, I am not a violator, even if I am running up and down the highways at one hundred miles per hour. The way to bring out the fact that I am a real scofflaw—to me and others—is to establish a legal speed limit. If I persist in my reckless driving habits after that, I just prove what my attitude was all along.

What the legal limit does is show my true colors... stir up the mud in the bottom of my character bucket... strip away my moral facade and show how godless I am at the core.

So, in injecting His law into the human picture, God caused transgression to increase. I don't mean He caused us to sin, He just defined it; He just drew some boundaries, knowing that we had a heart that wouldn't respect them. All He had to do to make self-conscious transgressors or violators or scofflaws of us was simply to draw some lines. Our own hearts carried us out of bounds. He let us, posterity of Adam, discover our complicity with Adam... that our condemnation *in* Adam was not a legal fiction but a partnership under the curse that was truly deserved.

Yet, God's design was not to rub our noses in our guilt, so to speak. Rather, His intention was to awaken us to our own depravity, to drive us to despair of ourselves... to sensitize us to our moral dead-endedness and prepare us to receive the abundance of God's grace, which was revealed to us in the appearance of Jesus Christ.

But where sin increased, grace increased all the more, that, just as sin reigned in death, so also grace might reign through righteousness to eternal life through Jesus Christ our Lord.

Right here is where we see the goodness and kindness of God. The more those divine boundaries incited our sinful passions, the more sin dominated our wills, and our transgressions piled up, and their stench mounted up to heaven; it was God's merciful plan to be there to meet the believing sinner... to blot out his sin and clear his conscience with the covering of Christ's righteousness imputed to the sensitized and repentant transgressor.

Sin "reigns" in that it masters our will and leads us into the prison house of death—death in all its ramifications. Death is the environment in which the sinner lives and moves and has his being... all of what we call "life" is nothing more than a hollow imitation in which we exhaust ourselves trying to escape its tenacles... keeping out of its reach while all the while rushing right into its arms in its many disguises. Sin "reigns" like a malignant tyrant... it seduces us, enslaves us, and at last mocks us and betrays us and at last abandons us to rot in the grave, and life marches on without us... leaving us at last to rendezvous with the judgment of God without a leg to stand on.

But for the believing sinner, the grace of God in the form of forgiveness... in the form of the imputed righteousness of Jesus Christ, surmounts and covers the multitude of our sins, be they ever so many. Death gives way to life through Jesus Christ our Lord, whose righteousness covers our sins and whose presence dwells now within us. Grace now reigns. Life supplants death.

God never met a repentant sinner whose guilt was piled so high that His forgiveness could not surmount it and top it, whose sins were so extensive that the arms of His grace could not surpass its borders and erase them.

The whole scheme of God's salvation was that as the sin principle embedded in our natures reigned over us to produce death—in the sense of separation from the life of God and affliction with all the penal miseries of sin—so now, His grace might reign in our lives through justification, resulting in the participation in eternal life— participation in the divine nature, the divine life.

So, the Law and all its sinful effects are just a foil for the glorious grace of God.

Well, someone might argue (and some did) that if our sinful conduct serves a foil for the grace of God... if God magnifies our sin so that He can glorify His grace by forgiving our sin, then would we not do God a favor by sinning more, rather than less, thereby "creating for Him an opportunity to shine," so to speak... by providing an occasion to make Him look good by His willingness to forgive our sins, no matter how great?

That is the point of the question in 6:1.

Wrong turn! No such logic is intended or implied in the divine plan of salvation. There is nothing about the grace of God or the logic of justification by grace that provides any incentive or excuse for sinful behavior. Forget it!

Transitional Logic: If people die because they are in Adam and live because they are in Christ (a thesis expostulated in 5:12–19 and based on the typology Paul recognizes in the two heads of the race), what is the function of the Law? If in the final analysis, people don't die because they *personally* are transgressors of the Law and don't live because they *personally* keep God' law, the Law given through Moses seems superfluous. So why did God throw it into the mix? What meaningful purpose does it serve? Where does it fit in the salvation equation? The answer surprises.

The apostle's response: The first function of the Law is to convict (or convince) men of their sinfulness, that is, their moral bankruptcy or that fallenness inherited from their first father, Adam.

How did the Law fulfill this function?

Its presence stirred up the mud in the bottom of our character buckets. It incited the sin principle in us. It excited our "contrarian" spirit where the will of God is concerned. It smoked sin out of hiding. So, with the advent of the Law, transgression, in the legal sense, multiplied as sin ran roughshod over the law of God and defied His express desires.

But God has interdicted this deadly situation. How? In Christ, He stood at the ready like a fireman with His hose, dousing a roaring blaze and smothering the billows of sin with a flood tide of forgiving grace. If, through the Law, He exposed the magnitude of our sins, His grace was always more than sufficient to pardon it. His grace is always greater than our sins. It is always bestowed upon those in Christ in a measure equal to the need and beyond our transgressions.

The Law is meant, then, to confirm our depravity and lostness. His grace is there to affirm our security and forgiveness in Christ.

Now some might misunderstand or twist this truth in such a way as to infer that since sin calls forth grace, one ought to continue in sin in order to keep the fountain of grace flowing.

This is an antinomian mentality that views sin as a kind of lightning rod to attract grace. Since the exercise of His grace glorifies God, whatever stimulates its outpouring magnifies Him. A subtle and perverse twist of logic, but one that the apostle emphatically rejects as a valid extension of his logic or intent.

---

[147] The alternative textual reading (*echomen* = "let us have" versus "we have"), which some commentators support, lends good sense, but not the best in this context. The apparent intent of the author is to expound the momentous blessings (4:7) that accrue to the justified, not to exhort them to appropriate subjectively the wealth they have in Christ, as important as that is. Both thoughts are biblical. The only issue is which is most compatible with his argument at this stage.

[148] The perfect tense of *echo* implies the continuing effect of a past action up to the present.

[149] Moulton and Milligan, *The Vocabulary of the Greek New Testament*, 545.

[150] Even in extra-biblical Greek *elpis* usually connotes an *expectation* rather than a mere wish or ardent desire as the word "hope" does in normal English usage. I remember a footnote to this effect in a course on the Attic orators when I was translating a speech of Lysias. Unfortunately, I cannot find that in my files at the moment, but I remember the text was *The Attic Orators*, Oklahoma University Press.

151 Trench, *Synonyms of the New Testament*, 203.

152 Cf. *Evangelical Dictionary of Theology*, "Hope," 532.

153 Grammatically the phrase could mean either 1) our love for God or 2) God's love for us. The following context is decisive that Paul is speaking of God's love for us subjectively apprehended.

154 The love of God is not essentially an emotion or affection; it is a way of behaving toward another. . . a behavior that is willing to put aside selfish interest for the well-being of another; a behavior that is kind, merciful and unselfish even with respect to one's enemies.

155 Hodge, *Epistle to the Romans*, 136.

156 Commentators differ about whether the "righteous" man and the "good" are essentially synonymous or distinct types. As for the latter, I have trouble making any meaningful distinction between the two. Cranfield takes the second in the sense of a personal "benefactor," but that seems to me to be a reach. Who would find that here except one forced to discover a difference?

To me it makes perfectly good sense in context (and I see no forbidding lexical or grammatical difficulties) to understand Paul to say, "For it is unlikely that anyone would volunteer to die for a perfectly deserving man. Perhaps (I will allow) for a really good man some would be so bold as to sacrifice their own lives. But the death of Christ went way beyond that." This sense seems to me to best suit the context.

The second "for" isn't easy to account for on either interpretation. I take it as something between a confirmation and a concession—a confirmation in the sense that it would be possible, but really notable if one rose up to take the place of good person in death; a concession in the sense that it is not unheard of or unthinkable in such cases.

157 Whenever the Apostle uses the word "saved" with reference to future time, as here, it can be confusing if we are in the habit of conceiving of our salvation strictly as a momentary event that occurred at a specific time in the past. Of course, it did happen in past time in the sense that we were justified, reconciled, and regenerated all in a moment of time when we placed our faith in Christ. That is the foundation which guarantees all the rest of our redemption. These elements of our salvation are just the first cars in a whole train of the program of "salvation." And that is the key word—program. Our salvation should be conceived of as an urban renewal project with a beginning, a middle and an end. We are a divine renewal project. The program began with our justification, reconciliation, and regeneration. The middle or present tense, so to speak, is our sanctification, a phase in which the indwelling Spirit is making righteous the person whom God declared righteous. The conclusion is glorification in which our transformation into the likeness of Christ is completed and we enter God's presence and into the full measure of our eternal inheritance to reign with Christ.

Think therefore of "salvation" as an on-going program more than a historical event.

[158] Cf. Smythe, *Greek Grammar*, 379, paragraph 1689:2,c for an example of *epi* used with the dative to express "reason, motive, end. . ."

This exact Greek construction is found also at 2 Cor. 5:4, Phil. 3:12 and 4:10 as well as Acts 7:33. A very similar one appears in Romans 6:21 where the construction differs only in the fact that the plural relative pronoun is used instead of the singular. In every case except Acts 7:33 the sense is logical rather than spatial, furnishing a reason or motive attendant to some action or sentiment.

[159] As Hodge expresses (although rejecting) it: "He [Adam] being not simply **a** man as one among many, but **the** man in whom humanity was the act of all the individuals in whom human nature subsequently developed itself." *Epistle to the Romans*, 151.

[160] This amounts, Hodge responds, to translating *harmatano* "because all *are* corrupted." *Epistle to the Romans*, 149.

[161] Hodge's unaccepting summation of this viewpoint, *Epistle to the Romans*, 149ff.

[162] Ibid, 149.

[163] Ibid, 152.

[164] Some commentators understand this of self-condemnation for sin. That is, men do not recognize or assume guilt for sin unless there is an objective law to define transgression. But the fact is, there is natural law and based on that law, men do discover themselves worthy of death (1:32)

[165] Someone might object that just as one can opt out of Adam one can opt out of Christ. The point is that in Christ we are secured not by what we do, but what He did.

Romans Chapter 6

(6:1) *What shall we say then? Are we to continue in sin that grace might increase?*

"What shall we say then?" That is, "What conclusion shall we draw from this?"

Bruce:

> This is not a completely hypothetical objection, for in fact there have always been people to insist that this is the logical corollary of Paul's teaching about justification by faith; and unfortunately, in every generation, people claiming to be justified by faith have behaved in such a way as to lend colour to this criticism. James Hogg's *Private Memoirs and Confessions of a Justified Sinner* (1824) provides the outstanding literary example of such deliberate antinomianism; a notable historical instance may be seen in the Russian monk Rasputin, the evil genius of the Romanov family in its last years of power. Rasputin taught and exemplified the doctrine of salvation through repeated experiences of sin and repentance; he held that, as those who sin most require most forgiveness, a sinner who continues to sin with abandon enjoys, each time he repents, more of God's forgiving grace than any ordinary sinner. The case-books of many soul-physicians [Bruce cites in a footnote apparently as an example Hannah Whitehall Smith's *Religious Fanaticism* (1928)] would reveal that this point of view has been commoner than is often realized, even when it is not expressed and practiced so blatantly as it was by Rasputin (brackets my insertion).[166]

However, Bruce's assumption that the apostle is trying to rectify legalizing tendencies among Christians is dubious, I think. The scenario that he envisions does not, to my recollection, appear in the

NT with exactly this twist. Though plausible, it never, to my knowledge, takes this form of Christian reasoning.

More likely, Paul has in mind the objections of Jews and Judaizers whose clever but specious logic could easily (and perhaps often did) confuse the Church. It may have been a form of *reductio ad absurdum* (reducing to absurdity) on the part of his enemies who would raise this question in this form to show that his gospel logic leads to this very conclusion. Paul anticipates it and defuses it.

Also, he may have anticipated a more naïve but quite absurd inference on the part of some Christians that the logic of grace implies that we ought to cooperate in any way possible to glorify God, including sinning, so that He can exercise the glory of His forgiveness in Christ.

> (6:2) *May it never be! How shall we who died to sin still live in it?*

The fallacy of the inference above is inherent in the logic of the redemptive transaction.

"Died to sin..." Compare the footnote on page 197 for the notional content of this phrase. Fundamentally, I think, this phrase signifies our *legal identification with the death of Christ.* In this judicial transaction, the penalty for our sin is inflicted on the Savior as our legal Substitute (or Stand-in) at the cross. When a sinner embraces the Lord by faith as His Redeemer, one accepts Christ's real death for sin legally as one's own. He took the "hit" for our sins. He took the fall, and it counts as if it was our own. In that transaction, God accepts the death of Christ as our own... considers the price of sin paid in full and lifts from our lives the sentence of death, which hangs over us.

"How shall we still live in it?"

Should one wonder what it is about our escape from the penalty of sin that implies, as the apostle's question suggests, that the believer must not (yea, cannot) persist in the practice of sin, the answer is close at hand.

The apostle's question implies that our death to sin is more than an accomplished fact. It is a historical and irreversible legal reality, but also one with a moral purpose into which we voluntarily entered. In other words, he implies by his question that our legal death to sin was also a moral engagement; or at least was supposed to be if, in fact, we entered knowingly into the redemptive transaction. Our acceptance of Christ's death as our legal substitute implies a consent to, and moral partnership in, the divine purpose of redemption, namely, to set us free not only from the penalty of sin but also the service of sin.

Hence, the question "how can we persist in living in sin when, in fact, "we... died to sin?" is implicitly an open repudiation of the very idea.

If this connection has somehow been lost on us, then perhaps the problem is an imperfect grasp of the import of our Christian baptism. That rite makes a "statement" (or was supposed to) about our future relationship to sin.

Now he proceeds to develop the significance of Christian baptism as it relates to a life of sin.

(6:3–4) *Or do you not know that all of us who have been baptized into Christ Jesus have been baptized into His death? Therefore we have been buried with Him through baptism into death, in order that as Christ was raised from the dead through the glory of the Father, so we too might walk in newness of life.*

"Or do you not know... " The language suggests something that is taken for granted in Christian faith. Faith is founded on knowledge just as a house rests on a foundation. Where knowledge is deficient, faith will be faulty.

His question implies a substandard base of spiritual understanding in those who would even ask if we should continue in sin in order to give God greater opportunity to display His grace in forgiveness. Such a "faith" is not sound or firmly grounded because it is not properly informed. There is no way to separate sound faith from sound doctrine. I repeat, one can know sound doctrine and not be a person of sound faith; one cannot, however, be a person of sound faith without sound doctrine.

"Baptized into Christ..." This is a NT era metonym for "confessed Christ by faith." Baptism was the normal venue of Christian confession. In the waters of baptism, faith was formally (and normally) professed. If one wanted to receive Christ under the impetus of Christian preaching, one accomplished that through the ritual of baptism. Baptism was the casing, as it were; the confession was the core. [167]

Christian baptism symbolizes our union with Christ and (by implication) our fusion with His universal Body. Its function is not to formalize induction into a local church membership but induction into Christ (and His Body); though, in the nature of the case, those who become members of Christ should affiliate and identify with a local church.

"All... were baptized into His death?" That is, in accepting His death as a legal substitute for our own, we enter all its ramifications... we embraced its purpose (or should have).

Implicit in our death to sin, symbolized in water baptism, was a self-conscious moral realignment, a commitment to Christ's agenda (v. 4) in death.

So, the bottom line is that "died to sin," though highlighting the forensic aspect of our salvation, that is, our legal identification with the death of Christ, signals (proleptically) our moral empowerment and realignment.

In short, "died to sin" is a phrase which signifies an absolute break, not only with sin's legal penalty but also sin's moral power (not in the sense that we are incapable of its seductive influence, but in the sense that its dominion is broken, i.e., we are no longer subject to its *involuntary* control and our wills are no longer tipped in its favor).

Buried with him by baptism...

This metaphor, it has been argued, indicates the mode of baptism then practiced, namely, immersion. This evidence alone is insufficient, however, to support that conclusion. "Buried" could be merely a metonym for Jesus's death with which we were legally united in baptism (cf. 6:5, where "united" represents the Greek word *sumphutoi,* which literally means "planted together"). That metaphor, as Murray rightly points out, does not likely refer to baptismal mode, so why should the previous one be taken differently?[168]

"Through the glory of the Father," that is, the power of God by synecdoche (the whole for the part).

"So we too might walk in newness of life." Although the wording, I think, primarily spells out the divine intention inherent in our legal union with Christ's death, the implication is plain that we ourselves shared that purpose. The moral intention was sovereignly initiated but, by grace, individually owned in our baptismal confession.

For the force of "too," see verse 10, where we see that death divorced the Son of God from any and all personal connection with sin (He *legally* became sin for us, our sin bearer, the focal point of judgment upon it) and now raised from the dead, the agenda of the resurrected Christ is to live for the glory of God the Father. As those united to Him, His purpose is our purpose, and we ought to keep in step with it.

(6:5) *For if we have become united with Him in the likeness of His death, certainly we shall be also in the likeness of His resurrection.*

The "for" expresses confirmation—confirmation of the cause-and-effect relationship between legal union with His death and spiritual union with His life.

"For if we are planted together in the likeness of his death, indeed we shall be also [raised in the likeness] of his resurrection" (my translation of the original with clarifying words in brackets).

The apostle invokes an image of sowing to depict our legal identification with Christ in His death, resulting in our organic union with His resurrection-life. In farming, one brings forth a living plant from dead seed. That is the picture.

One hears perhaps an echo of 1 Corinthians 15:36: "That which you sow does not come to life unless it dies."

So, the condition of spiritual resurrection is legal identification with Christ. Everyone legally connected with Christ in His death will be organically connected with His life. One experiences the first stage of the resurrection (new life) because of being united to the life of the resurrected Christ through the indwelling of the Holy Spirit. A rough analogy might be the quickening of life in the dead seed while it is still under the ground; finally, it germinates into a full-blown plant.

The initiation of this new life signifies a work of regeneration. Its continuation bespeaks an ongoing work of sanctification, leading ultimately to glorification. The link in our union with Christ is the Holy Spirit, who is continually present in the believer.

"Shall be..." The future tense of the verb should not be taken to refer primarily to our eventual physical resurrection—the birthright of our justification. Rather, the context of the future is the previous verb, a perfect tense (*gegonamen*). Whenever the condition in view (the state of legal identification) pre-exists, the author assures, we can be reassured its natural consequence will invariably follow.

We might paraphrase the logic: "Whenever the condition of having died with Him preexists, then, certainly, spiritual resurrection will follow as a logical consequence. In other words, we can count on this: if we know we have been united with His death, we know we shall be united with His resurrection (with all that means) as a matter of course."

In other words, the future tense is a *logical* future, not an *eschatological* future, referring to our end-time bodily resurrection. Yet, the phrasing does exclude the latter for the simple reason that our spiritual and physical resurrection are not biblically conceived as distinct events but as the same event working itself out in two stages.

We have a similar use of the future in 6:8 ("If we have died with Him, we believe that we shall also live with Him"), where there is no serious doubt the primary reference is to the present, not the eschatological (i.e., end times) future.

What is crucial here is to recognize that in Paul's mind, our resurrection, while culminating gloriously in the physical resurrection of our physical bodies (in an incorruptible form, 1 Cor. 15:42ff.), is *initiated* in a spiritual form in our regeneration (resulting from our spiritual union in Christ).

(6:6) *Knowing this, that our old self (anthropos) was crucified with Him, that our body of sin might be done away with (katargethe), that we should no longer be slaves of sin... (tou meketi douleuein).* (parentheses mine)

Here, he reinforces his case against the original inference by augmenting his assurance of moral empowerment (implicit in our union with Christ's death and life) in amplification of its moral effect and intent. It, therefore, reaffirms the absurdity of the original question (or inference). Our death to sin entails a new man with a new power and a new purpose.

"Knowing this..." By this phrase, the apostle indicates not what is necessarily given or common knowledge among believers but redemptive realities that need to be grasped by all.

Were it the former, the question calling forth this chapter could hardly have been raised. So, it really has a kind of hortatory (or subjunctive) force, such as "Let us also understand these realities so relevant in that connection."

Our old man was crucified...

"Our old man," I judge, is the unregenerate person, the person we were prior to the new birth, before becoming a new creation in Christ.[169] The person we once were will never again exist. This thought is powerfully articulated by Paul in 2 Corinthians 5:14–15, 17, and 21:

For the love of Christ controls us, having concluded this, that one died for all, therefore all died; and He died for all, that they who live should no longer live for themselves, but for Him who died and rose again on their behalf... Therefore if any man is in Christ, he is a new creature; the old things passed away; behold new things have come... He made Him who knew no sin to be sin on our behalf, that we might become the righteousness of God in Him.

In that case, how do we account for the fact that believers are called upon to put off the old man, as if the old nature were coexisting side by side with the new (Eph. 4:22)?[170]

The best interpretation of such difficulties, as I always say in teaching hermeneutics, is the one which explains the most and leaves one with the fewest problems. In this case, I believe a metonymical explanation (once again) best harmonizes the superficial inconsistency in Paul's conceptuality.

A metonym is a figure of speech in which the name of one thing is used for another (like a cause for its effect, a sign for the thing signified, etc.). Because the two have become so mentally identified with each other, that one name can be used to signify the other.

For example, we sometimes talk about going to the altar instead of getting married or going for the bottle instead of consuming alcohol.

In this case, I think the old self (in Greek, the old man) is a metonym (the condition) for old, sinful habits (the consequence). Now, sometimes, habits can remain, even though the condition that generated them has been altered.

I was reared in southern West Virginia just after the Great Depression era. I noticed that many folks, once dirt poor during the Depression but now prosperous, retained reflexes or habits stemming from the trauma of grinding poverty.

In that environment, one sometimes encounters a scenario something like this:

A rich man will be acting (i.e., very conservatively) like a poor man, guarding every penny as if it stood between himself and starvation. Exasperated with his excessive penuriousness, an impatient wife might fire off:

"Come on, John! Put off the poor man. You're rich now. Act like it! Stop thinking like the poor man you once were. Get rid of that fellow. Bury him. We don't have to live like that anymore. We're not in the Depression, and you ain't broke anymore."

Note that John *is* a rich man. He is no longer poor. Poverty and wealth do not coexist in the same person. Yet, the penurious habits born and cultivated in poverty are not easily relinquished. So, he may have to admonish himself occasionally—or be admonished by others—not to revert to the habits so well established and remembered from his former situation.

To say, "Put off the poor man" is just a metonym for the habits and mindset carried over from that former condition. The condition of poverty no longer exists; however, all the effects and consequences of that condition do not pass away with the condition.

Such an explanation, I believe, better accounts for the surface inconsistency in Paul's language on this subject.

If one wants to take the position that the old self (i.e., "man" in Greek) still coexists alongside the new, then it raises other problems more difficult to solve.

For example, how does one explain the use of the adjective "old"? To refer to a "man" still alive and well? That is awkward. Surely it would be more natural if we were to imagine an individual with two "personalities" but one of recent origin to refer to the congenital one as the "older" as opposed to "newer," especially if both asserted themselves from time to time.

On the other hand, it is more natural to describe a former condition as "old." If one has vacated a house or property, one naturally refers to the former as the "old" house or property. And how often have we heard a person now trim and physically fit allude contemptuously to their <u>former</u> obese and out-of-shape condition as "the old me"?

Moreover, it seems most unnatural conceptually to visualize the believer as two persons (i.e., an old man and a new man co-existing side by side). It seems that one must be one or the other. People like to talk about an old and new nature. The Bible does not use that nomenclature. It speaks of a new creature in 2 Corinthians 5:17.

But how can we be a "new man" when so much of the old is still in evidence? That nagging reality is the main reason, I think, why some interpreters insist on a new man/old man bifurcation model. To think of the old man as a thing of the past is to their way of thinking too perfectionistic. They are trying to give an account of our residual proneness to sin. If we are a new man without any opposition from the old, that situation seems harder to account for.

The reality they want to allow for must be acknowledged. But that can be accounted for in the new man. Just as a full-grown man may manifest childish immaturity without being a boy, just as a refined intellectual may retain vestiges of the barrio boy he once was without being one, so a new man can harbor residual influences and effects of his former condition without remaining in it.

The new man is "new," not because he is *totally and completely* transformed, but because he is *fundamentally and centrally* changed. The flesh remains but no longer reigns. It reneges, but it no longer rules. It agitates, but it no longer dominates. The soulish old man has died and been replaced by one whose spirit has been made alive in Christ, inhabited by the Holy Spirit, and ruled from that center. The "capitol," in other words, is in new hands, but the flesh still conducts guerilla warfare against the Spirt, sniping at the will of God at every turn. Now it is just a matter of time until that control extends to all the towns, villages, and countryside of the heart. Believers are truly "new men." All that is the same as before are the outer trappings and infection of the flesh. But the heart and center have been radically transformed. Yet, because of the presence of the flesh and its appetites and cravings, our wills, if not vigilantly monitored and reinforced by the resources of grace, are susceptible to being seduced.

Like the rich man, we, therefore, always need to be warned to "put off the poor man." We are now a rich man. The poor man no longer exists. But when conditions are wrong, we can relapse into the habits and mindset of the former condition.

"Crucified" is past tense, not present, having in view an event already having taken place. This is a metonym (sign put for the thing signified) for "put to death." It looks back at our legal identification with Christ on the cross when the penalty of sin was fully discharged in His self-sacrifice.

Why mention our release from the penalty of sin when it is victory over its enslaving power (i.e., its ability to enforce its evil demands upon our wills) that is the ultimate aim?

Again, because justification is the basis and handmaid of sanctification. Justification is "the track sanctification runs on."[171]

Legal death and spiritual resurrection are so inseparably linked that to declare the former is to guarantee the latter.[172]

"The body of sin" could mean the flesh dominated by the power of sin, or sin viewed metaphorically as a crucified corpse to be disposed of.[173]

I think the former interpretation is more probable because Paul seems to locate the power of sin in the body. The body is the seat of sin, not its source. Sin leverages the will through the appetites and weaknesses of the flesh.

Our grasp of this section is weakened if we think of sin as *activities* rather than a wicked willfulness expressing itself through the flesh in deeds and desires. Sin is not to be equated with Satan. Satan exploits the presence of sin in us.[174]

"May be disabled"—not presently in an absolute sense but ultimately, yet immediately in the sense that we are freed from the power of sin as a ruling force, that is, as mentioned above, one able to impose its will and enforce its demands upon our wills.

In that latter sense, sin has been disenfranchised permanently, yet it has not been eradicated as a powerful undertow through our flesh. We are still susceptible to its blandishments and solicitations. But no longer are we slaves to its demands. Now we are able to please God through a renewed heart and the superior power of the indwelling Spirit. Sin can no longer hold our wills hostage to its desires.

Calvin: "Although the mortification of our flesh is only beginning in us, yet the life of sin is destroyed by this very means, so that our spiritual newness, which is divine, may afterwards continue forever"[175]

In order that we may no longer be slaves to sin...
Far from any thought of encouraging unrighteousness, the divine design was to break the stranglehold of sin over our wills, to empower us with the ability to say "yes" to the will of God.

(6:7) *For he who died is freed from sin.*

This confirms our emancipation from the power of sin (in the enslaving sense) by a reminder of our justification from the penalty of sin associated with our identification with His death.

"For he who died [sc. to sin] has been justified [*dedikaiotai*] from sin" (parentheses mine. My translation of the English text).

In a legal union with Christ, the penalty of our sinfulness has been justly settled. With the penalty of sin out of the way, empowerment to righteousness follows since the *dead* man is united to Christ in His resurrection and all the moral power contained in that life.

Again, if Paul, to our surprise, seems to anchor our power over sin to justification (implicit in our death to sin), it is because—I say it again—he sees our redemption as a continuum in which the legal transaction is the condition of the moral union with Christ. Again—with the late Vernon McGee—"justification is the track sanctification runs on." [176] Justification and sanctification are linked as indissolubly as life and breath.

John Murray puts it differently but appears to acknowledge the same connection:

"This judicial aspect from which deliverance from the power of sin is to be viewed needs to be appreciated. It shows that the forensic is present not only in justification *but also in that which lies at the basis of sanctification*" (emphasis mine).[177]

(6:8) *Now if we have died with Christ, we believe that we shall also live with Him...*

Having drawn out the implications of our legal participation in the death of Christ, the apostle now shifts His focus to our spiritual participation in His resurrection. He wants to amplify the moral empowerment and obligation implicit in it.

"We believe" implies no lack of certainty. Rather, it is intended to flag a fundamental element of Christian conviction. In short, this is a *given* in the Christian faith.

"That also we shall live with Him..." The logic of union with Christ is this: those who participate in His death also participate in His life. The former is legal; the latter is literal. The future tense is obviously logical, not eschatological. It is a consequence that follows when a condition is met. We live with Him now, not eventually.

(6:9) *Knowing that Christ having been raised from the dead, is never to die again, death no longer is master over Him.*

"Knowing that..." I agree with Cranfield (*pace* Murray) that this expression does not specify the *basis* of the confidence that we shall live with Him, but in accordance with Paul's style, "is another consideration relevant to what has just been said." [178]

The real foundation of that faith is the logic of our union (stated in the previous verse, namely, that participation on the death end of Christ's redemptive transaction is a pledge of participation on the life end).

The point is that having died once, He will never again be subject to it. For a moment in time, by a covenant with and in the foreordination of the Father, He became sin (legally). He never sinned, but He agreed with the Father to become the Sin Bearer, to let all the punishment for sin fall upon Him. The sting of sin, even for One whose relation to it was only legal, is death. So as the Sin Bearer, death for an unspeakably horrible "moment in time" lorded over Him. But death could not hold Him. He died but still contained within Himself the power of an indestructible life. He rose from among the dead. Now He is immune forever to the power of death. It is not merely that He conquered death and lives again. Much more than that, He is the very fountainhead of life... the new Adam is a life-giving spirit, not like the old one, a merely living soul (1 Cor. 15:45).

Monday morning significance? Awesome! If His life is uninterruptible, so is ours, for we live because He lives. We are organically joined to Him. Our lives are forevermore in immutable and undetachable union.

But don't believers die just like everybody else? Doesn't death lord it over us? Ah, no! The body is mortal, but the spirit lives. I don't mean that it simply exists forever, but that it *lives* eternally. Life is more than existence. It is participation in and communion with the life of God Himself. *Living* is life in union and communion with God... life in harmony with the Source of life itself. Such a reconnection is found only in union with Christ... a union which can be established through justification by faith.

This is the point of Romans 8:10:

"Now if Christ is in you, while the body is death on account of sin, the spirit on the other hand is life on account of righteousness (i.e., justification)."

> (6:10) *For the death that He died, He died to sin, once for all; but the life that He lives, He lives to God.*

Here, He reaffirms the *finality* of His death and affirms the *intentionality* of His life. His redemptive transaction on our behalf was an all-sufficient atonement for sin. It never needs to be repeated. It never will be. It was "once and for all."

Now the immutable intention of the Son is to devote the life He now lives to God (i.e., the Father). The obvious implication is that, since the life that is in us is His life, we ought and do share the same spiritual intention as the life that has quickened us and abides in us. There is no way, then, that the justified person can logically conclude—or morally continue—in sin as a voluntary lifestyle. We have a new power and a new purpose. We can't possibly remain the same. We are in harness to the power and purpose of the resurrected Christ Who lives within us.[179]

> (6:11) *Even so consider yourselves to be dead to sin, but alive to God in Christ Jesus.*

In the original the text reads "Likewise you (emphatic pronoun) consider yourselves. . ."

Now the apostle appeals to them to adjust their thinking to the realities of this two-sided union with Christ. This is not an exercise in positive thinking; it is not a psych job. He is exhorting us to catch up mentally to the new spiritual reality.

"And it is not by reckoning these facts to be facts that they become facts. The force of the imperative is that we are to reckon with and appreciate the facts which already obtain by virtue of union with Christ" [180]

Paul wants them to awaken *fully* to its implications, to live in light of the facts. That way, they will never fall for any fiction or fallacy that might induce them to continue in sin or ever feel at home with the hangover reflexes of the old man.

"Likewise" (*houtos*) begs them for mental alignment with two aspects of Christ's redemptive transaction:

1) Likewise (just as with Christ to whose death you have been legally united), let your death to sin also mark a break with sin as your ruling principle.[181]

In our case, sin ruled over us morally. In His case, it ruled over Him legally as our ordained Sin Bearer. The ultimate expression of sin's rule is death. Christ died a real death. In that brief period in which death held Him in its grip, sin ruled over Him. But now that He lives, He is eternally finished with sin as His ruling principle (legally speaking).

Paul pleads: "Let that be true in your case also. No more of this nonsense about continuing in sin. A really dumb inference! An impossible thought to one who looks at the implications of our two-sided union with Christ."

2) Likewise (just as with Christ to whose life you have been united in His resurrection), let your life also be directed forevermore to the glory of God.

"Reckon" is obviously imperative from the context. There is little dispute about that, nor should there be.

> (6:12–13) *Therefore do not let sin reign in your mortal body that you should obey its lusts, and do not go on presenting the members of your body to sin as instruments of unrighteousness; but present yourselves to God as those alive from the dead, and your members as instruments of unrighteousness to God.*

Having demonstrated the absurdity of the original inference (6:1) based on our double union with Christ, along with the spiritual enablement and intention, coupled with it, the apostle, building upon the general admonition of 6:11, now extends its application.

The present tenses remind the believer of the need of constant vigilance against the old reflexes and the encroachments of the flesh in the service of sin.

The imperative serves notice of a radical change in the order of things: we now have a choice. Sin is no longer a master whom we are unable to resist.

Does the form of exhortation not imply that the dominion (which is not the same as the presence or influence) of sin, which our union with Christ effectively terminated (6:6, 14), is a continuing reality or threat?

No. The point is that the believer can *voluntarily* allow sin to rule (i.e., direct our behavior), soliciting our accommodation to the desires and weaknesses of the flesh. Sin does not have dominion in the sense that its enslaving power is unbroken. We have a choice now. We can say "no" to our old master. We also can say "yes." As long as we are encumbered with the flesh, its weaknesses, and appetites, that temptation will always be a real and present danger.

So, then, sin does not have *involuntary* dominion over the will of the believer and never will. This condition is decisively terminated. It is precisely because it no longer has authority over us that we should not allow it to usurp our obligation to obey our new Master. We must not allow sin to commandeer our body and use it for evil purposes. Rights to them belong now to God.

I concur with John Murray's insightful comment on 6:12:

> It is not to be supposed that sin is conceived of as reigning in the believer and that now he is exhorted to terminate that reign of sin. This would run counter to all that has been set forth in the preceding verses... It is only because sin does *not* [emphasis mine] reign that it can be said, "Therefore let not sin reign." In other words, the presupposition of the exhortation is not that sin reigns but the opposite, that it does not reign, and it is for that reason that the exhortation can have validity and appeal. To say to the slave who has not been emancipated, "Do not behave as a slave" is to mock his enslavement. But to say the same to the slave who has been set free is the necessary appeal to put

into effect the privileges and rights of his liberation. So, in this case the sequence is: sin does not have dominion; therefore do not allow it to reign. Deliverance from the dominion of sin is both the basis of and the incentive to the fulfillment of the exhortation, "Let not sin reign." [182]

Paul's appeal reminds me of a scenario that must have occurred more than once after President Lincoln declared the Emancipation Proclamation. Black slaves were, by his executive decree, set free from slavery to their white masters.

If I am any judge of human nature, I imagine someone would have to remind more than one ex-slave that he or she was now free and didn't have to dance to their former master's tunes. Freedom can be granted, but for one inured to the mentality of a slave, the old reflexes don't die all at once.

Several years ago, I was playing basketball with some students. One was a young man who had several inches and twenty or thirty pounds on me. Yet I was always able to "bully" him around the basket and move him pretty much at will.

Being a coach at heart, that bothered me. I shouldn't have been able to do that. I was way past my prime. He had the height and weight. He should have been able to shut me down good. So, I had a talk with him.

"Ron," I inquired, "why do you let me push you around like that? You're a big guy, fellow. Why don't you get tough in there and say, 'My way, or you'll pay!'?"

"You know, Mr. Andrews," he responded thoughtfully, "that's a very interesting thing. You know what the problem is? I didn't grow up until very late, just suddenly. Before that—you may find this hard to believe—but I was just a runt kid. Then, one day, I just took off. My eyes tell me I'm a good-sized fellow, but in my mind, I'm not used to it yet. In my head, I'm not what I am in the mirror. I am still that little kid I used to be. So, I get intimidated."

That's approximately the situation the apostle is trying to counteract. In reality, we're something radically new and different. But our minds are not always fully acclimated to that change. So, we fall back on the old reflexes. We get intimidated by our weaknesses and give in. We give in to temptation prematurely; we are sure we're already beaten. Actually, we are empowered for righteousness now.

Recently, I was watching a boxing match between two obscure fighters. One was 9–0 with 9 knockouts. The other was something like 12–3. The latter guy was knocked down three times and TKO in the first round. What the announcer said was interesting. It was something like this:

"— is a better fighter than that. But you can tell he is expecting to get hit... to be taken out, and he is responding to nothing punches as if they are knockout blows. He is embarrassing himself. He can fight better than that. His mind is defeating him before a punch even lands."

Sometimes it's like that in the Christian life also. We've already made up our minds what we can handle and what we can't. We don't give grace a chance. We're knocked out with phantom punches that many of God's saints stand up to every day.

"In your mortal bodies"—Hodge comments:

> Paul does not teach that the body is the source of sin, nor its exclusive or principal seat; but it is the organ of its manifestation. It is that through which the dominion of sin is outwardly revealed. The body is under the power of sin, and that power the apostle would have us resist; and on the other hand, the sensual appetites of the body tend to enslave the soul. Body and soul are so united in a common life, that to say, "Let not sin reign in your mortal body," and to say, "Let not sin reign in you," amount to the same thing. When we speak of sin as dwelling in the soul, we do not deny its relation to the body; so neither does the apostle, when he speaks of sin dwelling in the body, mean to deny its relation to the soul. [183]

Do not go on presenting... but present...
Our bodies are portrayed as an armory, our wills as ordinance officers. When the flesh requisitions our members for the service of our deposed ruler, we should no longer accommodate it or

acquiesce. We have switched our loyalty. We no longer belong to the old dominion. That ruler no longer has authority to employ those weapons for his purposes. We are now obliged by virtue of our new relation with Christ to reserve our members for the service of righteousness.

When I was in college, I was working one summer at Appalachian Electric Power Company on the maintenance crew. One of my jobs was to clean the floors in the control room. My boss had instructed me in the proper procedure.

The fellow in charge of the control room was a small man with a Napoleon complex. He wanted everybody in the control room, including me, to know who was in charge up there. Although I didn't know it at the time, he was infamous in the plant for trying to throw his weight around. A smart college boy was the ideal target for his one-upmanship games, so I came into his sights.

Although I was following my boss's instructions to the "T," George made a big scene of stopping me in front of the whole control room staff and bawling me out for stirring up too much dust. It was total nonsense, but he needed some excuse to assert himself.

He had an attitude. I wasn't prepared to give in to it since I was proceeding exactly the way I had been told, and I was not his employee anyway. I explained that to him nicely, but he was determined to overrule my boss Frank, and have it his way. So, I promptly took a seat in one of the control room chairs (much to the delight of the crew) and invited him to go find Frank (or if he wanted, I would go find Frank), but until Frank told me otherwise, I would do it Frank's way, not his. He was furious... and I was an instant hero throughout the plant.

(6:14) *For sin shall not be master over you, for you are not under law but under grace.*

For sin shall not be master (kypieusei) over you...

The Greek verb means to *rule, lord it (over), control,* or *dominate.* It is the same verb that is used in 6:9, where Paul says of Christ: "death no longer is *master over* Him." We also encounter it in 14:9: "For to this end Christ died and lived again, that He might be Lord both of the dead and of the living." The sense is clear enough. Paul declares that the power of sin as a sovereign principle, one able to take charge of our minds and rule our wills so completely that we are incompetent to do God's will is a condition that is terminated. It is not simply that this *should* not happen; Paul affirms categorically that it *will* not happen in the case of believers.[184]

This is a statement of "assured fact" (Murray), not a "volitive" or "jussive" future,[185] which expresses a command. Grammatically, the latter is technically possible but contextually unsuitable. The explanatory conjunction "for" renders an imperative sense implausible. It is naturally rejected by most commentators.

Nor should the future be construed in a *prospective* sense, as though assuring ultimate (i.e., eschatological) liberation from the enslaving power of sin rather than immediate emancipation from its involuntary service.

On the contrary, the freedom[186] anticipated by the future tense *starts* in the present (i.e., at the moment the conditions required for the change go into effect, namely, when the believer is united to Christ or, put another way, comes "under grace") and extends into eternity. That ongoing perspective accounts for the future tense. In its absolute sense, this freedom will be realized only at the coming of Christ when the believer is glorified (1 John 3:2): "we know that if he should appear, we shall be like Him…"[187]

The present tense ("for sin is not dominating you") would have been sufficient to affirm our liberation at the moment. But that would affirm too little. The future tense, however, standing at the threshold of changed conditions, looks all the way to the conclusion and sees our cross-won emancipation holding firm to the very end.

Imagine an NFL coach of a great Super Bowl team famous for protecting its quarterbacks. He must test a green, but extremely gifted, rookie. Looking into his eyes, the coach recognizes a diffident look which says, "I sure hope the defense doesn't kill me." Knowing what a great and dependable offensive line he has in front of him, the coach confidently reassures the nervous player:

"Son, you got the best offensive line in the league protecting you. They could make Mickey Mouse look All-Pro. You have all the equipment you need to do the job. So, relax and give it your best shot. Don't let the other team intimidate you because I'll guarantee you this: that defensive line will not dominate you."

The coach does not mean that after a long while, in the very end, the defensive line will cease to dominate the quarterback. No, no. Obviously, what he means is that from the moment he enters the game to the very end, he will not be dominated. They won't be dancing around over his broken carcass.

Now that doesn't mean that the quarterback will successfully execute every play or that he will never be outsmarted by the defense. It just means that the offensive line will set the tempo and always be in control of the game. The defense will never so outmuscle them that they can dictate the outcome.

This clause, an assurance that our resistance is not in vain, represents an incentive to refuse our bodies as instruments of sin and reserve them for holy engagements. Any struggle is less onerous when one is confident of the conclusion.

No way would I cherish the thought of duking it out in the ring with reigning World Heavyweight Champion Mike Tyson back in the day. In fact, I'd as soon not be in the same room with him.

But imagine the unthinkable. Suppose some great guru of boxing art claimed to have discovered an ancient boxing "secret" so simple and clever that anyone privy to it—even a broken-down jock—could accomplish the impossible: defeat Mike Tyson. Suppose to prove his point, he picked out a random pudge—me.

Now this fellow is no bag of gas. His track record commands respect. So, I believe in him.

Now he warns me up front that I will take some hits. Some will hurt, but he assures me none will maim or kill me. On the contrary, he confidently affirms that I will win.

"So," he encourages me, "don't pack it in the first time you get nailed. Don't plead, 'No mas!' Keep fighting back and stay on the attack. For Tyson, I assure you, will not dominate you. For you are not fighting in the old way. You have the winning edge."

Would anyone risk it? Sure—if one believes him. If one were confident of the outcome—that it would make one "rich and famous"—how many would crawl across England on broken glass to do battle?

That is sort of the psychological angle Paul is working here. When victory is assured, the warrior is dauntless. Yet, again, it is not a psych job; it's an effort to put their minds fully in touch with the new realities.

This is not the battle for the Alamo. That is, this is not a losing battle we are supposed to fight bravely. This is not a touch of insipient existentialism. For in Christ, God is at work in us, causing us to will and do His good pleasure. So, it only makes sense to cooperate with His operation in us (cf. Phil. 2:12).

For you are not under law, but under grace.

This statement explains the ground of his certainty that sin shall not have dominion over us. In union with Christ, we are free from the circumstances that guarantee our moral defeat. "Under law" is a condition that relegates us to a task like that punishment assigned to Sisyphus in ancient Greek myth. He was doomed to roll a great stone up the hill of hell, a forbidding feat Zeus knew he could never bring off.

"Under law" is a code phrase. It signifies a condition wherein the natural man seeks his salvation by living up to the exacting demands of the Law without the empowerment of the new life (grace) via the Holy Spirit. For any infraction, whatever he incurs, is the death penalty.

"Under law" is an approach to acceptance with God wherein God says to the natural man, one unregenerated and unaided by grace and the Holy Spirit:

"Here is the Law... the essence of righteousness. If you insist on a do-it-yourself approach, do it, and you will live; miss the mark at any point, and you die."

The moral futility of this condition is described in Romans 7:7ff. The flesh, dominated by the principle of indwelling sin, is incompetent to attain to the standards of God's law. In this "under law" state, sin triumphs. The final and ultimate expression of its dominion is death.

However, "under grace" is the alternative approach... the only viable one. "Under grace" is a condition where the pardoned sinner is empowered by the grace of God to fulfill righteousness. "Under grace," God says:

"Here is the free gift of eternal life. Now in gratitude, keep my law. I have planted within you the desire to do it and the power to perform it" (Rom. 8:4; Ezek. 36:27).[188]

"Under grace," the Spirit, not the flesh, is now the ruling principle. That change represents moral enablement and realignment. It's our warranty of empowerment.

(6:15) *What (shall we infer) then? Shall we sin because we are not under law, but under grace? (parenthesis mine)*

If this sounds familiar, it's because we bumped into it first in 6:1.

However, the two questions, while essentially the same, arise from different directions.[189]

In the first instance (6:1), the question had to do with whether or not multiplying sin is an appropriate way to give God opportunity to display His glorious grace by repeatedly forgiving our mounting transgressions. For Paul had taught that no matter how high the mountain of our transgressions when we come to Christ, God's grace is always more than sufficient for the measure of our guilt. Well then (an opponent might retort or a confused believer could conceivably infer), if forgiving sin glories God, maybe we can do good by doing evil.

In the second case (6:15), the question is prompted by the assertion that we are not "under law." To many Jews and Gentile proselytes to Judaism, that statement might suggest that since the Christian is no longer subject to legal sanctions or the penalty of sin (i.e., the death penalty for transgressing the law of God), that we have a free pass to sin, that we are now morally unaccountable, and that we no longer have any incentive to adhere to the law of God.

This statement would jar the assumptions of Paul's Jewish opposition. The very words were couched in a way as to shake up and contradict their suppositions.

Tell people (the Jews would argue) that they are not under legal conditions before God, that the price of all their sins has been paid, and that they are no longer subject to the penalty of their transgressions because Christ paid the price of their guilt for them, why, that is to invite every kind of excess and a license to sin. People must know that they have to toe the line, or they'll pay the fine!

What Paul says is astonishing (from the Jewish perspective). He doesn't simply say that sin will not rule them *even though* they are not under law but *because* they are not under law. He implies that there is something about being under law that aggravates this sin problem we have. For the moment, however, he pushes that aside (he will come back to it in chapter 7) to refute this new slander on grace.

Does being "under grace" instead of "under law" really invite the believer to engage in lawlessness? Does the absence of the legal sanctions of the law under grace foster sin? Far from it, Paul is about to show.

> (6:16) *Do you not know that when you present yourselves to someone as slaves for obedience, you are slaves of the one whom you obey, either of sin resulting in death, or of obedience resulting in righteousness.*

Paul immediately rejects this implication. His line of rebuttal is this:

Anybody who would jump to such a conclusion (that grace encourages sin) fails to grasp what it means to be "under grace." Those under grace are not moral free agents; they are under contract, so to speak.

What has happened is that those "under grace" have just changed masters. They are under new management; they are not independent contractors, so to speak. They are not self-employed; they just have a new "boss."

"Do you not know..." Here is a little lesson in spiritual reality.

All people present themselves (consciously or unconsciously) to one of two masters: 1) sin (or disobedience) or 2) obedience to God. The unbeliever presents himself by a natural reflex to sin and goes about his life in spontaneous disobedience to God. It is an unbreakable bond. He is simply a slave to unrighteousness. What Christ has done is break the enslaving power of sin over the mind through a quickening work of renewal called regeneration and by infusing our heart with God's own power and presence (the residency of the Holy Spirit). Now we have a choice in the matter and the impulse to obey God.

What the believer (if, in fact, one is an authentic believer) has done, in effect, is to present himself to God as a slave to obedience. Like a newborn baby with all the inherent powers of an adult, we now are endowed with the capacity for righteousness, but it takes effort and practice to overcome our sinful reflexes.

We believers have been set free from our old master, sin. "Under grace" does not imply that we are without a master; rather, it merely certifies that we have been set free as slaves from our old master, sin, and are now indentured to a new master, righteousness. Thus, "grace" does not change the "demand" factor in the life of the believer; what changes is who has the right to command our obedience.

(6:17–18) *But thanks be to God that though you were slaves of sin, you became obedient from the heart to that form of teaching to which you were committed, and having been freed from sin, you became slaves of righteousness.*

Because we have obeyed the truth, we are no longer the slaves of sin but the servants of righteousness. Hence, we are not free to do anything the flesh wants to do; yet—as slaves of God—we are free to do everything we ought to do. That is the big difference. It is a humanizing bondage. It is the bondage of true freedom.

The wording here makes it clear that in 6:16, the apostle is not implying that the issue of whom we will serve is up in the air. Clearly, he did not mean to suggest that true believers at different times elect to follow one master and, at other times, the other so that they may alternate and vacillate between moral masters from one day to the next.

His intention is to make sure that his critics understand that being *under grace* is not a state of moral independence... not a state of moral autonomy wherein one is free to do whatever one chooses. It represents, in reality, a change of masters... a new moral alignment... a shift in allegiance... a presentation of arms to a new sovereign... a whole new agenda.

The phraseology here supports that. Note the past tenses. "You *were* slaves of sin" indicates a former condition; "you *became obedient* to that form of doctrine to which you were committed" implies a decisive shift of allegiance in the past.

That idea is strengthened in verse 17. The believer's bondage to sin is spoken of as a thing of the past ("having been freed from sin") and our presentation of ourselves as bond servants of righteousness as a historically established fact ("you became slaves of righteousness"). Who our master is (if, in fact, we are genuine believers) is not up for grabs each day, not an issue in court every hour. That has been settled.[190]

> (6:19) *I am speaking in human terms because of the weakness of your flesh. For just as you presented your members as slaves to impurity and to lawlessness, resulting in further lawlessness, so now present your members as slaves to righteousness, resulting in sanctification.*

Paul apologizes for comparing the high dignity of our service to God to a bond so demeaning as slavery. Yet, it is an apt metaphor in communicating to the totality of the commitment to obedience under grace.

> (6:20) *For when you were slaves of sin, you were free in regard to righteousness.*

"When you were slaves of sin..." Pre-Christ in our unregenerate state, the radical truth was that regardless of any higher opinion of our moral condition, we were, bluntly speaking, out-and-out "slaves" of sin, incapable of rising above that dominating sin principle in our fallen flesh. We could not deny sin having its way with us.

184

"You were free with regard to righteousness." Sin was our master. No one can have two.

Here, a question presses itself upon us. Why does Paul now (inconsistently, it may appear) urge us to present our members as slaves to righteousness (19) when in 6:18, he implies that this shift of master has already transpired? The point is this, I think: what we did *officially, generally, and historically* when we received Christ now ought to be carried out *functionally, specifically, and consistently* in everyday decision-making.[191]

For when you were slaves of sin...

His appeal is for believers to be as radical in their obedience to righteousness as they once were in their obedience to sin. We are still slaves; all that has changed is which master is calling the shots. It is righteousness, not sin, that now holds sovereign title to our instruments.

> (6:21) *Therefore what benefit were you then deriving from the things of which you are now ashamed? For the outcome of those things is death.*

The slavery metaphor could be misleading. Paul hastens to rectify the false impression that in Christ, we have simply traded one form of grinding thralldom for another. True, under grace, we have not simply escaped an old master; we have been indentured to a new one. But the situation, let no one think, is not as though we are jumping from the pot into the frying pan. The outcomes are totally opposite. One leads to holiness, which, in turn, leads to eternal life. The other issues in sin and death. This is what Jesus meant in part when He urged sinners to come to Him, for "My yoke is easy and My burden is light" (Mt. 11:30).

Here, Paul weds appeal with incentive. In retrospect, he reminds the believer that the work (of sin) was disgraceful; the payoff was death... death in all its temporal and eternal ramifications.

The form of the question suggests an incentive for the life of righteousness. "Who in his right mind would want to return to the old life?" is the implication. What possible attraction could a life of sin still hold for one who has tasted the good things of God, who has drawn from the well of new life, who has once been drawn into communion with the living God? Only a pig would return to wallow in the mire, only a dog would return to its vomit—precisely because their basic nature has never been changed. The pig is a pig still, and the dog is forever a dog. But when the old man has passed away, behold, we are new creations. Our whole perspective has changed. Now that we see sin in the light of God, it is a life that loses its luster and glamour in much the same way that Bourbon Street appears jaded, dirty, grungy, and worn out with sin in the clear light of day. The attractive place that it may appear by night quickly disappears (to my eye at least) in daytime; it seems a fit candidate for serious urban renewal. One (this one anyway) just longs to raze the whole mess and start over. Such is the basic new instinct of the believer relative to the life of sin.

(6:22–23) *But now having been freed from sin and enslaved to God, you derive your benefit, resulting in sanctification, and the outcome, eternal life. For the wages of sin is death, but the free gift of God is eternal life in Christ Jesus our Lord.*

"Freed from sin..." The reference here is to its power. We are set free *absolutely* in the sense that sin no longer is able to control our wills involuntarily. Our experience of this freedom is relative in that through this mortal flesh, sin can leverage us, and we are thus still subject to temptation, still prone to fall back into carnal reflexes well trained for sin over time. Yet in the *prospective* sense, it is absolute, for the end result is guaranteed. Redemption is a process as much as an event.

"Enslaved to God..." Our obligation to righteousness is <u>total</u>, our practice inconsistent because of the rivalry of the flesh.

"You derive your benefit, resulting in sanctification..."

Holiness is a great reward. With holiness, for example, comes peace with God (in the sense of inner tranquility), a sense of the presence and approval of God, the joy of the Lord, confidence toward God, and the blessing of God. Holiness is the handmaid of all that we really mean by "life." Without it, everything else is just a cheap imitation.

The payoff of life under grace is life, not death. The benefit is holiness; the outcome is eternal life, for "without holiness no one shall see the Lord" (Heb. 12:14). The outcome of sin is death in all its multidimensional aspects; the outcome of righteousness is eternal life manifest in the present time in an organic connection with the Spirit of God, in fellowship with God, and ultimately, in putting off every residue of this mortal flesh and perfect communion with God in His very presence.

Review of the Argument of Chapter 6

In rebuttal of the perverse inference anticipated in 6:1, namely, that maybe believers ought to continue in sin in order that good may come (reasoning that our wickedness serves as a foil for His graciousness and thus magnifies His goodness), the apostle answers:

1. (6:1–3) Far from encouraging continuation in sin, our faith union with Christ in baptism (a metonym for confession) signified a decisive break with sin. [192]

2. (6:4–7) Far from encouraging continuation in sin, our death to sin, symbolized in the rite of baptism, unites us with the resurrected Christ with the purpose and power of a new moral agenda.

3. (6:8–11) Far from encouraging continuation in sin, our death to sin, involving as it does our union with Christ, implies a perpetual commitment to holiness. For if 1) our life is united to His and 2) His unending life is devoted exclusively to the glory of God, it follows that our purpose should be aligned with His.

4. (6:12–14) Given this death to sin and the moral empowerment and realignment implicit in it, the believer's mandate is not to persist in his old ways but rather to live up to the purpose and power of the resurrection life.

To forestall discouragement arising from the stubbornness of the flesh and the insidiousness of sin, the apostle emboldens us with the assurance that sin, though it may resist mortification, ultimately will not prevail in its penalty and power.

His confidence in their moral triumph over sin rests not on their resolution but is founded upon the terms of their sanctification. They are not under law but under grace.

To be "under law" is to be confronted with the unforgiving strictness and unrelaxed sanctions (penalties) of the law armed only with the energy of the flesh to fulfill it. Such conditions assure the reign of sin both in its penalty and power since the flesh cannot rise above itself to produce the works of the Spirit even occasionally, much less perfectly (as "under law") requires. The Law says, "Do this and live."

However, to be 'under grace' to face the requirement of the law (written not in stone, but on the heart) armed with the enabling power of the Spirit, not as a condition of life, but as an expression of it. Grace says, "Live and do this."

The law gives sanctions and no power. Grace gives power and removes the sanctions.

Yet again, misrepresentation or misunderstanding must be forestalled.

5. (6:15) To insist that believers were not under law might be construed by some as license. Without the Law and its sanctions against transgressors, some might imagine that to be under grace was nothing but an open invitation to take moral liberties, since the risk of condemnation was removed. This question is similar to the one in 6:1 but different. There, the question was whether the logic of grace involved the premise that one should persist in sin in order to magnify the goodness of God in forgiving grace. Here, the question is whether or not being under grace and outside the sanctions of the Law was, in fact, an inducement to sin with impunity. Again, the apostle rejects any hint of antinomian logic.

6. (6:16–18) Far from encouraging sin, being under grace does not imply the absence of restraints but a change of masters to whom

obedience is obliged. Believers do not cease to be servants; they just change masters.

7. (6:19–23) Drawing upon our new relation to God as servants of righteousness (a metonym for servants of God), the apostle encourages believers to live out their new role aggressively in view of the blessings of sanctification versus the sorrows of unrighteousness.

---

[166] Bruce, *The Epistle of Paul to the Romans*, 134.

[167] Because the wording of the text might suggest that benefits of Christ's death accrue only to those who have been baptized, lending credence to the doctrine of baptismal regeneration, some believe that this text must be referring to the baptism of the Spirit rather than water baptism.

If that interpretation were our only alternative, we would surely have to adopt it, for the idea that salvation depends on water baptism is totally incompatible with what the rest of the NT so plainly teaches. If the Scripture represents an inerrant revelation, then obviously the message will be internally consistent. On that supposition, an interpreter is quite justified in seeking an interpretation harmonious with the rest of the canon.

However, this expedient (viz., that Paul is referring to the baptism of the Spirit) is both unlikely and unnecessary in this case.

Unlikely because the concept of Spirit baptism is foreign to this context; so much so that most of the better commentators don't even mention this interpretation as a possibility. Besides, the burden of proof is on interpreters who find Spirit baptism here, since in baptismal texts water baptism is normally in view.

It is unnecessary because a more plausible explanation is at hand. Baptism here is a metonym (sign for the thing signified) for a faith confession. If that doesn't solve the problem for us immediately, the reason is simple. In modern practice the moment of confession and the moment of baptism are so separated in time (from days to weeks to months to years even) that to the contemporary believer baptism has lost its original functional significance, namely, to signalize initial confession.

We must remind ourselves that in the NT era baptism and the confessional event were not normally at intervals from one another. *The moment of baptism was the moment of confession.* They took place simultaneously; confession being made in the waters of baptism. We have lost something here to be sure. And it is no wonder that it complicates our understanding of this text. It is no longer natural for us to fuse the two together like in "altar" and "vows". But to Paul and the NT church it was natural to refer to baptism as the moment of confession because they always went together, not by necessity, but by custom. We would be wise to recover that practice somehow and re-link those two events as much as possible, in my view.

[168] Murray, *NICNT: Epistle to the Romans, Vol. 1*, 215 fn. 3.

[169] So also Cranfield, Murray, et al

[170] Eph 4:22 reminds that we have learned Christ and have been taught in Him "that, in reference to our former manner of life, you lay aside the old self, which is being corrupted in accordance with the lusts of deceit, and that you be renewed in the spirit of your mind, and put on the new self, which in the likeness of God has been created in righteousness and holiness of the truth."

Compare this however with Colossians 3:9-10 which exhorts:

"Do not lie to one another, since you laid aside the old self with its evil practices and have put on the new self who is being renewed to a true knowledge according to the image of the One who created him."

[171] Vernon McGee, chapel address at Dallas Theological Seminary, c. 1959-1963.

[172] I think it is relevant again to remark, as I mentioned above in verse 5 in connection with spiritual and physical resurrection, that Paul has a way of understanding certain aspects of the redemptive program differently than we do. In our analytical mindset, we tend to compartmentalize, bifurcate or fracture up various aspects of it as if these features of God's redemptive provision are entirely separately and distinct elements or events.

I do believe the continuum concept is most helpful here. For example, when the Apostle retreats all the way back to the foundations of our justification to find empowerment for sanctification, I think it is because, in his own perspective, he does not distinguish justification and sanctification as sharply as we do. He simply sees redemption as a continuum, starting with justification and working out its implications in sanctification and so forth.

This perspective does not call for any particular changes on our part except perhaps the tendency to treat justification as a phase of our redemption, which relates only to the problem of forgiveness and sanctification to the problem of holiness—as though one picks up where the other leaves off. The fact is, if I understand Paul rightly, justification doesn't leave off. It is a platform on which sanctification is built, but not one from which it takes off. The two are indissolubly linked in their logic.

[173] Alternatives are to construe it as referring to 1) sin as a body or mass or 2) the whole man as controlled by sin and therefore the rough equivalent of "our old man." See Cranfield, *ICC: Romans Vol. 1*, 309.

[174] Satan is a personal spiritual being existing outside us who may because of the dominion of Sin actually invade the unbeliever. Sin, on the other hand, is an impersonal but enslaving Law in unbelievers and a resident principle of the flesh of believers. Its presence is the consequence of the Adamic Fall. It is the cause of death (Rom. 5:12).

Believers are no longer involuntarily ruled by Sin inasmuch as they no longer walk according to the flesh, but according to the higher and superior principle of the Spirit (which functionally equates with the life power of the resurrected Christ, which, through the Spirit, animates them). Sin remains _in_ believers, i.e., in their flesh; however, Sin is no longer _over_ the believer. We can now just say, "no."

Yet because we are still encumbered by the flesh, though it is no longer our ruling principle, we are susceptible to its influence, its desires, its weaknesses. Unless we appropriate our grace resources, deploy our faith in fending off our temptations of the flesh, leveraged by the Enemy, we can still be seduced and can _volunteer_ to do the things of the flesh.

It is because 1) we are now empowered to overcome the flesh and 2) because the victory that now is only partial will eventually become complete, that Paul sometimes uses language (e.g. 8:4) of our sanctification that sounds as if the power of sin is more broken than it is, that is, as if the believer were able to resist sin absolutely. Again, it is that continuum idea as his apostolic mind oscillates on that continuum between the relative but growing power of the believer over sin in the present and the final deliverance from its power in the end. Too often we tend to look at the present as a separate and distinct stage of only partial victory followed by another stage (glorification) when the presence of Sin is finally and absolutely separated from us. Paul on the other hand sees a dynamic continuum. He sees the enslaving power of Sin now decisively broken. Sanctification is proceeding toward its climax. In his own mind, God has already secured the end, even if experientially it is only relatively (but increasingly) realized before the advent of Christ.

On the other hand, it is because he sees clearly that in the interim, we are encumbered with the flesh (wherein Sin is still resident) that he comes back to the relativity—and dangers—of the present state. Thus, he exhorts us armor up and follow through on our intentions in Christ.

These exhortations function in the believer (Phil 2:12) like water upon thirsty plants. They cause growth in grace. God uses His exhortations as instruments of His sovereignty. In calling us to work out our salvation, He affects something in us which causes us to will and to do of His good pleasure. So then one way in which He breaks the power of sin in us (i.e., sanctifies us) is to exhort us to do what is necessary to become holy. There is something in us like that which is in the Word (namely, the Holy Spirit). Thus, His Word, i.e., His exhortation, is more than just appeal; it is a powerful, creative, drawing Word which causes us to will and to do what He wants. But it doesn't do it all at once. It works gradually but surely to affect His purpose in us.

[175] Calvin, _The Epistles of Paul to the Romans and Thessalonians_, 128.

[176] Vernon McGee, chapel address at Dallas Theological Seminary, c. 1969-1963.

[177] Murray, _NICNT: Epistle to the Romans, Vol. 1_, 222.

[178] Cranfield, _ICC: Romans Vol. 1_, 313.

[179] Because of our organic connection with the living Christ, it is an ominous sign when a professing believer betrays little evidence of that presence and power within. . . when they are unresponsive to the Word of God... the reproof of the truth... the reprimands of the indwelling Spirit. When there are no vital signs, it may be an indication of a still-born child (Jas. 2:26).

[180] Murray, *NICNT: Epistle to the Romans, Vol. 1*, 226.

[181] Some might have trouble with the analogy at this point since it implies that Sin once ruled over the sinless Savior. That, of course, is clearly contradictory. However, bear in mind 6:9b which refers to the sin which "ruled over Him" (6:9b). It did not rule over Him morally (as in our case) but legally (as our Substitute). For He who knew (i.e., practiced) no sin was made sin (i.e., was treated legally as if He were the sum and embodiment of all Sin) for us, that we might become (i.e., might be treated as if we were the sum and embodiment of) the righteousness of God in Him" (2 Cor. 5:21).

[182] Murray, *NICNT: Epistle to the Romans, Vol. 1*, 226-227.

[183] Hodge, *Epistle to the Romans*, 204.

[184] If someone retorts that this denial simply is contrary to our experience, that in fact we do see believers who have lost control of their wills and are in fact "dominated" by the power of sin, our rebuttal is twofold: 1) that position begs the question, for it assumes what is yet to be proved, namely, that such people are in fact genuine believers (as opposed to those who profess to be) 2) that even if we concede that some who appear to fit this category are the real McCoy, the analysis of their situation does not necessarily hold up. For a believer to be mired in sin (certainly a temporary possibility) does not prove that that person has lost control and is unable to resist Sin blandishments. Even if they themselves affirm their impotence against the power of sin does not make it any more so than the inability of a child who resists discipline, responsibility, and work by whining "I can't." Saying it's so doesn't make it so, for many a sluggard says, "I can't" who really can, but is unwilling at the moment to pay the price of resistance. That is quite a different situation from being unable to.

[185] As in the case of "you shall call (*kaleseis*) His name 'Jesus', where the future amounts to a directive.

[186] Not freedom from the influence of sin, but from its domination (i.e., power not merely to solicit our obedience, but to enforce its desires upon our wills). Confusion (not to mention, heresy) results when we fail to distinguish between sin's *insinuation* and its *domination*. It is one thing to be voluntarily vulnerable to some influence; it is quite another to be involuntarily subject to the will of another. Our freedom from sin pertains to the latter, not the former.

[187] This is one of those *already, not yet* spiritual realities we see in Paul's theology. Certain things have a present aspect, like, for example, our present participation

in the resurrection of Christ, though the fullness of that reality is not yet realized as it will be. Because, however, the believer has already entered into it and the fullness is eventually assured, certain things are spoken of in some contexts as already existing without any qualification, (i.e. as absolute when in fact it is only relative at the moment).

[188] Here we refer to a different phenomenon than that intuition of natural law I believe is referred to in Romans 2:15. What is implanted under grace through the residency of the Spirit is more than an instinct for the law or will of God, but a heartbeat for it. A renewed heart loves the law of the Lord, cherishes it and wants in its deepest being to fulfill it. The natural man may have a stronger "ought-er" in his breast, maybe from religious training (as in the case of the Jews), may admire God's Law in a distant way the way a drunk admires sobriety, a coward admires courage; the value is ingrained so that he cannot but admire it but yet he does not love it, seek it and pursue it. In the child of God however there is a strong "want-er" implanted in the heart and nourished by the presence of God's Spirit in union with our spirit.

The dissonance comes entirely from the flesh with its lusts, all of which are contrary to the desires of the Spirit.

[189] An analogy might be the question, "Shall I continue on the job?" In one case that question might be prompted by the fact that I haven't been compensated in some time; in another perhaps by the fact that the boss hasn't decided just how he wants a job done. Though the question is the same, the issues behind the question are quite different. Such is the case here. Paul is not being redundant. Same question; different issues.

[190] There is a potentially enormous error in overstating the case, however. Sin is still hanging around the premises, so to speak. It still exercises formidable influence via temptations arising from the lusts of this mortal flesh. What being free from sin means is not that we are free of its presence or its solicitations to do evil, or free of finding any allurement in the ways of sin. Rather, it simply means that 1) Sin as a power resident in the flesh is no longer able to take our wills captive; we have a choice in the matter. We can elect to do what is right and godly, and 2) that we have within us the *desire* to obey God alongside the power to do it.

However parallel with that godly desire in our hearts is a rival set of desires arising from the flesh. These reflexes are well-established. They are easily leveraged until we become practiced and trained in the new habit of righteousness. Yet for the latter we have the command of our wills. We now can say, yes, to obedience and 'no,' to sin and we have now an honest desire to deny the latter. We have presented ourselves to Christ for righteousness. But just as a man or woman must daily in practice reassert his or her marital vows in the hard times of marriage, so the believer also must reaffirm, in the details of life, the surrender to obedience he once made in general.

[191] It would be like exhorting a husband who gave himself to his bride at the altar during a wedding ceremony to "be committed" to his wife. In other words, to make functional daily what he made official on a promissory basis; to make effective in practice what was prospective in confession.

A side issue: how does one account for that fact the Apostle appeals to believers not to serve sin when he has already made it quite clear that sin will not dominate them since they are under grace. If sin will not lord it over the believer, why then must he exhort the believer not to allow it? This question involves a paradox not unlike what we see in Philippians 2:12-13 where we are admonished to work out our salvation with fear and trembling (i.e., great reverence), *for it is God who is at work in you, both to will and to work for His good pleasure*. If God is causing the believer to will His will and to work out His good pleasure in us, why admonish us to do His will?

The answer lies in this: the very appeal of the living word of God (Heb. 4:12) is the instrument whereby the Holy Spirit draws the heart into the circle of His purpose. It does not return unto Him void, even if the response is sometimes on a time-delayed fuse.

It is true that sin will not dominate the life of a genuine believer. One potent instrument God uses is ensuring that result is the counteracting influence of His word. His appeals are more than empty exhortations. They are a living force which have their intended effect on a quickened heart. An interesting analogy we see in Deut. 2:28 where Moses is admonished to "charge Joshua and encourage him and strengthen him; for he *shall* go across at the head of this people and he *shall* give them as an inheritance the land which you see." Note that the Lord did not tell Moses to exhort and encourage Joshua *so that Joshua might do so-and-so*. The outcome was already fixed. So why charge, encourage, strengthen him? Because God's word through Moses was not so much verbal gas, but the living word of God which itself was a critical factor in creating the result. So it is with believers. God is not a moral mendicant, pleading with us to do what is right. On the contrary,

His exhortations are an effective moral force, a living power which takes effect in our hearts as moral compulsions. Not all at once, not altogether, but gradually, sometimes almost imperceptibly, but inevitably and powerfully—if in fact the living word meets a living faith. The common denominator is the Spirit. God's word does not return void. (Isaiah 55.8-11) It registers even when we don't know it, though our own Richter Scale is not always sensitive enough to register its impact.

[192] This "break" has three aspects. The first is the juridic condition and foundation of the other two.

"Died to sin" first of all means we are no longer subject to the penalty of sin, having been legally identified with Christ's death.

Secondly, "died to sin" means that through our organic union with the power of the resurrected Christ we have been freed from the power of sin *in the sense that we are now able to do what was previously impossible, to work righteousness and to please God.* This freedom is not absolute (in the sense that we are now able to avoid sinning altogether). But it is great, growing, and destined for perfection when Christ comes.

Thirdly "died to sin" means that in our union with the resurrected Christ, we are volitionally aligned with his purpose to glorify God.

Romans Chapter 7

Argument and Transitional Logic:

It is imperative that we follow the logic carefully. Otherwise, one will be thrown 'off the scent' in 7:14ff.

In 6:12–13, Paul exhorts believers to deny sin the opportunity to rule over (*basileueto*) their mortal bodies. They can prevent this regressive outcome by refusing to turn over the members of their bodies to sin as weapons of unrighteousness. Positively, they can assure it by volunteering the members of their bodies to God as weapons of righteousness.

Prior to the advent of grace, such an appeal would have been an exercise in futility and moral naivete. Any efforts in that direction would at last have stumbled over the weakness of the flesh. But now, the apostle assures them, they are morally empowered. For, as he reminds them in 6:14, "sin shall not reign over (*kyrieusei*) you." In other words, our two-way union with Christ has broken its enslaving hold on us for now and forever. Sin may not have been expelled from the premises, but it is no longer on the throne and giving orders that we are unable to countermand by an act of the redeemed will.

The reason we can now successfully resist sin's solicitations to do evil is because of radically changed conditions. "For you are not under law, but under grace." Those two states are as opposite as night and day in their moral equations and consequences. The former is a recipe for failure, and the latter is a warranty of triumph.

Now for anyone who had grown up conditioned to respect the Law, Paul's rationale would be jarring. Paul could anticipate at least three objections[193] from the Jews. They would protest:

1) That telling people they were no longer "under law" was an irresponsible and open invitation to transgression;

2) That those under the Law could not and had no authority to disengage themselves from that perpetual bond; and

3) That the moral effect of the Law is, contrary to what Paul implied, to restrain sin, not aggravate it. In 6:15–23, the apostle has been dealing with the first issue. Now in chapter seven he takes up the second and third.

In 7:1–6, he shows that not only can one be set free from the Law but *must* be to bear fruit to God. Under law, the passions of sin ran riot, producing death in us. The Law antagonizes the sin principle residing in the flesh, stirring the pot, so to speak.

Under grace, however, we are disengaged from the old order, that is, the rule of the flesh, and joined to the power of the Spirit, a holy newness supplanting the oldness so that at least we are endowed with the power to bring forth fruit to the glory of God.

Now this line of argument would evoke a natural objection. Paul makes it seem as though there was something evil about the Law. Paul disposes of that argument in 7:7–13, showing that it was not the Law itself that was evil. In fact, it was holy, righteous, and good. The problem was not in the Law but in the man under it, that man was dominated by sin. And sin leveraged the demands of the Law to stir up a firestorm of contradictions in us.

Note: Right here is where so many otherwise good teachers and commentators, in my opinion, miss the point and make this section out as typical Christian experience. They fail to track the lead-up logic carefully and confuse Paul's description in this section as a classic case (as do most lay folks) of universal spiritual *conflict* rather than a clear picture of all-out spiritual *conquest* ("I am of the flesh, sold into bondage to sin." 7:14). Huge difference! That conquest condition describes no believer.

Thus, in 7:14–23, he illustrates this latter reality, showing that the under-law state cannot possibly produce righteousness. To make his point, he uses theoretically the *best*[194] representative of a man under law, a legally conscientious Jew (such as Paul was before his conversion). It doesn't matter really whether this "I" was Paul himself or not. The point is that he envisions one like himself in his pre-Christian experience.

Here's the crux of the matter: *His point is to show the incompetence of the Law to sanctify.* That reality the Jews did not get. They thought the Law a help to righteousness, not a hindrance.

To strengthen his case, as I said above, he personalizes the ultimate moral futility of even the most high-minded Jew under the Law (himself, for example). Reach as he did, an example of the most idealistic Jews. Paul shows that in the end his effort at law-keeping was a big flop. Wretchedly (v.23).

Good and holy as the Law of God is in itself, the 'flaw in the slaw,' as the old saying goes, is our old sinful flesh, that awful, indwelling, mastering sin principle in him and all mankind, no matter how morally idealistic. When it comes to keeping the Law, the best man in the flesh just can't cut it. The only answer to this wretched state of condemnation is in Christ who has set us free from the law of sin and death (8:1-3).

To answer the objection to his assertion that the believer is "not under law," namely, that a believing Jew cannot just up and sever his covenantal obligations (i.e., without legal sanctions), Paul crafts an analogy to show how, in the case of Jewish believers, the saints have been *legally* released from the Law.

The main problem with the analogy is not the final point (#3 above) but figuring out what the various elements of the analogy correspond to.

> (7:1) *Or do you not know, brethren (for I am speaking to those who know the law), that the law has jurisdiction over a person as long as he lives?*

"Who know the law..." Their familiarity with the Law enables him to assume that they should understand the lifelong obligation involved in the phrase "under law." The only way a Jew got out from under the obligations of the Law (and the weakness and sanctions) was the same way a mafioso gets out of organized crime... by death.[195]

Here, Paul seems to give away the farm, argument-wise. He appears to play right into the hands of the opposition, conceding that the long arm of the Law applies *as long as the person under it lives.* The only escape hatch is death.

(7:2) *For the married woman is bound by law to her husband while he is living; but if her husband dies, she is released from the law concerning her husband.*

To reinforce his premise, he takes as an illustration the legal bond that exists in the law between a man and his wife. Only death can release a woman lawfully from her husband. Any other termination of that bond must involve transgression of the Law.[196] In the case of death—and this is a crucial point—the widow is absolved of any other obligation to that law (the law regarding her bond to her husband).

(7:3) *So then, if, while her husband is living, she is joined to another man, she shall be called an adulteress; but if her husband dies, she is free from the law, so that she is not an adulteress, though she is joined to another man.*

Should a wife leave her husband for another man,[197] that would make her a transgressor. We would call such a woman an adulteress. That accusation would not apply, however, if her husband died. She could be lawfully wed to another and subject to no such tarnish on her reputation. The death of her husband makes all the difference.

Now comes the application of the analogy.

(7:4) *Therefore, my brethren, you were also made to die to the Law through the body of Christ, that you might be joined to another, to Him who was raised from the dead that we might bear fruit to God.*

"You" refers to the Church, the whole assembly of believers. The church or people of God are spoken of in Scripture as the bride of Christ; Christ is the bridegroom. Paul here has that metaphor in mind (Rev. 18:23).

The first husband is the sin-bearing Christ, the one who legally became "sin" in our place, the one who bore the judgment of God for us. When He died, He bore in His person the penalty that we should have suffered as transgressors. When He died, our obligation to the Law was settled. Death is the greatest penalty the Law can extract, and righteousness is all that the Law can require. Christ bore our penalty and fulfilled the Law's requirements for us.

His death freed us to be united to the resurrected Christ, to be united with the power of His life, so that we might bear fruit to God, that is, bring forth works that would glorify God and please Him.

Of course, that statement of purpose implies something astonishing to the Jewish mind, namely, that somehow those under law were at a moral disadvantage. That is precisely the shock he intended.

(7:5) *For while we were in the flesh, the sinful passions, which were aroused by the Law, were at work in the members of our body to bear fruit to death.*

"While we were in the flesh..." In one sense, we are still in the flesh in that our mortal body remains, and the sin principle continues with us. As our ruling principle, not so. What Paul refers to here is *in the flesh* vis a vis *in the Spirit* as our ruling principle. See this clearly stated in Romans 8:8–9.

Under law, contrary to Jewish concepts, was a losing formula. It was an arrangement destined to fail. The load was way too great for the engine (the flesh) to pull. Worse yet, the engine was always in reverse. The result was we backed over the hill of disobedience every time righteousness called.

(7:6) *But now we have been released from the Law, having died to that by which we were bound, so that we serve in newness of the Spirit and not in oldness of the letter.*

"Released from the Law, having died to that by which we were bound..." The death penalty has been paid; justice was satisfied at the cross. We, in effect, died there *in Christ*. When He died, we died for legal purposes. Death releases the believer from any claims the Law may have had against us. That bond (under law) ceased with our legal death.

So that we serve in newness of the Spirit and not in oldness of the letter.

Having died with Christ (legally), we have been united with His life really. The power of the resurrected Christ is present with us in the form of the presence of His Spirit in us... the Holy Spirit. No longer are we shut up, as we were under the law, to the old conditions of moral weakness. At that time, we confronted the demands of God's law with only the energy of the flesh to help us conform. The flesh was totally ineffectual for fulfilling the Law beyond conforming to its outward letter. It could never enable us to rise to the spirit of it.

The reason that now we can produce fruit that is pleasing to God is because we are vested with something radically new. We are yoked to the power of the Spirit of Christ, who has taken up permanent residence within us. Newness has supplanted oldness. This is not reformation; this is transformation.

"Newness" refers to all the provisions of grace available to believers in this covenant when the Spirit has come in the fullness anticipated in the OT upon *all* the people of God.[198]

"Oldness" refers to the old (legal) covenant, where God's law was etched in external stone rather than inscribed on the renewed heart as a godly impulse and aspiration, and the heart was scrupulous about keeping the form (i.e., the letter) rather than fulfilling the spirit of it.

Believers then are free from the law, by the death of Christ. They are no longer under the old covenant, which said, "Do this and live," but are introduced into a new and gracious state, in which they are accepted, *not for what they do, but for what has been done for them* (emphasis mine). Instead of having the legal and slavish spirit which arose from their condition under the law, they have the feelings of the children of God.[199]

> (7:7) *What shall we say then? Is the Law sin? May it never be! On the contrary, I would not have come to know sin except through the Law; for I would not have known about coveting if the Law had not said, "You shall not covet."*

Paul, in 7:5–6, had stated that "under law,"[200] the passions of sin resident in our fallen flesh were actually "stirred up," not restrained and curbed, as his Jewish opponents of the gospel insisted. That condition (under law) didn't make people better; in reality, it just stirred up the mud in the bottom of their character buckets. It brought out "the devil" in them. It didn't make them more divine but more devilish.

Now that was a blasphemous and infuriating premise for a Jew to swallow. It seemed sacrilegious to suggest, as it did, that the omniscient God had gotten it wrong at the beginning... that He had messed up by putting people on a legal footing... that there was something wrong with the Law... something inherently evil about it. That was too much to swallow.

So, the question that now presses upon him is this: Is the Law inherently evil? If it excites so much transgression in us, it sounds as if God's Law is tantamount to a sinful influence.

"May it never be!" Paul quickly rejects any such inference.

His first line of defense for the moral integrity of the law of God is that it took the law to unmask sin, blow its cover, and expose its presence in us as an anti-God principle.

"On the contrary, I[201] would not have come to know sin except through the Law." The Law was God's holy instrument to reveal the presence of a transgressive principle lurking in his being. It serves as a kind of litmus test of the heart. Through the knowledge of the law, he first awakened to himself as a sinner. That was not a bad office of the Law.

In certain kinds of training for jobs that require people to keep cool under pressure, people are placed under stressful conditions that are designed to surface undesirable attributes that ordinary circumstances may mask. The test is not evil because it reveals unfitness and brings out the worst in the candidate. We don't trash the test; we admire it and trash the candidate.

Paul gives a specific example of the honorable function of the Law in exposing sin to his own moral consciousness... of making him aware of the presence of evil within him.

On the contrary, I would not have come to know sin except through the Law; for I would not have known about coveting if the Law had not said, "You shall not covet."

He would not have recognized covetousness, for instance, for what it was had it not been for the Law's prohibition of it. It raised his consciousness to the presence of covetousness in his heart. The net effect of the Law was increased activity on the part of sin in the form of intensified covetousness.

(7:8) But sin, taking opportunity through the commandment, produced in me coveting of every kind; for apart from the Law sin is dead.

"But sin..." In one word, Paul goes right to the bone of the human predicament. This is what is amiss in our lives... this is what entered into the equation of human nature with Adam's disobedience and corrupted our nature. This three-letter word spells "anti-God." From this root springs the lusts of the flesh, the lusts of the eye, the pride of life, a trinity of evil, which covers all the manifestations of sin in human life.[202]

Taking opportunity (aphormen) through the commandment...

The Greek word *aphormen* in classical literature literally refers to "the starting point or base of operations for an expedition... then... the resources need to carry through an undertaking..." [203] I remember encountering it often in the former sense in the works of Thucydides and Herodotus. It refers to a well-positioned and well-equipped take-off point for a mission.

The sin principle residing in our flesh, as Martin Lloyd-Jones puts it, [204] *using the law as a fulcrum,*[205] was able to move our resistance and produce the result that it was anxious to produce."

"Produced" (*kateirgasato*)—A strong word here that shows the sovereignty of the sin principle. It was not nagging and tugging at our minds, just tempting us and soliciting our complicity in its designs with respect to evil desires. It got its way with us.[206]

"Coveting of every kind" (*pasan epithumian*)—Concupiscence is what coveting refers to. It embraces every form of carnal lust...

every form of evil desire... every kind of overreaching that transgresses the lines God has established.

Why is it that human nature is so much like the feeding habits of horses and cows? No matter how much grass they have inside the fence, for some reason, they always find the grass greener on the other side. Why is it that the more money we get, the more we want? Proportionately, the poor are always more generous with God than the affluent... pastors have always known that. Why is it that forbidden fruit is so enticing? There is this transgressive principle in our flesh... this anti-god root in us that, before Christ, comes in and rules our minds and uses the law of God like a stick to stir up the crud in the bottom of our character buckets, as I like to put it. It uses the law of God like a sports team uses the printed challenges of its bitter rival on the dressing room bulletin board to feed its furious determination to make its opponents eat crow.

The sin principle in him, he found, seized the moment. Reacting to "forbidden fruit," sin took advantage of the Law's prohibition of coveting, watered, and fertilized it, and caused that sin to germinate in kaleidoscopic variety in the soul.

"Sin is dead." In context, nearer and remote, it is clear that Paul is not saying that in the absence of codified divine law, the sin principle would have been non-existent. No, it was there all along. What he is referring to is awareness of the sin principle in one's self-consciousness.

> When Paul says that he would not have known sin, if it had not been for the law, that does not mean only that it is the law which teaches us the difference between right and wrong, and that with the criterion of the law we should not know rightly what is sin. He means that sin would not have been the power that it actually is in the life of man, if the law had not helped to that end. There is indeed sin, without the law, but it slumbers. It is present as an evil covetousness; but it has not had the opportunity to reveal itself. Man does not realize what a frightful power has him under its might and rules him. But then the law comes and exposes sin that was heretofore hidden. The

commandment confronts man with its "You shall not covet." But what is the result? Not that covetousness vanishes, but on the contrary, it is brought out of seclusion. Just as the sun's rays call forth the possibilities that are in the seed and bring them to full growth, so the law calls forth the sin that slumbers. Now it has opportunity to develop its inherent possibilities; and the result is conscious opposition to God. *It is in relation to the law, that sin grows powerful in man.* [207]

(7:9) *And I was once alive apart from the Law; but when the commandment came, sin became alive, and I died...*

He is still talking in relative, subjective terms. Paul, as a Jew, was always under the Law, just as in another sense, the objective law of God has always been there before man in some intuitive sense.

But it does not always register... come home to the consciousness with full clarity and force. That is what the apostle has in mind. There was a time (he doesn't specify) when, as a Jew, the commandment of God had not taken firm grip on his moral senses and awakened his conscience.

In that state, he was "alive" in the sense that he had no sense of his guilt and no foreboding of divine judgment. He was secure in his moral blindness.

Then, at some unspecified point in his life, the commandment "hit" his moral consciousness. At that point, sin, lying dormant in the sense that he had no self-awareness of the innate antipathy in his breast of this predilection to evil... suddenly, sin was aroused in his being in vigorous opposition to it so that he was aware of its subversive activity.

"If by sin being dead means its lying unnoticed and unknown, then by *being alive,* Paul must mean that state of security and comparative exemption from the turbulence or manifestation of sin in his heart, which he then experienced. He fancied himself in a happy and desirable condition. He had no dread of punishment, no painful consciousness of sin." [208]

(7:10–11) *And this commandment, which was to result in life, proved to result in death for me; for sin, taking opportunity through the commandment, deceived me, and through it killed me.*

At that point, like Martin Luther much later, he died in the sense that he lived in mortal terror of condemnation and no doubt, like Luther, also tried frantically to find peace with God and earn his acceptance with God through a frenzy of legal works.

The Law, which, if obeyed, would have produced the fruit of life, became a weapon in the hands of sin that produced the fruits of death. Life as a quality of existence is not only eternal but, in its temporal manifestation, connotes a vital connection with God or communion with God and all that stems from that connectedness with the Source of Life. Death, on the other hand, speaks of disconnection with God and all the miserable ramifications of that alienation, not only hereafter but here and now in all the manifold miseries that accompany disobedience to God.

"Life includes the ideas of happiness and holiness. The law was designed [as a map of the way men should live] to make men happy and holy. Death, on the other hand, includes the ideas of misery and sin."[209]

(7:12) *So then, the Law is holy, and the commandment is holy and righteous and good.*

So, the problem is not the Law, after all; the problem is sin in us. The weakness is in the flesh. If a housewife sticks a fork in a tender roast to lift it from the pan, and it breaks loose and makes a greasy mess, the problem was not the fork which was designed to lift the flesh but the weakness of the flesh itself.[210]

(7:13) *Therefore did that which is good become a cause of death for me? May it never be! Rather it was sin, in order that it might be shown to be sin by effecting my death through that which is good, that through the commandment sin might become utterly sinful.*

Does it seem that he is saying that something essentially good could be the cause of so great an evil as death? That is not the point.

The real culprit or cause is sin... the principle of sin resident in the flesh. Sin took advantage of the Law... and used it as leverage. The purpose of allowing sin to use something so good to effect evil was to bring out sin in all its hideousness and cause the radicality of the problem to really appear for what it is.

"God has so ordered it, that the sinfulness of sin is brought out by the operation of the law." [211]

(7:14) *For we know that the Law is spiritual (pneumatikos), but I am of flesh (sarkinos), sold (pepramenos, perf. part. from piprasko = I sell) under sin. (parentheses mine)*

Further elaboration on the true source of our moral and spiritual malfeasance: The Law is not the problem; it partakes of the Spirit of God and is, by implication, pure and holy. Consider it exonerated from any imputation of sin.

The flaw in the case of the man under law resides in his nature. He is fleshly. That expression in context reflects a nature antithetical to the spiritual character of the Law.

The moral weakness of that *sarkinos* condition is further amplified by the following participial clause, which adds to the picture an inevitable and consistent circumstance accompanying that condition. That circumstance accounts for the moral futility of the best of people under law. It explains why *under law,* even the noblest of individuals cannot bring forth fruit to God despite their *intellectual* sympathy for the Law.

The bottom line is that we (in our original condition) are sold under sin. This is a portrait of stark moral slavery. This is a very strong expression of bondage to sin. [212] This is the situation of the person *under law*, not under grace. Mark that in bold.

Bear in mind that Paul's mission is still 1) to vindicate the Law as the *cause* (rather than a holy instrument put to wicked use by indwelling sin) of evil and 2) to show the moral futility of trying to please God under legal conditions. Those two issues are raised in 7:6–7.

> (7:15) *For that which I am doing, I do not understand; for I am not practicing what I would like to do, but I am doing the very thing I hate.*

"I do not understand..." As we would say, there is something that mystifies me, something that confounds and stumps me.

Here begins a sorry portrait of the moral futility of a man under law. To make that picture even more negatively impressive, the apostle uses himself (former self) as a representative case. He casts the description in the present tense, though not because he is speaking of his present condition.[213]

In this portrait of moral futility, the apostle recasts himself in his former state (thrown into the present tense for graphic effect) as a representative of a class, a very religious, legally zealous, high-minded Jew under the Law (like the rich young ruler, Nicodemus, and Paul himself once were).

The argument benefits from this nuance because it takes the best representatives of the class (those *under law*) and shows how miserably they fare pitted against the righteous standards of the law.[214]

This is a person, who, like those described in Romans 9:31 (are "pursuing a law of righteousness") and 10:2, possess a form of "zeal for God," whose sin-enslaved heart defeats his religiously-conditioned mind every time. He keeps contradicting himself, failing to live up to his own intellectually endorsed ideals, as expressed in the law of God.[215]

The apostle does not mean that the man under law cannot conform even to the outward standards of the Law. That is contrary to both scriptural representations and life experience. The problem is that in the final analysis, when one is awakened to the depth and breadth of the Law's requirements, one finds oneself in practice contradicting and falling short of the standards of the Law one has morally approved intellectually.

(7:16) *But if I do the very thing I do not wish to do, I agree with the Law, confessing that it is good.*

That fact that his moral practice in the final analysis is contrary to his intellectual assent to the standards of God's law is all-sufficient proof that whatever is wrong is not in the Law but within himself. Again, this is the big point, not describing spiritual conflict in a believer. That is way off the mark.

(7:17) *So now, no longer am I the one doing it, but sin which dwells in me.*

His conclusion with respect to this strange contradiction between what his conscience and intellect tell him he ought to do and where he actually comes down is a clear signal that *he is not in control of his life*. He is not the captain of his soul, the master of his fate. Sin is in the driver's seat. Sin is at the moral and spiritual controls of his life. Sin is able to push his 'override' button and get him to go against his own intellectual grain, against his own moral understanding. The bottom line is that he finds himself a *slave* and out of control.[216] Obviously, I think, we are not talking about a morally conflicted believer here; this is an idealistic, but wretched unbeliever in a moral cage fight with indwelling sin and losing badly, despite some culturally nourished good intentions. And, yes, one does not have to be a Pelagian to know that historically some Gentiles even were of that noble mindset.

(7:18) *For I know that nothing good dwells in me, that is, in my flesh; for the wishing is present in me, but the doing of the good is not. For I know that nothing good dwells in me, that is, in my flesh...*

This line furnishes further evidence that Paul is describing the way sin takes charge of a person under law or, to put it another way, a person in the flesh versus in the Spirit. By virtue of religious conditioning, the best that such a person can do is intellectually approve or agree with God's standards, but the acid test is performance. Water seeks its own level. That which is flesh is flesh, and it simply cannot and will not do the will of God. The flesh consistently overrides the intellect, unaided by grace.

Note that in biblical spiritual anatomy, the mind is not the same as the flesh but a part of us that is overrun and corrupted by the flesh to a greater or lesser degree. The flesh can never be renewed, but the mind can when the Spirit of God takes up residence in the believer (Rom. 12:2; Eph. 4:23).

There is nothing in this statement that is incompatible with the doctrine of total depravity, provided one understands that biblical teaching correctly. *Total depravity* does not hold that the wicked are as bad as they can be nor does it say that they lack any elevated moral thoughts or aspirations. This is clearly false, as human experience makes plain. *Common* grace does raise the moral plane in many and, thank God, it does! However, the bottom line remains the same:

Unaided by *special* grace, no unbeliever can keep the law of God no matter how strongly he affirms it, at least in its spirit.

"We know the good, we apprehend it clearly. But we can't bring it to achievement."[217]

That is precisely what Paul is emphasizing.

(7:19) *For the good that I wish, I do not do; but I practice the very evil that I do not wish.*

He reiterates for emphasis the plight of the most earnest moralist without grace, a life of moral futility and self-contradiction. Of course, not every unbeliever shares his approval of the law of God nor his confession of a shortfall. Paul is not describing here the experience of Everyman but the moral futility of the best of Natural Men, one schooled in the law of God, in moral sympathy with it through religious conditioning of the mind, but still under the sway of the power of sin residing in the flesh. His point is, I repeat, the legal way does not make people righteous, nor does it result in fruitfulness to God, even in the best and noblest of cases.

(7:20) *But if I am doing the very thing I do not wish, I am no longer the one doing it, but sin which dwells in me.*

Another underscoring of 7:17: He is not in control of his own life. Sin overrides his inbred religious sympathies.

(7:21) *I find then the principle that evil is present in me, the one who wishes to do good.*[218]

This is the crux of the matter. There is an evil root at the core of his moral being that ultimately wins out over his "values" training.

(7:22) *For I joyfully concur with the law of God in the inner man.*

Who doubts that Paul, Gamaliel, Nicodemus, the rich young ruler, or any number of the greater rabbis could have penned these words themselves? They were fiercely devoted to the Law. It was their pride and joy. Could any unbelieving Jew really say this, you ask? Let Paul himself answer that:

> But if you bear the name "Jew," and rely upon the Law, and boast in God, and know His will, and approve the things that are essential, being instructed out of the Law, and are confident that you yourself are a guide to the blind, a light to those who are in darkness, a corrector of the foolish, a teacher of the immature, having in the Law the embodiment of knowledge and truth... (Rom. 2:17–20).

Case closed.

(7:23) *But I see a different law in the member of my body, waging war against the law of my mind, and making me a prisoner of the law of sin which is in my members.*

There are two rival principles, one higher and one lower: the law of sin and what he calls the law of his mind. Do not confuse the latter with "the law of the Spirit of life," spoken of in Romans 8:2. The fact that they are not the same is evident from the fact that, despite the presence of the so-called "law of my mind," he still despairs of his wretchedness in verse 24 and cries out for deliverance. He finds it when (8:2) the law of the Spirit of life is added to the spiritual equation.

All Paul means here is that the mind can be so "formatted" and "programmed" by intellectual training and religious conditioning that it stands in opposition on the level of principle to the impulses of the flesh. Everybody knows that.

How many people hate lying, yet, in a bind, succumb to the temptation to do it? How many hate stealing but make concessions to theft when expedience strikes? How many condemn pornography but sneak a peek? Why is it that there is all this outcry against lawless sex and violence, but the vendors of sex and violence continue to rake in the cash? Because of these rival principles, values prove greater than our virtues.

Note carefully that what is described here is not the rivalry or tension between the flesh and the Spirit (to which it is only superficially similar) (Gal. 5) but between the lusts of the flesh and the inbred values of the mind. Note also that he is not describing mere *internal moral conflict* (one of the most common misreadings of this passage) but an *all-out conquest* of the man under law.

(7:24) *Wretched man that I am! Who will set me free from the body of this death?*

Not the words of a believer! The man under grace is not this wretched man. This person is not yet free from the body of this death. That he is not referring merely to the final resurrection it is clear from 8:2, where he declares the victory so absent from view in 7:24. "The body of this death" is a metonym for the "flesh" and the law of sin resident within it. The final resurrection only finalizes the victory already begun with grace.

(7:25) *Thanks be to God though Jesus Christ our Lord! So then, on the one hand I myself with my mind am serving the law of God, but on the other, with my flesh the law of sin.*

The victory secret is not law but grace a.k.a. "though Jesus Christ our Lord." Law just won't get it done; the secret of sanctification, the power for law-keeping is through the grace that comes to us in

Christ. Thus, the stage is set for fuller exposition of this victory in chapter 8.

But first, Paul encapsulates in summary fashion the situation that confronts even the best of men who are under law. They are caught in contradiction. They are trying to serve two masters. It is clear by now which one is prevailing—and always will—if one is under law. This situation is deadly. The outcome can only be condemnation.

The reason there is no condemnation to those in Christ (i.e., "under grace") is because God has rectified the situation. He has introduced into our lives a countervailing principle that enables us at last to live the way our renewed minds direct us. That is why there is now no condemnation to those of us in Christ. There is not only deliverance from the penalty of sin but from the enslaving power of sin as well.

Addendum to Chapter 7

NOTES ON ROMANS 7:14–25

I believe my exposition of this section has been ample to justify my position. The following addendum probably 'over-argues' the point. But for any who would like a more explicit and linear rebuttal of the other common view that this passage describes 'Christian' experience', here it is:

<u>VIEWS OF THE PASSAGE</u>

1. *It describes the moral situation of any man, regenerate or unregenerate, who tries to perform the requirements of the law in the energy of the flesh (i.e., natural man).*

According to this view, the language is elastic enough to portray either a regenerate person making a legalistic but futile attempt to measure up to God's standards or an unregenerate man confronted with and confounded by the unbending demands of God's law.

2. *It describes the spiritual defeat of an unempowered believer.*

This believer has never discovered and therefore never appropriated the power available through the Spirit (discussed in

Romans 8).

3. *It represents the experience of an unregenerate man—but not necessarily every natural man—but more particularly, the morally noble type the 'best' Jew was—a natural man "whose conscience awakened by the law, has entered sincerely, with fear and trembling, but still* in his own strength, *into the desperate struggle against evil."*[219]

APPROACH TO THE ISSUE

If one can show that view two is erroneous, then one has taken out "two birds with one stone." If one can demonstrate that this passage excludes regenerate experience, then view one is necessarily ruled out since that position allows that the passage *may include believers.*

Hence, my target is the second position. That would leave view three (by default) as the most likely interpretation.

THE WEAKNESSES OF VIEW 2 (describing regenerate experience)

A. This view of the transition between verses 7–13 and 14–25 misses the point of the argument and is, therefore, artificial.

1. How it sees the transition

Hodge and Philippi, who see a regenerate man in view, view the transition as an argument from the less to the greater.

As they see it, his argument goes like this:

The Law is powerless to sanctify; it only serves to increase the power of sin (7–13). [220] So far, we agree.

The conclusive proof (as they construe his logic) is the operation of the Law upon the regenerate man who, for a given period, forgets his faith and, as a natural man, faces the Law. Even with the sympathy which his renewed heart feels for God's law, he falls on his face morally and finds the Law cannot help him overcome his sins.

How much less can it sanctify the unregenerate man who doesn't even have a renewed heart?

2. Why this understanding of the transition is faulty

a. It omits what would need to be supplied to make it coherent; that is, it is just too elliptical (i.e., leaves out too much that must be supplied by the reader) to be plausible.

Godet calls this view of the transition clever but unacceptable. [221] The reason is this: if we take this view of the transition, Paul omits saying by way of transition what everyone but the most ingenious interpreters would need for him to say to make the progression of his argument intelligible. On this view, he needed to say between verses 13 and 14 something like this:

"Even since I have become a new creature in Christ, I cannot find any assistance in the Law; on the contrary, when I put myself under its yoke, it renders me worse."

There is no such transition, however. Paul is too logical in this thought to omit such a crucial bridge in his thought. His logic, we will grant, is not always easy to follow, not because he omits crucial transitions but because his ideas are profound or unfamiliar.

b. The crux of the argument in chapter 7 is the Law's powerlessness to sanctify the man *under law*, not the man under grace.

In this connection, one must not overlook the distinction between these two states: in the context of Romans 6 and 7, the law state is a graceless state—devoid of not only sanctification but all other grace benefits and resources, including regeneration and the Holy Spirit—a condition in which one is shut up to the weakness of the flesh and confronted with God's law written in stone rather than on the heart. "Under grace" implies the presence of the Holy Spirit and all the provisions, promises, and privileges that equip the believer for life and godliness.

Hence, to make the man in 7:14–25 a representative of grace (albeit an unenlightened one) confuses the argument. It is mixing apples and oranges. It blurs the sharp contrast Paul intends to draw between the inferiority of the legal approach in chapter 7 and grace scheme in chapter 8.

The point of this whole section (7–25) is to demonstrate conclusively *the powerlessness of the Law to sanctify.* Contrary to the legalists' insistence on the necessity of the Law as a hedge against sin, Paul shows that, far from curbing lawlessness, the Law (or rather, indwelling sin taking advantage of the Law) simply stirs up the sin principle. The Law plus the flesh plus the dominion of sin (and that is the equation of the "under law" condition) brings out the worst in us, not the best.

In support of his thesis, Paul (in 7–13) has "delineated… the deadly action of the law upon him from the time it established its supremacy in his inmost soul, and from that period during the whole time of his Pharisaism (presumably)." [222] His pre-conversion experience, then, is a classic example of the impotence of the Law to sanctify a man *under the Law.*

This (I repeat) is a code phrase in Paul that refers to a condition in which a man is confronted with the demands of the Law written in stone, armed only with the energy of the flesh (vis a vis *under grace*, which denotes a condition wherein the Law is written upon the tables of the heart and equipped with the power of the Holy Spirit).

If that indeed is his point, Godet asks: "How should he now pass all at once from this description to that of his inward struggles as a regenerate man?" [223] That would make no sense. He is not arguing that the Law is useless in sanctifying believers.

What Paul intends is to draw a sharp contrast between the *legal* and the *grace* conditions to illustrate graphically that the man under law cannot ever be sanctified—even under its most favorable conditions, that is, when the legal man possesses mental sympathy with the Law (like the rich young ruler, Nicodemus, and Paul himself in his pre-conversion days).

c. It would weaken rather than strengthen the argument for grace (versus seeking sanctification via law).

To inject an unenlightened *believer* into the argument to make the point that the Law does not sanctify does worse than confuse the issue. It even weakens his argument that *law is weakness—grace is power.*

How so? Well, if this person (in 14ff) is indeed regenerate, his moral futility is more of a comment on the potential impotence of grace than the weakness of the Law. Rather than sending a message that the Law is powerless to sanctify the best motivated and well-intentioned unregenerate man under law, it serves best to warn that even grace can't help a regenerate man who is counting on the incentive of the Law to make him holy.

As true as that is, it is quite beside the point here. Paul wasn't trying to show that in sanctifying believers, grace works *better* than the Law. His point is simply that a man under law (remember the significance of this phrase) can't rise to its demands. The Law furnishes no power. Sin reigns over good intentions. There is a malign power within that overrules the demands of the Law. The only exit from this flesh-ruled condition is *in Christ*, that is, under grace, wherein one enjoys a connection to the Spirit and a break with the dominion of the flesh.

d. It would be a form of argument irrelevant to his (indirect) target audience.

His argument, as I perceive it, ultimately envisions not Christian legalists but Jewish legalists who opposed the gospel and the grace principle of life through Christ. He is contending at this point, not with Judaizing Christians who want to mix law and grace, but with Jewish unbelievers who look to the Law as a means of righteousness and oppose Paul's teaching of grace as an invitation to lawlessness (cf. 3:8 for at least one form this accusation took). The apostle argues that, actually, it is just the other way around. To be under law is a condition that aggravates sinfulness; to be under grace is a condition that inhibits lawlessness.

If we rightly understand the opponent before the apostle's mind, that consideration produces another argument against Hodges' view of the transition here. How relevant would such an argument be against opponents who didn't even accept his original premise, namely, that in Christ Paul has experienced regeneration? That tactic would make sense (but not the case) only if one assumes that the apostle's imaginary opponents are Judaizing Christians mixing up law and grace. This epistle, however, is too highly evangelistic and apologetic in its tone to think that Paul was not speaking to lost Jews via this epistle to the Roman church. I grant that his agenda transcended this evangelistic aim; I am merely insisting on what seems obvious, namely, that it dominated his purpose.

B. This view depends upon a straw man (i.e., a situation that simply doesn't exist in the form presented).

Let's review their interpretation:

In Romans 7:14ff, Paul presumably describes the moral futility of a regenerate person (i.e., one under grace) who, although regenerated by the Spirit of God, indwelt by the Spirit of God, and illuminated by the Spirit of God, is so unaffected by grace, is so shut off from it, that he grovels under the dominion of sin and, even when he honestly consents to the righteousness of God's law, cannot manage to break out of its control but remains in uninterrupted disobedience.

Note the wretched condition of this person. What is described here is not merely a case of *moral conflict* (common to all believers) but a condition of *all-out moral conquest.* This person is, in fact, the helpless slave (v. 14 esp.) of that tyrannical resident of the flesh, sin. Paul has expressly declared this slavery to be at an end (Rom. 6:14).

Therefore, if one is going to take this view of Romans 7:14, one is struck with this straw man. Such a situation is unthinkable (in my theology, at least). To any who might be tempted to take such ground, I will only repeat an objection I made earlier, namely, that *such a line of argument would make a stronger comment on the incompetence of grace than the weakness of the Law.*

On the other hand, some who take this position would object that my portrayal of the situation of the "wretchedness" of the man in the "body of this death" is extreme. My response to that is: In what way? Note three indications of the extremity of Paul's portrait.

1) In verse 14, we have the words, "I am flesh, have been sold under sin." This is hardly consistent with 6:14, where our Magna Carta assures the believer that sin shall not reign over you. Nor is it consistent with 6:6, 18, which indicates that the dominion of sin (make a distinction between its continuing influence and its enslaving power) has been terminated.

2) The ensuing portrait is one of uninterrupted defeat; it is not a picture of mere conflict or intermittent failure; it is (and is intended to be) a sad diary of deadly, daily, durative defeat at the hands of the flesh in the face of the Law.

3) The woeful cry of despair in verse 24 ("Wretched man that I am; who shall deliver me from the body of this death?") bespeaks a deadly condition consonant with what I have described.

So, there is no softening the sad state of the person in Romans 7:14ff. This person is a slave of sin. This person is in a condition of uninterrupted sin. This person is crying out for a Deliverer ("Who shall deliver me...").

On the other hand, one cannot (in my view) admit my description of this person and still cling to the view that this individual represents a Christian. Such a position is possible only for those whose soteriology reeks of cheap grace and antinomianism and sees no necessary correlation between saving faith and godly works.

Yet, many of those who take the position I am opposing on Romans 7:14 find such a theology as repugnant as I do. Therefore, it always comes as a surprise to me to see them defending this position, for the language of this passage allows no watering down.

What we have, then, is a straw man—or else we are obliged to conclude that grace may make little moral difference, and some believers can and do continue under the dominion of sin.

Now perhaps someone might object that Paul is merely talking hypothetically about the way things would be if the believer were left to himself to confront the demands of the Law with only the weakness of the flesh available.

In this case, of course, the situation he depicts here would surely be realistic. But that would be pointless. What purpose would it serve to present a moral model that never really exists in the form presented? The fact is believers are never so alienated from their grace resources as this scenario would hypothetically suppose. The law of the Spirit of life (Rom. 8:1–2) *is* invariably alive and well and at work in every regenerate man. Such a condition as this hypothesis presupposes would never exist. It is, I say, a straw man. Hence, it proves nothing.

C. This view depends on a false assumption about the kind of experience described in this passage.

Those who take this view (that it depicts a regenerate person) assume that this "diary" merely reflects the outworking of the spiritual conflict between the desires of the Spirit and the desires of the flesh—a conflict here resolved in favor of the flesh when one attempts to conform to the law of God in the strength of the flesh. In short, this is a picture of normal spiritual conflict mismanaged.

I contend that the language here is much too strong for such reductionism. This scenario transcends mere conflict. On the contrary, it graphically portrays all-out spiritual conquest, as said earlier.

The victim is still a slave to sin, sold in bondage to it (7:14), the very condition that our death to sin and resurrection with Christ relieves (6:7, 14).

True, believers are still susceptible to sin. The flesh is still on the premises with all its appetites and weaknesses. But its dominion (i.e., its *enslaving* power—not its influence—has been decisively broken. Sin no longer has the believer under its *involuntary* control so that we, despite our consciences to the contrary, are *bound,* in the final analysis, to yield our members to its desires.

Yet that is precisely—and I think quite obviously—the condition of the person here described. He is a person still "flesh" and "sold under sin." His account of its enslaving power is monotonously consistent. It is a woefully graphic description of uninterrupted conquest. This assessment seems also more compatible with the desperate outcry of the "victim" when, in despair, he laments, "O wretched man that I am! Who *shall* deliver me from the body of *this death*?"

Surely that language is better suited to a morally high-minded man under law who, though culturally inured to its righteous ideals and awakened (as in 7:7ff) to its true demands, finds himself morally bankrupt before it and unable to match actions with good intentions. This person sees himself in the lethal grip of "the body of this death." This person is grasping for a solution.

This issue, I think, is crucial in this passage. If it is only describing the outworking of spiritual conflict, then one might more plausibly argue that a believer is in view (although it still would not suit the argument very well). However, if what we have here is a vignette of the spiritual *conquest*, then it radically tips the balance in favor of my proposal.

The currency of this view, particularly among laymen, has been based, in part,[224] on the sense that it squares well with everyday Christian experience—the experience of spiritual conflict, a tug-of-war between the Spirit and the flesh—and the experience of seemingly intractable sins and defeat.

As true to life as all that is, it fails to jibe with this passage. In fact, its very basis of appeal, as I will show, is evidence of its misreading. Let me explain that.

According to the "regenerate man" view that I am contesting, Rom. 7:14ff is theoretically a phase that *some* believers experience en route to maturity and the discovering of the victory secret of Romans 8.

In practice, however, most believers see Romans 7:14–25 as descriptive of their present Christian experience, not a previous stage of immaturity. I have confirmed this again and again in my classes. The believer interpretation normally would say that this situation represents *abnormal* Christian experience. Yet the reality is that <u>most</u> people read the passage as a "dead-on" account of their *normal* Christian experience.

This seeming "self-recognition" naturally explains the appeal of this interpretation to many lay people and accounts for their tendency to adopt it uncritically from their teachers.

So, what do we make of this perception? How does that undermine the interpretation it endorses?

Consider the implications. If this description does, in fact, describe <u>abnormal but nevertheless Christian</u> experience, its message is quite absurd. The message is not that the Law cannot produce holiness nor that there is only victory in grace. Rather, the message is that <u>for the average believer</u>, not even grace makes a difference! (For, remember, most will tell you that Romans 7 describes the Christian life, as they know it, to a "T"!)

The implication is that the gospel (or the grace scheme) is scarcely more potent than the legal system in sanctification. What else can one conclude if it is a fact that the Romans 7:14–25 description fits most believers better than Romans 8?

Inasmuch as this conclusion is absurd, we must find a plausible explanation for this common misunderstanding.

Fortunately, it is not hard to account for. Being well acquainted (and exasperated) with a veritable tug-of-war within and recidivism in sin, it is natural that believers might confuse the portrait of total all-out conquest (i.e., slavery to sin) with the much less serious problem of conflict (especially in light of Gal. 5, which speaks of the conflict between the desires of the flesh and the Spirit).

The error lies in assuming that this text is talking about the same warfare. It is not. The man in Romans 7 is overwhelmed by the desires of the flesh, but the law of the mind is not the law of the Spirit. The mind is the revelationally informed and elevated intellect of a sincere Jew (it could be a noble-minded Gentile) who gives intellectual assent to the ideals of God's law but, in the final analysis, finds good intentions overrun by the flesh's ambitions. It is not to a man under grace but one under law. The man in Romans 7 is "flesh" and "sold under sin"—still its slave—a hostile power which Paul guaranteed in Romans 6:14 would not have dominion over the believer. If 7:14ff is a believer, it belies that assurance.

But surely it says something that ordinary Christians resonate so consistently with this description? Certainly, that point can't be dismissed lightly. Yet it is so obvious how they manage to do so. Coming to the text, in many cases, with a background of "pre-interpretation" in this direction, most read it casually rather than carefully. And on the surface, it reads like a story of conflict. However, closer attention to the language indicates a much more serious problem—conquest.

D. This view would have grace making a greater difference between the moral empowerment of the (presumed) believers in Romans 7:14ff and 8:1 than between the unbeliever of 7:7–13 and the (presumed) believer of 7:14ff.

On this view there is a radical change in the moral equation between 7:14 and 8:1. Both are believers (presumably), but the former is morally incompetent, although rich in good intentions. Yet the latter surges with moral enablement.

However, the moral difference between the unregenerate experience described in 7–13 and the regenerate experience in 14–24 is scarcely discernable. One is as impotent as the other. Neither has a clue. Such an inference, in my judgment, defames the work of regeneration, the initiatives of the indwelling Holy Spirit who causes believers to will and to do of His good pleasure (Phil. 2:12), and the provisions of grace in which God has bestowed on believers "everything pertaining to life and godliness" (2 Peter 1:3).

Yet this view creates a "believer" who is capable of little more than lawful ideals. It is generally agreed that Paul describes his pre-conversion experience with the Law in 7–13. If in 14–25 Paul passes to his Christian experience, then one is struck by the absence of crisis, the want of any indication of a profound change of situation. It is as if the pre-conversion experience and the post-conversion experience leave this man on virtually the same level that he was before. There is little to indicate a spiritual resurrection, little to indicate that the man in 7–13 has been in 14–25 harnessed to the greatest power in the universe!

Yet this view, which sees little meaningful moral change between sinner (7–13) and Christian (14–25), sees a major breakout between 7:14–25 (Christian ignorant of grace) and 8:1ff (Christian aware of and appropriating provision of grace).

So, obviously, on this view, there is a greater spiritual gradation between the saints than between the saints and the sinners. I find that inference at variance with the analogy of Scripture.

This would mean that the gospel is the power of God unto salvation to all those who believe and happen to discover the truth about the operation of grace (a discovery few profess to make—if we judge from the number of those who acknowledge Rom. 7:14ff to describe their spiritual states).

Now should someone object that that is the very point, namely, that the Christian is little changed from the sinner without the operation of grace, I would respond again that:

1) It posits a straw man, for no believer may be so removed from the operation of the spirit of life as to leave him in this enslaved condition; certainly, conversion represents a radical change amounting to a spiritual resurrection (8:1–4).

2) This situation, as Godet says, would highlight not so much the impotence of the law but the weakness of the gospel. [225] I heartily agree!

E. Its appeal to the present tense on behalf of this view is open to serious objection on two sides (Incidentally about thirty years ago I had a friendly dinner time debate on Romans 7:14ff with a beloved English theologian who hung his hat on this very point (present tense.) whose theology was stronger than his Greek, in my view.):

1) It proves too much—more than this view wants, ultimately. Let us explain:

According to this view, the present tense is strong evidence that Paul's own Christian experience is in view.

For the sake of argument, let's concede that the present tenses prove that this passage describes Paul's Christian experience. Let's see how that argument based on the present tense proves too much.

If the present tense disallows one from locating the experience in Paul's unregenerate past, then the same present tense also excludes his regenerate past. The only alternative this logic leaves one is the conclusion that this passage is descriptive of Paul's spiritual *present*. If so, and if the passage indeed describes abnormal Christian experience, then one must infer that Paul himself has not yet gained the victory "secret" of Romans 8.

Or else one is now driven to the position that Romans 7 speaks of normal Christian experience, in which case, one wonders what to make of the "advance" of chapter 8 and the strange and self-contradictory language of Romans 7.

The bottom line is that if one takes refuge in the present tense, one cannot have it both ways. One cannot disallow unregenerate experiences based on the present tense and turn right around and insist that they must refer to Paul's earlier or *past* Christian experience vis a vis his current situation. This is inconsistent. This argument simply proves too much.

2) It is not unusual to describe a typical or representative experience in the present tense.

As Godet says, "Paul cannot forget... that what for him is a past [experience] is a present [experience] for all his sincere fellow countrymen of whom he is himself the normal representative." [226] He puts this typical experience in the present to make it more vivid, much like many writers in narrative used the historical present of past events for dramatic effect. In other words, grammatically it is a usage sometimes described as a dramatic present tense.

THE CASE FOR VIEW 3

Now I will state affirmatively the case for the view that Roman 7:14ff represents the experience of a high-minded unregenerate man under law, that is, one like Paul before his conversion.

Most of the evidence, but not all, will necessarily be repetitive inasmuch as it was brought forward in rebuttal to view 2.

I think this view is more likely because:

A. It seems to best suit the argument of chapter 7.

That argument is as follows:

The Law cannot, as pious Jews wrongly assumed, produce righteousness. On the contrary, it just aggravates the problem of indwelling sin. The flaw, however, is not in the Law but in the flesh. The Law is good in itself, but we are bad in ourselves. The natural Jew (the man under law) is enslaved or dominated (cf. 7:14) by an inner principle of sin that foils any good intentions his conditioning by the Law might generate.

This passage serves his argument by providing a first-person example (cast in the present tense to heighten the dramatic effect) of the futility of the man under law in trying to live up to its demands. The weak link is found once again to be in the flesh, the home base of the sin principle, not the Law itself.

It is important to his argument to adduce the best type of representative of the "under law" condition, namely, a legally serious and morally idealistic Jew. This serves to strengthen his argument that the Law cannot sanctify the man who is under law, even under the most favorable circumstances.

B. Contrary to what the common objection that the religious sentiments expressed herein are too elevated for the natural man, the evidence is otherwise.

There is no language here incompatible with the experience and sentiments of more idealistic unbelievers, especially among pious Jews.

(E.g., v. 15, 18—wishing or higher religious impulses may be present in unbelievers. Cf. Nicodemus, the rich young ruler, Mark

226

10:17, 21; Rom. 2:17–19; 9:31; 10:3. Noble men of ancient times—e.g., Seneca; also, Paul, Phil. 3:6, Acts 23:2; 24:16.)

The plain fact is that very similar language has been used by unbelievers. Consider the following examples mentioned by Godet:

"Desire counsels me in one direction, reason in another." —Ovid

"I see the better part and approve it; but I follow the worse." —Ovid

"I know what I ought to be, but, unhappy that I am, I could not do it." —Plautias

"What then is it that, when we would go in one direction, drags us in the other?" —Seneca

"He who sins does not what he would, and does what he would not." —Epictetus

Plato, in fact, represents the human soul as like a chariot drawn by two horses, the one of which draws it upward, the other downward. 227

C. However, Paul uses other language not appropriate for the regenerate condition.

For example, he describes the victim in verse 14 as "sold into bondage." That portrait is scarcely consistent with his insistence elsewhere that believers are no longer under the mastery of sin (compare 6:7, 14, 18, 20; also 7:24).

D. The present tense can be simply explained as common for illustrations that are a) representative in character and b) intended to enhance dramatic effect.

In any case, insisting that it must mean that Paul is writing of *Christian* experience (versus his unregenerate experience in 7–13) proves too much, as I have shown earlier. Refer back to the rebuttal section on this point.

E. Galatians 5:17, assumed by many to be parallel, resembles the situation here only superficially. There, the issue is simple chronic conflict, which requires a moral choice. Here, the issue is total conquest, which requires a new power source.

F. Understood as a characterization of the regenerate man, any regenerate man whatsoever, 7:14–25 would highlight the incompetence of grace more than the impotence of the Law.

The reality would be that grace may leave me as wretched and enslaved to sin as I was before. It may not necessarily make any moral difference for some people. And that conclusion, I believe, is against the analogy of the apostolic witness.

G. The first view (that this passage may have believers or unbelievers in mind) is a fatal admission that the language *can* describe the natural man.

If it can apply to unbelievers then I believe it must because that position, it seems to me, best accounts for the textual evidence. One of the most serious arguments against my view has been the objection that the language is too elevated for an unbeliever, which I believe I have disposed of.

A review of the big picture (i.e., the structure of this passage) may clarify some things obscured in the traffic of the small picture (analysis).

STRUCTURE

The Proposition: I am "sold under sin."
The Development:
The unhappy slave shouts his misery with monotonous repetition of the one idea—he would do good, but he cannot.
The proof falls into three dirges, each closing with a sort of refrain:
15 – 17
18 – 20
21 – 24

The solution is in 7:25, the first line. The second and third lines summarize the situation before taking up the thread of the solution set forth in 7:25. The "law of the mind" is not "the law of the Spirit." See Ridderbos on Paul's theology.[228] It is not a redeemed mind but that of a pious Jew thoroughly informed and elevated by the Law.

This solution is amplified in 8:1ff with all its redemptive ramifications.

Efforts to find a development in these verses are artificial.

> "For the power of this passage lies in its very monotony. The repetition of the same thoughts and expressions is, as it were, the echo of the desperate repetition of the same experiences, in that legal state wherein man can only shake his chains without succeeding in breaking them. Powerless he writhes to and fro in the prison in which sin and the law have confined him, and in the end of the day can only utter that cry of distress whereby, having exhausted his force for the struggle, he appeals, without knowing Him, to the Deliverer."[229]

By the way, the doctrine of election is consistent with all these propositions:

The natural man will never, on his own initiative, turn to God but, by nature, withdraws from God (Rom. 3:8; John 3:19–20).

God, on His part, will never reject or turn away anyone who seeks Him (John 6:37, 44).

The instinctual aversion of natural men toward God is so automatic, their love of their own way so addicting, that they cannot and will not turn to God except by the sovereign and countervailing initiative of God Himself (John 6:44).

Men do not perish because God refuses to allow them to be saved (2 Tim. 2:4; 1 Pet. 3:9) rather because they hate light and recoil from it (John 3:20).

Any person who is willing to be saved on God's terms will be saved (Rom. 10:8–13).

God may seal sinners in their sin because they hate the truth and love darkness (John 3:19) and refuse to trust in Christ (John 3:36; 2

---

[193] Sometimes in Paul's writings he informs us specifically and directly about the views he contests (e.g., 1 Cor. 15, Rom. 3:8). In other instances, like this one, we can fairly easily infer the objections he anticipates from the arguments he puts forward. To me it seems apparent that 6:15 thru 7:23 all takes rise from 6:14. Noting the correlation Paul sees between the reign of sin and the reign of the law over a person, I think the usage in 7:1 of the same unusual verb "rule over" (*kupieuei*) he had employed in 6:14 strongly supports this connection.

[194] An important qualifier here. The man described in this section is not just any Jew, but, as mentioned above, the best religious representative of the class. . . an earnest Jew like Paul or Nicodemus. If the best example can't achieve righteousness through the stimulus of the Law, none can.

[195] For OT saints "under Law" the escape hatch was by grace through faith just as it is for us. Grace was available through divine application of the benefit of Christ's death *by anticipation*. See Romans 3:25 where Christ's death is said to satisfy divine justice retrospectively in the case of the sins of OT saints whose transgressions God forgave earlier.

[196] This passage is not intended per se to address the issue of marriage and divorce, but its principles apply. Other than by death, there is no way that a marital partnership can be dissolved before God without transgressing God's law. That does not imply however that *both* partners in a divorce situation are equally accountable for the dissolution of the relationship. One may be the transgressor, the other the victim of the sin. The point remains that marriage was meant, according to the law of God, to be "until death do us part." It can never be dissolved by any other means apart from willful transgression on the part of one or both parties.

To apply this principle to believers does not mean that they are *under law*. "Under law" would mean that they were subject to the sanctions (death) for violating the law (or any part of it) and would have no moral power with which to keep it, other than the energy of the flesh. *Under grace*, I re-emphasize, does not mean that the believer is absolved of moral obligation to do God's timeless will (as expressed in the law), but that it is now a labor of love and not a labor of self-salvation and that it is undertaken in the new energy of the Spirit.

[197] Here the analogy is assuming an unviolated relationship.

[198] The key difference, as I see it, between the OT and NT work of the Holy Spirit lies in this fact. Not all the covenant people in the OT possessed the Holy Spirit; in the NT *every* member of the New Covenant is vested with the Spirit. . . no exceptions. Not every Israelite was true Israel (that is, a real believer). Every single member of the universal Church, the Body of Christ, is a genuine believer

in whom the Spirit of God resides. Of course, the same cannot be said of the local church, which is invariably a mixed multitude.

[199] Hodge, *Epistle to the Romans*, 219.

[200] In a sense anyone who is not "under grace" is "under law" if by "law" we understand the moral law of God. Not everyone, of course, could be said to be under the Old Covenant with all its statutes and ordinances. However, anyone who would approach God and would seek His acceptance would have to come either on terms of *law* or *grace*. So, in that sense the phrase "under law" covers even Gentiles who face the same strict and unbending demands of God's moral law and have no power to fulfill them except the energy of the flesh. In context Paul's first reference in this terminology is always the unbelieving Jews who oppose the Gospel. However, it covers the only two alternatives left to all men in seeking salvation. People are "under law" by default when they are not "under grace."

[201] The question is raised as to whom "I" represents here. Does the pronoun represent the natural man confronted by the moral law of God, or is it Paul speaking from his earlier vantage point as a religiously devout (but as yet unbelieving) Jew, or does it portray the first convicting work of the Law in the heart of believer? Hodge says the latter and calls this position the Augustinian view adopted by the Lutherans and Reformed and one "still held by the great body of evangelical Christians."

I consider myself a fellow traveler of the Reformed tradition in most respects. However, at this point I must demur. Those in this tradition are so afraid of Pelagianism (the heresy that the natural man is even without grace competent to perform the will of God) and the use that those of that tendency might make of some of the language in the chapter that they wind up missing the point and Paul's argument in trying too hard to deliver his words from misuse.

As I will show later there is nothing in his language that is inconsistent with our doctrine of total depravity or everyday reality. I have the highest regard for the mind and scholarship of Charles Hodge and many others in this camp, but at this point I think misguided theological interest has misled them and skewed honest exegesis. The whole point of the argument depends on assuming a man under law, for the Apostle's interest at this point is convincing us that there is no sanctification, no possibility of producing fruit to God under law. In doing so, he may have suggested to some that there is some fault in the law. He hastens to show that the flaw for the man under law lies in the man himself, not in God's law. Then he will proceed to portray in the case of a high-minded, religiously conditioned, but unrenewed Jew (like he was) the moral futility of the best representatives of those under law. Any way you slice it, the result is always the same: wretchedness and failure. Law will not produce righteousness or fruit to God.

It confuses everything when one makes this person as believer. I know I am being redundant here, but repetition in the service of clarity is a good thing.

[202] Right here is one of our areas of contradiction with secular psychology and modern liberal thought, both of which in general share a very optimistic view of human nature. The prevailing assumption is that if people are bad, it is nurture rather than nature which made them that way.

The Bible teaches otherwise. Mankind is corrupt by nature. Certainly, nurture can reinforce nature, but the tendency to evil is inborn. It is endemic to the human condition and is the reason why we must have human government; otherwise, anarchy would reign, and might would be right and only the strongest would survive.

Modern secular psychology typically has this great aversion to guilt as the enemy of self-esteem. The Bible sees man's problem as fundamentally moral and spiritual; psychologists see it as psychological. Man's problem is the loss of his innocence, in the biblical view. In the psychological model, his problem is the loss of his sense of self-worth. Everything stems from that.

And one of the worst feeders of low self-esteem is guilt. Hence, their mission— and they enthusiastically chose to accept it —is an all-out assault on every theory and every broker of guilt on the planet. That includes especially theological doctrines about the sinfulness of man and preaching that evokes the specter of humanness fallenness and stirs up feelings of guilt.

We believe the only sound way to deal with guilt is go to the root of the problem, confront it head-on and resolve it in God's way, not deny it, evade it or shift the blame onto others in the typical psychological way.

One never changes reality by denying it. The truth is that self-worth is not sustained by achievements or psychological mantras. In the final analysis it is founded on our perception of our creation in the image of God (which lifts us above the animal world and biological materialism) and upon a right relationship to Him.

When we have trashed our Creator, we are indeed morally corrupt and vile, and the only path to redemption is by way of confession and submission. Only then can self-worth be re-created and sustained.

We must set people free from their burdens of guilt. Hence, they deal in a great deal of blame shifting. (Please notice that they play musical chairs with guilt— they absolve their patients at the expense of the self-esteem of someone else. That way there are always enough clients to go around, I suppose.)

But this psychology perspective is wide of the mark. One does not change reality by denying it. One does not escape the burden of guilt by shifting it where it does not belong. The only way to deal with guilt is not to shift it, but to resolve it. That involves accepting blame where blame is due.

[203] Arndt & Gingrich, *Greek-English Lexicon of the New Testament*, 127.

[204] Lloyd-Jones, *Romans: The Law: Its Functions and Limits*, 121.

205 "The Law comes and addresses a man, and at once the antagonism to God that is innate within him, and natural to him, the spirit of rebellion, is aroused and aggravated, and his assertiveness comes into play. This is because man 'in sin' desires to be autonomous; he is not prepared to bow to anyone. He is self-satisfied, he is self-contained, he is independent; and so, he resents the idea of Law. That is why many people say that they do not believe in God. They resent the idea that there is anyone to whom they must bow the knee.... The natural man hates this notion that there is anyone, even God, before whom he has to bow down and submit himself... he wants to live his own life in his own way... And so, he says that the whole notion of God is nothing but a projection of the Victorian idea of a father. That is what clever people, the psychologists and others are saying. The Victorian father repressed his children, he gave commandments, and his word was law. His children had to do what he said. Most people, they say, have projected that into infinity and say that that is God. Of course, it is something purely psychological! In saying all that, they are, of course, showing this enmity, this hatred of God, this spirit of rebellion that is innate in us. So, the great characteristic of an age like this, which does not believe in God, is lawlessness, dislike of discipline and order in any shape or form. We have almost reached the state in which they [sic] do not believe in punishing anyone; a murderer almost becomes a hero who engages public sympathy. The prisoner gets more sympathy than his victim. Thus, the whole idea of right and wrong is rapidly disappearing from the human mind." (Lloyd-Jones, *Romans: The Law: Its Functions and Limits*, 126.)

206 Paul should not be understood to imply that the natural man succumbs to every temptation, goes headlong after every desire sin may present to his mind. This is not true. To transgress God's law, one does not have to transgress it in every way conceivable; one has only to allow Sin's desires to become the lusts of the mind as well as of the flesh.

Another thing we must remember about sin and sinners is the restraining influence of the Holy Spirit upon sinners. This takes many forms from divinely created impulses at the moment to perceptions of self-interest to cultural and personal conditioning. This sovereign factor serves the plan of God and keeps men, with no credit to themselves, from becoming as bad as they might at any given time. Even when men do the right thing formally, however, they never, apart from grace, do the right thing for the right reasons, (i.e. with a right heart). In some respect Sin always manages to corrupt even the noblest aspirations of the best cultivated and conditioned of natural man.

207 Nygren, *Commentary on Romans*, 279.

208 Hodge, *Epistle to the Romans*, 224.

209 Ibid, 225.

[210] An old illustration I remember used by the late Vernon McGee in special Bible lectures on Romans at Dallas Seminary c. 1960-61.

[211] Hodge, *Epistle to the Romans*, 226.

[212] Note that this language is inappropriate as a description of Christian experience. It is the very situation that Paul emphasizes that the man in Christ (under grace) has been set free from—see Romans 6:6-7, 14, 17 (*were* slaves), 18 *(having been* freed from sin), 20 (*were* slaves of sin), 22 *(having been* freed from sin and enslaved to God); 7:5 (while we *were in* the flesh); 8:2 (the law of the Spirit of life in Christ Jesus *has* set you free from the law of sin and death), 8:9 (you *are not* in the flesh but in the Spirit)

[213] The present tense is very possibly attracted from the contrast. "The Law is spiritual, but I am. . ." If so, its import is nothing more than a contrast of two perennial states of being, that of the Law and that of the person under law.

The shift from the past tense to the present, so often placed in evidence as an exegetical exhibit indicative of a description of *Christian* experience, also has another easy explanation as *a historical present*. Of this usage, Smythe says:

"In lively or dramatic narration, the present may be used to represent a past action as going on at the moment of speaking or writing." Later he adds a note: "The historical present may be coordinated with past tenses, which may precede or follow it." (Smythe, *Greek Grammar*, 422.)

Several huge difficulties, it seems to me, stand in the way of interpreting this of Christian experience on the grounds of the present tense. Not only can it be naturally explained in other ways, but if one finds that the present tense implies a Christian, especially in view of the shift of tenses, then are we saying this is *normative* Christian experience?

If so, this interpretation implies that the wretched man of verse 24 is wretched still, that the great Transition described in chapter 8 is nothing but the great Ideal. No believer (or few at least) ever makes it in chapter 8! In fact, the great appeal of the *Christian* interpretation of chapter 7:14ff is that it seems on the face of it so descriptive of the conflict of Christian living. The problem, as mentioned earlier, with that is, *the passage is not talking about the conflict of Galatians 5, but clear defeat and total conquest.* There is quite a difference! The interpretation in question, if it is read as defeat, means that for most Christians, *under grace* is as weak a condition morally as under law. It makes little practical difference in the moral elevation of our lives. If it is read as mere conflict, it is totally beside the point (of the argument), for the Apostle is trying to show the holiness of the Law in itself, but due to a deadly flaw in us, its powerlessness to make us holy. It leaves us in a "wretched" condition—an expression of a state far more serious than moral tension.

If it is not read as *normative* Christian experience, but substandard Christian living when believers live after the flesh and in a legal mode, then we have the forbidding problem that most Christians buy into this interpretation (I say again) because this is precisely where they see themselves. If so, grace is again proven as weak and incompetent as the law and Romans 8 is a spiritual pipe dream. Something is wrong here.

If people see it as Paul's own analysis of his present Christian experience, then the Apostle himself never made the great Transition that he so eulogizes in Romans 8. Do we believe that? If one argues, no, no, Paul is talking about his *past* Christian experience, then one has conceded that the present tense can be used in this context to describe graphically an *historical* experience.

[214] That is the only case that fits the argument. It would be irrelevant to use Christian (under grace) experience to show the moral futility of life under law in the process of exonerating its holiness.

[215] Martin Luther in his days as a Roman Catholic monk greatly trembled before the Law of God, not to mention a lot of traditional standards of righteousness. He gave it his best shot with an energy and self-denial that few people know anything about.

Speaking later as a Christian concerning the Sermon on the Mount, wherein the spirit of the Law is laid bare, Luther acknowledged the moral futility of the natural man before God's Law:

"This word is too high and too hard that anyone should fulfill it. This is proved, not merely by our Lord's word, but by our own experience and feeling. Take any upright man or woman. He will get along very nicely with those who do not provoke him but let someone proffer only the slightest irritation and he will flare up in anger,... if not against friends, then against enemies. Flesh and blood cannot arise against it." (Cited by Roland Bainton, *Here I Stand: A Life of Martin Luther*, 34.)

[216] This is not an evasion of responsibility any more than a man stoned on alcohol and under its control weeps in contrition at publicly offensive and anti-social actions that are completely opposed to his standards and principles when he is sober. "I want everybody to understand," he might cry, "that that is not me. I am not like that. That is the alcohol." He is not denying responsibility but lamenting its enslaving power to take over the personality and make it contradict itself.

[217] Phaedra in Euripides' *Hippolytes*, 1.379-80.

[218] It is language like this that has disposed so many to opt for the "Christian" interpretation of this passage, feeling that the sentiments expressed here are too godly for the natural man. However, see my discussion in the Notes Addendum to this chapter's section where I show that this is clearly wrong. Above I have noted that such sentiments are not incompatible with the doctrine of total depravity. We have every right to resist Pelagian interpretations of this text, but this one does not involve that error if we rightly understand total depravity. Also, we cannot accept any teaching clearly at variance with reality. The Bible and reality will always agree, though both can be misinterpreted. One should always give the Scripture the benefit of the doubt, but where there is no doubt on the

experiential side, one must re-evaluate any interpretation of the Bible inconsonant with it.

For example, I know babies cry. You know babies cry. Everybody (even the deaf) knows that babies cry. So, if someone comes forward with an interpretation of Scripture that says babies never cry, I say their doctrine is false and they must go back to the Book and correct themselves.

So here. One day a young woman came to my office who had been coming to our services. She said she didn't know God and wondered if somehow, I could help her find Him. Her father, she said, was an atheist and she had no religious upbringing and didn't understand these things. As we talked, it was apparent that in the *common* grace of God she had a different mindset than the typical young single career girl out there today. She rejected their morals and didn't want to live like they did. She had higher, more elevated moral principles more in line with those of Scripture. Yet she was finding it hard to cross over the line and come to Christ and divorce herself from the world. She couldn't understand the contradiction within herself. I could. Right here it is.

[219] Godet (quoting M. Bonnet), *Epistle to the Romans*, 294.

[220] Hodge, *Epistle to the Romans*, 226.

[221] Godet, *Epistle to the Romans*, 281.

[222] Ibid, 281.

[223] Ibid, 281.

[224] The Reformers, following Augustine, were inclined to this interpretation apparently in reaction to Pelagianism. The doctrine of total depravity seemed to exclude the high moral tone of this person. Yet when one understands total depravity, not as the inability to sympathize with righteousness, but as the incompetence to perform it, even when the enlightened mind consents to its goodness, there is no conflict. It was an overreaction.

That reaction of course has been fed in more recent times by opposition to the holiness movements dating from Wesley. These have always featured some species of perfectionism which downplays the normality of sin in the Christian life and urges believers to seek the entire sanctification available to them.

Thus, I suspect both sides of this debate have obfuscated the passage over the years on behalf of theological "spin" (i.e., protecting theological interests, assuming too readily that their doctrines had already been safely established biblically.)

[225] Godet, *Epistle to the Romans*, 281.

[226] Godet, *Epistle to the Romans*, 293, brackets mine.

[227] Godet, *Epistle to the Romans*, 293.

[228] Ridderbos, *Paul: An Outline of His Theology*, 128-129.

[229] Godet, *Epistle to the Romans*, 282.

Romans Chapter 8

Here is where the apostle in triumph expounds God's redemptive solution to the spiritual trainwreck ("Wretched man that I am! Who will set me free from the body of this death? Thanks be to God through Jesus Christ our Lord!" (7:24-25)).

Let me explain that. Something had to change that sorry situation or those under the law were doomed. So, in chapter eight he declares...

The Conquest of Sin as the Ruling Power in the Believer's Life

To redeem man, to lift the sentence of condemnation from over our heads, God had to deal with sin on two levels: 1) on the legal level, He dealt justly with the *penalty* of sin, and 2) on the moral level, He had to break the enslaving *power* of sin so that the people whose sins He forgave did not remain enslaved to it.

The wretchedness of enslavement to the power of sin he depicted in 7:14... a picture of the moral futility of even the noblest and most high-minded Jew under law. If anyone had any illusions about the power of the Law to produce holiness, that portrait was meant to disabuse them. The problem was not in the Law itself but in the power of sin resident within the flesh. All the Law did was stir up sin to resist and flout the Law. It just stirred up the mud, it did not clear it up.

For any Jew with an awakened conscience and an intellectual commitment to the Law, being under law could only produce sin and exasperation... and *condemnation.* Obviously, God cannot take into His pure family and His holy presence persons whose nature is anti-God and whose spirit is anti-law.

Yet, thanks be to God, through Christ Jesus, God devised a fail-safe plan of redemption, which secures the former as well as the latter. For God, through the work of Christ, has broken the bondage of our wills to indwelling sin. Sin remains with us, yet not forever, and never again will it rule us as an indomitable principle.

(8:1) *There is therefore now no condemnation for those in Christ Jesus.*

"Therefore," I believe, looks back to the summation (v. 25) of the situation of 7:14–23. That situation is one of futility, where the Law of sin reigns through the flesh, overruling the good intentions of one trying to measure up to the Law. What Paul described there is a condition of complete conquest (not mere conflict), which leads to the dominion of death. Condemnation under those conditions would be assured.

Now, Paul, anticipating the provisions of grace in Christ Jesus, proclaims redemption for believers[230] from the threat of condemnation.

(8:2) *For the law of the Spirit of life in Christ Jesus has set you free from the law of sin and death.*

By "law," he means here something akin to "principle."[231]

"For" provides an explanation for the fact that those who are in Christ are no longer subject to the legal condemnation that must befall those trying to serve God on works terms—that is, to be justified by Him based on legal merit.

The defeating principle, namely, the principle of death-producing sin portrayed in 7:14ff in all its lethal results has been so neutralized by a superior principle that we are freed from its ability to rule us, that is, its power to enforce its demands upon our wills.[232]

Note again this motif of *freedom* from that which held us in 7:14ff (cf. 6:6–7, 14, 17–18, 20 (were), 21; 7:5, 6). In the present incomplete state of our freedom, from the power of sin, we are free of its *dominion,* not its influence. The former is a term of thralldom.

"The law of the Spirit of life" amounts to "the Holy Spirit who implants in us the life of God" with all its moral empowerment.

(8:3) *For what the Law could not do, weak as it was through the flesh, God did: sending His own Son in the likeness of sinful flesh and as an offering for sin, He condemned sin in the flesh. .*

.

"For" begins an explanation that accounts for the new freedom affirmed in 8:2, namely, freedom from the death-bearing law of sin.

"What the Law could not do" is contrasted with what God accomplished through the incarnation. What the Law could not do he has just described in chapter 7—it could not break the power of sin. The Law could not render men holy. Under law, people cannot bring forth fruit pleasing to God. All the Law does is excite our flesh to do evil. God fixed that problem. How, we will learn shortly.

"Weak as it was through the flesh" reminds us again that the Law's inability to produce sanctification in those under it was due to no moral defect in the Law itself but owing to the enslaving principle of sin resident in the flesh. The flaw in the Law was not in it at all, but in *us* all.

"In the likeness of sinful flesh..." The wording is careful, not docetic. He is not implying that the humanity of Christ was a phantasm. That take is against the whole analogy of Scripture, not to mention his own theology. What Paul means to convey is that while Christ shares our humanity, he in no way partakes of our fallenness.

"And concerning sin" The Father sent Him to deal with our sin problem. His mission was to make a substitute offering of Himself to propitiate the just wrath of God against sin (2 Cor. 5:21). An atoning offering, in other words.

"He condemned sin in the flesh"—He *condemned* sin in the flesh. Without justification, that is, settling the penalty of sin, there could be no dealing with the power of sin. Justification is the track that the train of sanctification runs on, as I remember an old Bible teacher once saying.

"Condemned"—in the sense that He judged it at the Cross, and in the process, *He decreed its destruction*. He took dead aim in dealing with the penalty of sin and on the power of sin residing in the flesh. Like city fathers putting up a condemnation order over a ruined site where urban renewal was planned, so God, at the cross, put a condemnation order upon that old sinful man that we were, poured out His judgment upon us *in Christ,* and thereby paved the way of renewal through the power of the Spirit. Murray's comment is too narrow when he says:

"There does not appear to be good warrant for supposing. . . that the reference is to the expiatory action of God in the sacrifice of Christ... the governing thought of this passage is concerned with deliverance from the law of sin and death and, therefore, from sin as a ruling and regulating power." [233]

Certainly, he is right in supposing that the main focus here is on the power of sin. What I think Murray overlooks, however, is that Paul always sees our justification as the foundation of sanctification. This linkage appears in 6:7 and is the only connection that really illumines it. [234]

The whole point from chapter 7 to this juncture is to underscore the incompetence of the Law to mortify sinful passions, a situation which could not result in anything but condemnation to those under the Law. Now God has accomplished in Christ what the Law could not—a condemnation order with respect to the power of sin that will result in the ability to fulfill the righteousness of the Law.

That interpretation agrees with all that follows through verse 11. The passage is intended to explain why believers (i.e., those who walk after the Spirit) are able now to please God, whereas unbelievers (those who walk after the flesh) cannot.

The Divine Intention in Our Emancipation

(8:4) *in order that the requirement of the Law might be fulfilled in us, who do not walk according to the flesh, but according to the Spirit.*

The question here is whether the apostle is speaking in absolute or relative terms. If the former, then in the term *condemnation,* he certainly had our justification in view as well as sanctification, for it is only through justification that a believer can fulfill the law of God in any unqualified sense.

Justification does more than subtract our guilt; it clothes us with the perfect righteousness of Jesus Christ so that there is not one shortfall in our standing before God. He is our righteousness, and all that God's law requires is fulfilled for us *by Him*. His perfect righteousness is imputed to us so that we stand before God holy and blameless in Him (Eph. 1:4; cf. also Eph. 5:27). Colossians 1:22 says:

> "He has now reconciled you in His fleshly body through death, in order to present you before Him holy and blameless and beyond reproach..."

If, however, he meant it relatively, then he simply intended to say that God purposed that at last His people would have new hearts (as promised in Ezek. 36:26) and would be morally inclined to adhere to the law of God and conform to the spirit of it (love) and not simply its external letter.

The essence of the Law is love (Matt. 22:27–28; Rom. 13:10). Jesus said that the badge of discipleship would be the mark of love (John 13:35; 1 John 3:23; 4:7–8, 11–12, 19–21). Obviously, Jesus anticipates that this virtue will be within the moral capacity of His disciples. Paul assumed no less.

I suspect Paul had both senses in view, and the language is elastic enough to allow for both. For, in the end, God intends that our practice will be made as perfect as our position. Certainly, his redemptive purpose is to remove every vestige of the flesh (1 John 3:3) and to perfect us in the likeness of His Son. That purpose is already in progress in the form of our sanctification; it will be consummated in our glorification.[235]

The whole thrust of 8:1–11 is that in the believer there is not only the *power* to pursue after holiness but—this is crucial—also the *proclivity*. Those who are according to the Spirit not only have the energization but, likewise, the inclination to follow the things of God rather than the things of the flesh. That such is the case and the reason for it is developed in the remarks which follow.

The Divine Provision for our Emancipation: A Comparative Look at the Conditions and Inclinations of the Believer and the Unbeliever

In us who are walking not according to the flesh, but according to the Spirit.

The relative clause does two things:

1) It explains the morally enabling principle in believers, which assures the achievement of God's moral goal in believers.

2) At the same time, observe that it defines an attribute, which sets us apart from the unbeliever.

God's purpose in condemning sin in the flesh so that the righteousness of the Law might be fulfilled was not confined to a class of "super saints" who opt to walk after the Spirit rather than the flesh. This clause does not limit God's purpose to a circle-within-the circle of believers. That is not the idea at all.

The point is to explain how God achieves this effect in believers while setting them free from the law of sin which produces death. He puts a different engine under their hood, so to speak. Their moral engines are driven by a brand-new fuel, to change the metaphor a bit.

"Who walk after the Spirit" is a description that extends to the *whole* class of believers, not just a spiritual caste within the ranks. None of them is any longer a person who walks *after the flesh*. That means that the flesh is no longer the principle that controls their attitudes and behaviors on an involuntary basis.

That is a descriptor of the natural man, and Christians are no longer in the state of nature. They are now, each and every one, people who *walk after the Spirit*. Their nature now partakes of the Spirit of God (2 Pet. 1:4). The dominant influence in their lives is now the Holy Spirit, not the flesh. They enjoy His uplifting and overcoming power.

Now get this: we are still *in the flesh* but no longer *after the flesh*. There is a rivalry of impulses and desires, one set stemming from the flesh, that is, that corrupted part of our being that is mortal, and one set deriving from the Spirit. The battle is not equal, but there is still a conflict. Sin will not be a master over the believer (6:14). The Spirit will eventually prevail. We will gradually be shaped and conformed into Christ's image. The victories of the flesh will be less and less; those of the Spirit more and more... if we are after the Spirit. Note verse 9, where *in the Spirit* is the theological equivalent of *after the Spirit*. This is clear from the context. All in Christ are in the Spirit.

Illustration: There is an adult in every infant, though, in childhood, the adult is not so evident, not even in adolescence. But the power of adulthood is irrepressible, and ultimately, it prevails as childish things are put away and a full fledged adult blossoms, though not without many lapses in maturity along the way.

So it is with the maturation of a Christian. New life is obvious in most cases—there is a definite change—but in spiritual infancy and adolescence so much of the old remains that, at times, that condition seems more of the essence, more of the nature, than the new. But, in time, the new man comes to maturity, never to perfection, but to a semblance of Christian manhood or womanhood.

The following text explains why this is inevitable that every person will follow nature. It's because water seeks its own level.

It's no wonder that those after the flesh can't rise above the flesh, nor any wonder that those after the Spirit are empowered and destined to overcome the dominion of the flesh, for:

(8:5) *For those who are according to the flesh set their minds on the things of the flesh, but those who are according to the Spirit, on the things of the Spirit.*

"For" launches a comparison of the two kinds of men—those after the flesh and those after the Spirit—whereby the apostle accounts for the moral incompetence of the former and the ability of the latter.

Those according to the flesh mind the things of the flesh and those according to the Spirit mind the things of the Spirit.

Each is governed by the desires that correspond to its nature. Those still in the flesh are ruled by the desired characteristics of the flesh (i.e., the old sinful nature); those now created after the Spirit share the desires of that Spirit.

Again, I emphasize in this section this thought: This condition of being "after the Spirit" involves more than moral ability; it also implies a certain moral *inevitability*. There is a new law of our inner being that does more than _enable_ us to do right; it *inclines* us to the desires of the Spirit. We are not merely empowered to do right; now our nature is so created that we are disposed to do what is right.

(8:6) *For the mind set on the flesh is death, but the mind set on the Spirit is life and peace.*

"For" explains the *gravitational pull,* which finds the flesh operating in its low moral orbit—the fleshly mindset is always drawn to those things that characterize death. "Death" is a word that encompasses all the fallout of human disobedience, not just our exit from temporal life. It starts with alienation from God, being cut off from His fellowship and blessing, subject to all the penal miseries of sin (i.e., the curse), continues with a darkened mind and conscience, a course of life lurching along blindly in self-destructive behaviors, emptiness, lack of fulfillment, and issues finally in one's being cast out into outer darkness away from any hope of retrieval and any vestige of His grace. That is death in all its ramifications.

In contrast, the mindset of the Spirit follows the desires of the Spirit. Paul does not intend us to understand that this pattern is absolutely consistent. That would be contrary to the analogy of Scripture and his own teaching in Romans and elsewhere. What is contrasting is tendencies... mindsets... the way the moral tree is bent.

I have tendencies, but I am not always consistent. I sometimes surprise myself in both positive and negative ways. But I (and my wife) can tell you what my tendencies are in certain circumstances. So, it is with the believer. Christ has changed our tendencies. Those tendencies are better developed in some than in others and are stronger in some respects than in others. But they are there, and they will progress under the training and empowering influence of the Spirit.

Those after the flesh (*hoi kata sarka*) are, by a law of their own inner being, unable to rise above their fleshly nature but are drawn inexorably, as if by a form of moral gravity, into the orbit of death. Again, water seeks its own level. As Jesus put it in John 3: "That which is flesh is flesh and that which is Spirit, is Spirit." They are different in kind, not just degree.

That those in the flesh could never please God is inevitable, for they are neither subject to God's law nor able to be (Rom. 7:14ff).

> (8:7–8) *Because the mind of the flesh is hostile toward God; for it does not subject itself to the Law of God, for it is not even able to do so; and those who are in the flesh cannot please God.*

"Hostile" = enmity" (*echthra*)—enmity in this case is defined, not by a hostile emotional disposition toward God's law (that is a very important distinction in light of 7:14ff) but rather by a negative moral outcome.[236] "Enmity toward God" in the final analysis is determined by the fact that the man in the flesh does not *functionally* subject himself to God's standards. He prohibited by a ruling principle within that renders him "unable to please God."

> (8:9) *However you are not in the flesh but in the Spirit, if indeed the Spirit of God dwells in you. But if anyone does not have the Spirit of Christ, he does not belong to Him.*

But for you (believers), no such disability exists.

"You" (*hymeis*) is emphatic in the original. But *you* (as opposed to unbelievers who are still "in the flesh," i.e., under the rule of the unregenerate nature) are not in the flesh, but in the Spirit."

This ability is guaranteed if, in fact, they are indwelt by the Holy Spirit. And they *are,* in fact, indwelt by the Spirit if they belong to Christ. There is no such thing as a believer with the Spirit and one without. The Holy Spirit is not an optional equipment for the saints. He comes to us with the price of admission, so to speak. Christ and the Spirit come to the believer in the same package.[237]

The logic formalized is as follows:

All who belong to Christ are indwelt by the Holy Spirit.

All who are indwelt by the Holy Spirit are "in the Spirit."

Therefore, all who belong to Christ are "in the Spirit."

> (8:10) *And if Christ is in you, though the body is dead because of sin, yet the spirit is alive (life) because of righteousness. (parenthesis mine)*

Our new relation not only enables us to live according to the Spirit but, by its inner logic, morally obliges us to do so. For, to the flesh, we owe nothing but our miseries; to the Spirit, we owe the presence of life, even amid death and the promise of the resurrection.

"If Christ is in you..."[238] The premise is assumed to be true and continues drawing out the *fail-safe* implications of life "in the Spirit."

The body is dead on account of (__dia__) sin, but the spirit is life on account of (__dia__) righteousness.

The first clause has something of a concessive[239] force and acknowledges the truth of 5:11, namely, that the believer in this mortal body is not immune from the destruction of it, but on the other hand, victory over death is guaranteed by the presence of Christ. Thus, the sting of sin is defeated.

Charles Hodge: "The sense in which the spirit is life is antithetical to that in which the body is dead. As the body is infected with a principle of decay which renders its dissolution inevitable, so the soul, in which the Holy Spirit dwells, is possessed of the principle of life which secures its immortal and blessed existence."[240]

"Dead on account of sin"— "Dead" in the sense that the principle of death resides there and will hold sway. Even as the body "lives," it is amid dying. "The wages of sin is death" (Rom. 6:23)[241]

"Life on account of righteousness"—He does not say the Spirit is "living," but more significantly, is *life.* Because the Holy Spirit, the fountain head of the principle of life, occupies the human spirit, the apostle seems to merge the two, as closely linked as they are. Often, it is hard to decide between the human spirit and the Holy Spirit in certain contexts because Paul sees the two in intimate organic connection. He seems to say that at the core of our new creation is the awakened spirit, once dead to God, now so irradiated with the Holy Spirit that it pulsates with the divine life.

"On account of righteousness..." This phase attributes the presence of life (in the form of the life-bearing Spirit) within us to the justifying work of Christ.

So, the thought is that while our bodies, owing to natural corruption through Adam, are destined for dissolution, the life-giving Spirit who indwells us through the imputed righteousness of Christ is the answer to the plague of death, which now holds no terrors for believers.

Although Hodge takes this phrase to refer to subjective righteousness or personal holiness, this would be misleading. There is no cause-and-effect relationship between the presence of life and personal holiness. Certainly, we would agree that true life exists only among the righteous, but not because of the latter but His justifying work, not ours.

> (8:11) *But if the Spirit of Him who raised Jesus from the dead dwells in you, He who raised Christ Jesus from the dead will also give life to your mortal bodies through His Spirit who indwells you.*

With the presence of the Spirit comes the warranty of ultimate victory over death in all its manifestations. Our mortal bodies will be raised by His life-giving power.

This verse highlights our privilege in the possession of the Spirit who vests our temporal lives with hope that transcends our mortality. In the resurrection of Jesus, the apostle lifts into view the divine model and pledge of our own resurrection.

The apostle, as a prelude to summoning the Romans, now, in effect, "to work out their salvation (viewed not as a salvific event but as an on-going redemptive program) with fear and trembling because God is at work in them to cause them to will and to do according to his good pleasure" (Phil. 2:12), reasons thusly:

"The flesh has nothing going for it. All your assets are on the spirit side of the ledger. The body is dead; the spirit is life. All the good things in your present and all your hopes for the future depend on the Spirit. You have nothing to gain from the flesh.

(8:12) *So then, brethren, we are under obligation, not to the flesh, to live according to the flesh —*

Noblesse oblige is a French phrase for the "obligation of honorable, generous, and responsible behavior associated with high rank or birth."[242] The apostle here expresses the Christian form of it. This summarizes the responsibilities of royal privilege... the moral obligations that attend our birth right as members of the family of God.

First, however, he waves off any dalliance with the flesh to gratify its appetite for transient, but destructive, pleasures. It's strictly a non-profit enterprise.

"Are under obligation..." (*opheiletai esmen*) that is, are debtors. Like crime, life according to the flesh does not pay. The only dividend we can show for it in the end is death. What we get from following its pleasures is reaping all the penal consequences of the curse, the pains, and miseries that attend lawlessness, estrangement from God, the dissolution of the body, and ultimately, absolute separation from God, including every vestige of grace and goodness as we now experience it through common grace.

Why should we be "suckers"? The flesh corrupts everything and gives nothing in return. Why pander to the appetites of the flesh, which, in the end, only destroy us?

Our obligation is to live according to the Spirit, for it is only through the Holy Spirit that we have a future. In the Spirit, we have the promise of bodily resurrection, of redemption from the curse of death. All that ultimately matters comes from the side of the Spirit, not the flesh.

So, let us see that we owe the flesh no favors, for it has done us nothing but damage. All our assets come from the Spirit. Our present mortal bodies will be trashed because they are corrupted by the flesh. Even so, we have the prospect of resurrection through the Spirit who indwells us. So, let us follow the Spirit rather than the flesh.

Paraphrase: "So, you don't owe the flesh a thing. Don't pamper your dead body as if the outcome of your life and hopes depended on pandering to the appetites of the flesh. You owe everything good in your present and future to the Spirit."

By way of incentive, he reminds us of the polar outcomes of the two alternatives. One course assures death, the other entails the assurance of life.

> (8:13) *For if you are living according to the flesh, you must die; but if by the Spirit you are putting to death the deeds of the body, you will live.*

"Must die" = are about to die (mellete apothneskein)

With *mello,*, the present infinitive could be translated "are destined to die."[243]

"The periphrastic future is used to emphasize that the consequence is necessary and certain, since it is God's judgement... the meaning is not merely that they will die... but that they will die without hope of life with God."[244]

"To put to death the deeds (Gk. = *praxeis,* pl. from *praxis* = acting, activity, course of action, act, deed, action, of the body *(somatos)*."[245]

Note that, here, the activity of the believer is presumed in cooperating with the Spirit of God. The Christian life is not a "let go and let God" proposition. We are saved through faith, not by works. But Christian faith is active. Faith without works, as James (2:26) tells us, is dead. It is a hollow shell devoid of reality.

The "body" is a metonym for the flesh. That is, the seat of the flesh's activity is named in place of the source to bring out, emphatically, I suspect, its doom as an instrument. Much of the activity of the body is right and proper in itself. It runs, walks, talks, eats, sleeps, sees, and performs necessary mechanical duties for us. The body is not evil in and of itself. There is no Eastern dualism here in the opposition of matter and spirit.

What is wrong is the intrusion of corruption in the form of what the Bible calls *sin.* One might say that the principle of sin seizing upon the natural drives and appetites of the body and pushing them beyond lawful bounds amounts to what we might call an uprising of the "flesh." The flesh stands for all that is corrupt in us, the seat as well as the source. This corruption tends to express itself commonly in pandering to the wants of the body instead of serving the will of God and in overindulging the appetites of the body. Hence, it is not unnatural for the apostle to speak of the deeds of the body in the same way he might speak of the deeds of the flesh.

To live after the Spirit is more than a moral obligation of God's people but is also a spiritual imperative. For those who live after the flesh is death. Those who follow the flesh can count on the fact that whatsoever they sow, they shall also reap (Gal. 6:7–8; cf. 1 Cor. 6:9–10; 1 John 3:7–10). The truth is that "without holiness no man shall see the Lord" (Heb. 12:14).

The point is not that we are saved by faith *plus* holiness but that those who are in Christ are those who walk *after the Spirit*, not after the flesh. Walking after the Spirit is therefore a vital sign, not an extra condition of justification and regeneration. For as the next verse says so emphatically:

REASSURANCES FOR THOSE WHO WALK AFTER THE SPIRIT

(8:14) *For all who are being led by the Spirit of God, these are the sons of God.*

Literally, in the original, this text says, "For as many as are being led (present passive) by the Spirit of God, *these* are sons of God."

The present tense is a *customary* present. [246] This is their habit or custom. It is the norm for authentic believers to submit to the leadership of the Holy Spirit. They are known by the "light" to which they respond. Jesus said it: "My sheep know my voice... and they follow Me" (John 10:27). He didn't say that some of His sheep would follow Him, and others would decline to be disciples. He simply said that His sheep respond to Him, which is one and the same thing theologically as saying that the sons of God are led by the Spirit of God.

There is a form of doctrine among modern evangelicals that holds that genuine believers come in two classes: the spiritual and the carnal. The former walk after the Spirit, and the latter walk after the flesh. In the end, the spiritual class will receive a great reward for their faithfulness; the carnal group will find themselves inheriting the kingdom but none of the "property," so to speak. Or to put it another way, discipleship is something that not all believers choose. There are believers, plain and simple, who never get with the program and really walk with God. They are saved, nonetheless, because they believe God's promise of salvation in Christ.

This is a gross error, I believe. The root error is the failure to the nature of biblical faith as involving at bottom responsiveness to the Word of God.

No one wants to deny that believers can and do, at times, dishonor the grace of God and think and behave sometimes in a carnal manner (1 Cor. 3:1ff). Nor would we contest the fact that a real believer might experience a period of extended spiritual sickness just as we might undergo prolonged physical illness and be somewhat incapacitated during that time.

That, however, is a different scenario than to postulate that a real man or woman of the Spirit can, for a lifetime, basically walk after the flesh in wanton disregard of the indwelling Spirit and still be counted among the children of God. To that premise, we (and I believe Paul says too) emphatically say, "No!" Who are the real sons of God? Paul answers like Jesus—you will know them by their fruits. (Matt. 7:20, a principle that is not only a false prophet detector, but a false brother indicator as well see Matt. 7:21ff).

"As many as are led by the Spirit of God" are authentic children of God. So many professing believers in the ranks of our churches fail to get that and go in their great presumption to a date with ultimate disaster (Matt. 7:21-23).

Question: If it is true that the people of God respond to the Spirit of God because of an affinity of their new nature, why must they be admonished to do so, encouraged to do what they will do anyway?

Answer: A child will walk, but fathers stimulate the development of that endowment by exhortation. We all think, but our teachers have intensified and honed the exercise of the thought process by admonition. Divine exhortation is part and parcel of divine sanctification. It represents more than an inert plea of a helpless

God. God's Word is His way of effecting His will in our lives. Philippians 2:12–13 is an example of this tension between divine appeal and causation. God appeals to us to work out our salvation (in that aspect called "sanctification") and then turns right around in the next breath and encourages us to cooperate with the Spirit because God is working in us *to cause us to will and to do of His good pleasure!*

If God is literally causing sanctification to proceed in our lives, why should He appeal to us to work it out? Simply because His Word is not hollow breath but a living force, a creative extension of Himself (Heb. 4:12) that serves to *affect* what He commands. There is something in us like that which is in the Word. That common denominator is the Holy Spirit. God says to the believer in effect, "Let there be light in us," and that Word will not return unto Him void but will accomplish whatsoever purpose for which He sent it (Isa. 55:10–11).

Even as it appeals, convicts, convinces, and converts the errant heart—maybe not all at once, but sometimes by degrees and stages. God is not in a hurry; He is never frantic. He can work explosively; He can work erosively. In the work of sanctification, He has generally chosen to work on the latter principle. Spiritual growth, like physical, emotional, and mental maturity, is a matter of process and time.

The hammer blows of God's Word do not break down the formations of the flesh all at once. Yet, ultimately and relentlessly, it pounds on the bastions of the flesh, undermining and weakening its buttresses, even destroying some of them outright.

The pervasive lack of response to His Word, lack of appetite for it, and indifference to the things of God is no argument against this perspective, for it assumes wrongly that all those in the church are part of the Church.

However, on balance, the leadership of the Spirit is more powerful in the truly regenerate than the influence of the flesh. That is what Paul is saying. It should also be pointed out that our knowledge of our own hearts is shallow and our ability to measure our lives in God's scales is unequal to the task. That is much more the case where others are concerned. So, it is for God to judge ultimately.

Meanwhile, let no one deceive himself who constantly stands at the beck and call of the flesh. That is not the habit of the sons of God. Let each man examine himself lest, in the end, he hears from God Himself those mournful words to hypocrites: "Depart from me, you workers of iniquity. I never knew you."

This verse explains or accounts for the life-and-death outcomes embedded in the lifestyle alternatives mentioned in verse 13:

1) living according to the flesh or

2) putting to death the practices of the body by the Spirit.

The fact is, the character of our lifestyle is a litmus test of the nature of our relationship.

Who is it who really belongs to the family of God? How can we distinguish the possessors from the professors? What is the most telling hallmark of the people of God? It is this: they are those who respond to the Spirit—who operate on His channel, who bear the fruit of the Spirit. They and they alone are the children of God.

Paraphrase: "On the other hand, if you align yourself with the Spirit, you shall live. For such alignment is a vital life sign of the sons of God. Walking in the Spirit doesn't earn you life but is the badge of those who enjoy it."

Analyzing the apostle's statement in terms of a formal syllogism, it is clear that our newness of life not only includes *moral ability* but also *the moral inevitability* of sanctification.

Only those who are led by the Spirit of God qualify as the sons of God.

Being led by the Spirit of God is mortifying the deeds of the flesh.

Therefore, the sons of God are those who mortify the practices of the flesh.

All A are B.

All B are C.

Therefore, all A are C.

The Reassurance of the Witness of the Spirit

(8:15) *For you have not received a spirit of slavery leading to fear again, but you have received a spirit of adoption as sons by which we cry out, "Abba, Father!"*

The first evidence of kinship or relationship is found in the external fruit of the Spirit (e.g., Gal. 5:22–23). A complementary and normative confirmation is the internal witness of the Spirit.

The Spirit who indwells us creates a spirit or disposition, not of dread, terror, and anxiety with respect to God like Israel experienced at the holy mountain (Sinai), not running from God like guilt-stricken Adam, but a spirit of privileged familiarity that is drawn toward God and blessed with the happy instinct to address him tenderly and affectionately as "Abba" or "Dear Father."

Abba is an Aramaic term of tenderness and affection for a father. *Pater* is roughly the Greek equivalent but lacking perhaps the connotation of tender affection connoted by the Greek. Hence, Paul combines them, maybe because it had become formulaic in early Christian expression. Possibly, *pater* was simply an interpretive addition for Romans who may not have been familiar with the Aramaic word.

In any case, the point is that the Spirit within us has created a spirit not akin to the apprehensive dread of a slave toward a cruel and harsh master but that of a favored child who has been adopted into full rank and privilege by a loving father... a child who comes with an affectionate and tender heart to God and greets Him joyfully as "Father."[247]

"Cries out" Almost every time my little grandson (then six years of age), saw me after any absence of a few days, he literally cries out almost involuntarily, "Grandpa!" and races into my manly (well, once upon a time) arms. So, it is the spiritual instinct of believers, fed by the Holy Spirit, not to cringe and be cowed by God and act like a craven slave but to cry out, "Father!" and race into His embrace with all expectancy that He will welcome us with all the joy that I receive my grandson.

The reason we know this is the confirming witness of the Spirit who reassures us of our identity and privilege.

(8:16) *The Spirit Himself bears witness with our spirit that we are the children of God...*

It is the normal office work of the Holy Spirit to confirm our adoption and subjectively strengthen the assurance of our salvation that we have objectively in the gospel. This ministry has already been alluded to in other language in Romans 5:5, where Paul tells us that it is the Holy Spirit who is responsible for pouring out in the hearts of God's people as confirming sense of His love for them.

Like a radio signal, sometimes the message of the Holy Spirit gets garbled in transmission, owing to some kind of interference or static, so to speak. The problem may be faulty (weak) faith or stem from disobedience. In the latter case, the reassuring work of the Spirit in its gentler[248] form is temporarily blunted by the Spirit's urgency to signal His grief and displeasure with our sinful conduct (Eph. 5:30; Isa. 63:10).

> (8:17) *And if children, heirs also, heirs of God and fellow heirs with Christ, if indeed we suffer with Him in order that we may also be glorified with Him.*

The logic embedded in that assurance reinforces the conviction of our safety in Christ and our obligation to live according to the Spirit and not to the flesh. If in Christ our status is so exalted, why is it that we must endure all this pounding? That question begs an answer, for it might seem contradictory to our riches in Christ.

"If indeed we suffer with Him..." The consummation of our redemption is not based on faith *plus* suffering, but the faithful are called to suffering (John 15:33; 16:33; Acts 14:22; 1 Thess. 3:3, 4; Psa. 34:19).

"If indeed" (*eiper*) here introduces an assumption or a given rather than a pure condition, just as in verse 9. One might translate it "since" or "seeing that." [249] Paul does not intend to say that our glorification is a reward earned through suffering but simply to remind us that suffering for the children of God is a given, a necessary precursor that we must endure enroute to the consummation of our redemption.

Implicit in this assumption, however, is the fact that perseverance through suffering is a badge of faith. That is why, in Matthew 24,

Jesus says of His persecuted disciples that those who endure to the end will be saved. The saints persevere, and perseverance implies suffering in the pathway of faith. If we deny Him on earth in the face of suffering, He has already forewarned, He will deny us before His Father (Matt. 10:32–33; 2 Tim. 2:12).

"That we may be glorified with Him..." We are better able to endure our present tribulations now because we know that they go with the territory and are in the plan and purpose of God a necessary antecedent to our glorification with Christ. The point is that we do not view tribulation as any kind of anomaly or contradiction of our exalted standing as children of God but part and parcel of God's temporal plan for His people. "In hope we have been saved... with perseverance we wait eagerly for it" (8:24, 25).

"Suffer with Him..." (*sumpaschomen*). The present tense implies that the Christian experience is marked by sharing His afflictions. We in whom Christ dwells live out His presence, though we must endure as aliens, at least in principle, the same kinds of adversities that He had to endure at the hands of a hostile world. For example, "all who live godly in Christ Jesus will suffer persecution." It is a given, not a possibility. We will be spiritual lightning rods and will attract the same kind (though not necessarily the same degree) of hostility from the world that He attracted. What else? How about loneliness, being misunderstood, rejection even from those nearest and dearest, privation, slurs and slanders, mockery by inferiors, desertion by friends, betrayal... that's for starters. These kinds of abuses are not specifically *Christian* sufferings until they take rise from following Christ. Ordinary affliction can be *Christian* when it is accepted in the spirit of faith that God allows all burdens for His own purposes and are endured in that spirit.

> (8:18) *For I consider that the sufferings of this present time are not worthy to be compared with the glory that is to be revealed to us.*

The conjunction "for" (gar) picks up the ironical concession that the sons of God imitate the sufferings of Christ enroute to glorification and explains why these adversities do not blow away our confidence and unhinge us from following Christ.

It is not simply that we know that the crown comes by way of the cross, but also that we understand through faith that the burdens that assail us pale into insignificance in view of the blessings that await us. This is the minimizing perspective that enables the people of God to absorb maximum "punishment" in following Christ.

Our salvation is not to be measured by what is happening to us now, but what we hope for lies yet in the future. We must remember our future lest we get overwhelmed by the present.

"Revealed to (*eis*) us..." As the preposition implies, we are beneficiaries of that revelation, not merely spectators of it. The preposition in this case has a discreet theological ambiguity about it that is quite apt. It expresses that the "glory" of God is manifested "toward" us, that is, that we are its goal or objects. But, also, it contains the notion of the inward or transforming effects of the glory of God to which we shall be exposed at the consummation. There is in this preposition here something of the idea that His glory shall be revealed "into" us as well as "toward" us... toward us and penetrating and transforming us is the more complete idea of this pregnant phrase... it comes at us like a cosmic laser, piercing our being and purifying and transforming us in His likeness.

(8:19) *For the anxious longing of the creation waits eagerly for the revealing of the sons of God.*

How does one explain the glory that is in store for the saints? To communicate more impressively the inexpressible magnitude[250] of that glory that awaits Christ's joint heirs, the apostle takes poetic license, using the technique of personification, and portrays the transforming event as so grand in its scope and wondrous in its effects that the whole order of creation eagerly anticipates the dawn of the great regeneration.

"The anxious longing (*apokaradokia*) of the creation waits eagerly (*apekdechetai*)..." The compounded Greek word translated "anxious longing" is comprised of three elements, which, at their roots, create a picture of straining the head in anticipation. The reason creation (by personification) is said to eagerly welcome the prospect of our revealing as sons of God is that creation itself has a stake in it, as we shall see. Much like a bride's attendants in her train share in the glory of the bride, so creation itself participates in the transformation.

"The creation..." (*ktisis*). By a logical process of elimination, Murray rightly, I believe, narrows this concept in this context to all that is that "non-rational creation, animate and inanimate" in the created order. [251]

"Revealing of the Sons of God"... The return of Christ will be, as it were, a cosmic "coming out party" for the sons of God who are in this present world incognito as such. The world scoffs at our profession now, but on that day the Prince will, so to speak, put the glass slipper on the foot of Cinderella, much to the horror and chagrin of her abusive sisters who must now face the wrath of the Sovereign for their mistreatment and disregard of his Bride. On that day, our status and privilege will be made known for all to witness. "When Christ, who is our life, is revealed, then you also will be revealed with Him in glory" (Col. 3:4).

> (8:20–21) *For the creation was subjected to futility, not of its own will, but because of Him who subjected it, in hope (elpidi = expectation) that the creation itself also will be set free from its slavery to corruption into the freedom of the glory of the children of God. (parenthesis mine)*

These verses explain with poetic license the eagerness of the rest of creation (in the limited scope defined above) for Christ to return and the sons of God to be revealed. That event marks not only our *glorification* but also its *regeneration*, that is, its release or liberation of all the side effects attendant to the fall of man and the curse under which God placed him.

In punishing man, God disordered creation itself, to some degree, to make man's lot harsher on earth and to leave in place a permanent signal of the problem affecting man on this planet[252] (see Gen. 3:17–19).

"To futility..." (*mataioteti*).

> [...]the simplest and most straightforward interpretation would seem to be to take *mataiotes* here in the word's basic sense as denoting the ineffectiveness of that which does not attain its goal... and to understand Paul's meaning to be that the sub-human creation has been subjected to the frustration of not being able to fulfill the purpose of its existence, God having appointed that, without man, it should not be made perfect. We may think of the whole magnificent theater of the universe together with all its splendid properties and all the chorus of sub-human life, created to glorify God but unable to do so fully, so long as man the chief actor in the drama of God's praise fails to contribute his rational part. [253]

"Not willingly..." (*ekousa*). That is, not through any fault of its own, as though it, too, was guilty of sin but subjected to corruption (*phthoras*) in its own way as man was in his way. The reference is especially to the bondage to disorder and decay. Nothing endures. Death invests everything. The original creation was perfect; after the fall of man, it was imperfect, partaking of an unshakeable corruption.[254]

"In hope..." This phrase expresses not a wish but poetically (by personification) signifies that the corruption of nature is not permanent but a temporary condition from which nature itself expects emancipation at the time of the manifestation of the sons of God.

> (8:22) *For we know that the whole creation groans and suffers the pains of childbirth together until now.*

Creation is likened poetically to a woman in the distress of hard labor looking for relief from her pain and a joyous issue of her travail. "Until now" means right up to this very minute, but does not imply its immediate termination. It continues to this hour—until the Lord comes.

The bottom line is that creation itself is in a distressed condition, owing to the curse, but like a mother in labor, anticipates a glorious outcome.

(8:23) *And not only this, but also we ourselves, having the first fruits of the Spirit, even we groan within ourselves, waiting eagerly for our adoption as sons, the redemption of our body.*

What is true of creation (poetically speaking) is true of God's children, literally speaking. Owing to the presence of the Spirit of God in us and His organic union with our human spirit, He sponsors within us an eager longing for our release from entanglement with corruption and the curse and our resurrection and transformation and manifestation to the world. What Christian doesn't long for that time? The time when the pains and distress of this temporal world are terminated, when we come into our own, regaled and renowned as the children of God, when the reality of our adoption into the family of God is inscribed across the face of the universe, and the enemies of God and righteousness are exposed for what they are and consigned to everlasting darkness and shame!

He whose heart does not relish that prospect should examine it; it may be dead toward God.

"First fruits" refers, as Cranfield says, "not to something offered by man to God but to something given by God to man, and the idea conveyed is that of the gift of a part as a pledge of the fuller gift yet to come. What the believer has already received is a foretaste and a guarantee of what he has still to hope for."[255]

I take it that by the first fruits of the Spirit, the apostle does not designate the presence of Spirit Himself per se as the first fruits of our salvation, but rather the effects of His presence in us, that is, His work on our behalf. His work in us and for us, which is the result of His presence in and with us, is a small sampling or foretaste of what is in store for us and accounts for that visceral longing for our adoption, that is, in the formal and public sense of the term when

God proclaims His ownership by raising us from the dead by the power of God and transforming us in Christ's likeness.

(8:24) *For in hope we have been saved, but hope that is seen is not hope; for why does one hope for what he sees?*

The "groanings" of the people of God, their dissatisfaction with these present temporal conditions, their distress with the corruption that remains with us, and the tears and pain that accompany it is not at all incompatible with our profession of *salvation*. The fact is, let it be once and for all made known, the Christian has been saved *in hope*. There is no disappointment with God, but there is distress with the pain and corruption of this present order, which will not be terminated until Christ returns.

Our distress does not contradict our status as saved people, as the redeemed. What is rendered certain by divine decree is not yet in any full measure enjoyed by the children of God. As for being saved *in hope*, Murray expressed the point well:

The uniform teaching of the apostle, as of Scripture in general, is that we were saved by *faith* (cf. 1:16, 17; Eph. 2:8). "In hope" refers to the fact that the salvation bestowed in the past, the salvation now in possession, is characterized by hope. Hope is an ingredient inseparable from the salvation possessed; in that sense it is salvation conditioned by and oriented to hope. That is simply to say that salvation can never be divorced from the outlook and outreach which hope implies. [256]

What we have now is by no means the measure of our Christian expectation. That our salvation is guaranteed does not mean that it is in any way fulfilled or completed. We came to Christ in expectation of something that has yet to be realized. We were suspended, as it were, in hope. The present is only the beginning; what holds us is the future, something we do not yet see materializing.

If what we have is all we get, then there is not room for *expectation*, for hope relates to that which is coming but not yet verified by sight.

(8:25) *But if we hope for what we do not see, with perseverance we wait eagerly for it.*

If hope is part and parcel of our package of faith, then perseverance ought to be our calling card. We can't confirm God's promises by sight, but by faith we expect Him to fulfill them. The fact that we are called upon to ride out suffering without the advantage of prior confirmation by sight does not surprise or trouble us. We knew from the beginning that this was a trip of faith... that our hope was out there in the indefinite future, out of sight and out of reach of sensory verification.

Consequently, we persevere in hope, awaiting God's time to fulfill His promises and to bring us into glory with Christ. Hope sustains the sufferer. "Perseverance" is a faith word. That is, it implies faith in the promises of God, the kind of confidence that endures agony and adversity in the assurance of God's faithfulness to His Word. So, like a deaf-mute in the face of suffering, the Christian signs his hope with perseverance.

Perseverance means that we sit tight, engage in the good fight, and wait for God to set all things right. In the meantime, we are not surprised if we find trouble like a prize fighter finds bruises, but we are sustained by the confidence that if we bear the cross, we will wear the crown. Not that we earn our salvation through suffering, but the path of faith goes by way of the cross.

(8:26) *And in the same way the Spirit also helps our weakness; for we do not know how to pray as we should, but the Spirit Himself intercedes for us with groanings too deep for words...*

In the same way" (hosautos)...
What is the correlation of "in the same way"? Some see the comparison this way: "As we wait patiently, so the Spirit helps..." Others take it: "As hope sustains us, so the Spirit also sustains us..." [257]

Both would make good sense, but the question is whether either of those senses best suit the context. Whatever the answer is, it seems to me the comparison must either 1) draw a correspondence between two sources through which the believer is "helped" (in the same way the Spirit helps us) or 2) find some analogy in the yearning for the consummation of our salvation, the intensity of which breaks out in the allusion to mutual "groanings" (for the phrase *stenagmois* in verse 26 seems clearly to echo its verbal cognate *systenazei* and *stenasomen* in verse 22) or both of the above.

That the second correspondence is intended seems too plain to ignore, and it is simplest to not press it any further. The idea is that the Spirit helps us in our present weakness but, in doing so, yearns with us for our revealing as the sons of God. In fact, I take it, the Holy Spirit fuels the "groanings" in our own human spirit.

"Intercedes in our weakness..." This intercessory work[258] is a constant (note the present tense). This is a work of habit on the Spirit's part. It is necessary because of our weakness in this current fleshly condition. We are not of the flesh, but we are still in it. It limits us; it creates static and interference. We do not see nor understand as we ought, for we are still a people in process.

"Weakness (*astheneia*)..." A general term for the whole spectrum of infirmities that burden us in this mortal condition.

The Holy Spirit takes up the slack, so to speak. We lack the spiritual intelligence and discernment to seek from God that which best promotes our salvation (that is, our advancement toward Christlikeness, that which brings us nearer the goal of the high calling of God). At times, we ask for things which seem important and are not; for things which seem in our present interests but are actually inimical to them; for things which seem to serve God's purposes but don't (like the disciples wanting to pray down fire on the Samaritans, or Elijah wanting an earthquake-level manifestation of God to bring Jezebel to bay). The Spirit knows exactly what we most need and prescribes that in prayer.

For we do not know how (ti) to pray for as we ought...

This explains some of our unanswered prayers. It also explains why sometimes we ask for comfort and receive pain, why we ask God to fill our cup and He "eats our lunch." We pray at times in the blind.

We do not always understand in what direction our true interests lie. We may miss, but the Spirit of God is always on target. Prayer is answered when our prayers and His intercession match up. Prayer fails when there is dissonance between what we seek and what the Spirit orders. Even when we are prayerless, the intercessory activity of the Spirit continues... maybe ordering into our lives that which drives us to our knees and teaches us the discipline of depending on God.

To try to understand this interplay of the divine and human spirit in the matter of prayer in terms of human psychology, Paul appears to be saying that Christian prayer occurs at two levels: there are self-conscious prayers, which we may write in a journal somewhere and which may or may not express the yearning of the Holy Spirit. Then there are inarticulate yearnings (groanings) in the bowels of our Christian subconscious, aspirations excited and fed by the Holy Spirit who is united with our spirit.

The reason the two levels of petition are not identical is perhaps because in this flesh, at the surface or conscious level of the Christian, there is static arising from the influences of the world, the flesh, and the devil that have a distorting effect on our internal transmission. Hence, we do not always read the Spirit well on the conscious level, and, therefore, our prayers sometimes are neither wise nor right.

Whether this model of the situation is approximate is speculative. What we know for sure is that when we pray, with incommunicable intensity, the indwelling Spirit prays alongside us. In case of dissonance, His intercession takes right of way in heaven because it always agrees with the mind of God the Father.

"As we ought... (*katho dei*)" that is, as is fitting. This refers not to the form so much as the content of prayer, for *ti* refers to substance, whereas *pos* would have been the proper word to indicate manner.

Situationally, we sometimes don't understand what is most appropriate to the need; spiritually, our values are not always in tune with the Father's at a given time so that we ask amiss (James 4:3).

The indwelling Spirit stands and intervenes in our weakness and prescribes for us what is right and fitting.[259]

(8:27) *And He who searches the hearts knows what the mind of the Spirit is, because He intercedes for the saints according to the will of God.*

God the Father, in the language of the cybernetic age, "interfaces" with God the Spirit. The Father scans the heart, that is, the core of our being, the seat of the human spirit, where the Holy Spirit is resident. The Father knows the mind of the Spirit; whatever the Spirit knows, the Father sees; whatever the Spirit wants for us, the Father wants for us. There is an absolute community of minds between them.

"Knows..." (*oiden*) that is, "understands" with approval. [260] The Father does not simply understand the petitions of the Spirit just because they correspond with His own purposes; nothing is hidden from the all-knowing God, especially the desires of His own Spirit. Our concept of seeing or knowing sometimes connotes the idea of perception with approval.[261] The intercession of the Spirit is approved by the Father *because* it is unfailingly in accord with His will. We know, as 1 John 5 tells us, that if we ask anything in accordance with His will, He hears (or approves) our petition (1 John 5:14).

"Saints" refers to all God's true people, as those who are set apart in the sovereign purpose of the Father in Christ by the redemption action of the Holy Spirt.

This terminology has no reference to those canonized by the Roman Catholic Church as what we might call 'super saints' by their standards. All genuine believers of any age belong to the universal Church (John 10:16; 11:52; Luke 13:28-29 and Eph. 2:13-22). All the citizens of the Kingdom of God, in other words, are 'saints' in the biblical sense.

(8:28) *And we know that God causes all things to work together for good to those who love God, to those who are called according to His purpose.*

"We know... " expresses a confidence embedded in normative faith. Here is a conviction that all believers ought to share, but one which it is possible that some with stunted growth may not yet have fully caught up to.

It is precisely because of this ongoing intercessory work, because of this interest of the Spirit in furthering our salvation (sanctification) and advancing us toward the mark of the high calling of God that Paul can affirm this great comforting truth.

"To those who love God..." This is a code phrase, if you please, for the whole class of believers, not an elite group among them who happen to love Him. Note that it correlates with the last clause which frames the thought of this verse on the other end "to those who are called according to His purpose." These two classes are coextensive. What applies to one applies to the other. Certainly, there is not one class of believers who are "called according to His purpose" and another whom He failed to call according to it. This commandment (i.e., to love God) lies at the core of the law of God, which is the requirement that is fulfilled (8:4) in those who no longer walk after the flesh but after the Spirit. The latter defines the difference between saints and sinners.

Kenneth Taylor in his *Living Bible* badly misconstrued this text (and, I am afraid, a number of others). The comfort here is not for a select group of Christians, *but for all.*

"All things work together (*sunergei)* for good..." The Greek could also be translated "He works all things together for good." In any case, the point is clear from the context that the Sovereign God so superintends our experience in conjunction with the intercession of the Spirit that everything works together for our ultimate good.

"Good" is to be understood in the eternal rather than the temporal perspective. In strictly temporal terms, not everything turns out to be good if good is defined by things like the overall balance between the subtraction of pain and the addition of pleasure. Good is to be defined in terms of whatever advances the work of redemption in us, whatever reproduces Christlikeness in us (v. 29), whatever fits us for the presence of God, and whatever draws us nearer to the goal that God has in mind for us. Good is whatever renders us more like God, more dependent upon God, more desirous of God, and more obedient to God. Good is *not* something that, in the end, winds up making us more successful or happier or healthier or richer in temporal terms.

"Work together (*sunergei*)..." God's providential ways are impenetrably complex and synergistic. They combine like the ingredients in a recipe to produce a certain food product. In the chemistry of divine providence, experiential ingredients mixed into our lives in certain proportions under heat combine to produce a result that is good in terms of advancing God's redemptive program in our lives.

In temporal terms, God's providence may result in our being poorer or sicker or lonelier than one would hope, but the promise is that God conspires to use everything He orders up for us to shape us into what He intended and fit us for His presence.

"All..." Everything has its place in God's wise plan. Corrie Ten Boom tells us how God used even the nuisance of a plague of fleas to deter the intrusion of harassing German guards in her barracks in a Nazi concentration camp, so God can use the most unexpected things as instruments of His sovereign purpose. For that reason, we give thanks in "everything."

"According to His purpose (*prothesin*)..." Verse 29 defines God's purpose, namely, that we should be conformed to the (moral) image of His Son. In short, Christlikeness is the objective. Elsewhere, it is expressed as His purpose that "we should be holy and without blame before Him" and "that we might grow up in all aspects into Him, who is head, even Christ," and that we might "attain... to the measure of the stature which belongs to the fullness of Christ," and that every man may be "complete in Christ." Our temporal happiness is not the mission; our everlasting holiness, which is the key to true bliss, is the purpose and program of God for our lives." Cranfield, I believe, misses the point when he defines God's purpose as His purpose of "mercy." [262] The question is, what is His mission of mercy?

An overriding motif of Paul's presentation of the gospel is the inviolable security or safety for those who have taken refuge in Christ in the ark of His justifying grace from the flood waters of God's judgment against sinners. That chord he strikes again and again.

We must remember that the alternative to the approach to God opened to men through the gospel is the avenue of law. On legal terms, man must strictly fulfill the law of God in all of its requirements or suffer the legal consequences. For a person coming to God on law terms, there is no possibility of salvation. No safety, no sense of security is possible. So, time and time again, Paul reverts to the built-in safety of the doctrine of grace. God has mercifully created for sinful men who will believe the gospel and embrace Christ as their Savior and Lord a fail-safe plan of salvation that has safeguards at every necessary point. It is safe and secure, not because we are now good enough to live up to the demands of the Law, but because our Sovereign God is gracious and able to make all things work together for good to those of us who, by His grace, have come to love Him, to those of us who have been called by Him according to His own sovereign purposes.

The rest of this chapter is devoted once again to accentuating that theme—the utter security of the man in Christ. "Be happy; don't worry; the game is rigged." The ark of grace is fail-safe. The only question is, are you in it?

> (8:29) *For whom He foreknew, He also predestined to become conformed to the image of His Son, that He might become the first-born among many brethren...*

"For" (*oti*)... The first question is, precisely what thought in the previous verse(s) does this text proceed to explain, for *oti* denotes a causal connection.

In verses 29–30, the apostle explains how we can be so sure that our Sovereign God is in control, in fact, was in control long before we ever knew He was involved in our lives and superintends the chemistry of our experience to gain the result that He had in mind for us before we ever knew Him.

Right now, we get hammered a lot as believers. Our outward circumstances are not regularly consistent with our position as sons of God. But we were saved in an attitude of hope. We knew then that today is not our day, that through many tribulations, we enter the kingdom of God. We must, with perseverance then, sit tight, keep up the good fight, and wait for God's time to set everything right. Meanwhile, there is a Helper for us in our afflictions and a comforting sense of security for us. The indwelling Holy Spirit intercedes for us in such a way that we can depend on the fact that no matter how crazy things seem to get, "all things work together for good to them who love God and are called according to His purpose."

This passage is intended to set you at peace, not only about your ultimate safety in Christ but also to set you at peace about the shaking and painful things that happen to you enroute before we come into our final inheritance. The thrust of this text is to remind us that God is always in control of the situation, that things are fine, and everything is on track and in order, even when it seems like life is going south.

Here let me inform the reader I am putting our forward momentum on a bit of a pause to focus on this word "foreknew." It absolutely critical at this point that we get it right. That is because so many good people have an emotional resistance to the notion of divine election that they go bonkers if we appear to be 'twisting' words to make the text read in a way favorable to the doctrine. I can understand that.

So, I need more than your casual attention to track with me on the meaning for "foreknew." It is not as simple as it looks. I want you to see how naturally the semantic range of the word 'know' shifts from simply 'know' to 'approve.'

However, to achieve clarity on this point, you will need to bring your full attention, footnotes and all. This is not brain surgery, but lack of focus can derail one enroute to the conclusion. To repeat, my goal is to show why it is that 'foreknew' does not mean in this context simply that God knew something beforehand. I am going to show that the word "foreknew" in this context can and does carry a meaning of "approve" (beforehand) or "choose" (beforehand), and that the latter senses are fully within the legitimate semantic range of the term.

Now that we all understand where I am headed, we launch our case.

"Foreknew" (*proegno* from *proginosko* = to know beforehand, in advance, then to choose beforehand)... This word can simply mean "to know [something] beforehand." Semantically speaking, it could speak of the *pre-vision* of God, as Murray puts it.[263] That is, it could refer to God's seeing or knowing something in advance.

The question is, does it? The semantic range of "know" in biblical (and classical Greek) usage is much broader than that. For instance, get this, both the Hebrew *yada* (=know) and the Greek *ginosko* are used in the sense of "to have sexual relations with." In classical Greek, the word (spelled *gignosko* at that time) includes such meanings as "to discern, distinguish, to form a judgment, to decree, etc."

My point is twofold: 1) words may have a range of potential meanings and may not be limited to one more common and familiar sense, and 2) the more familiar sense of a word is less decisive in determining its proper sense in any given occurrence *than the clues in the context.* Context, not a lexicon, is decisive. A lexicon tells us the accepted range of meaning, context is the ultimate referee about *the* meaning.

Now, in this case, there is one major clue that "foreknew" in this context *can't possibly have the sense of "those whom God had knowledge of in advance".* Why?

Well, God knows all things before they even exist, and He certainly knew all men before they came into being. Yet it is not true that those whom he knew about in advance, He predestined to become conformed to the image of His Son... and then called all those, then justified them and glorified the same. That would affirm the universal salvation of mankind, a doctrine which is contrary to the analogy of Scripture in general and the teaching of Romans in particular.[264] You see that clearly, I hope.

Can *ginosko* (know) mean "approved"? Does that fall within the range of its biblical usage? It does indeed. Behind its usage in that sense is the way its Hebrew correspondent *yada* is used. Get this too. When the OT was translated into Greek (the Septuagint version), *ginosko* was commonly the Greek substitute for *yada*.[265]

Let me provide two clear instances of this usage from the OT, and then I will cite other examples in the NT. The first is Psalm 1:6, "For the Lord knows the way of the righteous, but the way of the wicked will perish" (knows = *yada* in the Hebrew and *ginosko* in the Greek version), and Amos 3:2 (NIV), "You only have I chosen of all the families of the earth" ("*chosen*" = *yada* in the Hebrew and *ginosko* in the Greek version of the OT).

Clearly in Psalm 1:6, the poetic structure (antithetic parallelism) calls for a sense of "know" that is approximately opposite of the thought of condemnation in the second line of the couplet. The point, therefore, is not that the Lord is "aware" of the activities of the righteous. That would be a better point applied to the wicked but of relatively little comfort to the believer unless the idea of approval is wrapped up in "knows." And that is precisely the idea. Note also in the NASV, the editors have acknowledged this point in the margin, where their notation on verse 6 says, "Or, approves; or, has regard to."[266]

In the Amos passage, to take *yada* in the sense of simply "know" would result in a gross theological error. It would have God denying His own all-knowing character in saying "that you only I have known of all the families of the earth." God can hardly have said He was unaware of the existence of other nations! Clearly, the point is that Israel was the object of His special favor or approval. Seeing this clearly, the NIV translators rightly translated *yada* in the sense of "have chosen."

Now we will see the same sense found in NT usage. In 1 Corinthians 8:3, Paul writes:

"But if anyone loves God, he is known (*egnostai* from *ginosko*) by Him" (1 Cor 8:3). Obviously, it is theological nonsense for Paul to imply that God's knowledge of us is the consequence of our love for

Him. The converse would be that if we don't love God, He isn't aware of us... He doesn't know that we exist. That is absurd. What Paul means is that loving God is a badge of those whom God knows in the sense of recognizing or approving.

If the reader is tracking, I hope you are seeing that the Greek verb 'know' and its Hebrew equivalent 'yada' in some contexts 1) can have more than one meaning, as in all languages, and that 2) in these contexts cited, to translate them 'know' not only misses the point badly but 3) theologically, to do so would be absurd.

Similarly, in Matthew 7:23, Jesus says of those who, in the end, prove to be false disciples: "Then I will profess unto them I never knew you..." That "I never knew you" is not an admission of ignorance of their existence or of their names and habits. Rather it implies that His favor or approval or special regard was not set upon them. In other words, they had no special standing with Him.

In the preceding illustrations, it is a virtual lock that the Hebrew or Greek words *must,* in context, mean something other than simply "know" or "be aware of," and something akin to "approve or choose."

In my final example, it is not necessary that it means something else, but "approved beforehand" yields a superior sense in context. And that, hermeneutically, is the best option. In 1 Peter 1:20, the apostle, speaking of Christ as the Christian's Passover lamb, says, "He was *foreknown* (*proegnosmenou,* a participial form from *proginosko)* before the foundation of the world, but has appeared in these last times for the sake of you." The picture is that of One, who, like the Passover victim, was *chosen* or *selected* or *approved* beforehand, but sacrificed for us in these last times, that is, at the appointed time.

It is now clear I trust that we are not foisting upon "foreknow" any alien meaning when affirming for it the sense of "pre-approved" or "chosen beforehand." It can mean that when the context requires it, and this one seems to demand it. The context has to do with a class of persons who enjoy God's favor or approval. What makes it even more decisive is Romans 11:2, where Paul avows of unbelieving Israel: "God has not rejected His people whom He foreknew, (i.e., previously chose)." Proof that is in verses 5–6, namely, the existence of a blessed remnant according to God's gracious choice, that is, the existence of an *elect* remnant, proves that God's choice of Israel has not been jettisoned.

Now our pause finished, we resume.

Now what follows is intended to reinforce our sense of security and safety in the plan and purpose of God. For every single one of those upon whom God set His favor *in advance,* (that's the idea of election), He predetermined what He was going to accomplish in their lives.

"Predestined" (*proorisen* from *proorizo* = to decide beforehand)... *horizo* means (among other things) to "determine," "appoint," "fix," "set." Here, "predetermined" catches the sense.

God has a 'project' under way in our lives. It's called "salvation" or "redemption." Salvation, I reiterate, is a *process* as well as an *event.* It is an event in the sense that it has a definite starting point... a time when we become a child of God... a point of entry after which all the rest of the *program* is guaranteed.

What God has in mind for us is not evolution but transformation. What God has in store for us is not a blind continuum of gradual genetic mutation in the human race on into the indefinite eons that man presumes upon. No, what God has in mind is a grand and cosmic consummation that, at any moment, will issue in the ineffable glorification of His transformed people and the regeneration of deformed nature, a new heaven and a new earth and a casting out and trashing of everything that does not belong to the new order. *He has determined it in advance.* His holy purpose is fixed, and no force in heaven or earth can repeal or alter it.

"Conformed" (*summorphous* from *summorphos*)... At the core of His purpose is the determination, decided in eternity past (Eph. 1:4), that God would break the hold of sin upon us and reshape us gradually into the moral likeness (*eikonos*) of His Son. His aim is to reproduce Christ in us, to form the spirit of Christ in our characters. That project will be accelerated, compressed, and consummated by the purifying sight of His glorious presence upon His return (1 John 3:2).

"Firstborn" (*prototokon*)... This does not mean here (anymore than it does in Colossians 1:15) that the Son of God is a created and non-eternal Being, inferior to the Father and something less than God. Cults like to latch onto language like this to make their case for the sub-deity of Christ. This is an expression that refers to the heirship and the right of the firstborn in Hebrew society to inherit a double share of the Father's property.[267]

Jesus is God's Son in a unique and preeminent sense that none of us are. He is God's *monogenes* (unique) Son. As such, He comes before us in preeminence, that is, in dignity, in honor, and glory. The purpose of God from eternity past has been to surround His glorified Son with a host of other sons purchased by His blood and made like Him, to share His eternal joy and glory.

(8:30) *And whom He predestined, these He also called; and whom He called, these He also justified; and whom He justified, these He also glorified.*

"Called" (*ekalesen*)... Every single one that God chose and predestined to be conformed to Christ, He called. This refers to what theologians speak of as God's *effectual* call as opposed to His general call, whereby through the gospel, He invites them to repent and to be saved through faith in Christ. We know that because all these relationships are one-for-one... everyone called is also justified. In other words, all those in the class of the called turn up in the class of the justified and so on. The boundaries of each category are coextensive.

What is referred to is what Jesus spoke about in the Gospel of John in 6:37, 44, 45; 10:16, 27. We are called for conformity to Christ; we are called to fellowship with God's Son as co-heirs (1 Cor. 1:9). This calling is irrevocable (11:29).

Everyone called is also justified. All barriers to God's full acceptance are removed. We are fully pardoned, and the spotless righteousness of God's Son is imputed to the rest of His children.

Everyone justified He also "glorified." The puzzle is, why the historical as opposed to the future tense?

The answer, I believe, lies in the mind of God. What is future to us, in the mind of God has been settled in His purpose from eternity past. It is a done thing in the mind of God. The past tense has the effect of drawing our attention in a fresh way to the certainty of God's purposes for us. We call this kind of expression a prolepsis, that is, spoken of in anticipation as accomplished.

For example, a political candidate will say, "As president, I will do so and so." Well, he is not even elected yet. Proleptically, or by anticipation, he speaks of himself as doing something that is still in the future or maybe in his (or her) case, not at all.

Paul now brings his exposition of the gospel to a triumphant conclusion. He shows us in the final analysis the completeness of God's saving provision wherein there is total immunity from condemnation. Secondly, he reassures us of the inalienable love of Christ for us despite every circumstance that might stand in our way or appear to contradict it.

(8:31) *What then shall we say to these things? If God is for us, who is against us?*

The bottom line of all that he has said is this: God has hedged us up on every side with a fail-safe salvation. He is for us. If God Himself is for us, who could possibly stand against us and successfully oppose the consummation of our redemption? Who could put any block in our path that would defeat God?

(8:32) *He who did not spare His own Son, but delivered Him up for us all, how will He not also with Him freely give us all things.*

This is an argument from the greater to the less. If God has done the greater thing, He surely will not fail on the lesser thing.

If it is true that God cared for us so much that He spared not His only begotten Son but delivered Him up to death on the cross to put us in a right relation with Himself and make us members of the family of God, why would He not finish the job? Why would He sell short, so to speak, after spending so much to save us? What it cost to justify us is indescribably greater than the expense of glorifying us. How can anyone doubt that He won't freely donate anything and everything necessary to bring our faith to the finish line and glorify us with Christ? Logic says God will pull out all the stops to completely bring us into our inheritance as co-heirs of Christ.

We are assured of salvation, not because of the tenacity of our love and faithfulness, but because of His.

"His own Son..." that is, Christ, His preeminent Son, whose sonship is unique in that this Son is of the same nature, substance, power, and glory with the Father.

"Us all..." In this context, this phrase refers to the elect, but that does not mean that the sacrifice of Christ is not sufficient for "whosoever." In practice, only the elect respond out of true faith to the gospel and avail themselves of God's work of justification, though the Scripture affirms its sufficiency for all (whosoever).

(8:33–34) *Who will bring a charge against God's elect? God is the one who justifies; who is the one who condemns? Christ Jesus is He who died, yes, rather who was raised, who is at the right hand of God, who also intercedes for us.*

Do we in our frailty and weaknesses fear being vulnerable to indictment? Does the great Enemy of our faith sow seeds of doubt and guilt?

From the Law? No fear. Our transgressions have been borne by Christ. Its demand for justice has been served in His sacrificial death for us. Our sins cannot, therefore, condemn us. He Himself took our condemnation in His own body. The perfect obedience that the law of God demands has been fulfilled by Him and imputed to us through faith. In Him, its righteous requirements are fully satisfied.

From Satan? No fear. So what if he slanders us and advertises our every misstep and shortcoming to high heaven? God is the Supreme Court of One. He has declared us justified by faith. From His gracious verdict, there is no appeal... no double jeopardy.

From the accusations of our conscience? The fact that our conscience has not forgotten does not change the fact that God has forgiven those in Christ. Our conscience may broadcast our guilt in our souls, but Christ carried our guilt to the grave. And His resurrection proves that God has acknowledged the debt as paid in full. The accusations of our conscience should warn us of discipline and correct us, but they can never condemn us and disinherit us.

Whatever may be charged against us from any source... from the Law... from the conscience... from the enemy, no matter how valid our guilt, if any man is in Christ, he is sheltered from any condemnation. Christ not only paid our debt in full, but more than that, if more were needed, he stands as our Advocate before the throne. He is our Mediator and, figuratively speaking, makes intercession for us. I say "figuratively" because the case is not as though the Father were in a constant state of judicial ambivalence about us ("I condemn them-I condemn them not" etc.) or as if the Son is always having to literally plead the merits of His blood to deliver us from wrath on account of our sins.

The reality is that in His Person, as the crucified and resurrected Mediator, He represents before the Father a standing Testimony to the atoning sacrifice for sin made once for all. He "makes intercession for us" not in the form of verbal pleas to a reluctant and inconstant Father, but in His presence before the throne of justice. His being there at the Father's right hand is all the advocacy we need. His presence is a silent but everlasting statement that the price is paid in full, for His presence before the throne is a living receipt that the Father accepted His payment for our sins as our substitute.

> (8:35) *Who shall separate us from the love of Christ? Shall tribulation, or distress, or persecution, or famine, or nakedness, or peril, or sword?*

This, as in chapter 5:5, speaks of His gratuitous love for us, not our love for Him. Verse 39 seems to make this clear as does the parallel passage in chapter 5. In terms of his emphasis on the security of the believer, the pertinent point is not our love for Him but His for us.

"A father's or mother's love is independent of the attractiveness of its object, and often in spite of its deformity." [268]

He mentions these terrors because not only have they been the common lot of believers throughout history and things we should continue to expect to come our way, but they would also seem to be "wedges" that would drive believers off the ground of faith and cause us to turn our backs on God and lose our place in His affection.

That such is indeed the norm for believers even the psalmist (44:22 LXX) laments.

(8:36) *Just as it is written, "For Your sake we are being put to death all day long; we were considered as sheep to be slaughtered."*

We might say less poetically: They chew us up and spit us out; our life is cheap. All because we belong to You, the world makes us pay every day in some miserable way.

(8:37) *But in all these things we overwhelmingly conquer through Him who loved us.*

Ironically, that is not the effect. Instead of destroying our faith and driving us away from God and into the arms of wrath, God makes it strengthen our faith and our place in His affections. God has this thing wired so that everything works together for good, and nothing can separate us from His love.

He uses even these extremities so that we soar to greater heights of faith rather than wither away in unbelief and despair. The same threats that make a coward run cause a brave man to stand up and fight. So also, the adversities that knock the pins out from underneath a mere professor will strengthen the legs of a real believer and render him tougher than ever.

(8:38–39) *For I am convinced that neither death, nor life, nor angels, nor principalities, nor things present, nor things to come, nor powers, nor height, nor depth, nor any created thing, shall be able to separate us from the love of God, which is in Christ Jesus our Lord.*

To crown his affirmation of our safety and to render it more impressive, the apostle ransacks the whole order of creation in its various dimensions and finds nothing that could interdict the love of Christ for us.

The big surprise (and the most offensive) premise in this argument was his insistence that the Jews, no less than the Gentiles, are lost and in need of the pardon that God offers to sinners in Christ. The Jews need saving as badly as the Gentiles.

Overview of the Argument from Chapter 4-11

Having proved that point, the apostle proceeded to show that justification before God is not based on legal performance (or the basis of meritorious law-keeping) but strictly based on God's pure grace through faith in Christ. He went on to show that this concept of justification on the ground of faith (as opposed to justification on the ground of legal performance) was completely in keeping with the testimony of the OT and, secondly, that this free gift based on faith was for Gentiles as well as Jews, a real sticking point with the latter. He used Abraham, whom he shows to be not only the spiritual father of believing Jews but also the spiritual father of believing Gentiles, as a classic model of saving faith.

Abraham was asked in His day to trust in the God who has the power to raise the dead, and in our day, we are asked to trust in God in that same character when we are directed to put our trust in Christ whom He raised from the dead. The point was especially pertinent to the Jews because they could not accept a crucified Messiah and, therefore, would not buy into His resurrection. That is the specific point at which God throws down the gauntlet to them and to us—the resurrection. Faith does not exist until it comes to terms with the fact of Jesus's bodily resurrection. That is to say, that the crucified Savior rose from the dead and still lives at the right hand of the Father in heaven.

Next, the apostle proceeds to expound upon the absolute security and safety (picking up on 4:16) of this justification-by-faith scheme of salvation (vis a vis the insecurity of Jewish efforts to be accepted or justified before God on the basis of legal merit.) Paul shows us that we are hedged about on every side with saving benefits that anchor us and secure the final outcome. In this process, he appeals to an analogy between those in Adam and those in Christ. The point is this: just as those in Adam are certain (by virtue of Adam's disobedience being imputed to them) to share his death, in the same way, those in Christ (by virtue of His obedience imputed to them) share in His life. Hence, we are saved by virtue of position, not by virtue of our performance.

That raised an important question about why God bothered to give the Law. If people are condemned (die) because they are in Adam and are justified (imparted life) because they are in Christ, the revelation of the Law seems superfluous. It appears not to explain either life or death. So where does it fit in?

The answer is that God revealed the Law to Moses to awaken sinful humans, that is, to sensitize us to our transgressive nature. In other words, before a person will cast himself on the mercy of God and apply for salvation by grace through faith, he needs to discover his moral bankruptcy before the law of God. That was (and is) the primary function of God's law, that is, to expose our guilt and drive us away from any presumption that we are okay and point us to the arms of God's mercy, where we will find His forgiving grace (1 Timothy 1:9-10).

One might infer (wrongly) from this that the believer's security in grace bestows upon him a license to indulge freely in sin, since he no longer has the condemnation of the Law to fear.

On the contrary, the apostle shows in chapter 6 that, in accepting God's free grace, the believer renounces sin and dedicates himself to live according to the glory of God. He, in effect, died to sin, not only in the sense that its penalty was removed, but its enslaving power was broken through his union with the power of the resurrected Christ. The believer under grace has not only the intention of living in obedience to God but also incentives to depart from the ways of death.

If any illusion remains that somehow the Law promotes holiness better than grace, that somehow being under law is more likely to produce godly living than being under grace, Paul devotes chapter 7 to exploding the myth. He shows, first, that the believer's emancipation from the Law is not only entirely kosher, but it also affirms that it was totally necessary. His point is not merely that grace <u>can</u> promote holiness but, more importantly, <u>only</u> grace can. The truth is, contrary to Jewish thinking, being <u>under law</u> is a condition that can't help but result in moral bankruptcy and frustration.

He shows how the Law functions effectively in exposing our sinfulness, but it fails miserably in producing obedience. Yet the root problem is not with the Law per se. The flaw in the Law scheme is *with us*, that is, in our flesh. He then illustrates that futility from his own past experience as a high-minded Jew intent on keeping the Law. What he discovered was that his good intentions inevitably fell short of the mark, a mark that intellectually he genuinely approved. That showed that the problem (the inability to secure obedience) was not any flaw in the Law itself, but one that resided in him. It demonstrated that the Law, with nothing better than the flesh to perform it, was a moral equation inevitably doomed to failure.

By contrast, the reason believers are so secure and run no risk of condemnation is because God solved that problem. Victory was achieved when He sent His life-giving Spirit into our hearts to set us free from our enslavement to the death-bringing law of sin operative when we were under law (i.e., still in the flesh). This solution was rendered possible by the atoning sacrifice of Christ, which dealt with sin's guilt and enabled God to accept us and indwell us through His Spirit.

Paul explains that the Spirit is the decisive and victorious factor in setting us free from the power of sin. Water seeks its own level (John 3:6), and the man in the flesh cannot rise above it, even with the advantage of the revealed Law. The man of the Spirit is led and morally empowered by the indwelling Spirit of God.

But doesn't the suffering of saints take some of the bloom off that rosy picture? No way. Suffering is an inevitable part of the Christian experience as we await the consummation of our salvation. And what we have is not all there is; we were saved in a posture of great expectations. Thus, we must, with perseverance (of faith), await God's time to fulfill them.

Meanwhile, we need not feel insecure, for God is at work in our lives to accomplish His eternal purposes and, in the process, to make everything conspire for our eternal good. No matter what He lets loose on our lives in the interim; nothing can challenge or alter His verdict of justification. He will allow nothing to separate us from His love.

Now a great question lingers. The train of God's redemptive message, if one believes Paul's message, has come to Israel, and relatively few believed it. That train has now more or less moved on to the rest of the world, leaving behind the majority of his countrymen still lost in unbelief. Suddenly, God's chosen people don't seem to be so chosen after all. His promises of a great future for this nation would appear to have failed.

Is that the case? Did God's purposes for Israel fail? If not, how do we explain it? These next three chapters (9–11) are called a *theodicy*, that is, a vindication of God. Paul sets about to show that any appearance of failure in God's purposes is in appearance only, not reality.

Indeed, on the part of the nation Israel, there has been a big-time spiritual failure, but not any on God's part. In fact, the promises of God never did, Paul will prove, extend to the entire physical seed. The truth is, God's promises to this nation were always based on the principle of sovereign selectivity, a selectivity not based on human merit but His sovereign grace. And they always applied only to a remnant chosen by grace, Jew or Gentile.

Israel blew it by its stubborn determination to seek righteousness on its terms rather than His. The Gentiles are being saved because they have submitted to God on His terms. Israel is indeed devoutly religious but in a wrong and futile way. God's way is by faith, and that stipulation applies to all people.

Israel cannot complain that it did not get the message. The Jews had every chance to hear, for God sent them the message redundantly. The problem is, as a whole, they simply have not believed it. Even from their Scriptures, they had every clue to recognize what God was doing.

Even though the majority has missed the boat, still, God's elective grace is at work while His judicial blinding is in evidence of Israel's unbelief. In short, everything that is happening is consistent with what God has always done and predicted would continue to be.

Yet in the end, there is still to be a work of salvation among the Jews on a grand scale. They will again be grafted into his holy tree and flourish. Meanwhile, let us all learn the lesson: Kindness to those who continue in His kindness and severity to those who turn away in unbelief. The section closes with a paean of praise for the inscrutable wisdom of God.

---

[230] Had Paul been describing a regenerate state in 7:14ff, the transition would be quite puzzling logically. In that case we would expect him to weigh in with Christ's provision for the penalty of sin, reassuring us that we are "covered by the blood" no matter how much we fail. "Therefore there is now no condemnation because Christ has made atonement for our sins"—or something to that effect.

But that is not the connection at all. Rather the whole discussion revolves around the way God has conquered through grace the dominating power of sin that held us in its grip under the law when we were still unregenerate (after the flesh).

[231] In all languages (at least the ones I know) words usually have more than one sense. Context is the final arbiter of its meaning in any given case. The term *nomos* (law) can refer to 1) the OT revelation (Romans 2:15) or 2) the Decalogue (Ten Commandments) per se (Romans 13:8) or 3) the whole corpus of legal requirements, including ceremonial and civil codes, (Phil. 3:6) or 3) a principle or phenomenon known to prevail under certain conditions (Romans 3:27). Here Paul uses the word in the latter sense.

[232] Sin remains with us; it is still a "power" within. The difference now is that it is no longer an *enslaving* power. We are free from it in that sense. Moreover, the superior power of the Spirit is now resident within us. We are still *temptable* and we still fall back on old reflexes in response to sin's solicitations. But the sin principle is no longer sovereign. We can now say, "No," and fulfill righteousness. Now we sin as volunteers.

[233] Murray, *NICNT: Epistle to the Romans*, 277. See also p. 278 for judicial use to the word "condemnation" with reference to the power of sin.

[234] Paul, with his theological scalpel, does not always distinguish concepts always as surgically and cleanly as we might prefer. Hence, reference to the work of

justification, it seems to me, sometimes is used almost metonymically (cause put for the effect) for sanctification.

[235] Occasionally I will be communicating with my Executive Pastor about something I wanted done. Frequently when I bring one of those subjects up, he will smile and say emphatically, "It's done! It's all taken care of." He doesn't in every case intend to convey to me that everything has already happened, that the outcome is complete, but merely that in executive fashion all the wheels are turning, and the outcome is assured by his actions.

In that sense some things in the biblical frame of reference are "already, but not yet." The appropriate action has been taken to assure an intended outcome. We can speak of that outcome as though it were already done, for it is now in process and God will let nothing stand in the way of its completion. That, I think, is what we have here. At the strictly legal level, God's law is already fulfilled to the letter in Christ. At the practical level, it is now being fulfilled in the spiritual sense as opposed to the merely external sense (we walk in the love of God). At the comprehensive level it is God's purpose to cause us to fulfill all His will (Phil. 2:13) and that empowerment is already in place and working toward its appointed end.

[236] Analogous to the idea of enmity towards the law of God is the idea in Proverbs of "hating" one's child by the refusal to discipline him. It is not an affective word, but a functional word. To fail to discipline a child is the functional equivalent of hating that child. The result from failure to discipline will be one and the same as if one's despised the youth.

Likewise, one does not have to have an emotional antipathy toward God to qualify as having "enmity" toward Him. Failure to obey Him is the functional equivalent of hostility toward God.

The man under law in chapter 7 cognitively had a high opinion of God's revealed law, nurtured from his youth. Cognitively and perhaps emotionally he embraced it just as many sinners nod approvingly toward the Bible today and even think people ought to live "by the Book" and profess to admire those who do. Yet their failure to do so, yea, their downright inability to do what they approve and endorse proves that there is something anti-God in their "system" that is the functional equal of "enmity."

[237] This point the Apostle is stressing is very significant considering the Pentecostal and charismatic insistence on the need for a so-called second work of grace, another baptism of the Spirit (beyond the first one that 1 Cor. 12:13 speaks of), to empower the believer for service.

Any fair reading of this text and in fact of Romans 6–8 makes it clear that Paul sees all believers *empowered* for Christian living. That is the whole point. We are now able to live for God; we are set free from the binding shackles of the law of sin.

Paul certainly doesn't leave any impression in this passage that there is any deficiency, anything lacking in our capacity to get on with it, that there is something major the believer still needs to catch up with. In love but in truth I say to these brethren whom I believe to be misguided and misguiding on this issue, that what we really need to catch up with is not a second work of grace, but a first work of understanding Paul.

Can you imagine Paul leaving out such an important item of theology and Christian experience? They have built a whole movement around this premise, yet where is it in Paul? The Book of Acts must be interpreted in light of the explanatory theological content of the Epistles. Yet it is not there. Surely if it would be anywhere it would appear in Romans 8. However, the impression here is that the believer is fully equipped and ready for the road.

Let us please, please be done with our carnal love affair with the sensational, turn our backs on the habit of canonizing experience and people's doubtful interpretations thereof, reject these disreputable characters who set themselves up as contemporary prophets and return to the bedrock of the Scriptures for our religious authority. "To the law and the testimony! If they speak not according to this word, it is because they have no dawn (light)" (Isa. 8:20).

[238] "Paul's thought is. . . that through the indwelling of the Spirit Christ Himself is present to us, the indwelling of the Spirit being 'the manner of Christ's dwelling in us.'" Cranfield, *ICC: Romans, Vol. I*, 389.

[239] So also, Cranfield on this point.

[240] Hodge, *Epistle to the Romans*, 259. Hodge adds: "It is not inconsistent with the perfection of the redemption of Christ, that its benefits are not received in their fullness the moment we believe. We remain subject to the pains, the sorrows, the trials of life, and the necessity of dying, although partakers of the life of which he is the author. That life, which is imparted in regeneration, is gradually developed until it has its full consummation at the resurrection" (p. 259). It is no doubt this very tension between the perfection promised and the present incompleteness of our redemption that sometimes disappoints our expectations, that the Apostle speaks to from verse 17ff.

[241] Technically men die because Adam's sin was imputed to them; but this legality only anticipated the consequence of the Fall. Adam's nature, corrupted by transgression, was in the mysterious genetics of fallenness, transmitted to the race so that sinners by imputation always prove to be sinners by nature fully deserving the curse of death imposed on Adam and his seed.

[242] Webster's New Collegiate Dictionary

[243] Smyth, *Greek Grammar*, 436.

[244] Cranfield, *ICC: Romans Vol. 1*, 394.

[245] Arndt & Gingrich, *Greek-English Lexicon of the New Testament*, 704.

[246] Smyth, *Greek Grammar*, 421.

[247] I once had a man in my first church right out of seminary about whose relationship to God I had some serious reservations. Not because of this, but consistent with it I noted that every time someone called upon Him to pray, he jolted my spirit when he began his chilly prayers with a distant and unfamiliar address:

"God,..." God is God, alright, but Paul says the child of God knows Him on more familiar and intimate terms. We do not balk at calling Him "Father" in the tenderest way. In fact, the Spirit turns our spirit in that direction. It is a reflex of the Christian heart.

I would however caution those who would "daddy-ify" this near-untranslatable word. That excess runs in the same vein as calling His people God's "kids". In my mind, both have a grossly trivializing effect that diminishes His majesty on one hand and children of their royal dignity on the other. God can be intimate with us without using terms to express it which debase his otherness.

Paul's point is that God is not some awful, dreadful, distant, scowling, wrathful, indignant, stalking Other who threatens every minute to boil over on the sins of the wicked and smoke them. Rather our hearts teach us that we can come to him and address him affectionately and acceptably as our "Father."

[248] Discipline is a routine, but severer form of reassurance which is not always recognized as such (cf. Hebrews 12:6).

[249] Cranfield, *ICC: Romans Vol 1*, 407.

[250] Commentators (see Murray, *NICNT: Epistle to the Romans Vol. 1*, 301, fn. 23) have debated on the precise logical connection. Some see Paul's accentuation of the certainty of our future glory, other simply the futurity of it while others, like myself, see the point as highlighting the greatness of that glory. It seems to me that the latter connection makes better sense in context than the others.

[251] Murray, *NICNT: Epistle to the Romans Vol. 1*, 302.

[252] This explains incidentally how it is that on one hand creation is so incredibly ordered, revealing the hand of a Creator, while on the other there are aberrations and there is, as it were, a literal running down of creation. Creation is simply much too great, too complex, too precise, intricate, interdependent to postulate blind chance as its "author". That explanation is simply the silly choice of minds whose steadfast refusal to acknowledge their Creator leaves them no alternative but to resign themselves to an explanation that insults their intelligence (and ours). Yet, for all that, something is clearly wrong in such a fine 'clock.' That, in fact, is the very point that we are supposed to take our cue from.

All the destructive forces of nature are providential reminders of that the Creation is under the curse, that we are under sin and that the whole thing needs to be fixed, beginning with sinful man. That's the message.

[253] Cranfield, *ICC: Romans Vol 1*, 214.

254 One of the fallacies of some environmentalists is the myth that Mother Nature is perfect and harmonious in all her ways, that man is, so to speak, the fly in the ointment. What we need to do is get in phase with her. Well, the Bible teaches us that Nature, for all its wonders, for all the fingerprints of the Creator left amply in evidence upon her, still has its nose somewhat out of joint. All is not perfect with Mother Nature either. This myth is a cousin to the illusion about man that in his primitive condition without the socializing effects of culture, he was pure and uncorrupted, the Noble Savage.

255 Cranfield, *ICC: Romans Vol. 1*, 418.

256 Murray, *NICNT: Epistle to the Romans Vol. 1*, 309.

257 Cranfield, *ICC: Romans Vol. 1*, 421.

258 Christ also intercedes for us at the right hand of God. His office work seems to relate to the accusations of the Enemy against us. He is our Great High Priest who presents Himself as an atonement for our sins. The Spirit intercedes for us on behalf of our necessities on the path of salvation.

259 If the Spirit intercedes for us and His petitions are perfect, why should we bother? Is prayer on our part not a redundancy? No, we pray because prayer expresses a spirit of dependency on God, we pray because in prayer we offer not only petition, but praise to Him, we pray because petition provides God an opportunity to confirm His activity in our behalf. It is therefore crucial that we pray, even if we sometimes pray amiss. In omitting prayer, we would deny to God what rightly belongs to Him and deny to ourselves one of the mightiest stimulants of faith and growth.

260 See also Hodge, *Epistle to the Romans*, 279.

261 One says to his wife when he is late for dinner: "Honey, I was held up by a wreck on the freeway." She responds: "I understand the situation. Don't worry about it."

262 Cranfield, *ICC: Romans Vol. 1*, 430.

263 Murray, *NICNT: Epistle to the Romans Vol. 1*, 315.

264 No, no, someone objects. The word means "to know or be aware beforehand that people would accept the grace of God." Well, that predicates something more significant of the word "foreknew" than is present in this text. "Those" is the predicate of the verb. It is unqualified, except by the idea that "those" is a class co-extensive with "those whom He predestinated to become conformed. . ." By qualifying *those* with the modifying thought of "would respond to the grace of God," is content imposed on the text that is not in the text. The only way that is justified is in cases where an idea is clearly implied in the context but left to the reader to supply. Paul would not likely leave such a thought unsupplied for the simple reason it is not clearly demanded by the context.

So why do people add that notion to the predicate? Either because they are linguistically unsophisticated and think that a word that most commonly means simply "know" must for that very reason mean "know" here or because it is necessary to escape the theology of the other alternatives.

The alternatives are either (1) that it refers to mankind in general (which we have seen is theologically impossible) or (2) "foreknew" means "approved beforehand" which is emotionally impossible (to those who eschew the idea of divine election).

[265] The transition from the idea of "to know" to the meaning "to approve" is natural. From the idea of "knowing" we move to the thought of "recognizing" someone or something. From there it is an easy step to push its semantic range out a little further from the sense of "recognition" to "taking notice of," "regarding" and "acknowledging" in the sense of conferring one's approval upon. We see that movement even in English. Somebody inquires about some business, group, or entity that we know nothing about and want to know if it's legit. We ask some informed agent or agency. "Oh, yeah, we know them." Depending on the inflection, the idea conveyed by implication is that they are recognized in the field, they are approved in the thing they do. What does it mean when a school is said to be "accredited"? It means that they are approved and that means that some official body has recognized them. We get the idea of "recognizing" from the idea of "knowing." So, you can see we get from the root sense of "knowing" by natural steps of extension to the notion of "recognizing" in the sense of approving.

[266] See also Brown, Driver, and Briggs, *Hebrew and English Lexicon of the Old Testament*, 394.

[267] See this connection in Gen. 43:33, esp. Deut. 21:15-17, 2 Chron. 21:3, and esp. Psa. 89:27, a Messianic passage.

[268] Hodge, *Epistle to the* Romans, 291.

Romans Chapter 9

(9:1–2) I am telling the truth in Christ, I am not lying, my conscience bearing me witness in the Holy Spirit, that I have great sorrow and unceasing grief in my heart.

What Paul is about to say is incredible. Though he was himself a Jew and at one time very advanced in the ranks of Judaism, a man of learning and standing among his countrymen at that time, from the time of his conversion he was viewed as a major threat and enemy of the Jews... a traitor of the first rank. They detested him and assumed he detested them and would seek their harm and not their good.

That is where they were wrong. Paul was completely misunderstood.[269] Everything he did, he did because he loved his countrymen and longed for their salvation with a passion neither they nor we can comprehend to this hour. Knowing how his ministry was misconstrued by the Jews and that his writings would fall into their hands (as he must have hoped), he appeals to the Spirit of God to bear witness to the truth of his feelings of grief for their lost condition.

"In this preface he disentangles himself from the false suspicion of hostility toward the Jews. Since the subject merited an oath, and since he saw that his affirmation would otherwise scarcely be credited in face of this already conceived prejudice, he swears that he is speaking the truth."[270]

(9:3) For I could wish that I myself were accursed, separated from Christ for the sake of my brethren, my kinsmen according to the flesh.

This passionate concern for the spiritual welfare of his countrymen reminds us of Moses, another great servant of God (Exod. 33:32). Paul is saying that if he could bear their inevitable curse for them, if he could take their place and his nation could be saved in his stead, he would accept that—yet knowing that such is not possible in the purposes of God. His concern is that they might appreciate that his attitude toward them did not resemble theirs toward him. Everything he did was driven by an almost ineffable passion for their salvation, a passion that would pay the ultimate price for their redemption were it possible.

"My brethren, my kinsmen according to the flesh..." His truest kinsmen are his spiritual brethren in Christ, but Paul is not reluctant to own his Jewishness and call those "brethren" who share his physical descent.

> (9:4) *Who are the Israelites, to whom belongs the adoption as sons and the glory and the covenants and the giving of the Law and the temple service and the promises...*

The tragedy of Israel's lostness is accentuated by her wealth of spiritual advantages and privileges that should have vaulted the Jews to the forefront of the kingdom of God but instead, through their unbelief, were wasted. Hence, the majority of the nation was (and remains) now shut out of their kingdom.

I daresay that most of us know little of this kind of overwhelming love for the lost. We care but, in most cases, not with a caring that could honestly make this statement. I do not condemn us for lacking a passion that almost transcends understanding but simply remark 1) that such a model ought to profoundly humble all of us who fancy ourselves to have "topped-out" in Christian maturity, reawakening us to great new levels of possibility and aspiration in Christ and 2) that more than anything else, it is being possessed of the love of Christ that drives *true* Christian service, that purifies our motives, and that relieves our labors of carnal distortions that insinuate themselves into our work under its auspices and almost guarantees a godly impact. In short, it was not his great intellectual endowments (though considerable) but his passion that God used in Paul to enable this one man to kick such a dent in human history.

This observation raises the natural question about what it takes for us to grow in the love of Christ; what it takes for his passion to become our passion and drive us. The answer is not that hard. Growing in grace is growing in Christlikeness. The secret of growing in Christlikeness is knowing God. To know God is to love God, and to love God is to love what He loves. Those who know Him best love Him the most and enter most fully into His purposes and passions. Knowing God begins with knowing His Word, then doing His will as revealed in His Word. We learn God, if you please, by doing His will. In short, intimacy comes with obedience, and with intimacy comes a heart that is on the same "page" with the Spirit of God.

Paul's model reminds this pastor that although, by the grace of God, I am not what I used to be, I am still not anything near what I should be or want to be. That humbles me, yet it encourages me to realize that Paul put his pants on one leg at a time just like I do (as did Moses), that neither was super-human and that, by the grace of God, I can still move much higher to the summit of divine possibilities by the all-sufficient grace of God. The thing that most holds us back is not limitation but *aspiration* and all-out intention.

Paul underscores the magnitude of the calamity by cataloguing the opportunities and advantages the Jews have squandered.[271]

"The adoption (*yiothesia*)..." a legal technical term for adoption, here used in a religious sense. The NASV translators err in adding "as sons," for Israel _as a nation_ was adopted by God as his _son_ (Deut. 7:6–8). God chose Israel as a holy nation, and that election still stands (11:29). He did not, however, adopt or elect _each one_ of the individuals who comprise that nation. So, the NASV translation of _yiothesia_ is misleading at that point. Were that the case, it would imply that adopted (or elected) persons were dis-adopted or dis-elected. That is just the opposite of the point Paul intends to make.

God took the sovereign initiative to establish a paternal relationship between Himself and Israel, to be their provider and protector and guide.

"The glory" refers to God's manifestations of His presence among His people throughout their history, but especially during their wilderness wanderings. The movements of the nation were signaled by the cloud by day, which transmuted itself to a pillar of fire by night and also by the so-called Shekinah ("glory"), which, in the sacred tent, enveloped the Holy of Holies.

"The covenants..." The plural doubtless has in view not only the covenant established between God and Israel at Sinai, where He condescended to be their God, and they, in turn, consented to be His people and to honor His Law, which He revealed to them there through Moses, but has reference also to the Abrahamic and Davidic covenants as well as all the renewals thereof at different intervals.

God had "signed on" on their behalf and vested the nation with many precious promises. On their part, all that was required was to believe God and respond appropriately. As a whole, they failed on their part.

"The giving of the Law (*nomothesia*)" that is, the legislation. There was no reason for Israel to stumble with respect to God's will. They did not have to scout the heavens or plumb the depths of the sea but simply respond to what was set before them. This reminds them that God gave them the unique advantage of objective revelation as to His will and all that was necessary to please Him. They did not have to speculate, just cooperate (Deut. 30:11–14).

Moreover, the Law was for their good, their benefit. Obedience would enrich their lives; disobedience would destroy them. Divine guidance in living was an enormous asset, but in following a course of superficial legalism, they wasted it (Deut. 10:12–13; 6:24).

"The temple service" (*latreia*), literally, the service, referring especially to the sacrificial ritual surrounding the tabernacle (and later the temple) and all the worship attendant to it. The term possibly could be even broader in conception, but that is its core.

The advantage of this worship was not only that it was divinely prescribed, guiding Israel in the right way to approach God, but also beneficial in its pedagogical aspect. That is, the sacrificial system was freighted with important messages about man's approach to God, such as the fact that without the shedding of blood, there is no remission for sin, such as the fact that an acceptable sacrifice to God in remitting sin was a lamb without spot and blemish. Indicators such as these should have been a great "jump-start" in pointing the Jews to the need of a better sacrifice than those offered under the Law. They should have been the first to put two and two together and recognize the gift of God in the sacrifice of His Son.

"The promises" (*epanggeliae*)... Goes beyond the promises contained in the covenants to embrace specific Messianic promises, the promise of the Spirit, and other encouraging prophecies concerning the hope of Israel.

All these markers were embedded in her revelation, yet Israel was blind and missed it all.

(9:5) *Whose are the fathers, and from whom is the Christ according to the flesh, who is over all, God blessed forever. Amen.*

"The fathers..." Abraham, Isaac, and Jacob and the whole Hebrew Hall of Fame, and despite all these models of godly faith, Israel is shut from the kingdom reserved for believing Israel because of unbelief. Gentiles will enter in before them.

"From whom is the Christ..." that is, the Messiah. To them and through them, the Messiah came into the world, and His own received him not.

"Who is the blessed God over all..." (*ho on epi panton theos eulogetos eis tous aionas).* The NIV has "who is God over all, forever praised!" The NASB rendering is grammatically possible, but in my judgment, unnatural. Typically, the Greeks like to use the article with some nouns, especially those that function as proper names and nouns of quality. *Theos* is one with which we rather expect the article, especially if we are to put a comma after *panton* (as with the NASB rendering). Also, the Greeks have a tendency to frame qualifiers between the article and its noun. Add to those considerations the fact that the resulting translation would be exactly in accordance with Pauline teaching about the Christ, and would make his point about national honor and privilege even more impressive and tragic simultaneously, it is most likely what he intended. This adjective is used of God in Romans 1:25 and in 2 Corinthians 11:25. In fact, every time it is used in the NT, it either is used of an attribute or quality belonging to God or of one that should be ascribed to him. It is never used in the NT of a quality that God ascribes to another.

(9:6) But it is not as though the word of God has failed. For they are not all Israel who are descended from Israel...

The situation with Israel is a national tragedy. But the calamity of it resides in Israel's wasted privilege, not in the failure of God's Word.

Any who would argue that the Word of God has failed if the majority of Israel is shut out of the kingdom of God in unbelief and shut off from the fulfillment of the promises God made to Abraham and his posterity are working off a faulty premise. That premise would be the assumption that true or spiritual Israel is coextensive with physical Israel.

Ekpeptoken (ekpipto) = to fall off or from (something) like withered flowers that fall to the ground. Also used as a nautical technical term in the sense of to "drift off course" or "run aground." Then, it comes to be used figuratively in the sense of to "fail" or "weaken."[272]

(9:7) Nor are they all children because they are Abraham's descendants, but: "through Isaac your descendants shall be named."

In reality, the apostle proceeds to demonstrate, one must differentiate for purposes of identifying the heirs of God's promises between the physical descendants (or "seed") of Abraham and his children.

A clear indication of this distinction is God's narrowing of the seed (or descendants) to whom His promises would apply to those descending through Isaac. Ishmael, the progenitor of the Arab peoples, is excluded from the line of promise, as are those descended from Abraham through his concubine, Keturah.

(9:8) That is, it is not the children of the flesh who are children of God, but the children of the promise are regarded as descendants.

The key to understanding the faithfulness of the Word of God, with respect to their pervasive national failure and forfeit of their share in the inheritance God promised Israel, is to distinguish between those in Israel who are children based on biology (physical descendant) and that much narrower line whom God reckons as children with respect to inheritance (i.e., as sharers in His promises). Those two circles are by no means coextensive.

(9:9) *For this is the word of promise: "At this time I will come, and Sarah will have a son."*

What Paul means by "the word of promise," which applies to a narrower circle than the physical descendants of Abraham, he now illustrates. He shows how God limited that loop at His own sovereign discretion first, in the case of Isaac, confining the inheritance of His promises to that line of Abraham that came to him through Sarah, namely, Isaac.

(9:10–11) *And not only this, but there was Rebekah also, when she had conceived twins by one man, our father Isaac; for though the twins were not yet born and had not done anything good or bad, in order that God's purpose according to His choice would stand, not because of works but because of Him who calls...*

Later, we see an even more impressive example of this narrowing principle. Isaac's wife, Rebekah, gave birth to twin sons, Esau and Jacob. God, at His own sovereign discretion, intervened in the situation and turned human tradition upside down in choosing the one who was technically the younger as the heir over Esau, who was formally the eldest.

(9:12) *It was said to her, "The older will serve the younger."*

This divine choice between the two was a simple case of divine discretion... a case of pure and simple election, for it clearly had nothing to do with human merit since the divine choice of Jacob as the eventual heir was declared before the boys were even born and before either of them had ever done anything good or evil.

This was done by God with the intent of anchoring His purposes to the principle of sovereign election, to the principle of divine calling rather than the shaky and unreliable standard of human merit.

(9:13) *Just as it is written: "Jacob I have loved, but Esau I have hated."*

"Hated" in the sense of rejected; in biblical conception, "hate" and "love" are not so much affective (i.e., emotional) postures as behavioral patterns, that is, ways of treating persons. God's love is not so much a way of feeling about persons as a way of treating them. Jesus loved the hypocritical Pharisees whom he excoriated in Matthew 23, not in the sense that He felt affection for them, but in the sense that He laid down His life for their sins. The Apostle in 1 Corinthians 13 describes Christian love on the pattern of Christ. It is notable that the attributes of that love are described in terms of behaviors, not in terms of affections for its objects. Christian love does not exclude affection necessarily, but it does not necessarily include it either. What it does is resign self-interest and give itself up to truth and righteousness and seeks the highest interests of its object.

To "love" Jacob, therefore, does not express affection for Jacob but a way of dealing with Jacob that involved preferential treatment for him. To love Jacob meant assigning him favored status and a place of blessing.

To hate Esau was not necessarily to despise him emotionally but simply to reject him as an object of blessing.

A good example of this notion of love without the emotional connotation usually attendant to it is found in Proverbs 13:24: "He who spares his rod hates his son." Solomon is not contending that one who fails to discipline his child emotionally despises the child, but rather that lack of discipline brings about the same result as rejection. In many biblical instances, one could replace the word "hate" with the word "reject," and the sense would not be materially affected.

However, even if one sees in the word "hate" here in its normal emotional connotation, the existence of that antipathy toward Esau in the case of God Himself presents no so-called moral problem for the simple reason that 1) God knows that any human being still "on the drawing boards," so to speak, will inevitably share the corruption of the race, and 2) God owes absolutely nothing to any sin-marred mortal but has the sovereign right to dispose of them any way He wishes, to treat them in any manner He chooses, and since they are inherently corrupt, to despise them if He pleases. He is not morally answerable to His creation in any shape or form but is, in Himself, the essence of goodness and, by His actions, further defines what is right and wrong. He does not take His cues from us as to the moral standards by which we should hold Him to account. We should not presume to stand in judgment upon His ways but only give ourselves to the task of comprehending His ways so that we might have greater light for directing our own ways.

If the majority of Israel is, in fact, lost in unbelief, it appeared on the face of it that God's Word has failed and that He was unable to deliver on His ancient covenant promises to Israel.

Paul's answer to this was that God's Word[273] had not failed but that the Jews had mistakenly assumed that the inheritance of the promises of the Abrahamic covenant extended to the natural descendants of Abraham through Jacob. This was incorrect.

To bolster his argument, Paul shows that the biological children of Abraham and the children of God were never coextensive, that, in fact, there was always within physical Israel a smaller circle of _true_ Israel to whom alone the inheritance applied.[274]

Paul shows first that God sovereignly narrowed the circle of Abraham's heirs down to those in the line of Isaac, Sarah's miracle child, who was born according to God's promise through a supernatural renewal of Sarah's reproductive powers. Isaac then becomes a prototype of a line of heirs who, like Isaac, are called "children of promise" because they, too, are brought into being by the power and purpose of God as Abraham's heirs. Their inheritance is not founded on pedigree but on the gracious choice of God.

A Jewish opponent might retort that to appeal to Isaac as proof of such an elective principle was weak, for Hagar, the mother of Ishmael, was not Abraham's real wife. As Sarah's son, it was natural for Isaac to supplant Ishmael in the line of inheritance.

The apostle foils this objection by showing that this pattern of sovereign election continues under different circumstances altogether. We see it clearly in the case of Isaac's twins, Esau and Jacob. He shows there is no other explanation for the choice of Jacob over Esau other than God's sovereign purpose. It obviously had nothing to do with moral character or legal works, for the choice was made before either was born and before either had ever done anything right or wrong, good or bad. God decided the elder would serve the younger for one reason: it was His sovereign decision, and in rendering it in advance, He established the fact that His purpose is in accordance with the principle of sovereign choice, not based in any way on human conduct. He sovereignly decided well in advance to embrace Jacob and reject Esau.

The implication is that there is a line within the line chosen by God Himself, a holy remnant who are heirs of His promises. The issue of God's faithfulness rests on what happens to that believing remnant, that is, true Israel, not what happens to the natural progeny of the nation.

Now, this perspective raises a question of fairness... a so-called "moral problem" with respect to God's dealings. Is it fair for God to sovereignly discriminate among men like this? Doesn't God owe it to all men to give everybody a level playing field, so to speak, and treat everybody alike? Is it morally right for God to decide to prefer one above another, to bless one, to curse another, to soften one, to harden another, to draw one, to repel another?

> (9:14) *What shall we say then? There is no injustice with God, is there? May it never be!*

Paul raises the question rhetorically, only to reject any such inference.

The question is instructive at this point because if we find ourselves asking the same one, it confirms that we are tracking with his logic. One must resist "tweaking" Paul's theology in any way that removes the question. Then, we miss the point and distort his teaching. Better to come to terms with it than revise it.

Put in a more amplified way, the question is: Is God unrighteous? Is God unfair when He sovereignly decides to show mercy and compassion to one class of human beings and not to another?

> (9:15) *For He says to Moses, "I will have mercy on whom I have mercy, and I will have compassion on whom I have compassion."*

In Exodus 33:19, Moses, at a moment of personal and national crisis, besought the Lord to reveal to Moses His glory. Pleased by Moses's humility and his desire to know Him better, the Lord consents to manifest Himself more fully to Moses for his benefit but not before asserting the fact that this concession was based not on the goodness of Moses or any sense of obligation to him or Israel, but strictly upon the His own sovereign grace and discretion. God is not beholding to even Moses and sets the record straight from the outset.

"For" introduces the basis of Paul's rejection of the inference above. In the words that follow, God made it plain to Moses that He deals with men on the basis of grace, not merit. He owes nothing to any man. "Mercy" implies the absence of moral standing and any obligation that might be expected to go with it.

He deals out mercy and compassion at His sovereign discretion, not because He possesses all power and authority and cannot be held to account by any human tribunal... not because He is in position to be as arbitrary and capricious with His distributions of favor and disfavors as He pleases, but because man in his fallenness, in his corruption, in his sinfulness, in his lawlessness and godlessness, has no moral claim upon God's blessing and favor. Man, literally, is at the mercy of a holy God who is not morally obliged to show it to anyone. All men deserve damnation, whether they appear to or not in the eyes of their fellow man. One moment in the presence of a holy God would expose their profound corruption[275] and would consume them in a flash.

> (9:16) *So then it does not depend on the man who wills or the man who runs, but on God who has mercy.*

"So then..." introduces an inference from the previous citation (Exod. 33:19). Literally, the Greek reads, "So then, not of the one willing nor the one running but (*alla*—a strong adversative) of God who shows mercy." This is an ellipsis where the subject is assumed to be understood and must be supplied from the context. What he has been talking about is God's _choice_ or calling or election. Paul says that God's choice of heirs of His kingdom and its blessings is based strictly on the principle of mercy in God's sovereign discretion, not on any principle of human decision (wills)[276] or performance (runs).

> (9:17) *For the Scripture says to Pharaoh, "For this very purpose I raised you up, to demonstrate My power in you, and that My name might be proclaimed throughout the whole earth."*

Pharoah represents an example of discretionary choice. God made Moses an object of His grace. His antagonist in the Exodus drama was the Pharoah of Egypt. God declared through Moses that Pharoah had been brought onto the historical scene and elevated by the power of God to the throne of Egypt for a singular "throwaway" purpose (*eis auto touto*): to be His divine foil in a historical drama that would have the effect of causing the name[277] of Yahweh to be published far and wide in the ancient world. This Exodus event was staged by God for the purpose of making His power and character known. Pharoah was a key player in this great saga, and God had raised him up for his specific role of opposition.

Does this imply that God Himself made Pharoah wicked? God forbid! "For God cannot be tempted by evil, and He Himself does not tempt anyone. But each one is tempted when he is carried away and enticed by his own lust" (James 1:13–14).

All men are born in corruption by virtue of their connection with Adam. A sinful disposition is a given. God does not create it; it is the effect of the fall and passed along from one to the other through birth, just like genes. All God did was to take a man who was the embodiment of the spirit of anti-God and steer him into his place in history and eternal infamy. God took a certified dirt ball, providentially directed his formation according to his evil nature and engineered his elevation to power for the purpose of using him for His own good ends.

God, who has the sovereign right to show or not show mercy at His discretion, elected not to show mercy to this man whom He chose to elevate to the throne of Egypt. God sovereignly maneuvered him into a political position and so stage-managed his sinful dispositions in his interactions with Israel and Moses that God served His own holy purposes through Pharoah. Pharoah thought he was in control; all the time, it was God who was in control and using Pharoah and all his hatefulness toward God for the Lord's own purposes.

So, what does this mean? It means that God has the right to dispose of fallen, God despising men however He chooses. It is His moral prerogative to extend His salvation to them or to seal them in eternal perdition through hardening.

(9:18) *So then He has mercy on whom He desires, and He hardens whom He desires.*

The antithesis of "showing mercy" to a soul is to "harden" it. God "shows mercy" when He sovereignly acts to make His grace efficacious in the heart. That is, when He decides to shatter the rock of unbelief and remove the scales of blindness that keep sinners fettered in their resistance to God.

"Hardening" (*qasha* in Hebrew = in Hiphil form "to be hard, obstinate, stubborn" and *skleryno* in Greek = to harden or to stiffen [e.g., the neck]) is a figure for an attitude of resistance to God. It is a posture of obstinance toward divine overtures, of stubborn resistance, stubborn opposition to His yoke (cf. Hebrews 3:7–19).

In the Exodus narratives, Moses alternates the blame for the hardening of Pharoah's heart between Pharoah and the Lord (compare Exod. 7:22; 8:15, 19, 32; 9:12, 34, 35; 10:1, 20, 27; 11:10). Moses obviously saw no contradiction in this but saw a subtle interplay between the arrogant resistance of Pharoah to God and God's judicial amplification of that disposition for His own good ends.

God hardens a sinner in the sense that He keeps the pressure on the obstinate heart, forcing the issue. The unbeliever is put in a position where he must either submissively receive the light or hostilely resist it. In that sense, God causes it.

Man hardens himself in the sense that he resists light and grace of his own free will. God does not force him to hate light. Man chooses to despise it, and by repetitious resistance, one makes rebellion a habit and renders it more reflexive than reflective.[278]

Pharoah resisted the pressure of the revelation of the power and character of God. The more He resisted the light of God, the bolder he became so that every time God raised the level of His revelation, the resistance of Pharoah rose to meet it. Pharoah then hardened himself in that he rebelled against God of his own volition. God hardened him in that God forced the issue so that through repeated defiance, Pharoah perfected his stubbornness to the point that God's glory never made a saving impression on him, and he was further removed from that possibility at the end than at the beginning. One of the judicial punishments of sin is God sending along a wind to blow the tree in the way it is bent and to fix it in that position for some purpose that serves his own ends.

> (9:19) *You will say to me then, "Why does He still find fault: For who resists His will?"*

"If God hardens us, why does he blame us for being hard?"

> If it be true, as [Paul] had taught, that the destiny of men is in the hands of God, if it is not of him who willeth [i.e., by force of human will power], or of him who runneth [i.e., by virtue of human effort that one becomes a child of God], but [salvation is a matter] of God that showeth mercy, what can we do? If the fact that one believes and is saved, and another remains impenitent and is lost, depends on God, how can we be blamed? Can we resist his will? It will at once be perceived that this plausible and formidable objection to the apostle's doctrine

is precisely the one which is commonly and confidently urged against the doctrine of election[279] (brackets mine).

The rhetorical question is telling. Anticipating the one that Hodge notes is normally put forward in opposition to the doctrine of divine election, its presence serves again to confirm that we are understanding Paul, and he is, in fact, teaching what some take exception to. The wise response I offer is not to find a way around what his rhetorical questions plainly indicate that he is teaching but to humbly accept what we may find hard to understand.

"It is not the doctrine of the Bible, that God first makes men wicked, and then punishes them for their wickedness [as this objection implies]. The Scriptures only assert... that God permits men, in the exercise of their own free [moral] agency, to sin, and then punishes them for their sins, and in proportion to their guilt."[280]

(9:20–21) *On the contrary (menoun ge), who are you, O man, who answers back (antapokrinomenos) to God? The thing molded (to plasma) will not say to the molder (to plasanti), "Why did you make me like this," will it? Or does not the potter have a right over the clay, to make from the same lump one vessel for honorable use (eis timen skeuos), and another for common use (eis atimian)?* (parentheses mine)

Hodge rightly observes that Paul, like other sacred writers and Christ Himself, when dishonest or arrogant questions or cavils were presented, rebukes the spirit of the objection before he takes on the substance of it. [281] Mere clay should be still and know that God has potter rights.

Man has no right to reply against God, to tell Him whom He can or cannot hold accountable. In relation to the eternal counsels and the infinite wisdom of God, man is too ignorant to venture into matters so far beyond his understanding. To presume to blame God is the height of arrogance and presumption. Who is man to take issue with His government of the universe? [282] The very fact that God does a thing is sufficient evidence of its justice.[283]

303

In this objection are embedded a couple of myths, that is, the unwarranted assumption that God is somehow obliged to treat all men the same and if He shows saving mercy and compassion to one, he is bound to show saving mercy and compassion to the other. These assumptions distort the true relationship between God and man.

The objections assume that all men are inherently good or innocent, that all men seek salvation and would accept it if only God would extend His grace to them. That is pure mythology. The truth is that man is not inherently good (Rom. 3:9–18) but naturally anti-God in his moral disposition, and none naturally seek after God (Rom. 3:1) until He first seeks them, and every single one would heartily refuse His offer of grace unless He took the initiative and first drew them.

The potter/clay analogy puts the case in proper perspective. All men are before God like clay. By virtue of our *sinfulness,* we lack any inherent worth. Morally, we are frankly dirtballs on the inside, if not the outside, and possess no claim to God's grace. It is as much God's right to dispose of humankind for honorable or dishonorable purposes as it is the right of a potter to dispose of dirty old clay in any way he pleases. "It must be borne in mind... that Paul is not dealing with God's sovereign rights over men as humans but over men as corrupt sinners. He is answering the objection occasioned by the sovereign discrimination stated in verse 18 in reference to mercy and hardening. These, it must be repeated, presuppose sin and ill-desert." [284]

> (9:22–23) *What if God, although willing to demonstrate His wrath and to make His power known, endured with much patience vessels of wrath prepared for destruction? And He did so in order that He might make known the riches of His glory upon vessels of mercy, which He prepared beforehand for glory...*

The logic of these verses in connection with the preceding is as follows: It is not simply that God has the right to do as He pleases, but on the positive side, as we would say, His sovereign choices serve holy purposes.

Hodge, whose remarks on this passage are consistently insightful, summarizes excellently the argument embedded in these syntactically difficult verses:

He now shows that in the exercise of this right there is nothing unreasonable or unjust, nothing of which his creatures have the least right to complain. The punishment of the wicked is not an arbitrary act, having no object but to make them miserable; it is designed to manifest the displeasure of God against sin, and to make known his true character. On the other hand, the salvation of the righteous is designed to display the riches of his grace. But in the punishment of one class and the salvation of the other, most important and benevolent ends are to be answered. And since for these ends it was necessary that some [i.e., of the guilty] should be punished, while other [i.e., of the guilty] might be pardoned, as all are equally undeserving, it results from the nature of the case that the decision between the vessels of wrath and the vessels of mercy must be left to God... [It is also the case] that even in the necessary punishment of the wicked, God does not proceed with any undue severity, but, on the contrary, deals with them with the greatest long-suffering and tenderness[285] (brackets mine).

In the Greek text, these two verses are one long, tangled, but incomplete sentence. The "What" that begins the NASV and NIV translations is missing in the Greek text. Actually, the sentence begins with the "if" (*ei*) and turns out to be a long conditional sentence with no mate (apodosis).

Since the thought is grammatically incomplete (not to mention compressed at points), the interpreter is left with the problem of supplying from the context that which logically completes the sentence. The right solution is supplying an apodosis that agrees with and advances the argument without putting any unnatural strain on his words to do it.

305

The first issue is figuring out the right apodosis (the mate to the conditional part of the sentence). What should it be? In the immediately preceding context, the apostle is, via rhetorical questions, upbraiding the presumption of man and affirming indirectly the moral authority of God to do as He pleases.

Given that, I propose that a natural apodosis (mate to the conditional sentence) would be something in this vein (the parenthetical additions amplify assumptions I believe are present in his compressed phraseology:

What right does puny man have to object if God (determines to raise up and) endures (for a time) the vessels of wrath fitted for destruction, resolving to exhibit his holy wrath and make His power known and (resolving to do so) in order to manifest the wealth of His glory upon the vessels (He chose as objects) of mercy, vessels prepared beforehand (by His saving grace) for (the) glory (they were destined to inherit)?[286]

The thrust of his argument is this: Does God, if it pleases Him, not have the right to do that (what verses 22–23 say He did)? What claim does clay have upon the potter that would preclude His authority to do that? What moral claim does sinful man have upon a holy God that would contravene His right to put bankrupt men (mere clay) to whatever use He pleases? And lacking any moral merit, inherent or acquired, in and of themselves, how dare fallen men try to shift the blame to God for the fact that they are vessels destined for destruction?

"Fitted for destruction..." (*katertismena eis apoleian*). Bear this in mind: God never took something good and made it bad; He never took a valuable ceramic piece and turned it into dirty old clay; but He does take mere clay in His mercy and fashion it into exquisite ceramic. And He reserves for Himself the right, if He chooses, to take dirty soil and dump it, to consign toxic materials for waste purposes. Who can fault God for that?

Now, in the following effort to illuminate this somewhat tangled sentence, forgive my redundancy at points in my attempt to cut the Gordian knot and clarify the point.

One can perhaps follow the sentence better if one dissects it into its constituent parts.

"What right does puny man have to object, [if...]"

"If God bore the vessels of wrath fitted for destruction with much longsuffering [in order to]..."

Then come two divine purposes, resolutions for which God endured these vessels of wrath fitted for destruction.

"[He was] willing" (*thelon* = 'wanting' in the sense of purposing or determining):

1) to exhibit His (holy) wrath (against evil)

2) to make known His power

That is, God purposed through the medium (i.e. vessels of wrath) to declare His holiness and power. For these vessels of wrath to serve those purposes, God patiently endured what was offensive to His nostrils, even mercifully making evil men unwitting partakers of His common grace in the process. The bottom line is that God endured protracted offense (think Pharoah and his court). In the process, the wicked, meanwhile, receive from God better than they deserve while God works out His plan to lavish His glory on His undeserving elect. God wins with both hands!

So, to sum up, the crowning purpose behind His decision to exhibit His wrath (holiness) and to make known His omnipotent power is:

"To make known (*hina. . . gnorisai*) the wealth of His glory upon the vessels of mercy who were prepared beforehand for glory."

"Prepared beforehand (*proetoemasen*) for glory" speaks of His ongoing work of grace in our lives (including pain and suffering) that prepares us for His presence and His gratuitous reward with great glory. It is that work whereby the Spirit equips our faith, more precious in the sight of God than refined gold, to stand the test, and the saints are conformed gradually to the image of Christ. On such, God will bestow ineffable glory. In a left-handed way, it is amazing grace.

(9:24) *Even us, whom He called, not from among the Jews only, but also from among the Gentiles.*

Here, the apostle brings the discussion back around again to the main issue, namely, the faithfulness of God to His promises in the OT to the Jews.

Everything is right on track. Not all Israel is true Israel. True Israel is a remnant within Israel that God, in His sovereign mercy, chose for Himself as "vessels of honor" and rejected the rest according to His prerogative. But He never limited His saving purpose to the Jews alone. According to His sovereign discretion, He has chosen some "vessels of honor" from among the Gentiles also.

"Even us, whom He called..." The antecedent of the relative pronoun is "vessels of mercy." Though (in the Greek text), it is attracted grammatically to the case of *hemas* (us).

The "vessels of mercy" set apart for honorable use in the sovereign purposes of God equates with those who are "called." This term "called" refers in Paul's theology to an efficacious drawing of God, which results in a truehearted response of faith to Jesus Christ. It is what Jesus had in mind in John 6:44 and Paul earlier in Romans 8:29.

The Jews, as we have noted already, had a great a problem accepting the premise that Gentiles would be included among heirs of God's blessing, just as they did accepting the idea that Jews might be excluded at God's sovereign discretion.

So now, with the help of OT evidence, he now bores in on the point that God's promises and kingdom always envisioned the embracing of the Gentiles as well.

> (9:25–26) *As He says in Hosea, "I will call those who were not My people, 'My people.' And her who was not beloved, 'Beloved.' 'And it shall be that in the place where it was said to them, 'You are not My people.' There they shall be called sons of the living God."*

He cites passages in Hosea 2:23 and 1:10, respectively, as OT proof that 1) God primed Israel well beforehand of His intention to include, in His family, people who once were not numbered among His own and who did not enjoy the standing of "beloved" in His sight, and that 2) He would adopt people into His family who, at one time, were disowned.

That this language in Hosea was applied to the Jews themselves when God in judgment disowned them only to reclaim them later and renew His blessing upon them was no objection. For the rejection and subsequent reclamation of the Jews from the Babylonian Exile of seventy years was only an example of the pattern. It does not exhaust the meaning and intent of the prophecy, for those words were elastic enough to anticipate the adoption of the once-rejected Gentiles as well.

At the same time, it should have been clear from the OT prophets that God, in His saving purposes, had only a remnant—a smaller circle within the larger ethnic circle—in mind. The remnant would be saved, and the mass would be condemned in devastating judgment. Take the prophet Isaiah (10:22–23 and 1:9 respectively), for example:

> (9:27–29) *And Isaiah cries out concerning Israel, "Though the number of the sons of Israel be as the sand of the sea, it is the remnant that will be saved; For the Lord will execute His word upon the earth, thoroughly and quickly." And just as Isaiah foretold, "Except the Lord of Sabaoth had left to us a posterity, we would have become as Sodom, and would have resembled Gomorrah."*

It should have been clear from the writings of the prophets that God never owned Israel as a whole but promised salvation only to a minority, leaving the rest to withering judgment. That judgment, by the way, was richly deserved and long delayed in the patience of God as He worked the clock in fulfilling His benevolent purposes on behalf of the elect and His great name.

Even if the number of the sons of Israel (ethnically speaking) were as the sand of the sea, the remnant will be saved.

How much clearer could it be that God never intended to save Israel *in toto?* It would not have mattered how great her numbers were, God had sovereignly determined the (note the definite article) remnant that He would save. There is no infidelity with God. Even now, among Israel, as the gospel is preached, He is calling elements of that remnant, and they are responding to Christ. God is doing what He said He would do, but the Jews are still behind the curve in catching up to His intentions announced long ago.

"Lord of Sabaoth" means Lord of hosts or armies, sometimes an ambiguous phrase in its reference. [287] It may refer to the armies of heaven or earth or both or even to the heavenly bodies. In a context like this, the prophet uses the epithet to signify that behind all human or heavenly power is the sovereign hand of God disposing the events of history according to His plan. He makes everything His instrument, even the unwilling and unwitting.

"Except the Lord... had left to us a posterity..." Isaiah reminds that salvation is not the birthright of the Jews but a gracious and merciful interdiction of the fate they all deserved. The hand of judgment should have swept them all away with all the violence that descended on the ancient, wicked cities of Sodom and Gomorrah, biblical archetypes of evil.

> (9:30) *What shall we say then? That the Gentiles, who did not pursue righteousness, attained righteousness, even the righteousness which is by faith...*

Paul had affirmed the sovereign right of God to have mercy and compassion upon whomever He would. He is no man's debtor, Jew or Gentile. In the process of exercising His sovereign prerogative of choosing the objects of His grace, He had, in accordance with ancient prophecy, chosen as vessels for honor, not only some Jews but also, contrary to Jewish expectations, reclaimed some among the Gentiles. That He rejected the majority of biological Jews should not catch them by surprise, for the ancient prophets clearly anticipated this outcome.

"What shall we say then?" Commentators struggle with this connection and make it more difficult than it is. One needs to take one's cue, I think, from the answer and work back.

One shall say this: Gentiles who weren't pursuing righteousness have gained righteousness—the kind that is based on faith, whereas Israel, pursuing a legal standard of righteousness, fell short of the mark.

Now what does that summary observation answer to, in the preceding context? I think it aims to highlight in summary fashion the great irony that Gentiles are included among His elect and the majority Israel is excluded—in order to address the question of blame ("Why?"–verse 32). Is the sovereign election of God to blame for the rejection of the majority of Israel, which once owned the inside track on His salvation, or does the blame for her national failure somehow lie with her?

"The Gentiles..." obviously refers to those Gentiles who received Christ by faith. The point is that in his time, Paul found a readiness to believe among the Gentiles that was missing among the Jews.

"Attained..." (*katalaben* from *katalambano* = seize, win, make one's own), even the righteousness, which is by faith" (*ten ex pisteos*).

'The dogs' (i.e., Gentiles) have eaten the crumbs the children rejected, as it were, and found the bread of life that the children had no use for. No man can come into the family of God without a righteous standing. The only righteousness that will suffice is the righteousness of Jesus Christ, which is imputed to those who respond to God's offer of forgiveness in faith.

(9:31) *But Israel, pursuing a law of righteousness, did not arrive at that law.*

"A law of righteousness..." We might have expected simply "pursuing righteousness." This is a difficult phrase. Is it equivalent to "a righteousness based on the law"? I have to think it is. If so, why didn't he just say that?[288] My guess is that "a law of righteousness" stands in contrast to what the Gentiles responded to by faith, namely, "a gift of righteousness."

"Arrive..." (*ephthasen* from *phthano* + *eis* = to come up to, reach, attain).

311

(9:32) *Why? Because they did not pursue it by faith, but as though it were by works. They stumbled over the stumbling stone...*

The reason for Israel's failure to arrive at the *sine qua non* (the essential) for acceptance with God, namely, righteousness, is simple. They took the wrong road. They insisted on pursuing righteousness on the basis of works. They set the requirements of God's law in their sights, and in the strength of the flesh tried to measure up. All the while, the law of God pointed them in the direction of faith, but they were blind to the true path to righteousness.

So, let them not blame God for their exclusion from His kingdom. The OT anticipates that they would balk at God's saving provision, and that is precisely the way it has all come down—Israel insisting on being accepted by God on the basis of merit and God insisting that Israel repent of her sins and take refuge on that rock of salvation, which is Christ.

(9:33) *Just as it is written, "Behold, I lay in Zion a stone of stumbling and a rock of offense, And he who believes in Him will not be disappointed"* (Isa. 28:16).

Paul quotes the Septuagint (LXX), the Greek version of the OT, from Isaiah, a prophecy written about 700 years before the anticipated advent of Christ and Jewish rejection of Him. Because the Messiah would appear to them in a different form than they had built up in their minds, the Jews would take offense at Him and turn away from Him. Instead of embracing Him as the one sure foundation of their confidence of acceptance before God, they would balk at Him. The few who do believe in Him are promised, however, that they will not be disappointed. Their faith will not be embarrassed or come up holding the bag.

What the prophet predicted had come to pass exactly as forecast. Instead of appearing in majestic royal dignity and military power, Jesus came disguised in earthly humility and presented Himself as a spiritual Savior, not a political revolutionary. He came to save people from their sins and bring them into a right relationship with God, not to deliver them from the Romans and restore the material glory of the former Davidic empire. That paradigm shift was unwelcome to their carnal minds and contrary to their worldly aspirations. So, they refused Christ. They stumbled over the Rock who would have been their salvation in the flood tide of judgment.

"Zion" that is, in Jerusalem, the city of God... the site of the temple, which is symbolic of the presence of God.

Addendum to Chapter 9

Many folks struggle with the biblical teaching of divine election, many very solid people. My experience is that 1) their reaction is often the result of the unbalanced way that doctrine is presented, pitting the sovereignty of God against human free moral agency. That is an error in itself.

Years ago I came up with an analogy that just might put the issue in a different light, like approaching a familiar intersection from a new direction will put a different perspective on that traffic spot.

I offer it as an addendum, hoping it will put the whole matter in a different perspective that may relieve all the fright. At the end, my hope is that you may wonder instead why God saved any rather than fret about why He chose to save only some.

P.S. Do not try to make this little parable walk on all fours!

The King of Gaia and His Amazing Grace

Once upon a time, there was a great king, the benevolent sovereign of the vast realm of Gaia. His kindness to his subjects was legendary. Never once had he ever abused or misused any of his subjects in any way. If ever a sovereign deserved the undying gratitude and steadfast fealty of his subjects, this was one.

But sometimes citizens don't know when they are well off. So it was with the blind inhabitants of Gaia. They seemed ever in the throes of a bad hair day. Constantly, they mindlessly kicked and chafed at royal authority. No matter that their monarch had always governed them patiently, mercifully, and wisely, he was never good enough.

It was almost as if they were under some kind of evil spell.

For one thing, they were infected with the all-too-human notion that authority—any authority—is oppressive by definition. They imagined if they could just get the crown's laws off their backs, they would magically achieve the freedom and tranquility that had forever eluded them. Little did they realize that their gnawing sense of enslavement and itch for emancipation had its roots in an interior, not exterior, condition of their own making, not the king's doing.

In the background of this malaise, but no small part of the trouble, was a skillful, agitating outsider. This rogue, who despised everything and everyone good, was set on subverting the great king any way possible. Along with his devilish co-conspirators, his design was to drive a wedge between the king and his subjects. Though wildly overmatched against the mighty monarch of Gaia, this foul creature was nonetheless an enormously clever and deceitful scoundrel who was, however, more than a match for the naïve but evilly disposed citizenry of Gaia. This lying interloper insinuated himself and his perverse ideas into affairs with the insidious intention of sowing enough discord to achieve the overthrow of the king and seize his kingdom for his own evil purposes. He played the rebel-hearted citizens of Gaia like a fiddle, craftily leveraging their native disloyalty and their cravings for autonomy.

It goes without saying, they fell blindly into his deceitful charms and totally into his ideological and moral orbit. Following a course of misperceived self-interest, they allowed him to lure them with his evil smirk into his fatal trap. Little did they realize the false freedom he promised them was true slavery, and the illusion of the good life he advertised was really a death march.

One dark day, the wicked citizens of Gaia revolted en masse. Led on by his deceptions and insinuations, these Gaians repaid the endless kindness and generosity of their sovereign with loathing rather than love. Disowning him and the whole royal family, they refused haughtily to pay any tribute to the crown though, amazingly, the king continued out of his royal coffers and stores to make daily provisions for their needs and provide for their safety and security in ways they never knew or imagined.

Before continuing with this sad story, maybe this is the best point to paint in the background of this narrative. It may sound as though the king was but a helpless bystander in his own kingdom. Don't be fooled. Trust me: from the start he had a firm grip on all these unfolding events. Had he felt it the wisest thing to do, he could and would have prevented what happened. A person of uncanny foresight, he knew well in advance the heart and the actions of his subjects as well as how his enemy would try to exploit the estrangement of his citizens. None of this caught his majesty flat-footed, as they say. From the outset, the king possessed all the power, knowledge, and wisdom needed to interdict the whole sorry episode.

So why didn't he, one may well ask. Kings have never felt obliged to explain all their thoughts and actions to subjects and spectators, but I think from what he has disclosed we can put together this much:

Obviously, the king was not so determined to make his subjects knuckle under that he was willing to use his power to reduce them to robots. He did not want the love and loyalty of machines. That sort of "honor" would give him no pleasure.

But there was an even greater consideration. From the day he established the kingdom on Gaia, the purposes and actions of the sovereign were determined by his royal master plan. When finally executed in all its glory, this would be the wonder of the ages.

Though it has never been fully explained, nor is it possible to fully comprehend how it worked, we can say this much: somehow, the good the king intended to bring to pass mysteriously embraced all the evil things that he allowed to happen. With godlike wisdom, he knew how to make evil serve good ends.

Let me not miscommunicate here. In no way do I mean to suggest the king authored or prompted his subjects to do evil or anything like that. No, no. He was totally above reproach in everything. Nor am I saying that he simply foresaw these evil events and adjusted his plans accordingly. Admittedly, I'm getting a bit out of my depth here. Let me just frankly admit that at this point, I am a bit like an ant trying to explain the thoughts and actions of an elephant.

Suffice it to say, in executing his master plan, this marvelous sovereign possessed such an array of powers and knowledge that not only was he able to foresee in various combinations how this and that situation would play off each other and how certain combinations of events, real or potential, would interact, depending on this or that, but had the remarkable ability to order and shape events that would make certain the outcomes he wanted.

I guess the important thing here (before we return to our chronicle) is that the king was brilliant enough to assure the outworking of his plan without stripping the players of their wills and accountability. In other words, he knew precisely how to make actions and events certain without making them necessary.

That may seem like a distinction without a difference. So maybe a little domestic analogy will help here. Can you bring a little imagination?

Suppose I anticipate a day when, for some reason, it is important for my kids to go to the kitchen and get into the refrigerator at a certain time. I need to assure myself that when that certain time arrives, they will respond on cue. But they are not robots. At that point, I will not be in a position to force them to act against their will. Moreover, in this instance, I am not inclined to impose my will on them. So, how do I bring this off?

Bingo! I have a plan. Just inform them in a timely fashion that their favorite drinks and desserts are hidden in the fridge crisper. Now, they don't *have* to go to the fridge. They can say, thanks, but no thanks, we're not hungry. However, I have the advantage of knowing my kids inside and out. I *know* that information will draw them to the fridge as surely as honey draws bees. I will not force them against their will, but I know how to use what I know of their native dispositions and unbounded youthful appetites to make certain they cooperate with my purposes. My plan works to perfection, but they do what they do of their own volition. I did not make their actions necessary, but I did know how to make their response certain and guarantee the outcome I planned.

Well, it was something like that with the king of Gaia. You get the general idea. The king of Gaia didn't incite his subjects to do evil.

But he did determine to use the evil they were all too glad and literally hellbent to do for his own good purposes and make certain that whenever they did their evil things, it all came down on time and on the dime to service his good ends. Amazing beyond words how he managed that!

Now to pick up the drama again. This story is one of amazing grace.

As I said, the great king of Gaia had a secret plan he had never shared with anyone except his son, the royal heir. Over time, he gradually unveiled it incrementally in a fuller and fuller way, although the whole story has never yet been told or fully comprehended. What we do know is this:

The master plan called for him to give his rebellious, incorrigible subjects the opportunity and the freedom to ruin themselves and to make such a hopeless mess of their lives that it would afford him an unprecedented window to display a grace and kindness never before seen or imagined in Gaia or anywhere for that matter.

His idea was to extend to all his worthless subjects, even after all the havoc they had wrought and the dishonor and insults they had heaped upon the Crown, an incredibly gracious offer of full amnesty and of restoration of all the rights and privileges of citizenship. What stupendous mercy! Unimaginable, given their wicked behavior. They all deserved a man (and woman) to be roasted. Yet, here is their sovereign extending to his worthless subjects an offer of redemption. Amazing grace!

But that keynote was part of the whole plan. Crucial to his ends was winning over his disobedient subjects on such terms that when they finally turned, it would be crystal clear to the whole realm and beyond that their restoration to favor and privilege in the kingdom was accomplished strictly and solely by the king's power, his wisdom, and his knowledge and sovereign initiative alone. Their "salvation" was, he wanted it to be evident, in no way indebted to any merit or noble action on their part. The whole plan was built around just that premise and outcome.

The mechanics are by no means entirely clear, but I guess you could say that it all started unfolding long before the rebellion, an event, remember, which the king anticipated and had incorporated into his plan from the first.

One day well before this ugly turn of events took place, the king of Gaia directed a royal scribe to bring to the throne room an official state roll of all the citizens of his realm. As he looked down the list of his unworthy subjects, every so often, the king would order the scribe to record a name on a separate list. When he had finished, the sovereign told his scribe to entitle the second list "The Roll of the Elect and Heirs of the Kingdom." Of course, at that point in time, the scribe had no idea what to make of this, but, as commanded, dutifully returned the list to the royal archives for safekeeping.

In time, after the great revolt occurred, it was like Gaia sat in some great darkness. The inhabitants seemed in the grip of madness. It was anarchy almost. They not only were now alienated from the Crown, but it was evident thereafter that they were at war with one another and, yes, even at odds with themselves. The repercussions were ugly and pervasive.

From the outside looking in, the king of Gaia seemed to be faced with a great moral dilemma. On the one hand, he loved his subjects and desired to save them from the jaw and paw of the evil lion, so to speak. On the other, justice had to be served. Love and injustice cannot coexist. The question was, how could he extend his love and yet honor his sense of justice?

Here is where this story gets even more amazing. The son of the king was privy to and involved in the whole plan from the start. He was just like his father in every way.

As part of the plan, the son volunteered with the father's consent— are you ready for this?—to be the scapegoat for the people. He volunteered to step forward to the bar of state justice and, offering himself as a legal substitute, allow the judge to inflict upon himself the full penalty of the people's traitorous actions. This way, their criminality could be legally and justly pardoned. Provided, that is, the offenders would actually believe the report of what the son did for them and did not hate the royal family so violently that, for spite, they would reject any reconciliation.

So, upon a day, it happened. The son paid a dear price to facilitate his father's gracious plan to make it possible for those reprobate and totally undeserving subjects to be reconciled with his father and put back in good standing with all the precious rights and privileges of upright citizens.

Now, the plan really kicks into high gear. The next thing on the agenda is to get the word out. Heralds are posted to every corner of Gaia. Messenger after messenger publishes the good news, extending to the king's wretched, wicked subjects his gracious offer of full amnesty.

Their message was always the same: "A royal offer of amnesty is on the table. Just believe it and receive it. Full pardon. Whosoever will may come. The king's son suffered your penalty in your place. Believe the good news, embrace it, and be reconciled to the king. Whosoever will may come and be restored to the rights and privileges of citizenship in the Kingdom."

It said something about the ruination and incorrigibility of these wicked citizens that this offer flew like a lead balloon. Time and again, the messengers returned at the end of the day mocked, maligned, or maimed. Some never returned. They were murdered.

By this time, one would think that the patience of the great king of Gaia would have been totally exhausted. Smoke 'em and start over! Yet, this incredibly merciful sovereign never scrapped his plan but kept on page and just kept a rotation of royal heralds publishing the word, sometimes redundantly. Naturally, the whole royal court was astounded that he would put up with all this nonsense from such hopeless ingrates. Yet, throughout the realm, the echo continued to ring, "Whosoever will..." A bona fide offer steadfastly refused and reviled.

Well, not quite, thankfully. Occasionally, there was a major breakthrough. And that's the really stunning as well as mysterious part of this marvelous story.

Remember that list of "the king's elect" the royal scribe has taken down and stored for safekeeping in the royal archives? Well, here is what that turned out to be all about.

As the messengers of the king were busy throughout the land publishing the word and being persecuted and reviled for their efforts, periodically the king himself, with that list in hand, would make a majestic foray into some venue or other. He moved about with his retainers in an arrestingly purposeful fashion, as though he knew exactly where he was going and whom he was seeking.

And that he did. For in every case, as he ventured into hostile territory, though always well protected, he would search out some recalcitrant subject on that list, maybe even one bold enough to revile him to his face as the king rode up to him or her. It was always so amazing to watch him work. It was nothing short of miraculous how he could approach a hostile and look him or her straight in the eye in a way that disarmed them completely. Whatever their attitude had been before, when he confronted them in that ever so personal, irresistible way of his, their hearts invariably melted before him. In the tenderest way, he would just say to them:

"You are mine. Repent. Trust me and follow after me."

Every time they would fall in behind his retinue and march off with him like soldiers heading into battle, totally turned around. There they were, following him through the jeering crowds, meek as lambs and brave as lions. Unbelievable!

Each time the royal party moved on, the king would scratch through another name on that list.

Still, the message went out:

"Whosoever will... come, follow me. Repent and receive pardon."

And still the resistance and contempt continued unabated.

In the midst of it all, the king continued to seek out his elect and confront them face-to-face. Who could believe the irresistible power of that certain gaze? How it melted all their hostility... how ashamed his former adversaries were of themselves when his eyes looked right into their souls. Every time, it was the same thing. Not once did he fail to rescue his man or his woman.

Yet all the time he was calling out his elect, the gracious invitation continued to be offered in every place his heralds went. "Whosoever will..." If they would only respond, they could be spared. But spared they refused to be.

On the last day the offer was still open, the king glanced at his watch. Obviously and ominously, time was about to expire—the time to bring the curtain down on the part of his master plan. Again, for one last time, he announced through his messengers:

"Whosoever will, come and receive amnesty. Please, come! Time is wasting. The opportunity for pardon is about to expire shortly."

Seeing no response and hearing nothing but more abuse, at last, he says:

"That's it. Time's up."

And directly as he rides away with all his elect in tow, he gives the fateful signal to his army in the rear to move in and do at last what justice cried for:

"The rest are yours. Punish them to the full extent of the law."

One thing was evident as one watched all this. The hardness and the corruption of the subjects ran so deep and thick that not one of them would ever have been "fixed" on their own. They were incorrigible in their wickedness and intractable in their contempt for their sovereign.

One can only be amazed that the king ever bothered to save any of them. But he did—many of them. Yet, it was only by his own sovereign initiative that he selected some (who knows for what reason—certainly not any merit in them) to rescue from themselves and somehow turn them into subjects worthy of him.

---

[269] Believers and servants of God are perennially misunderstood by the spiritually blind who cannot see what we see and do not know what we know. Job was accused of being a sinner. Even Moses' own sister and some of the Israelites, who coveted power and influence themselves, accused Moses of taking a position of eminence in leadership that Moses never wanted, and that God had imposed upon him. Ahab once called Elijah the troubler of Israel. David was accused by Saul of subversive activity and hounded and harassed almost out of his mind. Jeremiah was accused of undermining the national morale of his country when he warned the nation about impending judgment because in the minds of the establishment his message was negative and not positive.

[270] Calvin, *The Epistles of Paul to the Romans and Thessalonians*, 191.

[271] This lament of the Apostle dramatizes the danger of spiritual presumption, a peril also underscored in bold pen in 1 Corinthians 10. Always the risk exists, in a

context of religious privilege, of presuming 1) that one belongs to the family by virtue of birth or external identity, or 2) that religious heritage is a sign of God's special favor and acceptance. The Jews took themselves spiritually for granted because they were formally allied with the Name of the one true God, because they were privileged to be the repositories of His special revelation, and because He had done so many great works in their behalf. They never stopped to check their spiritual oil and to examine their personal relationship with Him, but rested upon the relationship of Abraham, Isaac, Jacob and Moses and upon their external conformity to the requirements of His covenant and law, like circumcision and sacrifice.

Modern forms of wasted privilege rooted in presumption are taking one's self for granted 1) because one lines up intellectually (creedalism) with the faith once for all delivered to the saints 2) because one has been baptized and is a church member 3) because one was once privileged to be a party to some great movement of God (the logic being that God would not have bestowed that privilege had it not been a sign of His approval).

A right relationship with God always comes down to the same requirement: a loving trust in the living God. But there is no loving trust in the living God unless there is a corresponding obedient walk. A talking faith that is not a walking faith is a mocking faith. It has no reality (James 2:26).

[272] Arndt & Gingrich, *Greek-English Lexicon of the New Testament*, 243.

[273] That is, His Word with respect to the covenant He had made with Abraham and his seed.

[274] One would think that it should have been obvious to the Jewish people that not all of Abraham's seed qualified as true seed, in terms of inheritance of the promises of God. Apparently, the thing that was new to them was not the simple fact that God discriminated between the descendants of Abraham in allocating His blessings, but that He did so on the basis of sovereign *grace* or election as opposed to some merit or virtuousness on the part of those He chose. That is the bombshell in his argument.

[275] Like a person with some lethal disease may for a long time before the affliction has run its deadly course seem to outward appearance the very picture of health and vitality. Medical tests which examine the internal picture reveal a condition the eye would never detect. So, it is with "moral" and "virtuous" unbelievers who win the praise of men but are found otherwise by the all-knowing and penetrating eye of God. Their very rejection of Him who is the embodiment of all good, the Lord Jesus Christ... their refusal to be identified with Him and to share His agenda is the beginning of the great exposé.

[276] On the face of it (assuming the rest of biblical testimony is consistent with it), this expression would seem to exclude any notion of election based upon foreknowledge in the sense of foreseeing a human willing or affirmative decision with respect to faith. Paul seems to go out of his way to say that this choice or

calling of God rests upon a sovereign decision to show mercy, not any pre-disposing human initiative.

Of course, of those who enter the Kingdom of God, a decision of faith will be required. But this willing of faith on the human side comes to birth because of sovereign initiative on the divine side (Ephesians 2:8-10). We would never have come to Christ in faith except the Father had exercised His sovereign prerogative and mercy and drawn us to Himself. (John 6:44) And it is quite certain that when God moves upon the hearts of His elect, they will in His time abandon their unbelief and come to Him in every single case (John 6:37; 10:27). This is not "irresistible grace" in the sense that God "forces" an unbeliever to decide for God against his will but in the sense that God awakens a living faith in his previously unresponsive soul.

God does not make faith necessary, but certain (to borrow Milliard Erickson's distinction). The difference is significant. Though human analogies inevitably break down due to the limitations of human knowledge, if I knew you feared snakes and didn't want you sleeping in a certain bed, I could just hide a snake under the blankets and let you discover when you climbed in. By that means I would render certain that you would decline to sleep in that bed, but not necessary. If you were a herpetologist, you might have calmly disposed of the snake and sacked out or maybe even have welcomed its company. But knowing who you were, I so ordered circumstances to achieve a certain (but not necessary) result. You bailed out of that bed of your own free will, but you had the freedom of choice to stay if you pleased. I never deprived you of that freedom, yet I used my knowledge of you to get you to exercise your will freely in a manner that was agreeable with my own. So it is with God. He has placed many a snake in the bed of elect sinners to turn them to an attitude of repose. He never stripped them of their freedom of choice but used His power and knowledge to direct its exercise.

[277] The name of God includes more than the fame of Yahweh, but also His glory, the centerpiece of which is His holy character.

[278] My late father-in-law grew up on the tough side of the street. In his earlier years, before his conversion, he was something of a brawler. Ever fitness conscious, before it became faddish, he worked out in his own way every day. To strengthen his solar plexuses, he would hammer them several minutes a day with the edges of his palms. They became very hard.

One of my late uncles was very tough that way. He had strengthened his solar plexuses to the point that they could resist great force. In fact, in his youth in the early 1900's he made money betting the coal miners and lumberjacks around the West Virginia barber shops that he could double them up (trading blows to the belly) before they could hurt him. His core was hard, hard, hard.

Likewise, when men resist the pressure of the Holy Spirit on the conscience, it gets ever harder to the point that it is impervious to the Spirit's solicitations. Not because God is unable to penetrate the conscience, but because that callousness is a subtle judgment of God against unbelief. He refuses to penetrate. He hardens whom He wills. That does not mean that he makes unresponsive anyone who might otherwise do so, but simply that he takes one who is already resistant to grace and allows that individual through repetitious resistance to His invitations to strengthen that hardness to the point that the pressure of proffered grace is no longer seriously felt.

[279] Hodge, *Epistle to the Romans*, 317.

[280] Ibid, 317-18.

[281] Ibid, 318 (e.g., John 3:3; Matt. 8:19, 20, 22; 19:16; 22:29)

[282] Murray states the question in similar words. *NICNT: Epistle to the Romans Vol. 2*, 31.

[283] If one does not understand this statement, it is because we labor under the illusion that there is some moral standard or benchmark outside of God by which God Himself is bound and measured and to which He may be held accountable. We forget that God Himself in His moral being is the standard of love, justice, and goodness. Besides Him, there is no standard that is not entirely relative to persons and cultures and reduces to little more than the standards of political correctness at any given time. Our job is to try to comprehend His revealed actions in terms of His revealed character, but not to presume to contradict them. Even so, we must allow for our vast ignorance and the vast chasm between God and man and not presume to judge His behavior by our puny intellects.

[284] Murray, *NICNT: Epistle to the Romans Vol. 2*, 32.

[285] Hodge, *Epistle to the Romans*, 319-20.

[286] Expressed in more amplified terms, I see the teaching of these two verses in this way:

At the expense of enduring what He hates, for the good of His elect and the glory of His Name, God puts up with the vessels of dishonor much like a homeowner who is remodeling a house puts up with a dirty mess until his purposes are served. God employs the vessels of dishonor as exhibits of His holy indignation against evil (compare Romans 1:18-32). In doing so, He leaves a judicial witness of His character—a testimony which serves to awaken the dread of evil in His elect and to nudge them to repentance and to draw them into the arms of His glory (*i.e.,* grace and righteousness). For the sake of His elect upon whom He intends to lavish His glory, He tolerates the vessels of dishonor and their resistance to Him in order to use them as He once used the opposition of Pharoah as occasion to demonstrate His divine power in overcoming and dismantling the evil designs of the godless. In this way evil serves God's holy purposes. God however is not responsible for the presence of sin any more than a potter is responsible for the existence of clay. Even so, like the potter, God takes evil, like the potter takes clay, and turns it, as only He can, to good ends for His elect and His name's sake. Who has any right to object to that?

287 *Evangelical Dictionary of Theology*, 465.

288 Cranfield argues that this phrase means the law embodying righteousness and is not a code phrase for "legal righteousness." He sees the Apostle simply saying that Israel for all its efforts to fulfill the law that was intended to guide men into the paths of righteousness had in the end failed to be guided rightly by it and had fallen short for all their zeal. The question is, why? Verse 32 answers that. Because they approached the law of righteousness not in faith, but as if it directed men to seek righteousness based on the principle of works.

Had Paul meant what Cranfield thinks, I imagine he would have placed the accusative article *ton* before law (*nomon*), thus yielding "the law" of righteousness of the presence of God among His people.

Romans Chapter 10

(10:1) *Brethren, my heart's desire and my prayer to God for them is for their salvation.*

Israel's unbelief... her stubborn insistence on legal righteousness, Paul reminds us again (cf. 9:1–3), is something that weighs on his heart. It is both his passion and his prayer that the Jewish people may turn in faith to Christ and enter salvation.

(10:2) *For I bear them witness that they have a zeal for God, but not in accordance with knowledge.*

His sorrow for them is greater because they are so close, yet so far, from salvation. The tragic irony of their estrangement from the God of their fathers is the fact that they, as a whole, possess an undeniable zeal *(zelon)* concerning God, a real religious fervor.[289]

"Not in accordance with knowledge..." (*epignosin*). The trouble is that their religion is misguided. It floundered on the rocks of ignorance of God.[290]

The trouble was they did not really know God. Their God-image was distorted, and they proved it when confronted with Jesus. They recognized neither Him nor His will. They insisted on casting God in their own image and approaching Him on their own terms. Had the problem been mere intellectual miscalculation, it might have been solved by better light. But as their response to Christ and the gospel proved, they were not open to better information. In fact, it infuriated them... a reaction which proved that the problem was rooted in self-will and human pride more than intellectual disadvantage. They wanted God and salvation on their own terms and were not willing to have it otherwise.

(10:3) *For not knowing about God's righteousness, and seeking to establish their own, they did not subject themselves to the righteousness of God.*

Paul here explains the core problem in the matter of their ignorance of God.

Blind (*agnoountes* = being ignorant) to the principle of justification by faith, they set out on a course of justification by works. Behind all spiritual ignorance is human callousness toward God (Eph. 4:17–19). Men can't see because they really don't want to see… don't know because they really don't want to know and can always find enough blinders to shield their minds from reality shock.

The response of the Jews to the offer of free justification based on faith might be compared to the response of a proud customer who is required to present a coupon to receive a free gift at a store he has long patronized. This imaginary business establishment advertises a free gift in exchange for a free coupon available in the newspaper or at the customer service desk of the store. Customers are duly reminded that the coupon will be necessary, no exceptions, but are also advised that if they visit the store and forget their coupons, substitutes are available at the store.

You wait your turn in line when a long-time patron just ahead shows up without the required coupon, demanding his free gift. The clerk patiently and politely explains that she is not authorized to make exceptions, as much as she might like. However, she graciously informs the irate customer that if he will just step over to the counter, they will be happy to furnish him the required coupon.

He is not mollified in the least. He complains that he has been a good-paying customer at this establishment for fourteen years and that the store owes him something for his patronage. He cannot see why *he* should be denied a free offer for lack of a dumb coupon. It doesn't cost anything, and it is readily accessible. The problem is that he thinks he is too good and too valuable to this business to have to submit to terms that he finds demeaning.

Anxious not to alienate the customer, the solicitous clerk spots a spare coupon beside the register and, with some relief, cheerfully offers the spare to him so that she may provide him with the free gift.

But the proud customer will have nothing of it. He insists on obtaining the advertised gift on his own terms. What he wants, in effect, is a reward, not a gratuity. The store, as he sees it, is in debt to him for his patronage. He will do nothing that implies he is in debt to the store.

So, he takes the offered coupon and throws it to the floor and storms out of the store in anger.

That is similar to what the ancient Jews and modern man still do.

God requires a "coupon," as it were. It's entirely free and universally accessible, but it must be presented to Him. Men are proud and insulted by that, however free it may be. They feel God owes them something, that they have earned their keep, and they will not come to him as beggars asking for a handout.

> (10:4) *For Christ is the end of the law for righteousness to everyone who believes.*

This verse explains more fully where they missed the boat.

"Christ" refers (metonymically) to the revelation of Jesus Christ as the defining event that blew away the myth of legal righteousness for believers. It was the gospel of Christ that exposed the error of their way and caused believers to accept the alternative, namely, the righteousness of God, which is freely offered to them in Christ.[291]

They want to inherit the kingdom of God, but on their terms or not at all.

"The end... to everyone who believes." This does not imply that righteousness by works was ever a valid option but merely that those who believe God recognize that the legal approach is a dead end and have disowned it.

What Paul teaches is that belief in the gospel of Christ means the termination of the use of the Law as a legal standard for the purpose of achieving that righteousness necessary for salvation. It's o-o-v-v-e-r!

Moses himself declares the futility of that approach to justification:

> (10:5) *For Moses writes that the man who practices the righteousness which is based on law shall live by that righteousness.*

Now Paul explains why it is so fatal to persist on that track of works-based justification. The Law cuts no slack for the legalist who wants to earn his way into God's acceptance. Its demands are exacting. Moses made clear that its standard was absolute and unforgiving:

He who does these things (i.e., the requirements of the Law) shall live by means of (the Greek preposition _en_ [in, within, on, at, by, among] renders the Hebrew preposition, which can refer to the instrument (by)).[292]

Bottom line: Practice the Law, and you earn the right to live; fail to measure up and pay the supreme penalty. It's that simple. No ifs, no ands, no buts, no maybes. Perform or perish. Fail to cross one of the law's "T's" or dot one of its "I's," and it's all down the toilet. Miss at one point, and one may as well fail at all.[293]

"Shall live..." It is clear from his usage of it that Paul sees this phraseology as having eternal life in view. That squares also with his employment of the same OT passage in Galatians 3:12.

If the righteousness-by-works method sounds like "mission impossible," the righteousness-by-faith method speaks to us in much kinder and gentler and more accessible terms.

> (10:6–7) _But the righteousness based on faith speaks thus, "Do not say in your heart, 'Who will ascend into heaven?' (that is, to bring Christ down), or 'Who will descend into the abyss?' (that is, to bring Christ up from the dead)."_

If that legal approach to justification insisted on by the Jews demands what is impossible of us, the method offered us in Christ, namely justification by faith, says that everything necessary for our salvation is already accomplished, that a gracious God leaves no hard hoops for us to jump through.

To make his point, the apostle alludes to a speech once made by the prophet Moses to his ancient Jewish contemporaries. Moses told them that they had no right to grouse that they didn't know the will of God. God had made it simple for them. He reminded them that they didn't have to ascend into heaven to bring down the revelation of His will nor descend into the abyss to bring it up. God had laid it all out before them and put it right under their noses. All that remained for them was to confess it with their mouths and embrace it in their hearts.

Paul adapts that speech of Moses and puts its words in the mouth of God's "righteousness" (personified for dramatic impression). Like Moses, Paul, in a poetic way, puts righteousness by faith forward as God's spokesman in the marketplace. In the words of Moses, righteousness reminds the modern Jew (and Gentiles too) that access to God's righteousness demands nothing extraordinary from them, that God has not left for them to accomplish any essential condition of their salvation, like bringing the Savior down to earth and raising Him from the dead. Trust God. He has done all the heavy lifting. Just receive the free gift by grace through faith.

So, in a nutshell, what is the message of righteousness by faith?

(10:8) *But what does it say? "The word is near you, in your mouth and in your heart"—that is, the word of faith which we are preaching.*

The "word," namely, the revelation of God about faith and salvation, the gospel, in other words, is accessible. There are no Herculean hurdles, no forbidding mountains to claim, no arduous journeys to take, no inhuman burdens to bear. What remains for us (Jew or Gentile) to access the righteousness of God are the only things that were necessary for ancient Israel to access the will of God back in the day of Moses: acknowledge it with their mouths and embrace it in their hearts. Don't make it harder than it is.

The salvation message with its demand upon us is not inaccessible, nor does it lay upon us any unbearable burden. It's near, that is, easy. All that is required is to acknowledge "the word of faith," that is, the message concerning faith or the gospel, with their mouths and embrace it in their hearts.

What is this "word (divine message) of faith" that the apostles preached?

(10:9) *That if you confess with your mouth Jesus as Lord, and believe in your heart that God raised Him from the dead, you shall be saved...*

It is the message that if you confess with our mouth Jesus as Lord and believe in your heart that God raised Him from the dead, you shall be saved. This is what he meant by it being near, in your mouth and in your heart. That is, it's totally within your reach. Don't make it something impossible!

Confess with your mouth and believe in your heart...

Two attributes of authentic faith. An un-confessing faith is hollow. A faith that goes no further than the lips is hypocritical. True faith is willing, even eager, to own up to Christ. Real faith starts in the heart... at the command center of the mind, will, and emotions. Confession is not a condition of salvation in addition to faith. Rather, it is a symptom or vital sign of its presence (compare Matt. 10:32–33).

The faith that God requires is not a vague blend of positive feelings about God or an optimistic outlook about the ways things will turn out. It believes at its core that Jesus is Lord. That faith affirms that Jesus is *Yahweh*[294] revealed in the flesh (John 1:1, 14; 10:30; 14:7–9). Whoever denies this has not arrived at Christian faith. The same goes for the resurrection.

These points of Christian theology are not the whole of the gospel by any means. Paul doesn't mention the vicarious (substitutionary) atonement, for instance. The faith issues that he raises, however, are the major sticking points with the Jews (and most every unbeliever). If, by faith, they clear those hurdles, the rest of the gospel is a slam dunk. This is why in its evangelizing churches must resist making an end run around Jesus and the issues connected with His person and work in attempting to "bring people to God." *No one can come to God who trips over the Lordship of Jesus and His resurrection.*

Paul, be it noted, is talking about mature faith; there is infant faith, where the Holy Spirit has implanted a seed of living faith that gradually germinates and blossoms full-orbed. I think the disciples

331

themselves were examples of that seed of living faith, initially immature but nurtured by the Lord into steadfast, persevering faith.

(10:10) *For with the heart man believes, resulting in righteousness, and with the mouth he confesses, resulting in salvation.*

An example of synonymous parallelism characteristic of Hebrew poetry. The second couplet expresses a thought essentially synonymous with the first. It lends *emphasis* to the idea in the first line. It is likely, given the parallel thought structures of these two verses, that verses 9–10 reflect a baptismal formula or a hymn then in use by the ancient church.

"Righteousness," that is, justification or imputed righteousness. Here, it is virtually synonymous with the concept of "salvation" because justification, an essential element of salvation, is the foundation and warranty of the whole.

(10:11) *For the Scripture says, "Whoever believes in Him will not be disappointed"* (Isa. 28:16).

The connective "for" here justifies his application of the accessibility of the gift of righteousness to all *mankind* as opposed to ethnic Jews in particular. He again references the passage previously cited in 9:33 (Isa. 28:16) and camps out on the word "whoever."

(10:12) *For there is no distinction between Jew and Gentile; for the same Lord is Lord of all, abounding in riches for all who call upon Him...*

Paul will not allow us to miss the point of the all-embracing "whoever," making explicit what is implicit. Before God, there is no difference in the need or the way of salvation for Jews and Gentiles or, for that matter, men, or women, rich or poor, educated or ignorant, red, yellow, black, or white.

The Lord is Lord of *all*, not just the Jews. Moreover, He is bountiful in His riches toward all who call upon Him.

(10:13) *For "Whoever will call upon the name of the Lord will be saved."* (Joel 2:32).

To "call upon Him" is a pregnant phrase that implies a worshipper or servant of God, not a petition uttered in panic or crisis. That worship is driven by faith.

That is why he can say, "Whoever will call upon the Name of the Lord will be saved." Note how verse 14, the first line, verifies our assertion that behind worship, the apostle sees faith as a necessary precursor. Paul says people can't call upon Him in whom they have not believed.

The "name of the Lord" does not refer to a set of syllables but to the Lord in His revealed character. The object of faith is God as He has revealed Himself. That revealed character summons faith and faith invites worship.

There are many religions with many worshippers of various kinds of gods. The only kind of worship that counts is that which calls upon the true God. However, the worshipper does not worship the true God unless one honors Him as He has revealed Himself to be.[295] If I saw my wife constantly kissing and cuddling and serving another man and calling him, "Jimmy," I would not look favorably upon that. Frankly, I would be ticked to the max. So, God also burns with holy indignation when men fashion themselves a god to their own liking and pretend they are serving the God of the Bible (see 1:18-32).

Paul has just made the points that God's way of salvation is fail-safe... that salvation, via faith versus works, is totally accessible for Jews and Gentiles alike...that Christ is an equal opportunity Savior... that salvation doesn't require some daunting deed or heroic performance of us but simply to acknowledge Christ, in trust, and that God has done everything necessary for our salvation, and to embrace His justification from the heart, that is, that whoever will do that will be saved... period.

The ancient Jews took profound offense to Paul's message at three points: 1) that salvation was by faith rather than by works or law-keeping, 2) that Jesus was the Messiah—which is why they refused to acknowledge His deity or resurrection, and 3) that God would accept the Gentiles on equal footing with them or would receive Gentiles before them.

Paul now addresses himself to this latter issue of the acceptance of the Gentiles and his preaching to them. The Jews were very jealous of what they regarded as a special and privileged relationship with God. Their religion was like a private club. They would not countenance Paul running around the Roman Empire in his missionary journeys, extending God's favor to the despised Gentiles on a footing equal to them, and giving Gentiles the impression that God was inviting them to the Big Party and, worse yet, preaching that God had left those Jews who rejected Jesus off the guest list.

Their jealousy and anger were similar to the ire some students at all-male or all-female private schools sometimes feel when the once exclusive doors are thrown open to the other sex. Maybe a better analogy might be the kind of resentment snobs feel when their once-exclusive domains are opened to the general public.

Now the apostle defends his mission to announce the New Deal.

> (10:14–15) *How then shall they call upon Him in whom they have not believed? And how shall they believe in Him whom they have not heard? And how shall they hear without a preacher? And how shall they preach unless they are sent? Just as it is written, "How beautiful are the feet of those who bring glad tidings of good things!"*

Paul here logically defends his authority as well as his privilege to take the gospel to the Gentiles. In doing so, he implicitly lays down some important principles with respect to worship and evangelization.[296]

The apostle now proceeds to show that the mandate to preach to the Gentiles was implicit in *whoever.* If God intended, as the OT bears witness, to enlist the Gentiles as His worshippers, then preaching to them was both a necessary and honorable function. It was not a betrayal of the Jews to invite the Gentiles to come to God but a sacred duty to God.

Therefore, the Jews have no right to take offense when the heralds of God take the message out to Gentiles. It's not a dishonorable thing but a glorious office, just as Isaiah described it when he anticipated in his prophecies the proclamation of the gospel.

Paul is here magnifying his appointed work as he will later in 11:13–14. He wants to excite the jealousy of the Jews to turn back to the God of Abraham, Isaac, and Jacob, whom the Gentiles have now claimed. Once the Jews rejected Him, He, in turn, offered Himself to them.

Did you ever notice how little kids sometimes get jealous and want to reclaim an old toy they have discarded when some other little child comes along behind them and seizes their discard as a prized possession? That is something of the psychology here.

Isaiah 52:7, in its original context, referred to the joyful messengers announcing to Jerusalem that the exile was over, and its captives had been set free to return and rebuild. But like other prophecies in the OT, the language is not exhausted by that historical fulfillment, but it anticipates in its scope the advent of the Messiah and the salvation He would bring.

(10:16) *However, they did not all heed the glad tidings, but Isaiah says, "Lord, who believed our report?"*

But the reception of the gospel is by no means universal, even if the offer of it is. Not everyone answered the door[297] when the heralds came calling. The same prophets who anticipated the proclamation of the gospel also foresaw its rejection.

What is happening (in the day of the apostles) is all consistent with prophecy... the offer of the gospel to the Gentiles as well as the Jews... the rejection of the gospel by the majority. All of this Israel should have known about had the nation had eyes to see and ears to hear.

(10:17) *So, faith comes from hearing, and hearing by the word of Christ.*[298]

A brief summary statement of the external conditions essential for the creation of faith. In reviewing these, Paul prepares the ground for a fuller[299] demonstration that Israel is culpable for her unbelief. If there is unbelief on the part of Israel, and there is, it is not because they are out of the loop communication-wise.

Faith depends upon hearing, and hearing comes through (*dia*) the message about Christ.

So, what excuse does Israel have for its unbelief? Is the problem perchance that they haven't heard?

(10:18) *But I say, surely they have never heard, have they? Indeed they have: "Their voice has gone out into all the earth, And their words to the ends of the world."*

Has God left Israel without a witness... has He failed to let them know? No, the Jews cannot claim that they have never heard.

In words first used by the psalmist to express the universal scope of natural revelation, Paul describes the universal range of the early proclamation of the gospel.

Israel, therefore, cannot plea ignorance. Faith comes by hearing and hearing comes by the Word of Christ... Israel has heard the Word of Christ. So why doesn't she believe?

Maybe Israel just couldn't figure it all out; it was over her head.

(10: 19) *But I say, surely Israel did not know, did they? At the first Moses says, "I will make you jealous by that which is not a nation, By a nation without understanding will I anger you..."*

The OT is full of clues that Israel should have recognized... clues that would have turned her around and pointed her in the right direction... clues that would have tipped her off that the gospel is indeed the message of God.

Israel should not have been caught by surprise at the invitation to the Gentiles to receive the grace of God. This offer was clearly anticipated in the OT by no less than Moses himself.

Well in advance, Moses the prophet had warned the Jews who rejected Him that God, in turn, would extend His grace to outsiders and provoke them to jealousy and anger against the Gentiles by adopting the Gentiles and rejecting the Jews. They would seethe in indignation at the Gentile adoption of their God, which signified His adoption of the Gentiles.

That very response to the gospel on their part should be a sign to them that God is in this.

> (10:20–21) *And Isaiah is very bold and says, "I was found by those who sought Me not, I became manifest to those who did not ask for Me." But as for Israel he says, "All day long I have stretched out my hands to a disobedient and obstinate people."*

Similar prophecies are found in Isaiah. He anticipated not only the reception of God's grace by the Gentiles but its rejection by the Jews.

The bottom line is that the Jews have no excuse for not recognizing God's hand. Even their negative response is anticipated. One would think they might check their oil considering the OT predictions.

Why can't the Jews wake up and see how what's happening in the world with respect to the gospel all fits the prophetic pattern? In light of these prophecies, how could Israel be so blind? How could she not know? How could she refuse to hear?

They were without excuse. Case closed.

---

[289] The fact that Paul acknowledges their evident religious fervor, but dismisses its worth as a saving grace, is proof (if anybody needed it) that, in biblical theology, sincerity and religiosity don't amount to much in the salvation equation.

Certainly, the presence of religious sensitivity ought to give one a head start in 'finding God' (if we want to use that phrase) over those whose wires are down. But religious zeal headed in the wrong direction is of no more value for saving our souls than an errant fire engine full of eager fire fighters is for saving my burning house.

There is more room for optimism about one finally getting it right if one at least starts out half right than all wrong. Hence, it is a plus, in that respect, if men at least acknowledge God. If they respect His rulership and the duty of man to serve Him, just as prospects for longevity are improved if men look after their health rather than if they are indifferent about it, just as it is more hopeful if parents care about their children rather than neglect them, just as the promise of the quality of life is enhanced if people help police their environment rather than act as accomplices in its wanton destruction.

Still, one's zeal can be totally misguided and bring about the very effects one sought to prevent. One can seek good health but, in the name of good health, act upon bad advice and misleading information, and wind up ruining one's health. One can love one's children but, in the name of love, rear them foolishly and end up spoiling them. One can care about one's country but care ignorantly and wind up supporting a political course that only succeeds in destroying it. One can seek to be humanitarian and, in the name of humanitarian concern, actually set humanity back.

[290] Sanday and Headlam remark that this term refers to a higher and more perfect knowledge, and hence it is used especially and almost technically for "knowledge of God."

[291] Commentators differ on the meaning of this sentence. Does this mean that the Jews were wrong to use the Law as a standard for earning righteousness by legal works because 1) Christ fulfilled the meaning of the OT and a legal prescription for salvation missed the point, or because 2) Christ fulfilled the righteousness of Law, or because 3) the revelation of Christ (i.e. the Gospel) signals the futility of a works-based righteousness?

It really depends on whether "end" (telos) in this place means "goal" or "termination." The former fits the first two possibilities and the latter, the third. While all represent biblically valid perspectives, in my view, the third is clearly preferable.

That is the more common meaning of *telos.* Besides, Paul's burden here is not to explain the spectacles through which the OT is to be read, but the avenue through which righteousness is, or is not, obtained. He has been contrasting the two methods of seeking it, one is through faith (*ek pisteous*) and the other, through law (*dia nomou*). For believers the latter approach has been abrogated as a way of acceptance.

The phrase "for righteousness," it seems to me, is decisive in favor of the third alternative, in that it explains from what point of view Christ is the end of the law. That is, the end of it as a steppingstone to an earned righteousness that God will accept. Not that all men will relinquish that use of the law, but for those who trust in Christ that use of the law has been terminated once and for all.

The ensuing contrast between the two kinds of righteousness connects much more naturally with the third view than the others, it seems to me.

[292] Abbot-Smith, *Greek Lexicon of the New Testament,* 150.

[293] The reason why any shortfall breaks the whole Law is because all its constituent parts express the same demand... to love God with one's whole heart and mind and to love one's neighbor as oneself. If one fails in any respect to do that, then one has come short of the standard whose elements, in part and as a whole, are required.

If the standard for admission to a sports team is consummate athleticism and that attribute is assessed by measurements of speed, strength, and agility, a deficit at any one point is fatal since athleticism is not determined by any one characteristic standing alone, but by all together.

294 Yahweh (Hebrew) is rendered kurios (Greek) in the Greek version of the OT (the Septuagint). *Kurios* means "Lord."

For someone to say that they accepted Christ as Savior at a certain time, but never accepted Him as Lord until "x" time later is specious. Christ does not come in two installments, one as Savior and another as Lord. Faith acknowledges Him as Lord in His essential Being from the start. Moreover, one can hardly believe that He is God revealed in the flesh and refuse to believe that He has the right to rule one's life. That is a logical contradiction.

However, if one who says this means simply that one did not honor His Lordship consistently or passionately initially, then we will concede that the process of sanctification does progress unevenly and sometimes spasmodically in some lives. But if one means by such statements that there was a time in one's "Christian" experience when one disavowed His Deity and/or His right to govern their lives, then in my view one is tacitly admitting a hollow faith that had no root. Such people in that case did not, I believe, come to faith when they thought they did, but had what I sometimes call merely "a narthex experience of grace."

295 If I were some great notable or celebrity, I would not warm to a tribute paid to myself or any attachment to me that was based on a gross misperception of me and or rooted in ignorance of who I really am and what I was all about. Such would be honoring a myth, not the man. So it is with God.

296 So, the best way to enrich worship is to nurture and enrich a biblical faith, not tinker with the forms. Without faith, the forms or styles of worship are irrelevant. Whatever improves faith will improve worship, because real worship calls upon God, draws near to God, submits to His will by force of conviction, not by the power of elegance or emotional "forced labor."

Indeed, the forms of worship may need changed occasionally. However, they should not be altered under the illusion that forms have the power to "create" a worshipping heart, but simply because inappropriate forms may contradict faith or stifle its passions or may be too tired to contain its exuberance.

In such cases, one changes the forms, not out of a love of novelty or to accommodate the easily bored or to pander to the palates of proud aesthetes, but simply to give faith room to rightly express itself.

The danger exists that in seeking to revitalize moribund Christian worship we start at the wrong end of the problem, with art and not the heart. Art is a gift of God and, rightly used, a great ally of Christian worship. However, it is no substitute for a muscular faith in creating it. The risk with placing too much burden on art to pour new life into Christian worship is not only that it misdiagnoses where the root problem lies, but it can also create the illusion of a cure where none has been found. Art is capable of producing, particularly in those with well-developed aesthetic senses, a natural high that simulates the emotional elevation of spiritual worship but is in no way connected with faith or the Spirit of God.

As for evangelism, Paul's principles make it clear that the church cannot expect to reap when it does not sow, for men cannot become believers in a Savior about whom they have never heard. Therein lies the Church's mandate to be an evangelizing agency in God's behalf. A large part of our mission is to make sure that those who do not know the truth have an opportunity to hear it, both at home and abroad.

We are failing as churches on both fronts. Just as we have learned how to be missionary minded without being evangelistic in missions, we have learned at home how to be evangelical without be evangelistic.

Note also that Paul expects an *authorized* ministry of the Word. Today the majority of seminary teachers and students scoff at that idea. They are very egalitarian in their views. Perhaps one of the central reasons why so much has gone so wrong in our churches is because we no longer take seriously the question of divine calling. Today there is the tendency to believe that all the parts are interchangeable and that anybody who feels like it has the right to step into any role they like. That is not the implication I see here.

[297] *hypakousan (hypakouo)*. This word can be used "technically of the door-keeper, whose duty it is to listen for the signals of those who wish to enter, and to admit them if they are entitled to do so, simply *open* or *answer* (the door)..." Arndt & Gingrich, *Greek-English Lexicon of the New Testament*, 845.

[298] Faith is not born in a vacuum. It comes from hearing... not (hearing) just anything, but something. That something is the specific message (*rhematos*) about Christ... the message about His Person and His work on behalf of sinners. Any so-called 'faith' not anchored to that message is a bogus faith.

In this day of doctrinal reductionism, we should be careful of a strategy of theological disarmament that proposes to enlist men for God and summon them to faith without introducing them to Christ, the epicenter of the good news. In this New Covenant era one cannot believe in God without first trusting in the person and work of Christ, for God has made Him the touchstone of faith.

[299] It is a stylistic trait of Paul's to broach a subject and then pick the thread up later and develop it. For instance, compare Romans 6:14 developed in chapters 7 and 8.

Romans Chapter 11

(11:1) *I say then, God has not rejected His people, has He? May it never be! For I too am an Israelite, a descendant of Abraham, of the tribe of Benjamin.*

This is a question of the utmost import as to the character of God for, in the OT, God had specifically declared that He would never reject (in the Greek version of the OT, the very same verb is used as we find here, *aposeto*) His people. See 1 Samuel 12:22 and Psalm 94:14 (Psa. 93 in the Greek version). This is clearly a question of the veracity of God.

"Then" (*oun*) harks back to the reception of the Gentiles and the rejection of the unbelieving Jews and the implication that Israel is sweepingly rejected.

So, what's the story? Has God trashed the Jewish people and reneged on the promises He gave to Abraham, Isaac, and Jacob? Has God disowned Israel *en masse* so that now there is no future for them, and their hopes are dashed and their promises null and void?

Emphatically not. Paul himself is a Jew and an apostle of Christ. In his election and office, he represents living proof that God in His sovereign action continues to call out Jews for His name.

(11:2) *God has not rejected His people whom He foreknew. Or do you not know what the Scriptures say in the passage about Elijah, how he pleads with God against Israel?*

"God has not rejected His people..." That is, as a class, Israel is still a favored people... a chosen people. "The gifts and calling of God are irrevocable" (verse 29). God chose Israel as a holy nation, and as a nation, Israel is still vested with the promises of future blessings. However, just because Israel is an elect nation *as a nation* does not signify that every biological Jew belonging to that nation or in good standing with it was thereby one of God's elect people. God chose a nation for Himself, and that nation has a certain destiny which God will fulfill; however, God has reserved to Himself the right to choose which physical members of that nation He wants to include as spiritual members of it with rights of inheritance.

"Whom he foreknew..." (See comments on 9:29.) This word theologically refers to God's sovereign preselection of Israel as the vehicle of His revelation to the world. Remember that the word "know" is used in the sense of "recognize" and then "approve." With the prefix "fore," it comes to have the sense of "to pre-approve" or "to choose beforehand."

The sense of the clause is not to affirm that there is one class of Israelites whom God has not rejected, namely, those "whom He foreknew," (though that is true) but to explain his emphatic rejection of the thought that God has gone back on His prophetic word, that He would never reject His chosen people. Paul's point is that Israel is indeed an elect nation *as a nation,* and nothing has changed about that. Therefore, the purpose of God stands. He will do for Israel what He promised, no matter how impossible it may seem. That was his very point in 11:3–4.

"Elijah, how he pleads with God against Israel?"

To show that even now God continues His work in and through Israel, Paul appeals to the remnant concept illustrated in the story of the OT prophet Elijah. Elijah lived in a time of radical spiritual declension in the Northern Kingdom. Ahab and his domineering wife and queen, Jezebel, had virtually driven out worshippers of Yahweh and turned the Northern Kingdom into a cult of Baal worship. The king and his vicious queen had systematically tracked down and destroyed the prophets of God (1 Kings 18:4). Elijah was on Ahab's Most Wanted list, and they were trying to track him down when he emerged to confront the prophets of Baal.

God, through Elijah, humiliated the prophets and worshippers of Baal, showing himself to be the true God. The people summarily executed the false prophets, but the restoration of Yahweh worship that Elijah expected never materialized. Instead of Jezebel falling on her knees and acknowledging Yahweh as God, Jezebel threatened Elijah's life and redoubled her efforts to capture him. Whereupon Elijah, in great discouragement, abandoned the territory of the

Northern Kingdom and sought a hideout in the remote desert of the Southern Kingdom.

There, despairing in his depression of life itself, he complains to the Lord that all is lost, that Israel has gone to hell in a handbasket, so to speak, and that the worship of Yahweh has been effectively defeated and eradicated in Israel.

(11:3) *Lord, they have killed Your prophets, they have torn down Your altars, and I alone am left, and they are seeking my life.*

Elijah, as we would say, felt like *The Last of the Mohicans*... a voice in the wilderness... the last finger in the dike... and an imperiled one at that. The collapse of righteousness and godliness, the aggressive moral decay of the nation, and the resistance to his message had turned Elijah into a devout pessimist.

His appraisal of religious conditions in Israel was in the right direction but extreme. Elijah had underestimated his God, had lost sight of the fact that God was still very much in command of His purpose. Unwittingly, he was insulting the sovereignty of God, implying that Yahweh, in the words of unsuccessful hunters, got "skunked" in Israel. After all the dust has settled, God has nothing to show for His efforts. Or so it appeared to him in the belly of full-on pessimism.

(11:4) *But what is the divine response to him? "I have kept for Myself seven thousand men who have not bowed the knee to Baal."*

The Lord gives his demoralized prophet to understand that even in the darkest situation, the Sovereign God is not wringing His hands, as it were, in bitter defeat. Despite all the religious idolatry around Elijah and an undertow of evil in the land, still, God was in control and had reserved for Himself a larger contingent of militant saints than Elijah knew anything about... 7000 faithful men,[300] in fact, who had not bowed a knee to the false god Baal.

"Seven thousand men..." Cranfield remarks that this number is to be:

> Understood in the light of the special significance attaching to the number seven and to multiples of seven in the Bible and in Judaism, as a symbol of completeness, perfection. God's statement that He is preserving for Himself seven thousand men in Israel amounts to a declaration of His faithfulness to His purpose of salvation for His people, a declaration that that purpose will continue unchanged and unthwarted to its final goal.[301]

(11:5) *In the same way then, there has also come to be at the present time a remnant according to God's gracious choice.*

A remnant...

Within the larger community of natural Israel, there has always been and still is what there was in Elijah's day, namely, a holy remnant of believing Jews raised up and preserved by the initiative of the sovereign God. These Jews are the true people of God within the larger circle of Israel. They are a chosen circle within the larger circle. Their choice by God is based strictly upon grace, not works.

> It was God, by His own decision and for the accomplishment of His own purpose, who made the remnant to stand firm; and for this very reason its existence was full of promise for the rest of the nation. The existence of a remnant, whose faithfulness was not their own meritorious achievement, would have had no particularly hopeful significance for the unfaithful majority. But, precisely because this remnant was preserved in accordance with the election of grace and not on the basis of works, its existence was a pledge of God's continuing interest in, and care for, the nation... [302]

(11:6) *But if it is by grace, it is no longer on the basis of works, otherwise grace is no longer grace.*

"It" refers to God's choice of the members of this believing or spiritual remnant among physical Israel.

Paul emphasizes that grace and works are two mutually exclusive principles. If works or merit is in any way a condition of our acceptance with God, then "grace" is no longer "grace." The term is emptied of meaning, for it implies that God imparts to the sinner His favor freely, and the sinner has nothing to offer, which would in any way obligate God to receive him. In short, grace is for the undeserving, and work implies merit. The Jews, if they would be saved, must eventually come to terms with Scripture, that the Israel of God, true Israel, the Israel to whom the promises of God will be fulfilled is that remnant of Israel whose relationship to Him is founded on grace.

(11:7) *What then? That which Israel is seeking for, it has not obtained, but those who were chosen obtained it, and the rest were hardened...*

"What then?" In other words, where do matters stand in view of what I have said?

"That which Israel is seeking for..." goes back to 9:31 and refers to a legally secure righteousness, which would obligate God to save them and include them in His kingdom.

"But those who were chosen obtained it..." That is, those whom God took the sovereign initiative to draw to Himself (John 6.37-39, 44) and in whose hearts He awakened a living faith. What they obtained was a legally secure justification, not based on their own works, but based upon the work of Christ, who died in their place so that they might be pardoned and whose personal and immutable righteousness was then imputed to their account.

"The rest were hardened..." (here, *eporothesan*, whereas in 9:18, Paul used *sclerynei*). From the following citation, it is clear that God is the hardening agent just as He was in the case of Pharoah. However, we must bear in mind that even in those narratives, responsibility for the hardening alternates between God and Pharoah himself. The reason for the dual perspective is simple.

A noun cognate of Greek verb (*poroo* = to make stubborn or without feeling) is used in Ephesians 4:18 (*porosin tes kardias auton*). To hardening or *porosis* in the case of the Gentiles, Paul attributes their spiritual ignorance and futility of their minds, leading to their surrendering themselves to sensuality and every kind of impurity with greediness.[303]

God, we remind, is the author of the hardening, in that He sends what the sinner resists, knowing that the sinner will resist it, and render himself more impervious to obedience by the very habit of resisting. On the other hand, the sinner hardens himself in that he stubbornly resists the obedience that God calls for, hardening his will and habituating himself to obstinance in the process.

In any case, this hardening is a judicial penalty imposed by God and brought about by His providential action. As we shall see later in this chapter, hardening is not necessarily permanent. God can apply providential solvents at any time.

(11:8) *Just as it is written, "God gave them a spirit of stupor, Eyes to see not and ears to hear not, Down to this very day."*

This citation combines elements from Deuteronomy 29:4 and Isaiah 29:10. Hardness amounts, in Cranfield's words, to "spiritual insensibility."[304] The spiritually hard are "untouchables." One cannot reach them until grace shatters the rock.

Their obstinance has resulted in a deadly spiritual torpidity. Their eyes do not see the truth, and their ears cannot hear it. Spiritually, they are blind and deaf... not because God wouldn't allow them to hear but because they refused to see and hear.

(11:9–10) *And David says, "Let their table become a snare and a trap, And a stumbling-block and a retribution to them. Let their eyes be darkened to see not, and bend their backs forever."*

This was an imprecation or curse from David, in his role as a prophet, writing under the impulse of the Spirit of God, imposed upon the enemies of truth and righteousness and, by extension, to the enemies of that ultimate righteous One, the Messiah Himself.

What starts as an antipathy to God causes it to transmute itself into an inability to know God.

"Let their table become a snare and a trap, And a stumbling-block and a retribution to them." If we understand "table" as a metonym for "that by which they propose to sustain themselves," then the prophet is simply announcing, in an imprecatory way, that God will cause what they depended upon to become their undoing. That is one of the effects of hardness. It is a form of blindness that leads and causes men to call good evil and evil good and leads them into paths of self-destruction in the name of self-preservation.

"And bend their backs forever..." that is, make their load crushing.

"Forever" (*dia pantos*), that is, not eternally, necessarily, but continually, as long as God sees fit to impose His judgment on them.

(11:11) *I say then, they did not stumble so as to fall, did they? May it never be! But by their transgression salvation has come to the Gentiles, to make them jealous.*

The great majority of the Jewish nation of Paul's day were shut out of the kingdom of God through unbelief. They rejected the King of the kingdom. In the words of the prophet Isaiah, God has laid in Zion, that is, in Jerusalem, the crown jewel of the holy nation, the seat of the symbolic presence of God in the form of the temple, a stone of stumbling and a rock of offence (Isaiah 8:14), namely, Jesus the Christ (i.e., the Messiah). Over Him, the Jews had largely stumbled in spiritual failure. In Christ, they had turned their backs upon God and His plan of salvation.

Now Paul asks: Did this happen in the sovereign purpose[305] of God so that the Jewish nation might "fall," (*pesosin*), that is, never to rise again? Did this stumbling represent a final failure and rejection of Israel as a nation and the forfeiture of all its national promises? The contrast between *eptaisan* and *pesosin* appears to be between a falling from which one may recover and one which is final.

This answer is an emphatic "No!" It is true that right now, the fulfillment of God's national promises is on temporary hold. They are in suspension, but as we shall see, not *permanently.*

Right now, however, their rejection serves a strategic purpose. Had the Jews welcomed Jesus in faith as their Messiah, their obedience would have dramatically abridged and accelerated the prophetic timetable. The kingdom of God in its outward form would have been immediately established and precipitated the judgment of the nations, not offering salvation to them.[306] That is all speculative.

However, inasmuch as they refused their Messiah, God has extended the privilege of citizenship in His kingdom to the Gentiles. In proffering grace to the nations, part of His strategy is to provoke Israel to spiritual jealousy through the salvation of the Gentiles and to draw them back to Himself.[307]

(11:12) *Now if their transgression be riches for the world and their failure be riches for the Gentiles, how much more will their fulfillment be!*

"If their transgression..." Fundamentally, unbelief is disobedience, an overstepping (*paraptoma*) of the lines God has laid down. To reject Christ is to refuse to do the work of God, namely, to believe Him, to respond to His Word and His will as the expression of God's own, for He is the very Word of God.[308]

"Be riches..." *Ploutos* means "wealth" and, in this context, corresponds to the enrichment, which is eternal salvation (verse 11). Salvation is the ultimate riches, the *sine qua non* of all wealth. Jewish rejection of grace is the cause of its extension to the Gentiles.

The argument is from the less to the greater. If their transgression could bring to the Gentiles such abundance of life (*ploutos)* and their (spiritual) defeat (*to hettema auton*) such riches (*ploutos*), how much greater will their fullness (*to pleroma auton*) because of the enlargement of the Gentiles? Their rejection of Christ the King and the loss of the Kingdom through want of attachment to Him constitutes not only a trespass of God's will but amounts to a punishing spiritual defeat in the contest of faith. They did not rise to the challenge and suffered loss for it.

The question is, what does Paul mean by their fullness? *Fullness* stands in contrast to *defeat* at least and perhaps transgression also. In that case, inasmuch as trespass implies punishment and defeat implies loss, *fullness* we would expect to refer to the recovery of the blessings of salvation—the revocation of punishment and the restoration of citizenship in the kingdom with all the rights and privileges thereof.

"Their" (*auton*) in both instances anticipates (on the principle of corporate solidarity) those Jews who will be participants in that great latter day national conversion when the Jews will, en masse under the stirring of the Spirit of God, return in faith to the God of their fathers and belatedly acknowledge Jesus as their true Messiah (verse 26). It is not those who are presently unbelieving, I presume, who will be the ones to turn their hearts "back to their fathers," but perhaps those unbelieving standing in their place in the end times who will be converted.

At this juncture, Paul directs himself in particular to the Gentile sector of the Roman church. What he has to say serves 1) to explain his double-barreled strategy in magnifying his apostolic commission to the Gentiles, 2) to offer some perspective that should defuse any tendency on the part of Gentile Christians to become arrogantly disrespectful and abusive toward unbelieving Jews as if the nation and its promises were now null and void before God, 3) to warn them against the kind of spiritual presumption and cockiness that tripped up the Jews and led to God's severe dealings with them, and 4) to inform them that God's purpose for Israel still stands... is written in stone and that His strategy in sending the gospel to the Gentiles will at last bear fruit in a harvest of national conversion. It ends with a doxology in praise of the impenetrable ways and the unfathomable wisdom of our great God. God's mysterious dealings in history are always to be admired but never fully understood by the puny mind of finite men.

(11:13–14) *But I am speaking to you who are Gentiles. Inasmuch then as I am an apostle of Gentiles, I magnify my ministry, if somehow I might move to jealousy my fellow-countrymen and save some of them.*

Asked to explain the blessing of God upon his ministry, a pastor (whose identity I have forgotten) once said that he had no secrets except this one: "We just try to find what God is doing and get in line." That is approximately what Paul says of his intentions. In extending His grace to the Gentiles, God's purpose is to plant the seeds of spiritual envy in their hearts, to water and nurture them, and at last bring them to harvest. The apostle aims to play that card all the way to the finish line. He magnifies his office not in word only but especially in the zeal and energy with which he prosecutes God's plan in proclaiming the gospel to the Gentiles. In saving[309] the Gentiles, Paul hopes for a bumper crop of Jews excited to respond by spiritual envy. His passion for the Gentiles goes hand in hand with his passion for Israel. He is saying, "My aim extends beyond my shot."

(11:15) *For if their rejection be the reconciliation of the world, what will their acceptance be but life from the dead?*

"Their rejection..." refers to that present but temporary hardening of Israel in her obstinate unbelief. This is a circumstance that has triggered in the purpose of God the proclamation of the gospel to the other tribes and nations of the world and resulted in the reconciliation of Gentiles to God on a worldwide basis.

Paul wants his Christian Gentiles not to become bitter and resentful against the Jews in the face of their ferocious opposition to Christ but to share his passion for their salvation. To aid and abet that sentiment, he again offers some perspective, arguing from the less to the greater.

If the nations have benefitted so much by default from the rejection of Israel, think how much greater the consequence of their acceptance (*proslempsis*) would be! If their rejection (*apobole*) resulted in the offering of grace to the Gentiles and their consequent reconciliation to God, one can only imagine how great a blessing their acceptance will bring.

This prospective blessing Paul describes in terms of "life from the dead" (*zoa ek nekron*). What is he referring to? Obviously, the form of argument requires something transcending the boon of reconciliation. Reconciliation is but the first phase of our redemption... that which qualifies us for the whole train of benefits that follow in its wake. If their rejection brings the initiation of blessing, then their acceptance means the fulfillment. "Life from the dead," I take it, refers to the first resurrection (Rev. 20:6) and the inauguration of the Messianic reign of Christ on earth centered apparently in Jerusalem, according to the prophecies of the OT.

In other words, their national conversion will be the precursor of the Messianic reign of Christ on earth when the people of God, Jew and Gentile, have their day. The Gentiles, therefore, should not disdain the Jews as divine rejects who retain no honor or holiness or future with God, but those whose eventual conversion marks the consummation of our hope, the reunion of all God's people, past and present, and the return of Christ to rule and reign on earth with us in great glory.

Even today there are those in amillennial circles who seem not to get it and like some Gentiles in the day of the apostle are dismissive of God's great future plan for the nation of Israel. I would think they should re-read the Dry Bones prophecy of Ezekiel 37 to cure that.

Yes, now Jewish believers are folded into the Church with Gentiles into one great flock of our Great Shepherd (John 10:16). But when it all goes down and Christ returns, if I understand biblical prophecy relating to Israel, Jewish believers will have ascendency in His kingdom. So, Gentiles, don't get cocky. The last shall be first.

(11:16) *And if the first piece of dough be holy, the lump is also; and if the root be holy, the branches are too.*

That Israel indeed has a glorious future Paul now proceeds to confirm explicitly. Israel's rejection is temporary; her restoration is inevitable, for in the sight of God, this nation still retains her original holiness. Holiness means separated for God. Let no Gentile, therefore, despise Israel or write her off as old business. She still figures very much in God's redemptive plan.

Paul argues his case on principles of OT logic. As part of the OT sacrificial regulations, the Israelites were required to present to God each season the first ripe grains and fruits of their harvest. These were called "first fruits." These were set aside and consecrated to God for sacred use. "The grain taken from the fields as the first fruits was prepared and worked into dough, then baked into a cake for an offering (Num. 15:18–21)." [310] "This cake offered to God's representative (i.e., the officiating priest) impressed the seal of consecration (i.e., holiness) on the entire mass from which it had been taken."[311]

By that ritualistic analogy, Paul likens the present believing remnant[312] of the Jews to the first fruits of the harvest and compares the dough from which the first fruit was drawn to the nation itself. If one is holy in God's sight, so is the other. Therefore, Gentiles should not regard the Jewish nation as something common or profane nor defame and despise it as such.

By the same token, if the root is holy, speaking of the patriarchs with whom God established His covenant and the promises based upon them, namely, Abraham, Isaac, and Jacob, the nation descended from them, the branches, that is, the nation with whom those promises are vested, shares in that sacred standing before God. This does not imply that every individual Jew is "holy," (i.e., has a reserved seat in the kingdom of God) but simply that the nation sprung from the roots, that is, the patriarchs are, according to verse 28, set apart for a special glory on account of the fathers chosen and beloved of the God who is faithful to His covenant promises.

(11:17–18) *But if some of the branches were broken off, and you, being a wild olive, were grafted in among them and became a partaker with them of the rich root of the olive tree, do not be arrogant toward the branches; but if you are arrogant, remember that it is not you who supports the root, but the root supports you.*

Now the apostle confronts head-on an ugly but natural human tendency. Whenever, in the course of human events, one person or group has been rejected in favor of another, the preferred person or group will almost always feel, or be tempted to feel, superior to those whom they have supplanted.[313]

In the case of the newly privileged Gentiles, there was a tendency with some to despise the dispossessed Jews... to write them off as divine rejects and to succumb to the conceit that in them (i.e., the Gentiles), God had found something meritorious and more virtuous. Hence, the temptation to credit their own innate superiority for their newfound acceptance with God.

Embedded in this unwarranted disposition was the danger of the same kind of spiritual pride that tripped up the Jews and caused them to presume upon their own intrinsic merit rather than the path of humble faith in the grace of God to accomplish their salvation. Thus, Paul warns any Gentiles against any form of spiritual arrogance that may expose them to the risk of replicating the same fatal error themselves that caused the Jews to be rejected.

To make his point, Paul draws upon an arboricultural analogy to check this festering sore in the psyche of parts of the Gentile church. The (cultivated) olive tree was a recognized OT symbol of Israel as was the vine (cf. Jer. 11:16; Hosea 14:6). God had, in effect, disowned the unbelieving Jews the same way that an arborist would break off the dead and fruitless branches of a cultivated olive tree. In their place, He brought the Gentiles into His kingdom in the same way an arborist might graft the branches of a wild olive into a cultivated olive at the places where the dead branches had been displaced.

"Among them..." that is, among the remnant of believing Jews.[314]

"And became partaker with them of the rich (*piotetos* = fatness) root of the olive tree..." The point is that God has privileged the Gentiles now to share in the blessings (i.e., divine election to salvation) belonging to the roots (i.e., the patriarchs of the Jews).

"Do not be arrogant toward the branches..." Literally, "Don't go around vaunting yourselves over the branches as though God dispossessed the Jews and chose you because of some inherent merit on your part."

The temptation for the Gentiles would be to imagine that God did this because He found some virtue in them that the Jews lacked, that He found them superior to the Jews and to begin to congratulate their own presumed worth rather than thanking the sheer sovereign mercy and grace of God.

What they must not lose sight of is that Abraham, the Jew, not the Gentile, is God's chosen conduit of salvation for the nations. "In you," God promised, "all the families of the earth shall be blessed" (Gen. 12:3c). Jesus reminded the woman at the well that "salvation is from the Jews" (John 4:22). Let, therefore, the Gentiles, if they harbor any ill-will toward the Jews or entertain any notion of their superiority to them, bear in mind that to them, the Gentiles owe a huge debt of gratitude.

> (11:19) *You will say then, "Branches were broken off so that I might be grafted in."*

Obviously, Paul is aware of pockets of anti-Semitic feeling in the ancient church. Some of it was no doubt a carry-over from cultural prejudices, which had not as yet been leached out by the cleansing power of grace. Some of it was no doubt traceable to Jewish hostility to the gospel. It is natural to feel that people must be inferior or defective who cannot see what we see clearly and who are so biased as to oppose what is good and embrace what is evil.

No doubt Paul had heard some early Christian Gentiles rationalize their disdain of unbelieving Jews on the grounds that God Himself must have found them more worthy of salvation because He went so far (to continue the olive tree analogy) as to "break off the Jews" and to graft in the Gentiles.[315] They assume that God was motivated by something which He saw in them rather than by His own sovereign strategies in no way related to their own intrinsic merit.

> (11:20) *Quite right, they were broken off for their unbelief, and you stand only by your faith. Do not be conceited, but fear...*

It is true that God disowned the Jews not because they were inherently inferior to Gentiles but because they refused to believe God. "Without faith it is impossible to please Him, for he that cometh to God must believe that He is and that He is rewarder of them who seek Him" (Heb. 12:6).

Gentiles stand (accepted) strictly based on faith... on the basis of faith and faith alone. God will never accept anyone who refuses to trust Him; He will never deny anyone who will. Merit has nothing to do with it; faith accounts for their standing before Him.

"Do not be conceited but fear." Reverence before a holy God who is no respecter of persons is the proper stance before God, not a high opinion of oneself that imagines that God chose us on account of some good things He saw in us, values and wants to keep, as if we added some value to Him. We are very mistaken about the love of God when we fancy that His mysterious love has anything to do with something He finds in us.

(11:21) *For if God did not spare the natural branches, neither will He spare you.*

There is a warning in that for Jew and Gentile alike. God is no respecter of persons. The way to God is through faith, and Christ is today the litmus test God has sent to test our willingness to believe Him. He is "the way, the truth and the life, no man cometh unto the Father except through Me" (John 14:6). There is no bypass... there is no alternative. God says to everyone that if you want to be accepted into the family and kingdom of the living God, you will come *this* way.

Many appear to start in the life of faith, but they fail to finish. They talk the game, but they don't play it. Thus, Paul puts Gentiles on notice who may think that in some way their acceptance of God depends upon something else besides faith and might be prone to put their eggs in some other salvation basket. The lesson for the Gentiles is that God does not play favorites. He proved that when the natural branches, that is, the Jews, took themselves and their value in the sight of God for granted and failed to trust Him, He cut them off. He disinherited them. He refused to include them among the faithful of Israel.

If He did that to the natural branches, let the Gentiles take careful notice: He will lop the unbelieving Gentiles off the tree just as readily as the unbelieving Jews. Without faith, nothing is safe. So let everyone, the implication is, make his or her calling and election sure.

> (11:22) *Behold then the kindness and severity of God; to those who fell, severity, but to you, God's kindness, if you continue in His kindness; otherwise you also will be cut off.*

A healthy Christian faith stays balanced between the tensions in God's character and in biblical revelation.[316] One of those tensions (not contradictions) lies in the kindness and the severity of God. Look at the Gentiles and see the kindness of God in extending His grace and mercy to the undeserving. Look at the unbelieving Jews and see the severity of God in dealing with transgressors.

God is a two-sided God; His love is a two-sided love, just like the love of a wise parent. It is fused with kindness and severity, depending on the circumstances. On the one hand, He is tender, compassionate, merciful, patient, abounding in lovingkindness and faithfulness, and forgiving iniquity, transgression, and sin for those who love Him and trust in Him (Ex. 34:6-7). But that same God presents a very severe side to those who refuse to believe Him... who reject His words, His will, and His ways. Eventually, He comes down on them hard. Sooner or later, they will be cut off and that, without remedy, if they persist in their rebellion against Him.

The man who rebels against God and has no fear does not know God. The man who repents and has no peace does not know God. The man who knows God will fear sin or not fear it, depending on his relationship to his sin. The man who knows God will tremble at the thought of persisting in it and will find peace in turning from it.

"If you remain in His kindness..." (*ean epimenes te chrestoteti*). Kindness is a metonym for faith, the effect standing in the place of the cause, namely, faith. To continue in the sphere of His kindness is to continue in the sphere of faith (see Col. 1:13). He says "kindness" and not faith, I believe, simply to accentuate what is at stake in the alternatives.

Cranfield's comment[317] that this "brings out the true nature of faith as living from God's kindness," whatever merit it may have in itself, is, I feel, quite aside from Paul's thrust here.

(11:23) *And they also, if they do not continue in their unbelief, will be grafted in; for God is able to graft them in again.*

There is no problem between the Jews and God that faith cannot fix. Their disinheritance will be reversed if they abandon their unbelief. In natural arboriculture, it may be impossible to graft in dead branches, but God can. So, don't dismiss the Jews as an object of evangelistic mission or concern. All that stands between them and restoration to divine favor is a lack of faith and the Spirit of God can change all that.

(11:24) *For if you were cut off from what is by nature a wild olive tree, and were grafted in contrary to nature into a cultivated olive tree, how much more shall these who are the natural branches be grafted into their own olive tree?*

In fact, for God, it is easier to graft Jewish branches back into a Jewish tree than it was to graft Gentiles into it, contrary to its nature.

Cranfield put it this way:

"If the Gentile Christian can believe that God has actually grafted him into that holy stem to which he does not naturally belong, how much more readily ought he to believe that God is able and willing to do what is less wonderful—to restore to their own native stock the unbelieving Jews, when they repent and believe."[318]

(11:25) *For I do not want you, brethren, to be uninformed of this mystery, lest you be wise in your own estimation, that a partial hardening has happened to Israel until the fulness of the Gentiles has come in...*

"This mystery..." In Paul's nomenclature, a "mystery" is not something mysterious or an inscrutable subject matter but a divine secret now fully revealed to the people of God, and something that is now our secret too. It is our "secret," not because we want to hide it but because the world is not listening.[319]

Paul wants the Gentiles to know that in the plan and purpose of God, the nation of Israel is not cast off. True, their unbelief had precipitated a judgment of God in the form of a judicial hardening that, in effect, "froze" or paralyzed the hearts of the majority of the Jewish people in a posture of radical unbelief and opposition to the God of their fathers and led to the gracious favor of God being at that time withdrawn from the Jews and extended to the Gentiles.

However, the Gentiles must not delude themselves into thinking 1) that this development implies that they are inherently better than the Jews (becoming wise in their own eyes and congratulating themselves on their superior wisdom in recognizing and receiving the Messiah the Jews so vilely and stupidly rejected), and must not conclude 2) that the Jews are "old business" with whom God is finished... that God has rejected them forever.

To allay the latter misconception and stifle a tendency for Gentiles to pride themselves on their spiritual superiority in responding to Christ, Paul proceeds to make certain that the Gentiles Christians get the proper perspective on things, for bad beliefs are always the mother of bad behaviors.

As proof that God's heart is still with Israel (the inference being that their heart must follow the heart of God), Paul has drummed on these points:

1) That the rejection of the Jews clearly is not total but only partial... that right now, there is a remnant of believing Jews in the constituency of the Christian church serving as a kind of first fruit of the harvest.

2) That God's judicial action in rejecting the Jews and extending His grace to the Gentiles was really a left-handed form of strategy to bring the Jews back to Himself in provoking them to jealousy and stirring them up eventually to seek, once again, the God whom they spurned when they rejected in Jesus their Messiah.

3) That Israel's rejection is not final, only temporary.

This state of affairs will persist "until the fulness of the Gentiles has come in" (Luke 21:24).

The phraseology apparently refers to that point in history when God's saving purpose is fixed mainly on the Gentiles as opposed to the times of the Jews when His grace was focused mainly on Israel (Acts 13:48).

> (11:26–27) *And thus all Israel will be saved; just as it is written, "The Deliverer will come from Zion, He will remove ungodliness from Jacob." "And this is my covenant with them, when I take away their sins."*

Following that undefined point in the future, the Jews will be converted *en masse,* as Godet puts it. "He speaks of a collective movement which shall take hold of *the nation in general* and bring them as such to the feet of their Messiah" [320] (see Zech. 12:10–14).

In support of his premise that, eventually, God will bring about a great national conversion of Israel, Paul appeals to OT prophecy in Isaiah 59:20 (his wording being based primarily upon the Greek rather than the Hebrew version of the OT).

This prophecy indicates that:

1) That at some undefined point in the future, God is going to send them a Redeemer or Deliverer.

2) That He will turn away ungodliness from Jacob, a collective name for the nation of Israel.

3) That God will establish a covenant with them at that time, referring to the new covenant promised (Jer. 32:37–44; Ezek. 36:22–32).

(11:28) *From the standpoint of the gospel they are enemies for your sake, but from the standpoint of God's choice they are beloved for the sake of the fathers;*

Now Paul begins one of his summations—a kind of bottom-line status report on Israel's relationship to God.

There is, to be sure, a sense in which the Jews are the objects of divine wrath and deservedly so—that is, in respect to their response to the gospel, their hostility to God in Christ has placed them on the footing of enemies of God and under the wrath of God (John 3:36).[321]

The unstated implication is that their current exposure to the wrath of God is no excuse for Gentile contempt of them, nor feelings of moral and spiritual superiority. Bear in mind, Paul says, this consignment of the Jews to the status of enemies of God is a judicial verdict, which triggered the extension of God's gracious invitation of salvation to the Gentiles. In a manner of speaking, God, in wrath, weary of His ungrateful and unbelieving children who despised their food and threw it on the floor, went away empty, seized the moment to show His love and mercy to beggars whom He invited in from the street to fill themselves with His good things that the children rejected.

We Gentiles, therefore, should not respond to the Jews with either contempt or arrogance but with simple gratitude to God for making us partakers of the crumbs that fell, as it were, from the rich man's table. Beggars don't scorn those who don't eat their dinner but thank God for their good fortune. Such should be the attitude of the Gentiles.

The paradox is that, though the Jews are on one side of the coin, viewed and treated by God as enemies and under the wrath of God, let everybody understand that, in terms of His sovereign election, these people are still "beloved." God cares about them, and they still figure mightily in His redemptive plan.[322] Even in their enmity, Israel is the object of His love.

"On account of the fathers..." referring to the patriarchs, Abraham, Isaac, and Jacob, with whom God established his covenants of promise. Israel is not beloved because of her intrinsic worth or goodness. Israel is beloved because God chose her fathers and was pleased to set His affection on them and to bequeath to them in His grace certain promises. The love that belonged to the fathers extends to the nation formed around them and all their spiritual descendants in it.

(11:29) *For the gifts and calling of God are irrevocable.*

Underlying Paul's assurance of the love of God for Israel, and the fulfillment of her destiny, rests on this principle: God is not fickle, capricious, or a liar. If He gives something unconditionally... if He promises something unconditionally, then He does not later second-guess Himself and withdraw His gifts or His calling at a whim. Now some of God's gifts and callings are plainly conditional on human performance. God removed Saul from his kingship, for example. He shuffled the high priestly line from one family to another. But conditional appointments are not in mind here, but those that derive from sovereign election.

"Irrevocable" (ametameleta = without regret)[323]

"Gifts" (ta charismata) in this context most likely refers to the gracious privileges and benefits described in 9:4–5.

"Calling" (*he klesis*) refers here to His sovereign choice of Israel to its Messianic destiny.

(11:30–31) *For just as you once were disobedient to God but now have been shown mercy because of their disobedience, so these also now have been disobedient, in order that because of the mercy shown to you they also may now be shown mercy.*

Now here is the way this principle is going to work itself out inexorably in history. God's plan has the Jews being saved on the same pattern as the Gentiles. Just as once the Gentiles were dead and unresponsive to God, but God, in His mercy, took the occasion of Jewish disobedience to the truth to extend His grace to the Gentiles, a day is coming when the Jews, now in the role of disobedience that the Gentiles once occupied, will also themselves be extended the same mercy the Gentiles have experienced.

> "This time, then, it will not be the disobedience of the one which shall produce the conversion of the others. A new discord in the kingdom of God will not be necessary to bring about the final harmony... Israel went out that the Gentiles might enter. But the Gentiles shall not go out to make place for the Jews; *they will open to door to them from within.*"[324]

(11:32) *For God has shut up all in disobedience that He might show mercy to all.*

"God has shut up all in disobedience..." This means, I believe, that God has acted in history in both the case of the Jews and the Gentile to expose to plain view their transgressive character with all its pain. It means that God has acted to bring sinners into touch with themselves as sinners with all the consequences of their disobedience—and this for the purpose of offering pardon to their burdened souls.[325]

"That He might show mercy to all." That is, to Jew and Gentile alike. This purpose statement does not imply universalism, that is, the doctrine that God will eventually save everyone, but simply that God has so worked out His plan of salvation that His merciful remedy is available to every repentant sinner who will appropriate it by faith.

Here is how that sin-consciousness is intensified. Disobedience is the mother of all human suffering. I do not mean that all our miseries are directly attributable to our personal rebellion against God. What I mean is that suffering in all its forms (disease, natural disaster, social distress, political oppression, psychological dysfunction, domestic disorder, you name it) has its roots somewhere in somebody's sin. Much of it goes back to Adam and the curse that grew out of that. Much of it goes back to the sins of others; some of it goes back to our own choices. Sin breeds suffering because it is a violation of the created order... it goes against the grain, and it injures and damages even when it doesn't appear to do so.

Suffering is a form of severe mercy because in letting our sins weigh upon us, in shutting us up to all its miseries and fallout, God providentially prepares many for grace... He makes them hunger and thirst for righteousness... to long for forgiveness... to hate the harsh slavery of sin.

Suffering, then, is grace in disguise. God, in His wisdom, is herding the Jews into that prison house of disobedience, where they must bear the yoke of their sin. One day it will bear fruit. One day, like the prodigal son, they will wake up and come to their senses and see how foolish they are to slop the devil's hogs. They will return to their father in self-repudiation and be received with joy and celebration and great honor.

> (11:33) *Oh the depth of the riches both of the wisdom and knowledge of God! How unsearchable are His judgments and unfathomable His ways!*

Paul from the mountain height attained in his argument, beholds in one view the history of man from the beginning of Adam to the triumphant end in Christ as King of kings. This history is not man's, but God's in His dealing with man, a history of God's own wisdom and knowledge. Paul is the true historian of the races as well as the true philosopher. No man can be either who leaves God out. The Bible teaches more real knowledge about mankind than is to be found in all other books. [326]

"'Wisdom' adapts means to ends and 'knowledge' sees both in all their relations." [327]

The "judgments" (*krimata*) of God are, according to Stifler, the product of His wisdom... that is, His decisions in adapting means to ends are too complex for the microbe minds of puny man to trace out, and His ways, as Isaiah 55:8–10, are far too unfamiliar to men for us to fathom.

The only wise thing for man is to get in line with His decisions and ways, and not try to improve on them, and not sell them short when we don't understand them. That is why it is so important for us to find out what the Scripture teaches and stick with the plan, come

Hell or high water, as the saying goes. In the end, let us consider the Word of God true and know that everyone who contradicts will eventually be proved a liar, as David said (Psa. 51:4).

(11:34) *For who has known the mind of the Lord, or who became His counselor?*

The citation is from the Greek version of Isaiah 40:13. The question is asked in a context of marveling at the glories of His activity in the creation of the earth. Look at creation and all its wonders and ask yourself, "Who among men is equal to the infinite capacity of the Divine Mind?" inquires the prophet. How many among men had any intelligence that God needed so that He felt constrained to invite that person to be His counselor?

"Who could have fathomed this, that God would use even man's disobedience as a means of effecting His saving will. And in it all God's mercy triumphs. He does not suffer anyone to appear before Him with pretensions." [328]

(11:35) *Or who has first given to Him that it might be paid back to Him again?*

To whom does God owe anything? Has any man made any contribution to God that puts God in that man's debt? None.

(11:36) *For from Him and through Him and to Him are all things. To Him be the glory forever. Amen.*

His self-sufficiency... His independence of human assistance is affirmed in these doxological premises.

The truth is the sovereign, omnipotent, omniscient, omnipresent, self-existent, and self-sufficient God is the Prime Mover, the first cause (from Him) and even the secondary cause (through Him) of every good thing[329] (everything we rightly prize and everything upon which life depends). He is the purpose for which all the works of creation exist.

His heart's prayer is that God might be forever glorified by creatures. That mastering aspiration drove Paul like almost no other.

Who knows how we might change if that ambition mastered us to the point that everything we said, did, or thought was filtered through that grid.

"Amen" means "so be it" or "let it be thus."[330]

Proclaiming the gospel in its fullest sense goes beyond telling the world what God has done for us in Christ, but also what we, in turn, should do for Him in gratitude for His amazing grace. In these last chapters, the apostle fleshes that out so that we might honor God in our various relationships. He starts with giving ourselves fully to God who, in Christ, has given His all to us.

In light of the apostle's discourse in this chapter, it is difficult to comprehend how some in Reformed and amillennial circles manage to write out of the future any place for Israel. I am not talking alternatively settling for the dispensation eschatological scheme, which has its own set of issues, but urging simply taking chapter 11 at its face value and admitting that Israel as a nation is not finished in the plan of God, but a great future for that nation yet remains, as the OT redundantly promised. One may argue about what shape that will take, but this author is baffled how otherwise good and intelligent, devout scholars and teachers can blind themselves to the content of this chapter. I think it may be another example of the way sometimes we allow our theological systems to impose themselves on the text and draw unwarranted conclusions that distort the message. We see that same error distort, I believe, the teaching in chapter 7:14ff and the subject of election in chapter 9.

At this point the polemic (argument) of this epistle is essentially finished. The apostle has expounded the true gospel in terms of what God has done for us in Christ and how it works—the gift of salvation by God's pure grace through faith alone. Now he takes up the other side of the gospel—how we believers should respond to that gospel of grace, what response God expects of us believers as our faith operates through love—both vertically and horizontally. Faith, if it truly exists, logically demands a response. And here it is.

---

[300] It is very hard for discerning and realistic people with their ear to the ground to be optimistic in these days in the Western world and in the U.S. in particular

when the spiritual horizon seems ever-darkening and ominously portending. Add to the signs of cultural decay and outright opposition to biblical Christianity the corruption, the compromise, the theological disarmament, the market drivenness and moribund conditions so pervasive among the churches, it grates on the ear to hear the sincere, but naive announce "signs" of revival in our time. God knows we wish for it and pray for it, but it is naive in the extreme to "feel" it in the air. At least that is my opinion. Things, I believe, are due to get much worse before they will get any better—if ever they will in America again, which I personally doubt. I believe that the Spirit like a wind has come and gone as a big "blow" in this country. What is left behind are little breezes and occasional freak gusts, in my sense of things at least.

How wonderful it would be to be wrong. But I doubt seriously that we are. What remains for us is to hold the fort and preserve what remains and gather in the gleanings.

Still, one must resist in this pessimistic (but I believe totally realistic) outlook the temptation to lapse into an Elijah complex that sees only "us four and no more" carrying on for God. God, I repeat, is still in control of His purposes. He has called out in America a people for His Name, and they are many (though not nearly as many as Gallup polls and Barna Group research might lead us to think). He has called them, He will keep them, and they will stand up and be counted.

[301] Cranfield, *ICC: Romans Vol. II*, 547.

[302] Ibid, 547-48.

[303] Hardening is the word that best describes what is today taking place in the U.S. and in the churches. Exposure to the truth without obedience to it gradually produces, by a kind of divine law, an imperviousness to it.

It is remarkable how little effect the Word of the Lord produces in the average church and on the ears of the typical worldling today. Not because the Word of God is weak, but because in the judicial purposes of God, He has allowed men to resist the Word at will and the habit of resistance has become more and more reflexive and effective. Now the truth rolls off their conscience like water off a duck's back. The preacher can bring a firehose to the pulpit, and it is surprising, even shocking, how moderns can shake it off and not even get wet!

In the world there is little functional belief in God, except to blame and shake our fist at Him when life goes to Hell. In the churches even there is little fear of God, for when the judgment of God does not catch up with the disobedient immediately or in ways which we can obviously correlate with it, denial sets in.

Hardness is what the prophetic preacher in America is dealing with and that on a grand scale.

[304] Cranfield, *ICC: Romans Vol. 2*, 550.

[305] *Hina* surely refers to God's purpose rather than the result contemplated by the Jews. I cannot accept the view of Cranfield and Sanday and Headlam that it refers to the former for the simple reason that it makes worse sense. Why would

the Jews pursue their own ruin? To affirm that they did not envision their own ruination in stumbling implies, it seems to me, that they were self-conscious in their "stumbling," but did not foresee the deadly outcome. This makes no sense. Unless I am missing something, this is not a cogent view, despite Cranfield's assertion to the contrary.

The purpose of God has been constantly in view previously and it is *re-appearing* in the last sentence of this verse. It is a reach to see anything else as a referent, in my opinion.

[306] This assertion of the hypothetical impact of Jewish acceptance of the Messiah does not imply that God's options are limited by human responses, but simply acknowledges, without trying to unravel the untraceably complicated outcomes entailed in the interaction between human responsibility and divine sovereignty, that if the Jews had done what they were supposed to do, then God would have done what He promised them. Of course, His promises were always attached to faith, and faith-creating grace was always subject to His sovereign election, so that the outcomes were always perfectly within His control and His prophetic timetable was never actually in jeopardy from a Jewish "surprise." Even so, His plan from eternity past had linked the extension of grace to the nations to the circumstance of Jewish rejection of the good news of Christ and His Kingdom.

See Acts 13:45-48; 18:6; 28:24-28, all of which link turning to the Gentiles with the Gospel to Jewish rejection. Acts 13 exemplifies a precursor of the divine strategy of exciting jealousy among the Jews, a phenomenon which eventually God will use in turning their hearts once again back to their God.

[307] The psychology of this phenomenon is something like what we may have experienced as a child when spoiled with an excess of toys, we mistreated and abused them and indifferently left them laying around exposed to the elements and thieves. Seeing our contempt of our good fortune and the delight and pleasure a disadvantaged child found in one of our casual discards, our parent, to teach us to prize our possessions, boxed up a bundle of them and presented them to the underprivileged child next door who is overjoyed at his newfound wealth. There is a sense that he now has what belongs to us. Our jealously over our former toys is exacerbated not only by the fact he now claims as his what was taken from us, but also by the sheer joy he seems to find in it. It made us long for its return and a chance to renew our pleasure in it. See 10:19 and Deuteronomy 32:21.

[308] For the former point see John 6:28-29 and for the latter see John 1:1, 14; 3:11.

[309] Paul does not mean that he himself is the saving agent, but God's instrument. It would be like a 911 operator hoping to save some, whose lives are threatened with disaster, by summoning police, fire, or other emergency personnel to the scene of a crime, fire, or accident. He or she might well boast that "I have saved a few" when in reality they were never directly involved in the rescue.

[310] Harrison, *Romans: The Expositor's Bible Commentary*, Vol. 10, 121.

[311] Godet, *Epistle to the Romans*, 404.

[312] Some commentators, influenced by the root/branches analogy which follows and feeling that they must be parallel in meaning, see the first fruits as the patriarchs. Still others argue for Christ as the first fruit. Once we agree that there is no compelling reason to take the two analogies as exact parallels, but concede that they can be two complementary comparisons, it certainly makes good sense, if not better, to see the first fruits as the present believing remnant. Christ is a poor referent simply because He is not properly a product of the harvest of the Jews, but the source of it.

[313] The woman who wins the man, man who wins the woman, the employee who wins the promotion, the player who wins the position, the company that wins the contract, the city that wins the bidding war for a big employer typically feels superior to all his, her or its rivals. We naturally feel that somebody saw something in us that was lacking in our competitors. Although many winners in high stakes wars are gracious and disguise their feelings well, others assume an air of arrogance that make them unbearable.

[314] It is of interest theologically that in this metaphor Paul does not distinguish between Israel and the Church as the dispensationalist viewpoint does but portrays the Church as an extension of Israel.

[315] Their persuasion is more understandable when we get on their horizon and remember that God apparently refused to save some of the Jews and elected to save in their place some of the Gentiles. Both were initially unbelieving, but God elected the Gentiles over the Jews. That, they reasoned, must say something for their intrinsic worth and superiority to the Jews. God must have seen in them something He liked better than in the Jews. Wrong.

[316] God is transcendent, yet He is immanent; God accepts us as we are, but He will not leave us as we were; God loves the sinner, but He hates the sin. God knows what we need before we even pray, yet He wants us to persevere in prayer. God wants us to know that it all depends on Him, yet serve as if it all depends on us. God is patient in following His plan, yet He is not slack about fulfilling His promises.

[317] Cranfield, *ICC: Romans Vol. 2*, 570.
[318] Ibid, 572.

[319] In this regard an analogy might be the business "secrets" of a maverick entrepreneur which are known to his close circle but rejected by outsiders. They are "secrets" in that they embody important business realities known and understood by him and his associates but not appreciated by more conventional outsiders.

[320] Godet, *Epistle to the Romans*, 411.

[321] ". . . when the feeling of [enmity] is applied to God, we must eliminate from it all admixture of personal resentment, or of the spirit of revenge. God hates the sinner in the same sense in which the sinner ought to hate himself. . . This sentiment is only the hatred [that perfect holiness bears] to evil; and [bears toward] the wicked man in so far as he is identified with evil." Godet, *Epistle to the Romans*, 421. [brackets mine]

[322] Perhaps a rough political analogy to this "love-hate" relationship God sustains to Israel might be the relationship the U.S. government had with the South during the Civil War. Where the issue of the union and slavery was concerned the government viewed the South as an enemy. Where the vision of a nation was concerned, the South was beloved, and the Government fought to regain her.

[323] In this principle rests our security as believers. It is as secure as our faith in God and our faith is a product of His own creation (Eph. 2:8-10).

[324] Godet, *Epistle to the Romans*, 414.

[325] Godet cites the Danish theologian Nielsen: "The sinful nature already existed in all; but that the conviction of it might be savingly awakened in individuals, this latent sin required to be manifested historically on a great scale in the lot of nations." *Epistle to the Romans*, 415.

The way to Heaven in the wisdom of God ironically leads right through Hell, so to speak. God drives the self-sufficient and the self-righteous sinner with the whips of sin until they seek relief in the mercy of God from its lashes and cast themselves at the foot of the Cross where the blood of Christ washes away their sin.

I have seen cattle ranches where the fences and gates are so designed that the cattle can be herded in and out of pens and down lanes between the fences into chutes and loaded onto trucks and taken to market. Those pens, lanes and chutes remind me of what God does. He herds the unbelieving into the pens of pain and uses the prods of sin to drive them into the only direction of relief. . . toward the chutes of His mercy.

[326] Stifler, *The Epistle to the Romans*, 200.

[327] Ibid, 200.

[328] Nygren, *Commentary on Romans*, 408.

[329] The analogy of Scripture of course excludes in the expression "all things" God as the source of evil. See, for example, Jas. 1:13, 17 and 1 Jo. 1:5. In context Paul has reference to the works of creation.

[330] Vine, *Expository Dictionary of New Testament Wors*, 53.

Romans Chapter 12

(12:1) I urge you therefore, brethren, by the mercies of God, to present your bodies a living and holy sacrifice, acceptable to God, which is your spiritual service of worship.

"Therefore..."
Cranfield:

> The implication of this "therefore" is that Christian ethics are theologically motivated or—to put it in a different way—that the Christian's obedience is his response to what God had done for him in Christ, the expression of his gratitude... [it] makes clear right from the start the theocentric nature of all truly Christian moral effort; for it indicates that the source from which such effort springs is neither a humanistic desire for the enhancement of the self by the attainment of moral superiority, nor the legalist's illusory hope of putting God under an obligation, but the saving deed of God itself. [331]

"By (*dia* + the genitive = through) the mercies of God..." This appeal certainly looks back to the premise of chapters 9–11, namely, that salvation is based strictly on the exercise of the sovereign mercy or grace of God and not in any respect upon human pedigree or merit. Of course, there is no problem with seeing it also encompassing the scope of his entire argument up to this point, but the last section of chapter 11 hit the note of mercy especially hard and set up this transition.

As for the difference between mercy and grace, it is primarily one of perspective: "Mercy" is being delivered from a fate that we truly deserve; "grace" is receiving a benefit that we truly don't deserve. The plural form of the former word (*ton oiktirmon*) reminds us that the mercy of God is a redundant experience... it meets us around every corner. It is so regular and routine that we are prone to take it for granted and to presume upon it as a birthright.

"Through..." In appealing to the believer *through* the mercies of God, the apostle sees God's mercies as an intermediary, which speaks eloquently in God's behalf for a thankful response in conforming to His will.

"To present..." (*parastesai*). In extra-biblical literature this is a technical word for the offering of sacrifice, [332] though not in the Greek version of the OT. The infinitive is aorist tense, which accentuates a simple moral imperative. The form by itself leaves the question unanswered as to whether this presentation is to be viewed as a one-time consecration or one that needs daily renewal. No doubt it is both, that is, a self-conscious resolution at a point in time that needs daily renewal by virtue of the weakness of the flesh. Jesus urged his disciples to keep "watching and praying, that you enter not into temptation, for the spirit is willing, but the flesh is weak." These words (Matthew 26:41 of our Lord to His disciples in the garden of Gethsemane) apply here also.

"Your bodies..." (*ta somata*). Calvin: "By bodies he means not only our skin and bones, but the totality of which we are composed. He has used this word to denote by synecdoche [a figure for 'the whole for the parts, the parts for the whole'] all our parts, for the members of the body are the instruments by which we perform our actions." [333] [brackets mine]

When we present body with all its members to God, we relinquish title to God. Our body and its parts are no longer our own, but now are formally acknowledged as a divine property.

"Sacrifice..." (*thusian*). The vocation of believers is that of priests to God. "You... are being built up as a spiritual house for a holy priesthood to offer up spiritual sacrifices acceptable to God though Jesus Christ" (1 Pet. 2:5). "But you are a chosen race, *a royal priesthood*, a holy nation, a people for God's own possession, that you may proclaim the excellencies of Him who has called you out of darkness into His marvelous light... Keep your behavior excellent among the Gentiles... " (1 Pet. 2:9, 12).

"Living..." (*zosan*). The sacrifice believers as priests are summoned to offer contrasted with those of the Levitical priests in this respect:

what God wants from us is not the symbolic sacrifices of slaughtered bulls and goats or lifeless grains of the field, but a life dedicated to the glory of God.

Ironically, it is easier to die for Christ than it is to live for Him, for the martyr dies once, but the disciple dies to self daily. In the final analysis, only those who live for Christ on a day-by-day basis will likely step up to die for Him when the occasion presents itself, for if one will not sacrifice his self-will for Christ in smaller matters in the routine of everyday life, certainly one will not voluntarily forfeit his or her very life for Him in a test of great peril.

"Holy..." (*hagian*). In the OT codes prescribing sacrifices, it was always required that sacrificial animals be physically "unblemished." Personal holiness is the spiritual counterpart to that prerequisite. To be "holy" means to be "set apart" (Vine, op. cit, p. 37) from common or profane use and reserved for God and for righteousness. "This is pure and undefiled religion in the sight of our God and Father, to visit orphans and widows (the helpless and hurting) in their distress and to keep oneself unstained (unspotted, undefiled) from the world" (James 1:27, parentheses mine for clarity).

"Pleasing (acceptable) to God..." This is an appositional phrase that summarizes the effect of a "living, holy sacrifice," that is, the requirements of an acceptable sacrifice for a believer-priest.

"Your spiritual (*logiken*) worship." Christian worship, if it is Christian, is not rote ritual but a rational engagement of our whole being... a profound affair of the heart... a response of the soul to the living God. Nothing less is acceptable to God. Spiritual worship is engagement of the heart.

> (12:2) *And do not be conformed to this world, but be transformed by the renewing of your mind, that you may prove what the will of God is, that which is good and acceptable and perfect.*

Here, he begins to explain the starting point of personal holiness. Creeping around with folded hand, in robes and candlelight surrounded by incense, smells, and bells does not signify holiness or a retreat from this dark world and its godless ways. The starting point is a firm moral resolution in the believer's heart to resist conformity to the corrupt and twisted ways of the sinful society all about us. That saint declares to himself in the inward man: "I refuse to be a clone. By God's grace, I resolve to be different!"

And do not be conformed (syschematizesthe—molded after) to this age.

Holiness begins, then, with godly determination, as the old cliché goes, not to let the world press us into its mold.

The fashion of this age is self-fulfillment rather than self-denial, to do our own thing rather than God's thing, to get revenge rather than to grant forgiveness, to live for the moment than to live for the future, and to take the broad road that leads to destruction rather than the narrow road that leads to life.

But be transformed in newness of the mind...

How do we transform ourselves? There is no button we can push, no switch we can flip, and no string we can pull. The key lies in steadfastly denying ourselves the license to be conformed to the world. When we take that step, transformation begins. We can't get heaven in until we take steps to get the world out of our souls. This is the Great Divorce that must happen.

In order that you may prove what the will of God is...

When the mind is transformed, it runs the behavior into different channels. If you want to know what pleases God, find those who have hearts after God and see what kinds of conduct characterizes them. "Prove" can also mean "approve." Which is it? The two run together in a way. When the heart (matrix of mind, affections, and will) is in sync with the Holy Spirit, the outflow confirms the will of God. So, we can say, real Christian character is revealed by the behaviors we approve.

Diversity in the family of believers is a great gift of God, but given our fleshly pride, it can and often does pose a threat to our unity in the disruption of our harmony. So, our unity and diversity must be valued and upheld in a godly tension founded on the truth in Christ.

Paul strikes two chords in this passage:

373

1. He emphasizes the need to come to terms with equality in our unity.

2. He emphasizes the obligation to be exuberant in our diversity.

In 12:1–2, the apostle issued an appeal that summarizes the essence of Christian duty. He calls upon us to live as believer-priests. The vocation of a priest is to offer gifts and sacrifices that are pleasing to God (Heb. 8:3). The sacrifice he calls upon us to make is the offering of ourselves. That commitment will translate to a firm resolution to reject conformity to the world in order to cooperate with the mental renovation project the Spirit of God has underway in our lives.

That general appeal now leads to more specific instructions about Christian behavior and ethics.

Paul knows that human nature is ever consistent, even though redeemed. As long as we are encumbered with this flesh, pride, the tap root of sinfulness, is always present as a kind of gravitational undertow. Somehow, our flesh is never satisfied to be equal in value to others. With great ingenuity, we find ways to make distinctions among ourselves that lend us the excuse to feel superior to others.

Believers who are mature in their understanding of their faith will recognize that there is nothing in its premises that permits the perception that one child of God is in any way more precious or valued in His sight than another. All stand on exactly on the same level in terms of value, if not in terms of function.

It is that perennial gravity toward pride and self-exaltation that Paul addresses right off the bat in warning us against an overly generous appraisal of our own relative worth in the sight of God. The diversity of spiritual gifts, some more spectacular and significant than others, as we know from 1 Corinthians 12–14, was the occasion of some of this vaunting in the early as well as in the modern church.

(12:3) *For through the grace given to me I say to every man among you not to think more highly of himself than he ought to think; but to think so as to have sound judgment, as God has allotted to each a measure of faith.*

"Through the grace given to me..." An allusion to his apostolic office but couched in terms consistent with his call for humility. Whatever spiritual authority he has, he possesses on the basis of divine grace, not inherent superiority. Paul shores up his exhortation with a positive example of the Christian perspective. All he has, he received from God, and not because he deserved it, but despite the fact he didn't. "Grace" broadcasts the fact that the favor God showed him was unmerited. Humility is not expressed by denying our spiritual gifts and natural talents, however great they may be, but by acknowledging with Paul that we are mere custodians of a divine deposit for which we owe no credit to ourselves nor is any owed to us by others as if we had anything to do with it.

I say to every man among you not to think more highly of himself (hyperphronein = to think too highly of oneself, to be haughty) than he ought to think...

Paul sounds a warning against an inflated view of oneself that is at variance with reality, that is, flies in the face of the divine revelation, or to put it another way, ignores the premises of our faith.

"To every man among you..." This inclusive phraseology embraces the whole community of (Christian) faith, not just its leaders. Godet wants to limit the reference, without adequate justification, to gifted leaders.[334]

"Not to think more highly of himself than he ought (*dei*) to think..." That is, in light of what God has revealed and we claim to have believed. "*Dei*" is an impersonal verb, which means "it is necessary" or "one ought or should." [335] It denotes compulsion of some kind, whether situational, logical, divine, or arising from propriety.

But to think so as to have sound judgment... (sophronein = to be of sound mind, be reasonable, sensibly, serious, to keep one's head).

Sanity is defined by one's relationship to reality; reality, in turn, is defined by divine revelation. To entertain a view of oneself that exaggerates one's importance in relation to others is, in effect, roaming the range of insanity in that one is out of touch with reality as described by divine revelation. Paul calls for believers in their self-appraisal to be sensible and stay within the bounds of sound judgment. Forget personal or cultural criteria of self-esteem; don't get drunk on the wine of cultural values and assign to yourself a superiority that is out of joint with reality. Keep your head, square up with what is revealed.

As God has allotted (emerisen) to each a measure of faith (metron pisteos)...

The NIV translates this clause "in accordance with the measure of faith God has given you."

Emerisen is from *merizo*. It means first to divide or separate, then to distribute, deal out, assign, apportion. [336]

Compare also Ephesians 4:7, where the topic of spiritual gifts is also broached, Paul says:

> "Now to each one of us grace has been given (*edothe*) according to the measure (*metron*) of the gift (*doreas*) of Christ."

One must think, given the fact that the same topic is in view in both contexts, that it is the same writer and that the language is similar, that Paul is expressing approximately the same idea in both. My assumption is that "given" in Ephesians 4:7 corresponds to "allotted" in Romans 12:3 and that "the measure (*metron*) of the gift of Christ" corresponds metonymically to "the measure of faith." If so, "faith" is used as a metonym.

In metonymy, a writer speaks of one thing under another name for some reason. The expression, "That lady sets a fine table!" meaning "That lady is some cook!" is an example of metonymy. One might substitute the sign for the thing signified (i.e., speak of baptism [the sign] rather than confession [the thing signified]) or mention the cause rather than its effect (e.g., the gift of the Holy Spirit [the source] instead of the gift of "what is good" [His benefits]). Compare Luke 11:13 with Matthew 7:11 for this latter example.

In that case, "faith" as the secondary cause on the human side stands here for its effects in the grace of God, namely, measured spiritual gifts or endowments of the Holy Spirit.

Although, as Charles Hodge notes, this is not the generally favored interpretation of this phrase, "this general sense is well suited to the context, as the following verses, containing a specification of the gifts of prophesying, teaching, ruling, &c., appear to be an amplification of this clause."[337]

The most common interpretation, according to Hodge, is one that has Paul saying, in effect: "Let everyone think of himself according to the nature or character of the gifts which he has received." That sense, I think, offers an antidote to pride of gifts that is so subjective as to be useless and seems to me somewhat beside the point. If I understand 1 Corinthians 12–14 rightly, the major problem was not people in a spirit of envy, and it was not overstepping the bounds of their true giftedness in exceeding the limits that their faith gave them the confidence to believe that they possessed but feeling superior in the exercise of endowments that they actually possessed. Besides, even if the former were the problem, it would be a small remedy indeed to exhort a vain believer to consult the measure of his faith and stick strictly to its parameters.

As a practical matter, who knows how to do that? How many believers can even identify their giftedness with any precision, much less define the measure that God has set for them? And what keeps a vain person from drumming up the "faith" to believe that his or her gift is greater than it is? Surely, we know that in such cases, if that is the constraint Paul applies, it will hardly help since vanity makes us think that our giftedness is greater than it is and to lay the blame off on the confidence God gave us.

To me, if I rightly grasp it, this interpretation is nonsense and the prescription for pride totally impractical. I would have no idea how to apply it personally in any halfway objective fashion—or even in a subjective fashion with any confidence that I was right. To this hour, I can't tell anybody with any certainty the extent of my giftedness, nor do I know any way to be sure that I stay safely within its limits. I think I am scarcely alone, and this spells doom for this view.

Why not say it straightforwardly as in Ephesians? Because, I suspect, he wanted to highlight the fact that the diversity of Christian gifts had God, not man, for its primary cause and that God's endowments had as their secondary cause on the human side not special virtues in the believer but were a consequence of that dignity we all share in common—namely, our faith in Christ.

Hence, I would paraphrase the sense like this:

Beware of pride of gifts. Don't think that you are superior because of any special spiritual gifts you might possess. Keep your head on straight and remember that God has allotted to each and every one of His servants certain spiritual endowments—measured endowments that owe nothing to any virtue you possess but have their origin and cause in that divinely created dignity common to all Christians, namely, our faith in Christ.

(12:4–5) *For just as we have many members in one body and all the members do not have the same function (praxin from praxis = activity, function, business), so we, who are many, are one body in Christ, and individually members one of another. (parenthesis mine)*

"For" is an elaboration by analogy. Paul sees a comparison between the nature of the church and the nature of the human body in that both are examples of diversity contained within an overarching unity, and the members of both are related to each other in a complementary, interdependent way that should minimize any tendency for one member to feel self-sufficiency or complete without the contribution of the others.

God designed the Church[338] on the analogy of a human body. That is why the Bible calls the Church the body of Christ. It is not an organization, but a highly complex and mysterious *organism* contained within local organizations but by no means coextensive with it. Christ corresponds to the Head of the Body, and it is He who, through His Spirit residing in each and every part, directs its members in their various special functions. All the members complement one another, and the healthy growth of the Body is impeded to the extent that the members fail to perform their functions. No member is self-sufficient, and all owe their life and appointed function and serviceability to the Head of the Body.

"In Christ" represents an apostolic reminder that this diversity in unity is not natural or humanly contrived but a supernatural creation.

The thought of Paul in these verses has its amplification in 1 Corinthians 12:12–31.

> (12:6) *And since we have gifts that differ according to the grace given us, let each exercise them accordingly; if prophecy, according to the proportion (kata ten analogian = in right relationship to or in agreement with) of his faith. (parenthesis mine)*

Diversity is the norm in the body of Christ and has its source in the grace of God in response to our faith. Now, Paul admonishes us to exercise those gifts in the manner appropriate to them.

If someone possesses the gift of prophecy, then let them exercise that gift in strict agreement with the premises and principles of the faith once and for all delivered to the saints. "They are to be careful not to utter (under the impression that they are inspired) anything which is incompatible with their believing in Christ." [339]

Like certain other endowments of the Spirit, the parameters of the gift of "prophecy" are not easy to establish, that is, it is no simple matter to define exactly where it starts and where it leaves off in relation to other gifts.

But I think we are safe in agreeing with Cranfield[340] that:

> The prophet was distinguished from the teacher by the immediacy of his inspiration: his utterance was the result of particular revelation. It might be a prediction about the future of the community (e.g., Acts 11:27ff), of an individual (Acts 21:10ff), or an announcement of something which God required to be done (e.g., Acts 13:1ff). It was characteristic of prophecy that it was directed to a particular concrete situation. Though he was dependent on special revelations, the prophet's mind—

unlike that of the speaker in tongues—was fully engaged, and his message was addressed to the church's understanding. By it, the church was instructed (1 Cor. 14:31), edified (1 Cor. 14:3), exhorted (1 Cor. 14:3), comforted (1 Cor. 14:3), or rebuked. Thus, prophecy fulfilled a truly shepherding function.

"The faith..." (*he pistis*). I agree with Cranfield[341] that this noun is not referring, I believe, to any special charismatic faith (i.e., a special endowment above and beyond saving faith), but to the body of truth believed. The first would be calling upon the prophets prone to call attention to themselves or prone to exuberance, not to exceed the comfort (and safety) zone of their confidence in speaking for the Spirit of God. That is possible, but the definite article tilts, it seems to me, the issue in favor of the other and provides a more objective standard of constraint.

Still, it may be that *analogian* should be translated "in proportion to," and the article merely serves to identify the prophet's individual confidence about the communications of the Holy Spirit. In that event, Paul's admonition is to play it safe and do not, for any motive or reason, go beyond what one is absolutely confident represents the voice of God. The prophet Nathan once, with good intentions, made that very mistake in 1 Samuel 7 when he gave David the initial go-ahead to build the temple, only to be corrected that night by the Lord.

(12:7) *If service (diakonian from diakonia), in his serving; or he who teaches, in his teaching...*(parenthesis mine)

"Service..." It is not easy to determine whether the apostle here is referring to a gift of helps or service in the more general sense or in the narrower sense of those specially equipped for the office work of a deacon who was charged with the distribution of alms and assisting the needy.

The point here is probably twofold: 1) to remind people to stick to their knitting, so to speak, and not to presume to exercise gifts not recognized in them, and 2) to urge the gifted not to quench the Spirit by sitting on their giftedness, but to honor the obligation implicit in the gift by serving or ministering to the needs of others energetically. God desires that his servants put His assets to work for Him.

Likewise, the teacher is obliged to busy himself in that function that the Spirit of God has programmed him to perform. The member has no right to be AWOL or usurp out of envy the function of another. The eye makes a bad ear, and the ear makes an inferior eye; the foot makes a sorry hand, and the hand a poor excuse for a foot.

(12:8) *"or he who exhorts (ho parakalon from parakaleo), in his exhortation; he who gives, with liberality; he who leads, with diligence; he who shows mercy, with cheerfulness." (parenthesis mine)*

The difference between the gift of exhortation and teaching, where they differ, is, as I understand it, in these distinctions:

Teaching aims at getting the truth straight in people's minds and hearts, whereas exhortation aims at getting that truth down into people's hands and feet. Teaching calls us to recognition and conviction of the truth; exhortation calls men to action based on what they know and believe. Teaching aims at getting the believer rightly informed about life; exhortation aims at getting us rightly engaged in life. Teaching aims at getting us to understand the truth; exhortation at getting us to act on the truth.

It is worth noting that biblical exhortation always uses the Word of God as its starting point. Using truth as its point of departure, the exhorter extends its implications into the life situation of the hearer, using the comforts, incentives, and warnings of the Word to prod the heart and will of the hearer to respond in the way that is situationally honoring to God.

Life experience teaches us that spiritual gifts do not always come singly but appear in clusters, but the mix shows up in kaleidoscopic variety. A teaching gift may be blended with a gift of exhortation,[342] but each in different measures in different people so that the gifts in their combinations may be as variegated as the flowers in a rose garden.

"He who gives..." (*ho metadidous* from *metadidomi* = impart, share, used of almsgiving to the needy). I tend to agree with Murray that, here, Paul is referring to a special gift of generosity that the Spirit implants in some saints (as opposed to those who administer alms since this last work seems to have been covered under the work of "serving").[343]

"With simplicity..." Is he exhorting those vested with this gift to give liberally or practice their generosity out of pure motives? The phrase is again ambiguous (*en aploteti* from *aplotes* = simplicity, sincerity, uprightness, frankness, then generosity, liberality; "Hermas is esp. fond of this word, mng. Simple goodness, which gives without reserve."[344], and both appeals would be appropriate. However, because a gift of liberality implies the existence already of a spirit of generosity and any appeal in that direction would therefore be a redundancy, it makes more sense to exhort givers to avoid the greatest trap which besets the generous, namely, the temptation to employ their liberality with ulterior motives, seeking by their largess to buy friends, favor, power, or exemption from accountability.

It is easier for the giver to give than to do it purely for the glory of God, whereas for the teacher or the exhorter, the greater temptation is neglect of God-given capacity rather than expending oneself in what is difficult.

"He who leads..." (*ho proistamenos* from *proistemi* = to be at the head [of], rule, direct; to be concerned about, care for, give aid). *Proistamenos* represents a compound of a Greek preposition (*pro* = before or in front) and a verb (*histami* = to put, place, set, stand). From the combined ideas, we get to put, place, set, or stand before, and from that, we get by a natural transition the idea of leading or ruling. This is the very word used in 1 Thessalonians 5:12–13:

> "But we request of you, brethren, that you appreciate (or recognize) those who diligently labor among you, and have charge over you in the Lord and give you instruction, and that you esteem them very highly in love because of their work."

It is also used in the same way of fathers managing their homes (see 1 Tim. 3:4, 5, 12) and in conjunction with rewarding those elders who rule well with double honor (1 Tim. 5:17).

"With diligence..." (*en spoude*). It is much easier to bear a title than to bear the responsibility that goes with it. If God has made you a spiritual leader, your temptation will be to enjoy the power of office but to shirk its burdens... to bask in the privilege of being somebody with clout without doing anything of substance.

"He who shows mercy..." (*ho eleon* from *eleeo* = to be merciful, to show mercy, to help someone [out of pity]). Another spiritual endowment is the gift of showing mercy. Some people have a special feel for this, an uncommon touch bestowed by the Spirit of God. However, showing mercy is often a hard and inconvenient labor, especially when we can't just swoop in with a splash of great mercy, get out, and get on with our lives. When the need for mercy becomes a major inconvenience, a bottleneck in our lives, then comes the temptation to react to the need, to blame the victim, and to respond, if at all, with acts of mercy in a spirit of resentment.

That is why Paul counsels bearers of this gift to avoid the snare, especially endemic to those who, by the nature of their special gift, tend to be called upon and taxed again and again. Let them remember the Spirit of Christ and let the Spirit exercise mercy through them "with cheerfulness" (*en hilaroteti* from *hilarotes* = cheerfulness, gladness, gratefulness), not glumness. (By the way, one 'hears' our English word 'hilarity' in this Greek word, but the former is quite detached from the Greek etymology. A 'hilarious' giver is a corny stain on the term).

The danger exists that members of the body will exaggerate their relative importance and will undervalue the importance of others in the overall scheme of things.

The analogy of a human body with the divine scheme of the Church is used to put the relative importance of all the parts into perspective.

Each member of the body of Christ has its function and gifts that fit that divine appointment.

Nowhere does the Bible discuss or emphasize the "trick" of identifying one's spiritual gifts, leaving us to infer, I think, that the Spirit's manifestations are a spontaneous faith-driven inclination.

The closer we walk in alignment with the Spirit, the more likely we are to find our identity—gift-wise—in Christ. It is a simple matter of attunement.

It is apparently possible that, for various reasons, people run ahead of the impulses of the Spirit in spiritual gifts just as oftentimes they run ahead of the evidence in the matter of natural gifts and presume upon gifts that they do not possess or, as implied here, in excess of what God has given them. When this happens, it is largely for the same reasons: admiration, envy, and the desire for applause or to earn a reputation for nearness to God, which can then be translated into influence over others for personal advantage.

It is also possible that the Spirit is willing to express Himself in and through us, but the flesh is weak and balky, particularly in those kinds of manifestations, where a toll is taken on us at that level.

Use of spiritual gifts is a matter of stewardship. We are custodians. It is a serious thing to put the Holy Spirit under lock and key, as it were, for the comfort of the flesh.

There are special gifts of the Holy Spirit.

They differ from natural gifts in that they are directly a manifestation or activities of the Holy Spirit working through the medium of a personality.

These gifts can be suppressed or restrained.

Each repository is obliged to exercise them. One can easily see how this discussion, on the use and implied abuse of spiritual gifts in the Body, evokes these exhortations about undergirding them in the spirit of sincere Christian love and framing all with humility and righteousness when people treat us badly.

> (12:9) *Let love (agape) be without hypocrisy (anypokritos). Abhor (apostygountes) what is evil (to ponepon); cleave (kollomenoi) to what is good (<u>to agatho</u>). (parentheses mine)*

"It is difficult to express how ingenious almost all men are in counterfeiting a love which they do not really possess."[345]

How important is love in the Christian equation? It is the *sine qua non* ("without which nothing") of our religion. Love is the first principle of the Christian life... it is the litmus test of knowing God and being a child of God... a touchstone of having been regenerated. It is the Christian's rule of life, the very badge of discipleship (John 13:34–35). Bottom line: *No love, no Christian.*

Because understanding of this exhortation is so fundamental, I feel the need to expand on this admonition a bit, for if contemporary Christians are confused about anything, it is what one scholar, D. A. Carson, termed the difficult doctrine of love. [346] So this text presents is a good opportunity to clarify the subject and dispel some popular misunderstandings.

Love is a reflex of the Spirit of Christ who indwells us... it is the Holy Spirit projecting through us the character of God, for God is love (1 John 4:8). The expression of this love is imperfect because its medium (us) is still encumbered with the resistance of an opposing principle in the form of this sinful flesh. Consequently, the motions of love sponsored by the Spirit within get distorted or stuffed on occasion in its passage from the Spirit through the static inference of the flesh.

The world, in its conceptions of love, understands neither what love is nor how it is rightly expressed, nor without knowing God, does it grasp the moral impossibility of manifesting the love of God. The notion that one can imitate the love of Jesus without embracing Jesus as one's Lord and Savior belongs to the world of myth as much as the notion that man, unaided by mechanical means, can fly without wings. No one can express the love of Jesus in the corridors of life apart from union with the Spirit of Jesus. The world, at its best, can only superficially mimic it, but no unbeliever can attain it; it can only be reproduced through us by the Spirit of God. That which is flesh is flesh, that which is Spirit is Spirit (John 3:6). Water seeks its own level and can rise no higher than the principle to which it belongs.

Without regeneration by the Spirit of God, the requirement of the law of God (which is love, Romans 13:8–10) is an impossible standard. The best the world can do is love its friends, not its enemies, and never for selfless ends (Matt. 5:43–48). In a nutshell, Christian love is to love God with all one's heart, strength, and mind and to love one's neighbor as oneself (Matt. 22:36–40).

To expect any unregenerate person to even begin to do that is like asking them to shoot a spit wad and hit the moon on a dark night. The world has no right conception of what love even looks like. Only a born-again heart can even begin to approach the standard, though none of us in this flesh will ever come close to hitting the bull's eye.

Which brings us back to the words of John Calvin that I quoted at the beginning:

> "It is difficult to express how ingenious almost all men are in counterfeiting a love which they do not really possess."[347]

That is exactly why Paul hastened to append to his exhortation a word of warning.

"Without hypocrisy…" In ancient Greece, as you may already know, actors were called "hypocrites."[348]That was because actors pretended to be something they were not, to feel things they did not in real life, to do and be things they did not do in everyday experience. Acting was a form of pretense that, on stage, the audience accepted with no prejudice. Paul is telling us to love in reality, not with pretense. In the streets, don't be phony about it. What he has in mind is well expressed by John in his first epistle (3:16–18):

> We know love by this, that He (Jesus) laid down His life for us (the ultimate model of self-sacrifice in pursuit of the well-being of the undeserving); and we (obliged by His example to follow in His steps) ought to lay down our lives for the brethren (at the very least). But whoever has the world's goods (disposable material resources), and beholds his brother in need and closes his heart against him, how does the love of God abide in him? Little children, let us not love with word or with tongue, but *in deed* and *in truth*" (brackets mine for clarity).

Paul was aware of the danger, encumbered as we are by the resistance of the flesh, to be content with talking a good game and not walking the talk. He tells us, in effect, to quit talking trash and play the game. Let our feet, our hands, and our resources do the talking for us.

Let's put our money where our mouth is.

This raises a crucial point of clarification. Biblical love, as I have already intimated, is not, at its core, a way of feeling but a way of behaving. I do not suggest that love is vacant of sentiment but merely insist that in the final analysis, the most telling factor in determining its presence or absence is how one treats the objects of our alleged love, not how we claim we feel about them. I personally don't put as much stock in the way parents say they feel about their kids as the way they treat them. A sensible young woman will put much more weight on the way her lover treats her than how he says he feels about her. Likewise in Christian love, the acid test is not sentiment but behavior toward God and toward our neighbor as in Matthew 22:36ff.

If love is, first and foremost, a behavior, it is not any kind of behavior we decide to make it. It is not defined by political correctness or someone's narrow social agenda. It is defined by imitation of the character of God, and the imitation of the character of God is expressed in conforming to the spirit of His law.

There is no such thing as "love" that does not manifest itself in faithful obedience to God. The essence of Christian charity to my neighbor is Christian conformity to what God says is right. I can't serve the well-being of society or my neighbor while disobeying God, for the law of God defines not only what is right in His sight but what is good for my neighbor and myself. Anything short of that is self-destructive and socially destructive.

> "By this we know that we love the children of God, when we love God and observe His commandments. For this is the love of God, that we keep His commandments; and His commandments are not burdensome" (1 John 5:2–3).

This is something like telling a man how to know if he is in love with a woman. The test, he says, is do you do what she tells you and enjoy it, that is, you don't find it an irksome yoke.

And this is love that we walk according to His commandments (1 John 5:3).

> "But whoever keeps His word, in him the love of God has truly been perfected (completed)" (1 John 2:5). (brackets mine for clarity)

The Lord revealed His character to Israel as a God who shows "lovingkindness to thousands, to those who love Me and keep My commandments" (Deut. 5:10). The last phrase is appositional, making concrete what is abstract in the first.

"Abhorring what is evil..." The original is especially strong, meaning to "hate violently, to loathe, to be disgusted with." The participial connection is modal, indicating, in part, the form that love ought to take in practice.

Love is, first of all, moral in its character. Love is not wrapping one's arms around social injustice, moral perversion, marital infidelity, ethical corruption, domestic violence, substance abuse and corporate mistreatment of workers, and saying it's okay. Love draws the line on evil in whatever form. Biblical love draws the same lines God draws, not the ever-shifting standards of the political correctness police.

No one loves the creations of God who is not offended by what offends their Creator. Any loving person abhors what God calls evil. What the Bible teaches on that score is what God teaches. And that is the final word.

"Cleaving to what is good..." The same goes for cleaving to what He loves. The original word for "cleaving" is the participial form of *kollao*, which means "to join fast together." In one classical reference in the Greek poet, Aeschylus, we find the word translated "is indissolubly bound to woe." [349] The idea is firm adherence. Find me the person who is best in touch with the heart of God... who best understands what God hates and what God loves... whose heart resonates with those same divine principles and passions, there is a person who truly loves God and loves people in the sense that Christ commanded us.

"No criterion of our alignments is more searching than the antithesis instituted between good and evil."[350]

As I suggested earlier, we have some really false and misleading ideas about Christian love. Some of those models are centered on emotion, and some rotate around the wrong substance.

One such notion, I noted above, is that love comes down to affection. Indeed, we use the word in that sense to describe people in love, but the defining feature of God's love is not so much affection but a way of treating people. The ultimate expression of that love is expressed in John 3:16, 1 John 4:9–10, and Romans 5:6–8. Not to suggest affection is not missing in God's care for His people, but that affection per se is not the defining principle of what love is.

Another expression of unhypocritical love is:

(12:10) *Be devoted to one another in brotherly love; give preference to one another in honor...*

"Be devoted" is the plural adjective "*philostrogoi*," meaning "loving tenderly, affectionate," and speaks "of the love of parents and children, brothers and sisters." [351] Though affection is not the essence of Christian love but rather joyous obedience to God, our love for God ought always to translate into an affection for all the family in Christ whom He loves. If the Spirit of God dwells in our spirit, then we should in our own affections reflect the tender affections of God.

The practical question is raised as to how one can be exhorted to summon affections that, in fact, may not exist and which we do not have the power to call forth by a simple act of the will. The answer in all such cases (see 12:2 "be transformed..."), I think, lies in embracing the ideal... in moral commitment to the divine ideal on the human side. From there, the Spirit of God will cause us to will and do His good pleasure (Phil. 2:13). Our job is to aim to do right, and God will help us close in on the mark in the process of sanctification.

Another important point is to remember that embedded in and standing behind and above the dead, cold, material letters on the pages of the Scriptures is that mysterious living, active, re-creative and transforming power that we call the "Word of God."[352] It never goes forth without producing its intended effect... effects not regularly discernible or measurable even to the human objects affected by it, yet never inconsequentially[353] (Isa. 55:11).

Hence, these very exhortations are like seeds in the heart of genuine believers, watered and fertilized, and bringing forth in their time the very harvest that they asked for. What the Spirit calls for goes forth with reproductive effect. The Word, again, is like a seed fertilized by the Spirit, which causes Christian virtues to be conceived in the womb of the heart and to bring forth fruit to God in time. The Spirit working through the Word creates over time what He commands and elicits what He exhorts.

"Give (*proegoumenoi*) preference to one another in honor (time)..." The Greek participle means "to lead on," "to bring forward" in classical Greek, and that is the idea here. The appeal is to be exuberant in showing honor, respect, and deference to our fellow saints, much as a parent would delight in leading one of their children into a place of honor or vice versa.

His burden is to check any tendency to promote ourselves at the expense of others. By far, the best way to combat that vice is not by mere suppression of the urge to exalt ourselves or by rushing out to find some way to humiliate ourselves, but simply by substitution, namely, taking the path of greatest resistance—honoring others.

> There is no poison more effective in alienating the affections than the thought that one is despised [he means looked down upon or viewed with contempt]... As there is nothing more opposed to brotherly concord than the contempt which arises from pride, while each esteems others less and exalts himself,

so modesty, by which each comes to honour others, best nourishes love. [354] (brackets mine)

(12:11) *Not lagging behind in diligence, fervent in spirit, serving the Lord...*

"Not lagging behind..." (*okneroi* = shrinking, hesitating, unready) in diligence (*te spoude*).

These three injunctions are closely related, and none are far removed from the original admonition about love and brotherly affection.

Paul's words elsewhere are often the best commentary on his sense in another place. So, here, his burden is the same as in Galatians:

> "And let us not lose heart in doing good, for in due time we shall reap if we do not grow weary. So then, while we have opportunity, let us do good to all men, and especially to those who are of the household of the faith" (Gal. 6:9–10).

Sometimes we are tempted to "bag" it because we are tired, because something else seems more rewarding to the flesh, because we are not appreciated, or because it's a hole we can't fill (a need we can't fix). Whatever the excuses that make the flesh balky, none alone or all together is ever sufficient reason to hold back in doing the good that we have means and opportunity to do. "To him that knows the right thing to do, and does not do it, to him it is sin" (James 4:17).

There is no place in the ranks of discipleship for the laid back, the casual, the indifferent, or the half-hearted. As they say in the sports world, when titles are on the line, God wants His servants by grace to "step up," to "take it to another level."

"Fervent in spirit..." (*to pneumati zeontes* from *zeo*). "Fervent" translates a participial form of *zeo*, which means to "to boil," "to boil or bubble up," used of the sea or other water or passion. [355] In Acts 18:25, Apollos is described by this very language as a man who, in his ministry of the Word, was "fervent in spirit" I take it that Luke was saying that Apollos was an intense man, an ardent man of unflagging zeal and passion for his work.

It was apparently in this very area that Paul had to admonish Timothy (2 Tim. 1:6–7), whose ardor had begun to flag out of fear and timidity.

"Serving the Lord..." Paul, I believe, inserts this generic exhortation in this context because it brings into focus the motive that ennobles Christian ministry and sustains its energy and passion—that is, the consciousness that it is the Lord we are serving, not an institution or people per se, nor trying to feel good about ourselves. Rather, it is the King's business that we are discharging, and it must be carried out in a fashion befitting His ministers.

The more important we see the one who sends us out on business, the more important we see the business and the greater the gravity and zeal with which we discharge it.

The bane of Christian service today is that, by and large, it is not seen in this light, though we use the phraseology. If, for once, we really saw ourselves as "serving the Lord" rather than some more parochial or trivial interest, it would reenergize our labor.

(12:12) *Rejoicing in hope, persevering in tribulation, devoted to prayer...*

"Rejoicing in hope . . " (*te elpidi chairontes*).

As Christians, we cannot sustain the life of faith unless we keep our eyes fixed on our future. There will be times when this life can so strip us down and pick our bones that the only thing that sustains us is the prospect of Christ's return... the expectation of the New Order... the consummation of our redemption in glory... when evil is finally put down, when the enemies of God are judged and universal righteousness reigns. That hope we must always keep before our eyes, for through many tribulations, we enter into the kingdom of God. Here on earth, hell lashes out at us... the residuals of the curse still encumber our existence, but whatever happens, no matter how bad things get or what we lose, in the end, we win... and we win big.

We are the future... we shall inherit the earth even if the world right now succeeds in disinheriting us. Whether we lose our health, our jobs, our status, our friends, our houses, our security, or whatever, nobody can take away our birthright... we still have a city that has foundations. Let us rejoice in that hope.

"Persevering in tribulation. . " (*te thlipsei hypomenontes*). The reason we must keep focused on our hope is because we are going to catch assaults of Hell in the present. Paul, strengthening the souls of the disciples (in Lystra, Iconium, and Antioch), encouraging them to continue in the faith, said, "Through many tribulations we must enter the kingdom of God" (Acts 14:22; 1 Thess. 3:3–4; John 16:33).

It is a trademark of genuine faith that it does not crumble under the load of adversity. Tribulation is God's great sorter. That is why the Bible says that those who persevere to the end shall be saved. Real faith hangs tough; false faith gives out.

"Devoted to (*proskarterountes* = persisting obstinately in) prayer. . ." See 1 Thessalonians 5:17 "pray without ceasing". Compare also Luke 18:1–8; Matthew 26:41–44; and Luke 11:5–13. It is not as though God is reluctant to grant the petitions of His children, but it is the case that 1) our time is not always His perfect time, 2) that it often suits His purpose in our lives to leave us under the load for some time, and 3) that His answers, when they come after much waiting in prayer, are more impressive for that very reason and more sustaining when, in the necessities of His plan, we again must await His wise timing. Meanwhile, keep camping out on the threshold of heaven and pounding its doors with unyielding faith in the character and power of God.

(12:13) *Contributing to the needs of the saints, practicing hospitality...*

The Bible has much to say about the grace of generosity, especially as it applies to ministering to the needs of those in distress. Nothing so exposes our profession of love as a charade than our withholding from or niggardliness with helping those in unfortunate circumstances (James 2:14–16; 1 John 3:17).

"...the needs of the saints" Red alert. Biblical teaching on this great grace has in view primarily the saints taking care of saints. Two or three years ago I wrote an unpublished paper on this very subject, specifically a careful study on NT teaching sustaining my thesis. General humanitarianism does not meet the standard of this virtue. The target is not the needs of the general public, though at times those needs right in front of our faces may cry out for our attention, especially in times of disaster, like war or famine or natural havoc.

I have never understood how Christian churches so often neglect the brethren in favor of helping people in the streets. That is upside down. In the early churches outsiders commented on the ways believers cared for their own kind. For the Carthaginian Church Father, Tertullian (c. 160-225 AD) wrote:

"Look," they (non-Christians) say, "how they (Christians) love one another" (for they themselves hate one another)..."[356]

"Practicing hospitality..." (*ten philoxenian* = love of strangers). This exhortation had special urgency in Paul's era when society consisted mostly of two classes, the rich and the poor, and the majority of Christians fell into the latter category (1 Cor. 1:26–28; 2 Cor. 8:1–2). Public inns did not dot the travel landscape.

(12:14) *Bless (eulogeite) those who persecute (diokontas) you; bless and curse (katarasthe) not. (parentheses mine)*

The natural reaction to hostility is to return the "favor." That is precisely what is wrong with it; it is the natural way, the way of the flesh, not the supernatural way, the way of the Spirit. There is in us all a natural moral gravity called "the flesh," which pulls us into the vortex of the power of sin and insists that we always lower ourselves to the world's level and fight fire with fire, return malignity with malignity, and contempt with contempt. We can never in this flesh rise totally above that impulse, nor will we always succeed in doing better than simply turning the other cheek, if that.

Still, on the human side, it is our Christian responsibility to embrace this moral ideal as the standard to aim for and leave it to the grace of God to overcome the gravitational pull of the flesh and to draw our hearts in the right direction. And we will grow contrary to our natural bent if once our heart is fused with an inner sympathy for it and a commitment to it.

By such exhortations, God's Word first reformats our conscience and then enlists a will agreeable to His purpose in the project of conforming us to His character. That is the function of all these seemingly unrealistic exhortations. Also remember the nature of the Word is a dynamic, not static, force in *causing what God commands* —the Word is a living word, active, not passive, sharper, and more penetrating than a double-edged sword (Heb. 4:12). It effects or brings about (incrementally) in the hearts of believers the very conduct and conditions it demands: "for it is God who is at work in you to cause you to will and to work for His good pleasure" (Phil. 2:13).

For a human being to "bless" another is to pray for good things to happen to them, whereas to "curse" is to call upon God to cause evil events to befall them. The spirit of love always covets God's blessing[357] upon men in the form of forgiveness, redemption, or correction. To ask for blessing upon our enemies, in other words, is not to ask God to confirm them in their wickedness by causing them to flourish and prosper in their evil ways, but to turn them from evil into the paths of righteousness, where true happiness and blessedness really lie. To bless our persecutors is another way of saying that we should ask in love that God would turn the hearts of our enemies and make them His (and our) friends.

Incidentally, this precept is not contrary to the spirit of the imprecatory Psalms, where the psalmist calls down God's judgment on the wicked. The difference is all a matter of perspective. What Paul is addressing here is the strong temptation, arising from the flesh, to get back at those who make life miserable for us... to succumb to the desire to see them afflicted with the same miseries (or worse) that they have inflicted on us. Where personal injury is concerned, we are not to be spiteful or vindictive but always to seek the best interests of even our enemies.

The standpoint of the imprecatory psalms, as I see them, is not a reaction to personal injury per se (though sometimes they are cast in personal terms) but, upon closer examination, appears to me to be the prayers of those who see in the actions of the wicked against the righteous, inveterate opposition to God and righteousness. In effect, the imprecatory psalms turn out to be, in my judgment, pleas of the righteous for God to set the world right, to let justice reign, to put down evil, and to make a cosmic statement that wickedness does not pay and that God rules and overcomes all the evil machinations of evil men against God.

In short, Paul is speaking to men who are tempted to feel malice and to return evil in retaliating against personal injury. The imprecatory psalms are asking God to reign in the wicked who show by their viciousness toward the righteous that they are unalterably opposed to God and everything that is good. We pray for the salvation of sinners who hurt us. We also pray for God's justice to intervene and judge the wicked who refuse to acknowledge God. Christ Himself died for sinners and prayed, "Father, forgive them, for they know not what they do" (Luke 23:34). Yet He Himself will return one day and subject those who do not repent to the most horrifying judgment in the name of justice, and all heaven and all the saints from all ages will rejoice in the overthrow of the wicked. The two perspectives are totally compatible.

Observe how the text assumes persecution as a normative fact of Christian experience. That agrees with the rest of the Scripture, what Paul told Timothy, "All who desire to live godly in Christ Jesus will be persecuted" (2 Tim. 3:12).

Persecution is not always overt but sometimes subtle; at other times, it is open and aggressive. It can take the forms of social ostracism or business or professional discrimination or physical intimidation or intellectual ridicule, and so on.

Satan will not allow, over time, godly aspirations and activities to live in peace and quiet. It does not always speak well of us if, as believers, we live day after day, week after week, and year after year in unmolested comfort, unchallenged by the enemies of Christ.

If we are truly "in the game," so to speak, one can expect persecution in one form or another to come calling.

Jesus forewarns us not to be surprised by this hostility. He explains the reason why we will attract it. We are aliens here with a difference that offends the conscience[358] (John 15:18ff).

The Lord also reminds us that persecution is a very positive sign of the reward in store for us when we attract from the world the same lightning as the ancient prophets, as did our Lord Himself (Matt. 5:10). We are in the best of company!

> (12:15) *Rejoice (chairein) with those who rejoice (chaironton), and weep (klaiein) with those who weep (klaionton). (parentheses mine)*

Rejoice...

Another mark of Christian love is caring for the welfare of others to the point that our sympathies are so tied to them that we spontaneously enter emotionally into their joys and sorrows. We all understand the naturalness of this in that realm where love is natural—among loved ones and very close friends. Paul just extends the obligation outward to everyone else.

The point is that we have a standing obligation to follow the rule of love and no right to limit the circle to whom the duty of love applies, especially in the family of God.

Christian love in its most mature form will always rejoice in anything good that happens to others... will always delight in the benefit of honest joy brightening the lives of fellow creatures, for the good that happens to our fellows can always elevate life and will never in and of itself corrupt it (though people themselves may turn good for evil purposes).

> "Not to welcome a brother's happiness with joy is a mark of envy; and not to grieve at his misfortune is inhumanity."[359]

The best antidote is not so much the attempt to suppress envy as much as substitution by asking God for grace to rejoice in the good that happens to others. Some overt expression of that, I have learned, helps break the rock of emotional resistance.

Weep with those who weep.

Our tendency is to be either indifferent or establish a comfortable distance between those in pain (so that we are not forced to deplete our emotions, our resources, or our energies in pumping water back into the well). As inhumane as either is, it is the gross insensitivity of "singing songs to a troubled heart."

"Like one who takes off a garment on a cold day, like vinegar on soda, is he who sings songs to a troubled heart" (Prov. 25:20). The metaphors speak of actions that have a detrimental, maybe even destructive, effect on their objects.

It is terribly cruel to effuse to those during great loss about one's great blessings. Thank God, but don't pour salt into the wounds of the sorrowful. To boast of great achievements to one trying to cope with great failure, to tout great victories to those struggling with great defeats, to sing of great openings to those in great straits, or of great relief to those in great pain—is the height of insensitivity. To laugh when others are crying, to rejoice when others are weeping is simply brutal. There is a time for everything, a time to weep, a time to rejoice, but each in its place and time.

(12:16) *Be of the same mind (to auto... phrontontes) toward one another; do not be haughty in mind (me ta hypsela), but associate with the lowly (tois tapeinois synapagomenoi). Do not be wise in your own estimation (ginesthe phronimoi par' eautois). (parentheses mine)*

"Be of the same mind" In Christ, value distinctions are verboten. People may have different ratings in socioeconomic terms like upper class, middle class, or lower class, but the currency of the world has no relevance in the kingdom of God in which every citizen is a child of God with all the dignity, rights, and privileges thereof. The worth of men in the eyes of God rests on two foundations: 1) that they are His creatures and bear His image, however marred, and 2) that some men are organically united to Jesus Christ ("in Christ") and therefore derive unique value from that indissoluble union with His Spirit. Since all God's children are beneficiaries of the same body, the same Spirit, the same Lord, the same calling and hope, the same faith and the same baptism, we all have identical value in the eyes of God. There is no upper class or lower class. All are cosmic aristocrats on the same level.

It is human nature to find occasion to make artificial distinctions among ourselves, to find any excuse available to feel superior to others. Human nature can't stand it if it can't find somebody to look down on. That is what all competition and the desire for achievement is all about, however benign. The lust for excellence in terms of the desire to be superior to others for the purpose of enjoying the feeling of appearing better than they are, is of the flesh and should be shunned by any Christian.

Do not be haughty in mind, but associate with the lowly.

Ambition has been called by Joseph Epstein "the fuel of achievement."[360] The lust for achievement in turn is fueled by the desire to be better than others, the need to have somebody to look down on. Ambition and achievement are secular sacreds. We never even think of challenging them as real virtues, so ingrained they are in our value system. Yet ambition is the mother of much sin.

Some will ask: Don't people need ambition to drive them to accomplish things that need to be done? Yes, but only one—the ambition to glorify God, to excel in godliness, to be distinguished in discipleship. Here we are driven by one mastering aspiration—to return to our Creator that which rightly belongs to him and that which rightly comes from us as His creatures. In that goal, our true humanity is realized; in that project, our highest good is realized and our greatest contribution to the well-being of mankind on this planet.

Again, the best way to combat carnal elitism and pride of superiority is not to attempt simply to suppress these feelings but to substitute a self-conscious effort to associate with those the world regards as the "lowly." Remember how radical Jesus was about it. He told us, when we throw a banquet, not to invite our friends and all those from whom we might find something to gain but to invite the outcasts who could never reward our kindness.

"The lowly" may be those of low socio-economic station... those considered of no account or importance in worldly terms... those who will not enhance our standing by association. The point is not that we should reject those of high estate in favor of those of low estate but consider them of equal worth in the sight of God and associate with one as readily as the other.

"Be not wise in your own estimation" Behind all social arrogance is a mind that refuses to be anchored to or instructed by the wisdom of God but carried away by the illusion of intellectual superiority and self-sufficiency, which goes the way of the world in these matters.

(12:17) *Never pay back evil for evil to anyone. Respect what is right in the sight of all men.*

Retaliation in the face of the perception of willful personal injury is a reflex of the flesh, the citadel of the sin principle that still has residency in us, and will, until we put off this mortal body. Human pride wants to assert itself and make others pay who do not appear to respect our persons, our property, our values, or our space. Generally, the natural man wants to make sure that no one ever enjoys, for long, any satisfaction from whatever they sought when inflicting some loss on us. Our impulse is to make sure that those who mess with us never get to enjoy the sense that they have gained anything by hurting us and to make them, if possible, regret their actions. Retaliation is all about salvaging human pride. Again, human pride is the tap root of sin, going all the way back to the Garden of Eden. Human pride always seeks to save face, insists on elevating oneself in the eyes of others, and refuses to accept humiliation in any form as the price of doing the will of God.

"Respect what is right (*pronooumenoi kala*)..." The idea is that we should take forethought in our behaviors to cut off from the enemies of God any excuse for *justified* reproach. We should make it our aim to confine our speech and conduct to those things that conform to the moral parameters of Philippians 4:8:

"Finally, brethren, whatever is true, whatever is honorable, whatever is right, whatever is pure, whatever is lovely, whatever is of good repute, if there is any excellence or anything worthy of praise, let your mind dwell on these things." Or, as Paul might say, "take precaution to make sure in the sight of all men that your speech and conduct falls within those lines."

"The meaning is... that Christians are to take thought for, aim at, seek, in the sight of all men those things which (whether they recognize it or not) are good, the arbiter of what is good being not a moral *communis sensus* of mankind, but the gospel."[361] See especially 2 Cor. 8:21 and compare Matt. 5:16; Rom. 13:12–13; 1 Cor. 10:31–32; 1 Tim. 5:14; Titus 2:10–12; 1 Pet. 2:12, 14; 3:16.

However, the phrase "in the sight of all men" does, I believe, acknowledge the truth of Romans 1:32, that deep down in the human consciousness is an intuitive awareness of fundamental right and wrong, "the ordinances of God," which overlaps with the moral revelation of the gospel. Where those two intersect, Christians must take great pains so that they do not lose their credibility and give unbelievers *truly* moral ground for slandering and rejecting the gospel.

(12:18) *If possible, so far as it depends on you, be at peace with all men.*

(See James 3:18 and Matt. 5:9.)

A healthy Christian heart cherishes peace and strives to perpetuate it in all human relationships, but not at any cost. As Calvin puts it:

"We are not to strive to attain the favour of men in such a way that we refuse to incur the hatred of any for the sake of the Christ as often as this may be necessary [... and...] good nature should not degenerate into compliance, so that for the sake of preserving peace are complaisant to men's sins."[362]

Also, sometimes evil men may force us, contrary to our peaceful desires, to defend our persons or those of others. In such cases, resisting evil is not of malice but out of necessity to arrest evil and prevent injury to us and others.

> (12:19–20) *Never take your own revenge, beloved, but leave room for the wrath of God, for it is written, "Vengeance is mine, I will repay, says the Lord. But if your enemy is hungry, feed him, and if he is thirsty, give him a drink; for in so doing you will heap burning coals upon his head."*

Never take your own revenge, beloved, but leave room (dote topon) for the wrath of God... (Compare 1 Sam. 25:26–31; Lev. 19:17–18; Matt. 5:38–42.)

In the Christian ethic, there is no place for vigilantism. Just as in the American system of justice, prosecution of wrong is to be left with the appropriate civil authorities, so believers are not to usurp the role of judge and jury and exact their own justice *(ekdikesis)* for wrong done to them. The proper settlement of all such matters resides with God alone.[363]

"Leave room . . " that is, back off and give God time and space to express His just indignation in His own perfect way.

When adjustment is needed, the Lord can create "poetic justice" better than we ever imagined. So, let it lie. Move on and let Him clean it up.

"You will heap burning coals on his head" He means to say either that 1) by so responding to the malignity of our enemies (i.e., those who make themselves such), we will ensure the outpouring of God's just retribution upon their hateful, impenitent heads or that 2) such behavior on our part will bring about the kind of shame and contrition that will lead either to repentance or at least to self-condemnation by his own conscience.

The second interpretation has been preferred by most interpreters since the first lacks Christian charity, being motivated by the desire to see our enemies punished rather than redeemed, a spirit clearly contrary to verse 15, for instance. This citation comes from Proverbs 25:21–22. The favored interpretation fits there as well.

However, one could understand Paul to be saying, "Back away and leave justice to God. He is the rightful judge. You just be sure to return good for evil, not evil for evil. If your enemy is hungry, feed him, and if he is thirsty, give him a drink. Don't withhold good from your enemy when it is in your power to render what he has need of. Rest assured that if he doesn't repent, your righteous behavior will bring down a scorching accounting for his wickedness. Justice, rest assured, will be served. The reign of the wicked is short-lived."

Either sense is biblical, I believe. The question again is simply which is most congenial to this context. Probably the former.

(12:21) *Do not be overcome by evil, but overcome evil with good.*

Bengel (cited by Cranfield) commented that to retaliate is to be overcome both by one's enemy and one's nature. [364] The defeat is compounded in that not only do we wave off the promptings of Spirit and yield to the passions of the flesh, but we also let our enemies reduce us to their moral level.

Good "overcomes" evil, not in the sense that it brings about the abolition of evil, but in the sense that 1) in doing good, one successfully resists getting pulled into the orbit of evil and making common cause with it, 2) that one escapes its consequences, and 3) that one remains as a beacon of light in dark world, reminding lost souls of the prospect of judgment and marking the way of salvation.

If, in its broadest sense, the gospel reveals not only what Christ in His redemptive work has done for us as well as what, having been reconciled to God through Him, ought now in thanksgiving be done for Him, some difficult questions are raised. We are no longer of the world but still very much in it, and discipleship is challenged at every corner. Historically, one of the most challenging has been the frequent clash between the Secular City and the City of God. How are we to negotiate that space in a manner that gives unto Caesar that which belongs to Caesar and gives to God what belongs to Him?

For example, had you lived back in the days of the American Revolution, should you have sided and fought with the American revolutionaries or with King George?

Had you lived in Boston in those days working on the docks, should you have participated in the Boston Tea Party?

If someone started a movement to overthrow the present government other than by democratic process, should you as a Christian participate?

Much of our Christian tax money is used by our governments, federal, state and local, to support enterprises, activities, and institutions that many of us could never in good conscience support. Should we withhold our taxes in protest?

If your government demands that you do something that is contrary to God's law, are you obliged to obey it?

Such questions are evoked in the next chapter.

---

[331] Cranfield, *ICC: Romans Vol. 2*, 595.

[332] So Sanday and Headlam, *ICC: Romans*, 352, who cite a passage in Josephus' *Antiquities*, IV. vi. 4; Cranfield adduces other extra-biblical sources in support of the same point.

[333] Calvin, *The Epistles of Paul to the Romans and Thessalonians*, 264.

[334] Godet, *Epistle to the Romans*, 429.

[335] Abbott-Smith, *Manuel Greek Lexicon of the New Testament*, 99.

[336] Ibid, 285.

[337] Hodge, *Epistle to the Romans*, 387.

[338] The Church in this sense does not correspond to any local church but transcends them all and consists of all true believers everywhere in those churches. The organic Church (capital 'C') excludes members of local churches who have no real relationship with Christ by faith. This is the invisible Church, which is a spiritual entity, a true spiritual organism which exists by the plan of God in the visible local churches but is never co-extensive with it. Hence a local church should not look upon itself as the 'Body of Christ' per se, but an impure and incomplete reflection of a part of it.

Not every member of a local church knows God or has a living connection with Christ, the Head of the Body. Every member of the invisible Church does, however. The local church is an organization for this world; the invisible Church is a transcendent organism that is forever.

[339] Cranfield, *ICC: Romans Vol. 2*, 621.

[340] Ibid, 620.

[341] Ibid, 621.

[342] See, for example, 1 Tim. 4:13; Tit. 1:9. Also note that the gift of prophecy may entail exhortation as well, 1 Cor. 14:3. The point is that spiritual gifts are not always air-tight 'packages' that admit no overlap or mutuality of function.

[343] Murray, *NICNT: Epistle to the Romans Vol. 2*, 125-126.

[344] Arndt & Gingrich, *Greek-English Lexicon of the New Testament*, 85.

[345] Calvin, *The Epistles of Paul to the Romans and Thessalonians*, 271.

[346] Carson, *The Difficult Doctrine of the Love of God*, 9.

[347] Calvin, *The Epistles of Paul to the Romans and Thessalonians*, 271.

[348] Vine, *Expository Dictionary of New Testament Words*, 242.

[349] Liddell and Scott, *An Intermediate Greek-English Lexicon*, 441.

[350] Murray, *NICNT: The Epistle to the Romans Vol. 2*, 128.

[351] Liddell and Scott, *An Intermediate Greek-English Lexicon*, 865.

[352] I take it that this thought is the same thing Luther had in mind. See Roland Bainton's recap of Luther's conviction in *Here I Stand*, p. 173.

[353] Even where it apparently fails, its rejection serves God's hidden purposes. Sometimes the Word goes forth to condemn the hearer and to seal them in their rejection, not to deliver them for their sins and into life more abundantly. (2 Cor. 2:15-16; John 9:39; Luke 2:34; 1 Pet. 2:7—what is true of the Living Word applies equally to the function of the Written Word). In other words, the Word deforms as well as transforms. Never forget that.

[354] Calvin, *The Epistles of Paul to the Romans and Thessalonians*, 271.

[355] Liddell and Scott, *An Intermediate Greek-English Lexicon*, 343.

[356] https://www.oxfordreference.com, accessed 2/17/2024.

[357] The prayer assumes in the asking that God always blesses in accordance with His own character and principles. What that means is that any prayer for blessing upon our persecutors is, in the final analysis, a plea for God's mercy and grace (in forgiveness and enlightenment) to visit them, to change His (and our) enemies into friends and to bestow upon them the riches of Christ.

[358] One of our little early teenage girls hit the mark recently when she passed me in the narthex. She was only half teasing, I think. Apparently, there was something she was supposed to have done and didn't or did and shouldn't have. As she suddenly bumped into me, she blurted out:
"Oops, I don't want to see you. You hurt my conscience!"
In her mind I stood symbolically for God and His interests. Whatever it was, she didn't feel exactly in alignment with those, and my pastoral (John 3:20) face painfully reminded her of that. Hence, though playfully spoken, the impulse to avoid me. On a macro level that is the Christian's problem in this world. Darkness hates light because light exposes. It hurts eyes that, like bats, are accustomed to

darkness. The world always wants to lower the shades. Christians have the effect of always raising them and annoying, literally, the Hell out of unbelievers. It makes them furious inside. They pick at every wart and pimple on your character, feel some comic relief when some believer falls into temptation himself or when somebody is exposed as a religious fraud. That gives their conscience some ease because they are better able to convince themselves that the difference is not real.

[359] Calvin, *The Epistles of Paul to the Romans and Thessalonians*, 274.

[360] Epstein, *Ambition: The Secret Passion*, 1.

[361] Cranfield, *ICC: Romans Vol.2*, 646.

[362] Calvin, *The Epistles of Paul to the Romans and Thessalonians*, 276.

[363] The question may be raised whether believers are hereby instructed to absorb passively all wrongs inflicted upon them and are denied the moral right to seek redress at the hands of constituted legal authorities. The point of this admonition is not, as I perceive it, to refuse us any recourse to legal remedies (Paul took refuge in his rights as a Roman citizen, Acts 16:35-40) but to rule out a spirit of vindictiveness and vengefulness in rectifying wrongs. People can seek legal relief from those who wrong them, not out of malice or a spite, but out of physical, emotional or economic necessity and/or because others are affected as well as themselves and also because it furnishes a chance to arrest or inhibit some form of evil that is making life hard or miserable for many besides oneself.

Also, we must remember, as chapter 13 will remind us, that civil government is an arm of divine justice, however fallible and imperfect, and may be appealed to as such.

It is the spirit and intent of our response to those who injure us that is most important, not the form of it. Anytime our motive is simply to avenge ourselves and to salvage our pride by taking matters into our own hands, it is wrong. Leave it to God, directly or indirectly (by turning the matter over to the proper authorities).

[364] Cranfield, *ICC: Romans Vol. 2,* 650.

Romans Chapter 13

This chapter, I believe, will teach us as disciples, who are strangers and aliens in this present world, to carefully understand the relationship of the believers to civil government and be ruled by divine principles.

Until the government demands that we do something contrary to the biblical principles, precepts, and practices, a disciple has no license to go rogue and become a resister of civic duty or a Christian vigilante.

J.W. Allen wrote that this chapter "contains what are perhaps the most important words ever written for the history of political thought" though he admits that few statemen ever took their political opinions from Paul.[365]

> There was a peculiar necessity, during the apostolic age, for inculcating the duty of obedience to civil magistrates. This necessity arose in part from the fact that a large portion of the converts to Christianity had been Jews, and were peculiarly indisposed to submit to the heathen authorities [on grounds that their only real King was God Himself or a human representative that the Lord Himself chose] (cf. Deut. 17:15) It was a question, therefore, constantly agitated among them, "Is it lawful to pay tribute to Caesar, or not?" A question which the great majority were at least secretly inclined to answer in the negative... They were continually breaking out into tumults, which led to their expulsion from Rome, and, finally, to the utter destruction of Jerusalem.[366]

(13:1) *Let every person be in subjection to the governing authorities. For there is no authority except from God, and those which exist are established by God.*

"Governing authorities..." literally "higher power" (*exousiais hyperechousais*), that is, those in legal authority. We agree with

Bruce that in the present context, this phraseology most naturally refers to civil authorities, [367] though some have argued for the heavenly or angelic powers standing behind human kings and authorities. We should take the simplest meaning that answers well to the demands of the context.

"For there is no authority except from God, and those which exist are established by God."

Behind the institution of human government and its magistrates, Paul acknowledges higher authority behind all human "governors." In the final analysis, it is God who raises up and deposes the powers that be. All the factors on the human side of the equation that historians and other observers might assign as the contributing causes are, if accurate, nothing more than the providence of God using human agents or agencies and temporal conditions to work His will.

Since the ultimate governing authority to whom believers are subject and accountable is God, it goes without saying that the believer should defer to God in any case where "Caesar," the lesser authority, oversteps his bounds and countermands what man owes to God, the highest authority.

Everything Paul says here presumes that human authority is operating within its rights, though not necessarily doing what is right in the eyes of God. God's will is that His servants respect the authority He has vested with temporal rulers within their limits. To go bravado in resistance to civil authority that God has indirectly put in place is neither courageous nor prudent but reckless and foolish and brings reproach on our earthly enterprise.

(13:2) *Therefore he who resists the authority has opposed the ordinance of God; and they who have opposed will receive condemnation (krima) upon themselves. (parenthesis mine)*

"The ordinance (*diatage*) of God" refers to the divine arrangement.
Here is the practical inference from the premise that God is ultimately the source of constituted legal authority. To rebel against

God's representative while discharging his rightful function is to rebel God's order.

For example, during the Covid pandemic, there were grounds for many pastors and believers suspecting bad motives, if not bad information, on the part of some overzealous governors in checking the threat. Even so, until it was clear that the civil authorities, whoever they happened to be, were using the crisis to subvert our mission and our worship and treating churches, their pastors, and people in a more restrictive way (blatant discrimination) than other citizens and institutions, we must restrain our impulses to revolt or else find ourselves in false piety resisting God.

Magistrates are to be obeyed because their authority comes directly from God with His "Good Housekeeping seal of approval," as it were. That does not mean that God approves what human rulers do, but He appoints those who are in place at any given time and bestows the power and authority by which they govern.

Whenever a magistrate oversteps his bounds, demanding of citizens or subjects conduct at variance with God's law, disobedience, as biblical precedent clearly shows, becomes our duty (cf. Acts 4:19; 5:29; Dan. 1; 3:18–28). [368]

This duty to submit to a wicked ruler then is no more absolute than the duty of a woman to obey her husband or children to obey their parents is unconditional. For in Scripture, it is evident that human law always gives right of way to God's law. Paul assumed that inference went without saying, especially considering the divine function of rulers to promote good and not evil. [369]

(13:3a) *For rulers are not a cause of fear (phobos) for good behavior, but for evil. (parenthesis mine)*

Paul is speaking theologically and generally, not historically and absolutely. Government was not established to terrorize people for doing the right thing but to corral and punish those who do evil. "Good behavior" refers to whatever external conduct conduces to justice and the general social well-being of a people. Human authorities are not competent to regulate the minds and hearts of men, but their province is limited to public and private activities, which law and force of might can regulate, constrain, or restrain.

(13:3b) *Do you want to have no fear of authority? Do what is good, and you will have praise from the same;*

This question is addressed to those who fear and distrust civil authorities. This is a generalization. On balance, those who do good, that is, contribute to the public welfare, will not be terrorized by the power of the state but will even enjoy its commendation.

What Paul is saying, Peter also affirms in effect (see 1 Pet. 3:13–14). Peter concedes that civil authority does not always function as God intended. As a practical matter and historical reality, rogue governments and criminal or mad rulers do arise from time to time and misuse the base of legitimate authority for illegitimate and socially destructive ends. They call good evil and evil good.

(13:4) *For it is a minister of God to you for good. But if you do what is evil, be afraid; for it does not bear the sword for nothing; for it is a minister of God, an avenger who brings wrath upon the one who practices evil.*

Here, Paul speaks of the divine intention in raising up the institution of human government. Civil authorities are literally ministers of God, however unwittingly. Their role is to preserve the world, uphold justice, and restrain evil.

By and large, government does serve this function. That is why the world as a whole is not overrun with evil as happens when law and order break down and anarchy reigns (as formerly, e.g., in Rwanda and other lawless countries, where unbridled terror stalked the streets).

For it does not bear the sword for nothing; for it is a minister of God, an avenger who brings wrath upon the one who practices evil.

"The sword" is a metonym, the sign "sword" standing for the thing signified, the power to punish and coerce up to and including capital punishment.

God has vested human government with the authority to punish and to use whatever force necessary to restrain evil and enforce good behavior.

"An avenger..." "The state has been charged with a function which has been explicitly forbidden to the Christian."[370]

When God says "vengeance is Mine" (12:19) we are to understand that His interventionary justice is oftentimes exerted through His civil ministers who are the unsuspecting agents of His wrath. Individuals have the duty to love their enemy and to bless, not curse, the wicked who injure them. Civil servants have the responsibility to bring them to justice.

(13:5) *Wherefore it is necessary to be in subjection, not only because of wrath, but also for conscience's sake.*

Paul, by inference, extracts two good reasons for Christians to be compliant with civil authorities, one pragmatic and one moral.

1) It is a simple safety issue, that is, it's good for your health.

2) It is at bottom a conscience issue, that is, being right with God.

"The gospel is equally hostile to tyranny and anarchy. It teaches rulers that they are ministers of God for the public good; and it teaches subjects to be obedient to magistrates, not only for fear, but for conscience's sake."[371]

(13:6) *For because of this you also pay taxes, for rulers are servants of God, devoting themselves to this very thing.*

"For this reason you pay taxes" The Christian rationale for contributing to the support of a pagan or secular enterprise is to maintain a good conscience before God. It is a spiritual issue, for governors are unconscious ministers (*diakonos* and *leitourgoi*) of God. He has given them a role to play and holds them accountable. Our responsibility is to cooperate with His purpose, and one way we do that is by forking over what government requires of us to maintain its own existence.

"This very thing" (*auto touto*) is ambiguous in its referent. Most likely, the phrase refers to the nearest option that makes good sense. That would be the collection of revenues to support and maintain the institution of government, administer justice, maintain public order, and restrain evil. Just as God has ordained that the church should support its ministers and their work, so He has ordained that citizens should support the work of civil ministers. The former is by means of tithes and offerings, the latter by means of tax revenues.

(13:7) *Render to all what is due them: tax to whom tax is due; custom to whom custom; fear to whom fear; honor to whom honor.*

The bottom line for the Christian is to "render to all what is due them." Or, put another way, to give unto Caesar that which belongs to Caesar and unto God that which belongs to God.

Our Christian duty ends where their rightful due ends, and what is due them ends at whatever point governing authorities begin to require of us whatever is contrary to the law of God and to demand of us that we withhold the fear, the honor, and even the resources that belong to Him.

The business of statesmen is to administer justice, maintain public order, and to restrain evil for the preservation of society. Civil magistrates inhibit our baser selfish and lawless instincts inherent in our fallen human natures; government enables us, in spite of our depraved condition, to live together in relative peace and harmony and also creates conditions under which that which is best and most noble in us can flourish for the mutual benefit of all.

(13:8) *Owe nothing to anyone except to love one another; for he who loves his neighbor has fulfilled the law.*

For Christians, Paul now articulates the overarching duty[372] that comprehends all others and of which those with respect to civil government (v. 7) are simply subsets. All have limits save this one, and it is unending and universal.

The sense of the apostle's dictum has no bearing, as some would teach, on the practice of taking on credit. That legal arrangement is not in view.

The business of a Christian whose citizenship is in heaven but for the present resides and serves God here and now is not to be an agent of divine retribution or a political revolutionary whose mission it is to overthrow tyrannical regimes, unjust judges, and self-serving politicians, but our mandate is to pay the interminable and boundless debt that one man always owes every man—the obligation of love. From this debt, one is never discharged. We owe it as much today as yesterday and tomorrow as much as now (cf. Matt. 7:12; Gal. 5:14; Matt. 22:40; 1 Tim. 1:5).

We may pay our taxes to whom taxes are due and be done with that; pay customs to whom customs are due and be rid of that obligation. We may render homage to an official dignitary and owe no more, or honor to some superior and consider ourselves finished with that. The one debt that we can never consider discharged is the obligation of love.

> (13:9) *For this, "You shall not commit adultery, you shall not murder, you shall not steal, you shall not covet," and if there is any other commandment, it is summed up in this saying, "You shall love your neighbor as yourself."*

The law that, for the Christian, transcends and supersedes all other laws in case of conflict is the law of God.

Are we still "under law" then? Let us not misunderstand. We are not obliged to keep the law of God in order to be saved or to maintain our standing as Christians. Our obligation is not legal. Nor is our salvation in any way dependent upon our success in adhering to its strict and uncompromising demands (i.e., "strict and uncompromising" for those who are determined to "earn" their righteous standing before God).

Our obligation is strictly moral and born of our love for God. We are morally obliged to imitate His character. Because God, in His mercy (12:1), has condescended to love us, to pardon us of our sins, to adopt us into His family, and to bestow upon us as children an eternal inheritance, it is our moral duty to honor the law of God as

His children and loyal subjects. Again, the essence of that law (Matt. 22:36–40; Rom. 13:9–10).

Even so, there is a risk of misapprehending what the Law is all about. In its moral essence, God's law is not a sterile list of dos and don't's. The Ten Commandments are God's way of helping us as children understand what love means. Our abiding duty to others is to "love our neighbor as we love ourselves."[373]

(13:10) *Love does no wrong to a neighbor; love is therefore the fulfillment of the law.*

Just as when we love ourselves, we seek to prevent injury to ourselves, so when we love our neighbor, we will not do them (deliberately) any harm or wrong.

Love is what the law of God is all about. There is a notion afoot that because we Christians are no longer "under law," that we no longer have anything whatsoever to do with it, that we are no longer obliged to conform to it, that being "under grace" places one in a position before God that is totally demand-less.

This position is a great misunderstanding of what not being "under law" is all about. "Under law" (see commentary on 6:14) refers to a situation where a man in the flesh is faced with satisfying the unbending demands of God's holy law as a condition of salvation. This condition is impossible. Anyone "under law" is doomed.

"Under grace," on the other hand, speaks of a situation where a pardoned and regenerated man in Christ has the law of God written in His heart and is endowed with the morally enabling presence of the Holy Spirit so that he is now empowered to obey the impulses of the Spirit, to walk in love or, put another way, to fulfill the requirements of the law of God (cf. Rom. 8:4 on this point).

The whole point in our redemption is to conform us to Christ, and that implies conforming us to the law of God or the law of love. Jesus said, "By this shall all men know that you are my disciples, that you love one another" (John 13:35).

So, our relationship to the Law as Christians is not one that requires its fulfillment as a condition of salvation, but one that enables its fulfillment as a fruit or evidence of regeneration. *Grace, then, does not remove obedience as the goal of our salvation but does remove it as a condition of salvation.*

That is why Paul is making so much ado about "fulfilling the law of God." It is the moral goal of our redemption, the *summum bonum* (supreme good), the *sine qua non* (indispensable condition) of our existence.

When we love, we are, in effect, fulfilling the law of God. That is what the Scripture means when it tells us that love "covers a multitude of sins." With one shot, we kill a lot of evil birds.

That does not mean that love makes up or atones for a host of sins, but that love is compendious in its moral reach and prevents a host of sins. In fact, every sin is a breach in some way of the law of love. Love, and you won't sin; sin, and you are unloving. Love is, as John tells us, keeping the commandments of God, not in their letter but in their spirit.

So then:

Let us remember that the obligation to love is one debt that we can never discharge, though, situationally, we can fulfill it. It is a debt that remains even as it is fulfilled.

Let us evaluate ourselves as Christians by the standard of the law of love—God's will.

Let us measure our love by our conformity to the law of God.

This furnishes an opportunity to clear up a text that is misinterpreted by some, a misunderstanding that paints its victims into a financial corner that puts them at a severe disadvantage in the marketplace and under the illusion that they are following biblical precepts when, in fact, they are not (Deut. 15:8; Luke 6:34, 35; Psa. 37:26; 112:5).

Our text also performs for us two important services:

1) It redlines, once again, the real essence of Christian love and disabuses our conceptions of some of the false images and notions that surround it.

Love is not saying nice things about everybody.
Love is not avoiding giving offense to people.

Love is not affirming everybody, nor is it refusing to condemn their behavior. The person who never says anything 'bad' about anyone lacks a moral compass. That is not a commendation, but actually a condemnation. Jesus, the prophets and apostles, regularly tore the hide off scofflaws and religious hypocrites. See Matt. 23 on that point. Love never condones evil but abhors it and is willing, when appropriate, to speak out against those who traffic in it.

Love is not even necessarily sweetness, gentleness, or compassion insofar as those traits are functions of personality rather than grace. Love is not sappy.

2) It calls attention to our continuing *moral* obligation as Christians to conform to the law of God, something that is denied by many who misunderstand what it means not to be "under law." And this misunderstanding leads to a lot of moral looseness spawned by a spirit of what we call *antinomianism,* a bane of modern evangelical churches, whatever that term means anymore.

(13:11) *And this do, knowing the time, that it is already the hour for you to awaken from sleep; for now salvation is nearer to us than when we believed.*

Concerning the imagery in this passage, Calvin explains:

By night Paul means ignorance of God [with all the vanity, futility, depravity, iniquity, and perversity that attends alienation from knowledge], and all who are held in this ignorance wander and sleep as in the night. Unbelievers labour under the two evils of being blind and stupid [and stumble in all the potholes of sin created by these liabilities]. This stupidity Paul designates a little later by sleep, which is the image, he says, of death [i.e., living under the condition and dominion of spiritual separation from the quickening light and life of God]. By light he means the revelation of divine truth, by which Christ the Sun of righteousness arises on us. By waking out of sleep he means that we are to be armed [for spiritual engagement with the enemy] and ready to do what the Lord requires of us. The works of darkness are shameful and wicked acts, for night, he says, is without shame. The armour of light means honourable, sober, and chaste actions, which are usually done in the day. Paul says, <u>armour</u> rather than works, because we are to fight in the service of the Lord"[374] (brackets my additions).

"And this do..." (literally, the Greek reads, *Kai touto*) [375] referring back to all that he has just exhorted them to do.

"Knowing the time. . ." (*<u>eidotes</u> ton <u>kaipon</u>*). He leads, however, with the spiritual perspective that drives the urgency of his appeal. For believers, the season (*kairos*) is no longer night, for we have been delivered (in great measure) from that darkness, which consists in spiritual blindness and ignorance of God. Unlike the sleeping world, which still resides in darkness, we know God and know what on earth is going on and what is coming down. The return of Christ is often appealed to as moral incentive. What an embarrassment and loss it would be for the Lord to return and find us napping (morally), unprepared for His coming.

For the Christian, the time for sleepwalking is past. Now it is time to rise from moral and spiritual slumber with all the sin, ignorance, and blindness those images imply and to put on the enlightened way of Christ (that is, to imitate the works of Christ) and to go forth into the world arrayed in the armor of light, that is, in self-control, faith and love, and the hope (or expectation) of that salvation ready to be revealed in the last time (1 Thess. 5:8; 1 Pet. 1:5; Eph. 5:14).

Our calling is to walk as children of light, to please God, not the world, shunning the evil deeds of the surrounding world and to expose their character by shedding light upon them as we walk (Eph. 5:8–12).

"Now salvation is nearer to us than when we believed." This is not the time to be asleep at the switch, so to speak, for our Lord may surprise us with His coming and find us unprepared to welcome Him.

We tend to think of our salvation as a historic *event* that occurred at a specific point in time in our personal past. And that perspective is correct insofar as our redemption is an experience that has a specific point of entry, that being the time when faith was born in our hearts by the in-working of God, and we laid hold of it at the foot of the cross, as it were, and laid claim to the offer of full and complete pardon God offered us through the atoning sacrifice of His Son. At that juncture, we were justified in Christ and reconciled to God; we were regenerated and occupied by the indwelling Spirit of God.

These past and unrepeatable events in our lives signaled God's laying claim on us as His own people, and our admission by grace into the family of God, with all the rights and privileges thereof. In other words, these happenings, all occurring in a moment in time, marked our *irrevocable* entry into the kingdom of God.

So, in a real sense, our salvation was a great and momentous event, a translation from a condition of lostness and condemnation into a state of "foundness" and justification—from a condition of living death to a condition of eternal life.

Still, our salvation is something bigger and grander than an event that took place in our past.[376] It is an ongoing *program* of human transformation, a project of spiritual *renewal* that God initiated in our past that continues to this present hour and will continue until its consummation in our ultimate glorification at the return of Jesus Christ, when that gap between what we are and all the He intends for us to be, between what we now have and all that He intends for us to inherit, will be instantly closed and our adoption will be consummated in the full glory of divine sonship and ruling and reigning with Christ.

So, our salvation is a *process* as much as it is an event... a process guided and driven by the Spirit of God toward a magnificent rendezvous with the plan God has for the future. With every tick of the clock, our salvation, in the programmatic or process sense, draws ever nearer to its crescendo.

> (13:12) *The night is almost gone, and the day is at hand. Let us therefore lay aside the deeds of darkness and put on the armor of light.*

"The night is almost gone..." This world is on the verge of passing away; history as we know it is about to come to a grinding halt; the day of the Lord is closing in as the history of redemption works on to its inexorable climax in the second coming of Jesus Christ and our glorification.

"What he is saying in brief is that as soon as God begins to call us, we ought to direct our attention to the coming of Christ, just as we conclude from the first rising of the day that the full light of the sun is at hand." [377]

The night is almost gone (proekopsen from prokopto = advance, progress).

Paul means that the period fixed in God's timetable for the dominion of evil is well advanced toward the date of its expiration. Things are winding down on the order of this present world as it slumbers on oblivious to the day of the Lord arising on its horizon.

"The day is at hand." Contrary to the opinion of some, this statement does not represent a mistaken anticipation of the immediate appearance of Christ on the part of the apostle. Hodge explodes the admissibility of this interpretation. [378]

All Paul means to say is that the coming of Christ is virtually at the doors relatively speaking in terms of prophetic precursors. If it delays, it is not because so much remains to happen that it must take a long calendar. As at a wedding, the bride may delay, but nothing much remains on the program but her entry. So it is with the coming of the Lord. Calendrically speaking, Christ is at the doors until the Father signals the moment for His grand entry. [379]

"Lay aside the deeds of darkness..." implies things which people with any sense of shame try to conceal by doing them under the cover of darkness or are so debased that only the shameless would not attempt to hide them. He refers here to the same vile and odious activities referred to in Ephesians 5:11–12, where believers are reminded:

"And do not participate in the unfruitful deeds of darkness, but instead even expose them, for it is disgraceful even to speak of the things which are done by them in secret."

(13:13) *Let us behave properly as in the day, not in carousing and drunkenness, not in sexual promiscuity and sensuality, not in strife and jealousy.*

Hodge classifies the behaviors that Paul rules out as appropriate day-wear under three headings: intemperance or immoderation, impurity and discord—or we might say sins of being out of control (with respect to the mind and emotions), out of bounds (with respect to sacred barriers), and out of line (with respect to human relationships). [380]

Paul's exhortation reminds us that if technology has changed beyond our imagination, mankind remains mired in the same old lawless ruts of moral and social self-destruction. Human nature never changes.

"Properly..." (*euschemonos* = decorously, becomingly). As it is not considered fitting for people to spend their day life indulging in the night life, so it is not becoming for Christians who are day people to live like night people. They are, in the words of Cranfield, "to walk honourably as those who in Christ belong already to God's new order."[381]

Here is a representative list on that moral Bourbon Street, called "the world."

"Not in carousing (komois[382] *= reveling) and drunkenness..."*

Chrysostom says: "Nothing... so kindles lust, and inflames wrath, as drunkenness, and sitting long at wine" (*Romans,* Homily XXIV).

"Let's party" is the spirit of the world, not the spirit of Christ. Paul is not condemning good clean fun nor camaraderie. What he disallows is riotous, boisterous levity... wild "whooping it up" in the reckless pursuit of a "good time." What he places off limits, by these words, finds its modern correspondents in such excesses as one encounters at fraternity bashes, drunken office parties, Mardi Gras revels, and wild victory celebrations that cross the lines of self-control.

"Not in sexual promiscuity (*koitais* = beddings) and sensuality (*aselgeiais* = licentiousness, wantonness, excess)..." Sensuality is pleasuring the bodily senses without restraint... giving license to every wanton appetite of the five senses.

"Not in strife and jealousy (*eridi kai zelo*)." Strife or contention and envy are usually related as effect and cause. Envy arises from the frustrated desire for preeminence over others. When we are envious, we resent it that someone else enjoys something that we covet but can't have or we desire to deprive someone of something that we want for ourselves.

(13:14) *But put on the Lord Jesus Christ, and make no provision for the flesh in regard to its lusts.*

To "put on the Lord Jesus Christ" is to imitate through the empowering presence of the Spirit the ways of Christ. The imagery is that of putting on a garment, of clothing oneself.

"Make no provision (*pronoian me poieisthe*) for the flesh in regard to its lusts."

Children of light should not accommodate the evil passions of our fallen flesh in any manner. There are those things that we as human beings desire because we are human and those that we desire because we are *fallen* humans. In the first category fall desires for food, drink, shelter, and companionship. In the second, fall inordinate or transgressive desires for the same things... and more. Either the flesh wants too much of these legitimate things or wants them so much that one will make oneself an outlaw to God to have them and to have them on one's one terms.

Denying the flesh and its desires works best when we neither "feed nor tease the dog." If you want to diet, don't keep ice cream in the refrigerator just in case you change your mind. That is called doublemindedness. Don't put temptation in your way.

" 'The flesh...' signifies the whole of our human nature in its fallenness, organized as it is in rebellion against God." [383]

Introduction to Chapter 14

Paul does not do us the favor of describing the specific historical tension which he is addressing. We are left with the task of determining that by inductive process, that is, filtering through the details and piecing the puzzle together into a mosaic.

Cranfield defines six different background scenarios[384] that in various combinations, commentators have argued for as the impetus for this passage. I myself see the weak as most likely representing Jewish converts whose religious training and devotion to the Mosaic law made it constitutionally hard for them to set aside and discontinue, in good conscience, ceremonial practices that seemed to them necessary to rightly honor God. These ceremonial observances and practices had taken on almost a moral footing in their minds, and they had to continue them to feel like good Christians.

That kind of person is, I think, approximately the same type as Cranfield sees in the background. As he sees it, Paul has in mind people who "could not, with a clear conscience, give up the observance of such requirements of the law as the distinction between clean and unclean foods, the avoidance of blood, the keeping of the Sabbath and other special days." [385] Such a person seems to best fit the contextual requirements.

Characteristics of the Weaker Brother:

His conscience

a. Restricts him to a vegetarian diet, probably because of his legitimate fears that meats sold in the public marketplaces may be presumed to have been initially dedicated to idols before they were released for sale.

They saw themselves at risk of defilement before God if they partook of meat that had been associated indirectly with idol worship. Unable by faith to dismiss idols as silly myths, they got all hung up on the history of the meat as belonging to something real, and they could not partake in good conscience. But other believers, from the perspective of a more enlightened understanding, wrote idols off as non-existent entities and would not do them the service of elevating them to a higher level by asking questions for conscience's sake.

b. Requires him to treat some days more sacred than others

It is not "weakness" in faith to respect biblically imposed boundaries, such those as Paul laid down in 13:13 or Colossians 3:5ff. What is described as a brother "weak in faith or conscience" is one whose unenlightened conscience has been conditioned by past experience (cultural or religious) to treat certain things as sacred (or defiled and defiling) that in themselves are of no consequence to God and are irrelevant as measures or criteria of godlines. The weak brother's conscience is burdened with insistent scruples imposed by cultural conditioning as opposed to biblical command. These traditional (vis a vis revelational) scruples he is unable to ignore or trample upon without feeling the voice of conscience condemning him for disobeying and dishonoring God in a matter that in and of itself is a matter of indifference to God.

c. Seems double-minded and at odds within itself... that is, his conscience is reflexive and bound by old religious habit, yet unsettled enough by the liberty of others strong in faith (i.e., in their strong assurance of their liberties in these indifferent issues) that he (the weak brother whose conscience [trained under the ritual codes of the Mosaic economy] has not yet caught up with the logic or premises of his Christian faith) is susceptible to being emboldened by the example and liberty of others to act against his own convictions, thereby wounding his conscience.

That could, in fact, be why the weak brother is frequently shrill in his judgment, that is, because he feels as much temptation as indignation.

That is why it is so important not to do anything to leverage the conscience of the weak brother to override its scruples, for the spirit of lawlessness breaks out as much in willingly ignoring a boundary that one wrongly thought existed as in transgressing a real one. This creates a breach between a man and God and drives him in flight from God, just as Adam hid from God. For the first instinct of guilt is to run from God, not to Him. And every trampling of the conscience damages it... hardens it... desensitizes and renders it less serviceable to God and the behavior that honors Him.

---

[365] Bruce, *The Epistle of Paul to the Romans*, 235-236. Here, Bruce quotes J.W. Allen from *A History of Political Thought in the Sixteenth Century* (1928), p. 132.

[366] Hodge, *Epistle to the Romans*, 406.

[367] Bruce, *The Epistle of Paul to the Romans*, 236.

[368] What about rogue or criminal governments which have kicked their appointed traces and perverted their divine functions and serve the purposes of evil rather than good?

1. Even criminal government, as history shows, is less oppressive and onerous to society as a whole than no government. Anarchy is the greatest terror of all.

2. It is never the place of Christians to be seditious or work to overthrow a government, as undesirable as that government may be. If it is the will of God to rid a people of wicked rulers, He will do it without them having to resort to sin and ungodly means to bring it down.

3. To submit to a criminal government is simply to obey it at those points where its will does not conflict with the will of God. God's laws always trump man's laws. Therefore, compliance does not entail complicity in its evil ways.

Does resisting our government include (in a democratic arrangement) voting against those in authority?

No. In a democratic society, civil authority exists by the will of the people, and the legal instrument that the government provides and encourages for registering the public will is the voting process.

Hence, it is neither a subversive nor rebellious act, but a legal process for asking for change when the status quo is not satisfactory.

[369] "It is plain for the immediate context, as from the general context of the apostolic writings, that the state can rightly command obedience only within the limits of the purposes for which it has been divinely instituted—in particular, the state not only may, but must, be resisted when it demands the allegiance due to God alone. 'The obedience which the Christian owes to the State is never absolute but, at the most, partial and contingent. It follows that the Christian lives always in a tension between two competing claims; that in certain circumstances disobedience to the command of the State may be, not only a right, but also a duty. This has been classical Christian doctrine ever since the apostles declared they ought to obey God rather than men." (Bruce, *The Epistle of Paul to the Romans*, 237, citing Sir T.M. Taylor, *The Heritage of the Reformation*, pp. 8 f.)

[370] Bruce, *The Epistle of Paul to the Romans*, 238. (cf. 12:17a, 19)

[371] Hodge, *Epistle to the Romans*, 415.

The thrust of this text has been widely (and grossly) misunderstood as a prohibition against financial indebtedness and term financing. Whatever may be said for or against the wisdom of creating a burden of debt in a given situation, this passage does not and was not intended to address that circumstance, except in sense of disallowing us to withhold from people *anything* that they are due from us for the simple reason that such behavior is a breach of the law of love. This is a case of jerking a text out of context and using its language for a purpose foreign to its intent. Even if the intent of the author was to speak to financial obligations specifically, the language here would in no way forbid the incurrence of debt, but only prohibits the habit of not paying back what is owed.

For example, when one finances a home or car on a long- or short-term mortgage, the creditor and the debtor enter into a mutual agreement to repay the money on a certain schedule by a certain time. Legally and morally the money is not "owed" nor "withheld" from the creditor until such time as the debtor fails to give the creditor whatever falls due at those intervals.

In fact, one might even argue, to the extent that the issue here has to do with fulfilling the law of love (and it has everything to do with it) that in some instances it might be more hurtful for a debtor to pre-pay a financial obligation in instances where a creditor is depending on the interest advantage in a financial agreement, a benefit which pre-payment will deny him.

373 Note that Paul's premise is that people do love themselves (cf. also Eph. 5:28-29). This fact can be taken for granted. Note also that the imperative of the law of God, namely, that one should love his neighbor as himself assumes that our chief deficiency and point of resistance is not psychological, but sociological.

So, what do we say about the hypothesis that some people suffer from a lack of self-esteem. . . that they do not love themselves. . . that they do not think as highly of their own personal worth as they ought (and need) to think?

Part of the contradiction here is misanalysis on the part of counselors. Deep seated feelings of inferiority may, in fact, cripple personal performance and hinder social relationships, but that phenomenon does not preclude self-love which consists in great solicitude about one's own well-being. The very fact that people who suffer from feelings of inferiority seek to be rid of them is, in itself, evidence that they love themselves.

Also, the apparent self-contempt with which people revile themselves for various shortcomings is often nothing more than upset human pride. The fact is, we care so much about ourselves, about how we are viewed, about how we want to see ourselves, that we literally reproach and punish ourselves for being or doing less than we, or others, expected of us. The problem is not at all that we don't care about ourselves, but actually the reverse: we care so very much, we take ourselves so very seriously that we revile and punish ourselves for our sins, excesses, weaknesses, foibles and frailties rather than humbly apply to God for His forgiveness.

374 Calvin, *The Epistles of Paul to the Romans and Thessalonians,*286-87.

375 As used here *kai touto* (in classical Greek *kai tauta*) is an idiom serving to introduce an additional circumstance heightening the force of what has been said (cf. 1 Cor. 6:6, 8; Eph. 2:8; Heb 11:12). The things Paul has been exhorting his readers to do... they must—and they will—strive all the more earnestly to do, because they know the significance of the time.

376 For our salvation spoken of in the present tense or, put another way, as a present experience, see 1 Peter 1:9; see 1 Pet. 1:5 for it is seen in the future tense as an experience yet to be obtained.

The point is that our redemption is a *program* and different aspects or stages of it are experienced at different points along the line. Some are past, some present and some yet in the future. All of it taken together constitutes what is called "redemption".

Yet the parts that are past are a pledge of what follows. For that reason, it is appropriate to speak of "having been saved" since the whole project is assured by the initial work. Hence our redemption is something that is "already"... already in the sense that the foundation is already laid and all the promises are guaranteed in full, but right now the whole package and impact is "not yet" in place or fulfilled.

377 Calvin, *The Epistles of Paul to the Romans and Thessalonians,* 287.

378 Hodge, *Epistle to the Romans,* 410-411.

379 "The true explanation, we believe, is rather that the primitive Church was convinced that the ministry of Jesus had ushered in the last days, the End-time. History's supreme events had taken place in the ministry, death, resurrection and ascension of the Messiah. There was now no question of another chapter's being added which could in any way effectively go back upon what had been written in that final chapter. All that subsequent history could add, whether it should last for a few years or for many, must be of the nature of an epilogue."

The author goes on to say that this *Naherwartung* (near-expectation) of the early church "is not the same thing as a certainty that the End would *necessarily* occur within, at the most, a few decades," though he acknowledges some did entertain that expectation and many others could have held out the possibility of an almost immediate return. Cranfield, *ICC: Romans Vol. 2,* 683-64.

380 Hodge, *Epistle to the Romans,* 412.

381 Cranfield, *ICC: Romans Vol. 2,* 687.

382 Used of a village festival which "ended in the party parading the streets crowned, bearing torches, singing, dancing, and playing frolics." Liddell and Scott, *Intermediate Greek-English Lexicon,* 460. It might be added that the festivities included bawdy music, coarse levity and much debauchery.

383 Cranfield, *ICC: Romans Vol. 2,* 689.

384 Ibid, 690-95.
385 Ibid, 695.

Romans Chapter 14

(14:1) *Now accept the one who is weak in faith, but not for the purpose of passing judgment on his opinions.*

"Weak (*asthenounta from astheneo = to be weak or powerless*) *in faith,*" meaning lacking in the assurance or confidence that one can do something that, rightly understood, the principles of the gospel would permit without offense to God.[386] This weakness can take the form of either a forbidding or an ambivalent conscience in matters that are of no account to God.

Saints with weak consciences must not be confused with weak Christians in terms of devotion. In fact, they may be among the most serious and earnest disciples. Their weakness consists not in a lack of affection for Christ but in a mis-trained and misinformed conscience, resulting in unnecessary scruples that inhibit their freedom to exercise the liberties Christ has won for them. Their overly forbidding consciences and their tendency to inflict those same restraints on others and to judge them negatively when others do otherwise can be a source of divisiveness and unhealthy friction in the life of the church.

As Cranfield speculates, this nomenclature ("weak in faith") probably originated with "the strong in faith" who disputed with them about their unnecessary scruples. At any rate, Paul embraces the validity of this terminology "while he disapproves of [the] unbrotherly insistence [of the strong] on expressing their inward freedom outwardly to the full, quite regardless of its effects on others."[387] (bracket mine)

"Accept..." (*proslambanesthe from proslambano = to receive or accept into one's society, into one home or circle of acquaintances.*[388] They are, after all, brethren in Christ and should be shown all the love and consideration of handicapped brethren.

"Not for the purpose of passing judgment..." (*eis diakriseis = for quarrels*). That is, not in a condescendingly contentious way, admitting them to our company or society for the purpose of quarreling about his faulty scruples and attempting to modify his conscience about such matters.

"Opinions" (*dialogismon* from *dialogismos* = thought, opinion, reasoning, then doubt, . .dispute, argument, so Arndt and Gingrich. [389] Cranfield would translate it "scruples." [390]

(14:2) *One man has faith that he may eat all things, but he who is weak eats vegetables only.*

In an imperfect world, where we "see in a mirror dimly...where we know in part" (1 Cor. 13:9, 12)...where understanding is piecemeal at best in all of us and we are all being gradually "renewed to a true knowledge of the One who created him" (Col. 3:10), we are going to have these gradations in spiritual understanding or IQ. Some are going to be more or less advanced than others at various points. On some things, we may run ahead of the pack; at other points, we may be behind the learning curve.

"Has faith that he may eat..." that is, has the inner assurance or confidence that permits him, based on his understanding of the gospel and its implications, to eat whatever without giving any offense to God.

"Vegetables only..." The Jewish ceremonial law did not require Jews to be vegetarians, but it was strict about involvement in idolatry. For scrupulous Jews living in a Gentile world, that risk was heightened by the ubiquitousness of paganism and its customs.

In private sacrifices certain portions of the animal were the prerequisite of the priest, but nearly all the rest might be taken away by the offeror, to be eaten at home or sold. In public sacrifices made by the state the skins and carcasses, which at Athens sometimes amounted to hundreds, were an important source of revenue and patronage, the skins being sold for the state... and the flesh being distributed to magistrates and others, who would sell what they did not need for home consumption. [391]

Therein lay the problem for some like Daniel and his friends, for instance. The diet prescribed for them by the pagan King Nebuchadnezzar and the royal kitchen consisted of meat and wine that had been offered to idols and they felt that in eating it they were defiling themselves with idolatry. Hence, they respectfully requested an exemption for the customary court menu and be allowed to substitute vegetables and water for the king's rich meat and wine. Nebuchadnezzar's agenda was to re-program and "Babylonize" the Hebrews and they were right in their situation to draw their lines.

Probably, what Paul is dealing with here is a case where there were Jewish Christians with similarly forbidding consciences and defilement with idolatry. They insisted on becoming vegetarians to avoid the risk of defilement (and evidently thought that others should go to the same lengths). They may even have cited the example of Daniel and his Hebrew friends as precedents.

(14:3) *Let not him who eats regard with contempt him who does not eat and let not him who does not eat judge him who eats, for God has accepted him.*

"Regard with contempt..." (*exoutheneito* from *exoutheneo* = despise, then reject or treat with contempt.)[392] The tendency in such cases is to be haughtily impatient with such brethren, to act disdainfully superior and be annoyed by their scruples, and resent the judgmental attitudes that one must contend with betimes when the weaker brethren interpret the exercise of our rightful Christian liberties as a sign of lesser devotion to God.

"Judge..." (*krineto* from *krino* = judge, pass judgment upon, esp. in the sense of pass an unfavorable judgment upon, criticizing or finding fault with.)[393] On the other hand, the tendency of those with stricter consciences is to adopt a holier-than-thou stance and assume those who take liberties that their consciences forbid do so only because they are less loyal to Christ than they.[394]

Hodge makes a piercing point to the effect that one has no right to make a behavior a ground of condemnation unless God has made that behavior an issue of communion. [395] Otherwise, lay off.

> (14:4) *Who are you to judge the servant of another? To his own master he stands or falls; and stand he will, for the Lord is able to make him stand.*

Criticism in such matters is more than a matter of being out of line; it is also a question of being out of place.

This rebuke is addressed to the *censorious* weak brother who challenges the spiritual integrity of the stronger whose conscience permits him to exercise his Christian liberties. The weaker are rebuked for usurping God's role—that is, sitting in judgment on God's servants. To God alone, the right belongs the judicial right to determine whether to approve or disapprove the conduct of His servants. To intrude into this prerogative is what is offensive to God. At this point the weaker brother deforms himself into just a willful brother.

It is more than just wrong; such judgment is totally unnecessary where brethren are concerned. God has not only the ability to make His servants to stand (i.e., keep the faith) but He also has the will to make it happen.[396] It is, as Cranfield puts it so well, not an issue of "the strong Christian's ability to stand but... the Lord's ability to make him stand."[397]

"Servant of another..." (*oiketen* from *oiketes* = member of a household, then specifically, house slave, domestic.)[398]

> (14:5) *One man regards one day above another, another regards every day alike. Let each man be fully convinced in his own mind.*

"Regards one day above another...*(krinei hemeran par' hemeran* = selects or prefers one day in comparison to another).

Hodge explains the reference well:

> The law of Moses "prescribed the observance of certain days as religious festivals [and] the Jewish converts were... [in some cases] scrupulous [about these and others were not]... Both

431

were to be tolerated. The veneration of these days was a weakness [only in that it showed a less mature grasp of the bearing of the Gospel upon ceremonial observances of the Law]; but it was not a vital matter, and therefore should not be allowed to disturb the harmony of Christian [fellowship], or the peace of the church."[399] (brackets mine for clarity)

For more specific examples of what Paul has in mind, Hodge cites in the same passage Galatians 4:10, where the apostle notes that "you observe days, and months, and times, and years," and in Colossians 2:16, "Let no man judge you in meat, or in drink, or in respect of a holy day, or of the new moon, or of Sabbath days."[400]

"Another regards every day alike..." (*hos de krinei pasan hemepan* = selects [in the sense of approves or recognizes] every day, i.e., every day is special as a day given by the Lord and to be lived for Him). All are of equal value, and all present the same opportunity to serve and live for God.

"Fully convinced..." (*plerophoreistho* from *plerophoreo* = to convince or to assure fully.)[401] The main thing is for each to respect the dictates of one's own conscience in these matters. The reason that is so important will be broached in 14:22–23. We will see that it is spiritually irresponsible to ignore the voice of a conscience that imposes false restraints, just as a pilot of a commercial airliner would be irresponsible to the public who ignored the voice of a faulty electronic warning system before he was certain that it was false.

We will see why the failure to respect conscience is damning in our relationship with God.

(14:6) *He who observes the day, observes it for the Lord, and he who eats, does so for the Lord, for he gives thanks to God; and he who eats not, for the Lord he does not eat, and gives thanks to God.*

"Observes..." (*phronon* from *phroneo* = to think, form or hold an opinion, judge, then to set one's mind on.)[402]

"Observes it for the Lord..." We are not dealing with libertines on the one hand and legalists on the other. Both parties are acting on what they believe to be right in the sight of God, one in liberty, the other in restraint. One thanks God for the specialness of the day, and the other (implied) would thank God for the specialness of everyday alike. One thanks the Lord for what He eats, and the one who refrains from eating does the same. Both are acting out of a spirit of service and thanksgiving, but in opposite ways, both acceptable to God in the spirit in which they are rendered.

(14:7) *For not one of us lives for himself, and not one dies for himself.*

This statement expresses both God's design and our devotion, ever-growing but imperfectly realized in this flesh. It is this compendious sense of servanthood... this root motivation that sets all Christian behaviors apart from any superficial likeness to those of the superficial moralist, who is driven by mere humanism and the desire to show himself superior to others.

(14:8) *For if we live, we live for the Lord, and if we die, we die for the Lord; there whether we live or die, we are the Lord's.*

Whatever the Christian does, if he does it Christianly, is animated by the sense that in life or death, he is totally at the service of His Sovereign. Two people may act in opposite ways (where biblical boundaries are not involved) from different consciences, but the common denominator is that both are driven by a sense of obligation to honor God in every respect.

(14:9) *For to this end Christ died and lived again, that He might be Lord of both the dead and the living.*

God is sovereign over all being, whether or not man recognizes that inescapable fact. However, that sovereignty is not what this verse is speaking of. There is a sense in which Jesus as the Messiah, the second Adam, the new head of a new race, is appointed Lord as a reward of His redemptive work. As the Son of God, He is Lord of all by virtue of who He is. As the Son of Man, He became Lord of a new race by virtue of what He did. This verse explains how He won the right of Lordship over us as well as the ground of our subjective acknowledgment of this sovereign-servant relationship, that is, how God made it functionally effective in our lives.

Christ died to remove that which stood between us and God, namely, our sin and guilt, and then conquered the ultimate enemy caused by sin, namely death, in the resurrection. Having laid the foundation for our redemption, He reclaimed us from the slave market of sin and made us partakers of the divine life through the regeneration of the Holy Spirit. We are His in any circumstance, whether in life or death.

"Might be Lord..." (*kupieuse* from *kupieuo* = be lord or master, rule, lord it (over), control.)[403]

> (14:10) *But you, why do you judge your brother? Or you again, why do you regard your brother with contempt? For we shall all stand before the judgment-seat of God.*

Our concern is not to stand in judgment upon our brethren (in either direction) but to prepare ourselves to be judged for our faithfulness to God's purpose, remembering that God will judge us by the same harsh standards that we inflict on others (Matt. 7:1–2).

> "For we shall all stand before the judgment-seat of God" (*pantes gar parastesometha* [from *paristemi*] *to bemati tou theou*).

Second Corinthians 5:10 elaborates this: "Therefore we have as our ambition, whether at home or absent, to be pleasing to Him. For we must all appear before the judgment-seat of Christ, that each one may be recompensed for his deeds in the body, according to what he has done, whether good or bad."

There will be no exemptions. All will appear, and the authenticity of our faith will be tested by our fruit. That is, I believe, what Matthew 25:31–46 describes and what John 5:29 anticipates under the heading of the two resurrections.

This is not to imply that salvation is based on faith plus works or simply by works but merely that faith has fruits, and each will be recompensed according to what his life says, not his lips.

Paristemi is used as a legal technical term in the sense of to "bring before (a judge)."[404]

> (14:11) *For it is written, "As I live, says the Lord, every knee shall bow to Me, and every tongue shall give praise to God."*

This citation from Isaiah 45:23 and referred to also in Philippians 2:9–11 confirms universal accountability to God. The whole human race eventually will be arraigned before our God, and the whole earth will at last pay homage to Him, even if forcibly in terror..

> (14:12) *So then each one of us shall give account of himself to God.*

In the face of such an awesome prospect, let us back away from judging our brethren and concentrate our energies on serving and being able at that time to give a good account of ourselves.

Examples of a modern weak brother might appear in contemporary scruples like these:

- Scruples against use of non-natural foods

- Scruples against educating children in public schools

- Scruples against social use of alcohol in any amount

- Scruples against anything other than traditional music

- Scruples against dressing down for public worship

- Scruples against the use of makeup

- Scruples against working on Sunday

- Scruples against certain forms of entertainment (TV, dancing, mixed bathing, etc.)

- Scruples against selling things in the church

- Scruples against Christmas trees

What all of these have in common are:

1) God does not give us clear prescriptions with respect to any of these things, though there are principles that should be applied in ruling for or against them in given contexts.

2) All are issues about which devout Christian consciences can and do vary and have been the occasion of internal conflict among Christians—arrogance on the side of those who have liberty toward those who have scruples, and recrimination on the part of those who have scruples against those who do not.

3) Devout Christians can do the opposite things in each case and sincerely do what they do with thanksgiving to God and in a spirit of service.

4) All represent differences in conscience, which, in order to be pleasing to God, we must learn to tolerate in one another and to embrace each other in brotherly affection in spite of different consciences with respect thereto.

> (14:13) *Therefore let us not judge one another anymore, but rather determine this—not to put an obstacle or a stumbling block in a brother's way.*

"Therefore..." That is, in view of the prospect of divine accountability for our actions. We will not be saved because we did good, for our salvation is not based on merit. God's examination of our works relates to the integrity or authenticity of our faith. We are saved by faith; the reality of our faith is judged by its fruits. That is to say, the best evidence of whether the tree is dead or alive is in the presence or absence of the fruits belonging to its kind. The proof is in the pudding, so to speak.

Certainly, it is not a good sign if those who call them believers give little evidence of "*faith-fulness*" in such matters. Neither is it a good sign of a healthy faith if professed believers go around biting and devouring one another with censorious words, putting obstacles in the path of brethren that might contribute to their shipwreck in the faith. Jesus once called Peter "Satan" because he was putting a stumbling block in Jesus's way. That was when, out of self-interest,

Peter wanted Jesus to avoid His date with the cross. Jesus sternly warned any who might cause any of His little ones to stumble, of the terrible judgment that would befall such (Matt. 18:1–7). See also 1 Corinthians 3:17, where church wreckers are warned of disaster.

"Judge one another" is a summary admonition directed at the tendencies of the strong in faith and the weak in faith respectively. While the former may look with arrogant disdain upon the weakness of those with uninformed consciences, the latter, in turn, may be more apt to call the liberty of the strong license and denounce their spiritual integrity.

"But rather determine this..." We have a play on the Greek verb _krino_ (judge) here—"let us not judge... but determine (literally, judge) this."

Paul seems to be saying: Let us resist the temptation to go around hanging unflattering labels on brethren who displease us in these matters of conscience. Check that destructive impulse. Instead of putting down, it is better to apply our faculties to judging how best to avoid behaviors that might spiritually trip a brother or sister.

Not to put an obstacle or stumbling block in a brother's way.

Here, Paul seems to address the strong especially, for he seems to see the weak in conscience as most at risk in these situations, that is, more susceptible to overriding their protesting conscience to their injury.

People are always more tempted to act in the direction of liberty than in the direction of restraint. Any undue pressure on folks to violate their conscience is setting them up for a fall. If my mistaught and misinformed conscience insists that it is sub-Christian for me to wear multi-colored socks, that if I do, I am sinning. And if you, who know better, laugh and mock at my ignorance, tempting me to ignore my misguided conscience, you lure me into sin. Not because wearing multi-colored socks was wrong, but because I really thought my conscience was the "voice" of God, and in that mindset, I did it your way instead of what I thought was God's way. Right there is the offense that could potentially, in a chain reaction, send a brother defecting from God.

(14:14) *I know and am convinced in the Lord Jesus that nothing is unclean in itself; but to him who thinks anything to be unclean, to him it is unclean.*

"I know (*oida*) and am convinced *(pepeismai)* in the Lord Jesus..." A very emphatic precursor to his affirmation that nothing is unclean in itself. By phrasing the matter this way, Paul apparently means to say that his view derives from the Lord Himself. The phrase "in the Lord Jesus (*en kupio Iesou*)" most likely means "before or in the presence of the Lord," referring no doubt to a result of revelational encounter. His revelational "reading" may be reinforced by Jesus's teaching recorded in Mark 7:14–23, where Mark draws the pertinent inference that Jesus on this occasion, in effect, "declared all foods clean."

"Unclean" (*koinos*) means "common," that is, something that one comes into contact with every day—or ordinary things, things not holy, even blatantly profane.

Nothing is unclean in itself... (di' heautou = through itself or inherently).

"Nothing" in this context does *not* extend its embrace to all of men's attitudes, behaviors, desires, or purposes, but clearly here refers to material foods and drinks that men consume. Nothing of this kind is inherently defiling so that it imparts to the consumer unholiness by virtue of contact.

The absence of inherent impurity, however, does not mean that consumption is necessarily right for everyone. See my earlier footnote illustration about wearing colored socks.

But to him who thinks anything to be unclean, to him it is unclean.

For the person whose mistaught conscience, perhaps owing to some previous cultural conditioning, makes them feel guilty in the act of consumption or usage—for that person in particular, it is a sin to partake.

Why is it wrong to do what our conscience forbids, even if our conscience is misinformed? Because to ignore the voice of conscience, however mis-trained it might be, would be to adopt a transgressive posture. If I mistakenly think it is the "voice" of God and ignore it, therein lies a transgressive or rebellious spirit. And spiritually, that is no light thing.

Suppose a parent told a son to be home at eleven, and the son thought his parents said seven. Yet he decided to ignore what he wrongly thought was their deadline and come home instead at eleven; his parents would not be disturbed at all, that is, until they discovered that he mistakenly thought he was supposed to be home four hours earlier. Yet he deliberately chose to ignore what he wrongly thought they required. When the truth came out, even though he had not actually violated their rule, his action would still betray a rebellious spirit. So, it would all be to the same effect. They would be as disappointed and displeased in one case as the other.

Here is the larger spiritual principle:

> (14:15) *For if because of food your brother is hurt, you are no longer walking according to love. Do not destroy with your food him for whom Christ died.*

"Is hurt..." (*lupeitai* from *lupeo* = to pain, grieve or distress.)[405] The grief or distress may result from derogatory criticism or from a sense of alienation from God, brought on by feelings of guilt for setting aside one's conscience under our social pressure.

"Do not destroy" (*apollue* from *apollumi* = ruin, destroy)[406] is strong language indeed (compare verse 20 and 1 Cor. 8:11).

How can a believer be destroyed or ruined? The analogy of Scripture prevents any interpretation that allows for a believer losing his salvation, once gained. One proof of this premise (among a host) has already appeared in this very section, where Paul assured us earlier that the God who is able to make His servants stand will, in fact, do that very thing (verse 4).

The only options left are for "ruination" in some lesser sense or to take "believer" in an accommodating (professing) sense (as in John 2:23 or 8:31 or like those "disciples" in John 6:66), where all those who profess Christ are taken at face value as "brothers" but always with the tacit understanding that the proof is in the perseverance of the saints. Many "professors" eventually prove non-starters. In the end, they do not "show" at the finish line. In short, all the professors do not turn out to be "possessors" in the end.

Even so, if I allow myself the loveless liberty to wreck their conscience carelessly, indifferently pushing them to ignore that protesting "voice" within and thus let misinformed guilt drive them like Adam running from God, I become the leverage Satan needs to ruin their approach to God. That is serious business and accountability to be an instrument in any spiritual crash.

Since it is difficult to identify any lesser sense that makes sense, and since we find such accommodating uses already in the NT, that interpretation is preferable. When a person tramples on his conscience, he sins. When one sins, guilt follows in its wake. Guilt, unless interdicted by confession and repentance, drives people in fear from God[407]—the very antithesis of faith. For it is only if our hearts do not condemn us that confidence before God can be sustained (1 John 3:21). Sin, like murder, committed once is more easily repeated, especially when one feels a sense of estrangement from God. In that posture, one is more susceptible to temptation from the Enemy. Sin often repeated hardens the sensitive conscience, blunting one's moral senses and puts the soul at ever greater distance from God and at greater fear and antagonism toward him.

In short, sin aborts the birthing of real faith and eventually squashes whatever it is that imitates faith in those who have been superficially touched by the work of the Spirit. Sooner or later, they apostatize, that is, fall away from God, an event precipitated by some offense given by another or some sin that someone helped lead them into or both.

Though such persons are fully responsible and accountable for their own ruin, any who "helped" them take the fall are also held accountable. God uses such offense as a filter to sort out the true and the false, but He does not excuse those who gave it.

The danger on the part of the strong is flaunting their liberty in such a way as to tempt those with a forbidding conscience but a vacillating will to act against their convictions. My conscience may deny me the liberty to do a given thing, but I may still, for some reason, wish that I could. Maybe my rigid conscience creates social stress for me (e.g., in entertaining or being entertained, not feeling that I can provide alcoholic drinks for guests accustomed to them, or that I can imbibe). The strong, by exercising their liberty unwisely, may make it harder for the weak-willed to abstain, even when it goes against their conscience. The strong may even go so far as to pressure the weak in faith (conscience-confident) to ignore their "silly scruples" and put them down and intimidate them in such a way that they give in to their desire to be accepted by men and abandon their desire to be pleasing to God in adhering to what they thought His will was.

The law of Christ compels Christians to put their responsibilities before their rights, the exercise of Christian love before the exercise of Christian liberty. In short, Christ expects us to check our liberties at the door whenever their exercise might put a brother at risk spiritually.

"Do not destroy with your food him for whom Christ died" puts the face of absurdity on the risk of assertiveness about our rights versus our responsibilities. The spiritual ruin of a brother is a price much too high for a diet of beef, even if nothing is wrong with a diet of beef. One should not insist on a happy stomach if it is going to cause a professing brother heart trouble.

Besides, how can we think it too much to ask us to lay down our liberties for the spiritual welfare of our weaker (in terms of conscience confidence) brethren when Christ went so far as to lay down His life for them? If Christ prized them so much, how can we despise them so greatly? Case closed.

(14:16) *Therefore do not let what is for you a good thing be spoken of as evil...*

"Be spoken of as evil..." (*me blasphemeistho* from *blasphemeo* = to injure the reputation of, to revile, to defame.)[408] This particular term seems to have outsiders in view. If so, "a good thing..." (*humon to agathon* = your good or your good thing) may well refer to the gospel.

In that case, Paul would be admonishing the strong not to push their liberties so far as to cause sin, divisions, and quarrels to the point that apparent brethren were in the language of Galatians, "biting and devouring one another" so that they were consuming one another and making a mockery of the Christian message in the eyes of outsiders, hence inviting its defamation (cf. Gal. 5:15).

The language could also refer to the liberty of conscience with respect to abandoning the ceremonial rituals in view. I think, however, the word "blaspheme," as it would more naturally suggest, the reviling of those outside the church, is against this view.

Something good in itself can bring one into dispute, because either one does it in excess (like gluttony), or because the indulgence of a liberty hurts others by tempting them to follow one's lead and to act against their own conscience, or by precipitating public quarrels that fester, break out in open hostility and verbal violence, and give unbelievers a good excuse to question not only the credibility of the parties but the gospel itself.

> (14:17) *For the kingdom of God is not eating and drinking, but righteousness and peace and joy in the Holy Spirit.*

"For" offers another reason for demoting these issues to the periphery where they belong. They are not of the essence. They do not establish the boundaries where God reigns nor serve as identifying marks of those whom God accepts.

"The kingdom of God" is that sphere where God's rule has taken effect in the hearts of men.

"Is not in eating and drinking…" The rule of God is not discerned or detected in what the citizens of the kingdom eat and drink. The badge of the Kingdom is not diet. The insignia of God is found rather in the possession and pursuit of righteousness, promotion of the peace of God, and in the overflow of that quiet, unquenchable joy which only the Holy Spirit can impart. So, if you want to find who belongs to the kingdom of God, don't check out their refrigerator but use these other insignia as your point of reference.

(14:18) *For he who in this way serves Christ is acceptable to God and approved by men.*

Conscience issues are irrelevant where these attributes exist. For the record, whoever bears these marks enjoys God's acceptance, whatever his weaknesses and the approbation of his fellow man.

Of course, the acceptance of God is assured in a way that the approval of men is not. Those who fit these characteristics do not deserve in any way the censure of men and generally will enjoy a reputation among them as good people. So, it was with Jesus (cf. Luke 1:52).

(14:19) *So then let us pursue the things which make for peace and the building up of one another.*

The welfare of the body is more important to God than the indulgence of individual liberties. Our primary interest should not be, "May we do this or that?" but rather, "Will our doing this or that be constructive?" Christ did not set us free to do as we please but to do what pleases Him and builds up others.

(14:20) *Do not tear down the work of God for the sake of food. All things indeed are clean, but they are evil for the man who eats and gives offense.*

This verse, in principle, circles back and more or less reiterates the thoughts of verse 15.

"All things indeed are clean." Again, "all things" is limited in its scope by the context to matters of diet. Dietary regulations of the old covenant served their purpose and now, under the new covenant, are no longer binding upon the people of God (cf. Mark 7:14). Nothing we might consume in the way of food or drink is defiled or defiling in and of itself.

Some liberties, however innocent in themselves, can become sinful, however, because by insisting on exercising them we allow them to displace more important things or, as here, we are willing to expose others to spiritual injury in doing these things. In those cases, what is clean in and of itself becomes defiled in the circumstances. It is a terrible and inexcusable choice to pamper our own appetites at the risk of potentially damaging the work of God.

(14:21) *It is good not to eat meat or to drink wine, or to do anything by which your brother stumbles.*

We should not admit everything our conscience permits if doing so knowingly creates a spiritual obstacle for our brother. Prime rib is fine unless I cause my brother somehow to choke on it.

(14:22) *The faith which you have, have as your own conviction before God. Happy is he who does not condemn himself in what he approves.*

The greatest happiness lies not in being free from the burden of unnecessary scruples but in exercising those liberties with the kind of Christian restraint that does not make us an accomplice to the downfall of another.

What Paul means is something like saying to your teenage son, who has just gotten his driver's license and a fast car to go with it:

"Son, you want to know how to have the most enjoyment with this kind of car? It's not going out there on the highway, taking your life in your hands, endangering the public happiness, and attracting the law. That just makes trouble for you and everybody else and, sooner or later, brings a lot of heartache for everybody. It just makes a bad thing out of a good thing."

"Don't ruin it, son. You'll have by far the most enjoyment if you don't go out there and show off all the speed you've got, but just rest content in the fact that you have all the speed you will ever need when you need it but have the maturity to curb and control it in such a way that you keep out of trouble with the law, and you never endanger the life and safety of others. In the long run, you will experience more happiness going that route than the other, which will only bring you and others to grief."

(14:23) *But he who doubts is condemned if he eats, because his eating is not from faith; and whatever is not from faith is sin.*

This principle affirms what I said earlier.

"He who doubts," that is, lacks the confidence before God that one can partake without trampling on the will of God.

"Not from faith..." That is, it does not issue from an affirming conscience that gives one an unequivocal green light to enjoy it.

"Whatsoever is not from faith..." that is, any conduct or practice that lacks the confidence that God permits this thing.

It is sin because acting contrary to our conscience, even if the voice of conscience is mis-trained and therefore mistaken about right and wrong, betrays a spirit of lawlessness. That exposes an underlying willingness to transgress what one understands to be the will of God in a situation.[409]

---

[386] "The weakness in faith. . . is not weakness in basic Christian faith [i.e. Gospel premises] but weakness in assurance that one's faith [i.e. Gospel principles] permits one to do certain things [that the Scriptures do not explicitly address]" (brackets my own clarifications of his sense as I perceive it.) Cranfield, *ICC: Romans Vol. 2*, 700.

[387] Ibid, 700.

[388] Arndt & Gingrich, *A Greek-English Lexicon of the New Testament*, 724.

[389] Ibid, 185.

[390] Cranfield, *ICC: Romans*, 701.

[391] Robertson and Plummer, *ICC:1 Corinthians*, 166. Citing Smith, *Dictionary of Greek and Roman Antiquities*, II. p. 585.

[392] Arndt & Gingrich, *Greek-English Lexicon of the New Testament*, 277.

[393] Ibid, 453.

[394] It is important to remember that we are not dealing here with issues where clear biblical boundaries are established, but cases where the Scripture does not speak, at least with specificity and clarity and therefore conscience must rule. Obviously, there are those who take liberties that Scripture does not grant and this kind of presumption is clear transgression and does indeed point to a lesser (if not an outright lack of) devotion to God. But that kind of situation is not in view here.

[395] Hodge, *Epistle to the Romans*, 419.

[396] This text bristles with strong implications for the doctrine of the perseverance of saints or the security of the believer. God will see that His own keep the faith. He does not start the program of redemption in our lives at such a price and leave it incomplete and us short of the finish line. Compare the argument of Romans 5:6-11.

Further (by way of application) this principle reminds us that in the whole process of discipling, we can take ourselves and our "spiritual technologies" much too seriously, as if God's work will shrivel up and die if we aren't able to come along side with our highly refined and rigidified methodologies to make discipleship happen. I am amazed at the relatively impoverished conditions under which some believers manage vis a vis the nutrient-rich environment under which some professors wither away and die. God draws and keeps those that are His. (John 10:27-29) This is no excuse for irresponsibility on the part of shepherds, for they are co-laborers in God's vineyard who shall be held accountable. But their inadequacies, ineptitudes and irresponsibility will in no way diminish God's harvest. He will reap what He planted. We can relax when we don't have it all together. God is the difference that makes them stick and grow.

[397] Cranfield, *ICC: Romans Vol. 2,* 704.

[398] Arndt & Gingrich, *Greek-English Lexicon of the New Testament,* 559.

[399] Hodge, *Epistle to the Romans,* 420.

[400] Our Christian "sabbath" would indeed fall into this category if we viewed it as more sacred than other days in the sense that it required more holiness of us than other days, were more demanding us in terms of consecration to God than other times.

Not so. Every day is an equal opportunity employer where holiness is concerned. What God asks of us on Monday, He asks of us on Sunday, namely, that we present our bodies a living and holy sacrifice, one acceptable to Him, that we "be not conformed to this world, but transformed by the renewing of our minds" (Rom. 12:1-2).

The transfer of the Christian day of worship by the apostolic community to Sunday to commemorate the resurrection of our Lord signals an egalitarian calendar.

Is Sunday special at all? Only in the sense that there should be a day when God's people give their minds and bodies a reprieve from life's labors, set aside worldly preoccupations and meet together in the presence of God to hear from Him as a body and to let Him hear from us in praise and prayer. That day could be any day. The early Christians picked the first (or Resurrection) day. We could all choose Monday or Wednesday or Saturday and Heaven would not have a hernia, so to speak. It's inconsequential.

The main thing is that Sunday is the day the world has come to expect us to do our thing and we ought not send the message, I believe, by non-attendance (Heb. 10:25) that it no longer matters to us a great deal to honor God with our public worship. It is a matter of testimony.

[401] Arndt & Gingrich, *Greek-English Lexicon of the New Testament,* 676.

[402] Arndt & Gingrich, *Greek-English Lexicon of the New Testament,* 874.

[403] Arndt & Gingrich, *Greek-English Lexicon of the New Testament,* 459.

404 Arndt & Gingrich, *Greek-English Lexicon of the New Testament*, 633.

405 Arndt & Gingrich, *Greek-English Lexicon of the New Testament*, 482.

406 Ibid, 94.

407 See the reaction of Adam and Eve to their guilt. They hid from God and Adam immediately began extenuating his guilt by shifting the blame to Eve and even God for giving her to Adam! This classic psychological dynamic of guilt causes hardening to set in.

408 Arndt & Gingrich, *Greek-English Lexicon of the New Testament*, 142.

409 For example, it would be as much the spirit of murder to riddle a mannequin one mistook for a real person as it is to pump an actual person full of holes. One would be as much a scofflaw to ignore a 20 mile per hour zone that one wrongly presumed existed as one would be if one blatantly defied the law that one knew existed. I would expose myself as a cheater if in taking an exam I used notes I wrongly thought were disallowed just as much as if I used crib notes that were not permitted. Likewise, it is as much the spirit of lawlessness to trample on my conscience when it misinforms me about the will of God as it is to ignore it when it informs me correctly.

Romans Chapter 15

The apostle brings now the preceding discussion about Christian liberty and the restraint thereof down to brass tacks.

> (15:1) *Now we who are strong ought to bear the weaknesses of those without strength and not just please ourselves.*

Here, Paul articulates an obligation embedded in the law of love, namely, to make charitable concessions to the spiritual weaknesses of others and to renounce self-gratification for the purpose of accommodating and supporting those who are weak. Look out for others before you look out for number one. Bottom line: Please your brother before you please yourself.

"What Paul is forbidding in particular is that strong Christians should please themselves by insisting on exercising outwardly and to the full that inner freedom which they have been given, when to do so would hurt a weak brother's faith."[410]

"We who are strong (*dunatoi*)" equates those in chapter 14, whose better informed faith grants their consciences the freedom to do all that God allows (as opposed to "those without strength" [of faith]), whose less informed faith and misguided conscience creates religious scruples about matters of indifference to God, such as matters of diet and observance of certain days they had been trained to treat as more sacred than others.

"To bear..." (*bastazein* from *bastazo* = 1. to take up 2. carry, bear, literally a burden; b. bear, endure; c. carry, bear in a weakened sense with idea of a burden; 3. carry away, remove.)[411] Galatians 6:2: "Bear one another's burdens and thus fulfill the law of Christ" (John 16:12; Acts 15:10; Rev. 2:2, 3).

The question is: Does "bear" mean simply to carry in the sense of helping the weak with their burden (i.e., this weakness of faith), or does it mean to carry in the sense of enduring, graciously putting up with by reigning in one's liberty for the good of the weaker brother. Against Cranfield and with Hodge, I prefer the latter since there is no other way to "carry" or help the weak with this particular infirmity except to charitably renounce self-gratification at their expense. Certainly 14:1 makes it fairly clear that this does not mean relieving them of their scruples in the sense of talking them out of them. Not that charitable dialogue with those weak in faith about these issues is ruled out, but Paul has recommended charitable tolerance rather than discussions as the best course of action.

I cannot agree that "endurance" necessarily involves condescension or any attitude of superiority. Tolerance of weakness is no different than a circumstance where one kindly accepts the limitation of life and endures unwelcome circumstances out of love for the infirmity of a loved one. What Paul calls for here is very much akin to his appeal of us to be "showing forbearance to one another in love" in Ephesians 4:2.

"The weaknesses" or infirmities, that is, "the prejudices, the errors, and faults which arise from weaknesses of faith or the mistraining of conscience" (cf. 1 Cor. 9:20–22). In matters where faithfulness to God was not at stake, Paul says it was his policy to accommodate his lifestyle to others, whatever sacrifices and limitations that might involve, for the purpose of removing every source of unnecessary offense that might get in the way and obscure the real issues so that he might have a better opportunity to expose them to the truth and bring them to Christ.

And [ought not] not [strive to] please ourselves [as the matter of most importance].

Here, Paul strikes the death knell to the cult of self-fulfillment and individualism. The doctrine of self-fulfillment says that the most important value in life is be happy and to resist any form of self-denial that will keep you from feeling totally fulfilled. It doesn't matter who you let down so long as you don't let yourself down. That perverse philosophy is the son of Western individualism, which says that it is more important to be yourself, to be true to yourself, and to do everything your own way than to let yourself be forced into somebody else's mold or will. We have received that doctrine as a virtual sacred. It goes almost as unchallenged as the idea that freedom is the unalienable right of every man and goes along with that notion as a corollary.

This is one of those many places where the Scriptures and the Christian way contradict our culture and fly right in the face of our democratic traditions. Duty to others comes before gratification of self. That is the law of God.

"We are not to do everything which we may have a right to do, and make our own gratification the rule by which we exercise our Christian liberty." [412]

> (15:2) *Let each of us please his neighbor for his good, to his edification.*

Paul restates this obligation in positive terms but adds a qualifying circumstance as a controlling consideration in deciding when and when not to accommodate one's neighbor and to restrain one's liberty in consideration of their scruples.

"Please…" (*aresketo* = strive to please, accommodate) [413]

"As the points of difference are not essential, as the law of love, the example of Christ, and the honour of religion require concession, we that are fully persuaded of the indifference of those things about which our weaker brethren are scrupulous, ought to accommodate ourselves to their opinions, and not act with a view to our own gratification merely." [414]

"For his good, to his edification." Here is the regulating qualification. The second phrase defines "for his good." What is good is whatever edifies, that is, whatever results in spiritual gain and improvement of the soul.

Christians are not called to be people-pleasers as if maintaining good peer relations were our guiding social value. Our mission is to please and glorify God. We glorify God by emulating His love toward our brethren and relinquishing any disposable liberty or pursuit on our part that might in any manner prove to be a spiritual hindrance or obstacle to our brethren.

"The good we should contemplate is their religious improvement." [415] This is not, then, a case of weak-willed compliance but an "exercise of enlightened benevolence" in the interest of our brother's spiritual welfare.

"We are not simply to ask what is right in itself, or what is agreeable, but also what is benevolent and pleasing to our brethren."[416]

> (15:3) *For even Christ did not please Himself; but as it is written, "The reproaches of those who reproached You fell on Me."*

Now, he presents to us the selfless example of Christ, both as a model to follow and a source of motivation.

The quote is taken from Psalm 69:9: "For zeal for Your house has consumed me, and the reproaches of those who reproach You have fallen on me."

In this ancient Psalm, the writer and prophet, the great King David, speaks as God's human representative and righteous servant. He declares therein his consummate and uncompromising devotion to the glory of God. He says, in effect, that his will has so merged with God's will, his love with God's love, his purpose with God's purpose, and his heartbeat with God's heartbeat that any reproach aimed by hostile men at his holy God pains him and grieves him as much as if he were personally the target of their animosity and insults, so unified are his interests with God's.

In the NT, the sentiments and actions of God's righteous servants like this one are often viewed as transcending the original writer and echoing by anticipation the sentiments and actions of that ultimate Man of God, the Christ, and in this case, David's heir and greater Son. If these feelings and behaviors were ever true of anyone, they were true of Christ, the consummate Righteous Servant above all. Hence, under the guidance of the Spirit, the propriety of appropriating as predictive of Christ what were originally attitudes belonging to another (David).

The point of the citation is not an exhortation to submit to a life of reproach from spiritual hostiles but rather "The simple point to be illustrated is the [self] disinterestedness of Christ, the fact that he did not please himself."[417] (brackets mine)

At bottom the argument is from the greater to the less. Surely in pursuit of that same objective (the glory of God), we should not hesitate to put up with the infirmities of the weak who love God since Christ Himself bore and put up with the reproaches of the godless who hate Him.

"Fell on Me..." in the sense that He so emptied Himself (of Self) in His devotion to God... that He so identified with the divine interests that the reproaches intended for God by hostile men... that He was so wrapped up in God's service that the mud thrown at God's face got all over Him emotionally as well, so merged were His interests with God's, His will with the Father's, His purpose with the divine purpose, and His love with God's. In the same way, we should vacate self-interest and be so committed to God's that we abandon the path of self-gratification in favor of building up the weaker brethren whom God loves.

Christ was totally vacant of self-interest in His service of God in whose commission we also serve. He never let the pursuit of self-gratification or self-fulfillment on the human side ever stand in the way of promoting God's interests or promoting His glory. He willingly exposed Himself for God's glory to the shock of humiliation and the vicious brunt of human hostility toward God in the service of God and providing for our needs.

"If it is the duty of a servant to refuse nothing that his master takes upon himself, it would be quite absurd for us to wish to exempt ourselves from the necessity of bearing another's weakness, for Christ, in whom we glory as our Lord and King, submitted Himself to this. He laid aside all regard for Himself and devoted Himself to this task."[418]

"By this he means that he had burned with such a desire to advance His kingdom, that He forgot himself and was absorbed in this one thought. He had so devoted himself to the Lord that he was grieved in his heart whenever he beheld God's holy name exposed the slander of the ungodly."[419]

(15:4) For whatever was written in earlier times was written for our instruction, that through perseverance and the encouragement of the Scriptures we might have hope.

In case anyone might think it was a stretch to reach back into the OT for that citation, which prophetically applied to Christ, as a justification for His principle of self-denial, Paul now enlightens us about the function of the Scriptures. His words ripple with significance for the whole project of Christian growth and discipleship.

"Whatever was written in earlier times" refers to the OT corpus that formed the Bible of the early church until the NT was written, widely distributed, and recognized by the Church as canonical (i.e., as vested with divine authority).

"Was written for our instruction..." (*didaskalian*). A similar thought is expressed by Paul in 1 Corinthians 10:11: "Now these things happened to them (i.e., their wilderness experiences) as an example, and they were written for our instruction, upon whom the ends of the ages have come." See also 2 Timothy 3:15–16. What applied to the OT writings is no less true of the NT documents. Same song, different verse. So much for contemporaries who largely dismiss the relevancy of the OT for Christian growth and edification. Heresy continues to bedevil the ranks and endanger souls (2 Tim. 4:1-4) .

"Instruction..." If the Scriptures exist by the plan of God for the purpose of instruction, then it must mean that knowledge is a fundamental condition of spiritual health and maintenance of the soul and a right relationship with God.

I make this point strongly, for there are those who not only lightly esteem the importance of the teaching of and nurture from the Scriptures but—and this is the underlying reason—attach no great importance to right doctrine... to correct understanding of God and the things that relate to walking with God. Somehow, they imagine that right feelings are all that matters, failing to understand that right feelings are the product of right doctrine, though apprehension of right doctrine is no guarantee of right feelings or devotion. As one of my professors in seminary used to remind us: "Gentlemen, you cannot act right if you do not believe right. No man acts better than he believes. I can tell what you believe in every case, not by what you say but by what you do."

One can teach people what is right, and they may not get it right, but unless they are taught the right way, they will not walk in it.

The Scriptures are our compass, "a light unto our paths, a lamp unto our feet" (Psa. 119:105). They make us wise instead of foolish. Only a fool despises teaching. You show me a person who does not gravitate to the Scriptures and resonate with sound teaching, and I will show you without exception a person who is shallow and unstable and susceptible to being misled and capable of misleading.

"That... we might have hope." The ultimate end of biblical instruction is to build incrementally our hope quotient. By "hope," it is meant to strengthen our expectation or confidence in God's ultimate faithfulness to His promises. The problem we face is that our knowledge of God and spiritual reality is partial... very incomplete. "Now we see through a glass darkly" (1 Cor. 13:12). Some things are clearly revealed... but there are obscurities... mysteries in the ways God works.

The Scriptures show us by precept, principle, precedents, and prophecy things we need to know to shore up our faith in times when present experience would seem to contradict or collide with what God promises. Those are times of real tension that challenge and erode our foundation of hope or expectation unless it is constantly being nourished and strengthened by the resource God has provided. That resource is the Bible. Nothing lifts our sense of hope, nothing shores it up, and nothing fits it for the road like the Scriptures diligently pondered and rightly understood.

Notice how the Scriptures accomplish this divinely designed goal: "through perseverance and the encouragement of the Scriptures."

The interpretative problem here is whether Paul means to connect perseverance with the Scriptures or with the reader. In other words, is he saying: "through the (the definite article is there in the original) perseverance and the encouragement that we derive from the promises, precepts, precedents, and personalities of the Scriptures," or does he mean "through perseverance on our part and the encouragement that the Scriptures provide"? The Greek is capable of being understood either way. However, since Paul is talking about how the Scripture functions to strengthen our staying power in maintaining and enriching our hope, I prefer the former interpretation.

But since "perseverance" is a quality possessed by the saints and not by the Scriptures, is this objection fatal? Not if we understand the phraseology metonymically, that is, as referring to the models of perseverance that we encounter on the pages of Scripture who, by their steadfast example, inspire us to emulate their perseverance or endurance in the face of the same mysteries and apparent contradictions as confronted them. By such precedents, the Bible has a tremendous fortifying effect on believers battered by the savage storms of life bearing down hard on their feeble faith and possibly eroding its foundations except for the protective seawall of inspirational models who have preceded us in this walk of faith and found God faithful in the end. Besides, it seems to me that if one prefers the former alternative, one still winds up with the second view by a process of inference, for perseverance does not exist independently of the Scripture but is a symptom of faith that is stimulated by the encouragement that the Word of God provides. And the Word of God in the apostle's day consisted, for all intents and purposes, of the familiar OT Scriptures (2 Tim. 3:14-17).

The "comforts" spoken of refer to the glorious outcomes of victorious faith that we, time and again, see in the biblical record, outcomes that reassure us that the sufferings of this present life, including the self-imposed restraints out of consideration of weaker brethren, are nuisances hardly worth a thought considering the glory that God has in store for us.

Consider several implications of this teaching:

The Scriptures are a grace resource designed to bring about the spiritual effects necessary to sustain the believer in life and godliness.

The Scriptures are a living resource that possesses the power to cause what they command, to produce what they prescribe.

The nurture of the Scriptures is the single most formative and effective discipling instrument and strategy in the church's arsenal.

When we neglect the Scriptures, it is the spiritual equivalent of one neglecting physical nurture and the vitamin intake necessary to sustain a healthy body. We cannot neglect the Scriptures and maintain a healthy soul.

There may be dozens of methods and programs which serve successfully as vehicles of biblical nurture, but we must never confuse the delivery system with the substance. It is the assimilation and internalization of the substance that changes lives, not the delivery system. One delivery system might be more suitable for one than another, but all are effective for the same reason, and the unsuccessful are ineffective for the same reasons.

Woody Hayes, the famed but now long-deceased former coach at the Ohio State University, was famous for his smash-mouth style of football. Everybody knew his game plan: three yards and a cloud of dust. Grind it out yard by yard, and wear 'em down. Well, for this pastor and many others the church's equivalent to that strategy is a steady diet of the Word of God. If the Word will not change men, nothing will.

(15:5) *Now may the God who gives perseverance and encouragement grant you to be of the same mind with one another according to Jesus Christ.*

Paul now mixes petition with exhortation, reminding us that, ultimately, it is the Spirit of God, working in conjunction with His revealed Word, who causes us to will and to do of His good pleasure.

Prayer moves God, not that He is manipulated by it but because He is pleased by it, especially so when our spirit agrees with His Spirit. Such prayer has almost the force of prophecy in that it sets in motion the answer to the very thing that it appeals for.

"To be of the same mind with one another..." He is not asking God to bring them all to exactly the same opinions about the matters over which their consciences differ but to bring them to the same purpose and devotion, that is, to honor God at any price.

"According to Christ" defines that spiritual concord as that which is consistent with the standard of Christ in his devotion to God... all out for His pleasure and nothing for self.

This prayer shows by implication that the spiritual effects the Scripture produces are owing to the God who is the ultimate author of the Scripture and the cause of its effects on the hearts of men. Scripture is His instrument through His Spirit. The two are bound up together. That is precisely why the Scriptures are more than they appear to be, just letters and words written on pages. More is there than meets the eye. It is a living Word... a powerful Word... sharper than any two-edged sword... penetrating to the deepest recesses of the human heart and consciousness (Heb. 4:12).

Paul thus prays that God will make His Word effective in the hearts of His people. The Word is not magic... it has no power of its own in its dead letter and paper pages. What power it has resides strictly in the fact that the Spirit of God stands behind it... that it is truth. It will take effect only in those hearts that God prepares to receive it and to benefit from it.

(15:6) *That with one accord you may with one voice glorify the God and Father of our Lord Jesus Christ.*

The supreme objective of the family of God is to blend heart and voice in glorifying Him. The strong accommodate the weak because our mission is not to please ourselves but to facilitate and enhance conditions that enable the whole body in one spirit as one great choir to glorify the God who is like Christ and appeared in Him.

"With one accord... with one voice..." (*homothumadon* = with one mind, purpose or impulse).

The one important thing is not whether we agree about all the issues but whether, in heart and in speech, we unite in such a way as to bring glory to God. We bring glory to Him when we emulate the selfless devotion of Christ to Him and to one another and speak to and about one another with charity and for the purpose of building up one another rather than tearing down.

"The God and Father of our Lord Jesus Christ." This phraseology reminds us that Christ and the Father are morally identical and on the same sheet of music in terms of passion and purpose. To honor One is to honor the other, and so with dishonor (John 10:30). As Christ is dedicated to the same principles, passion, and purposes as His Father, it is incumbent upon His followers to get on the same page. How can we do less than Christ? How can we insist on our rights and our liberties at the spiritual expense of others when the glory of God is at stake? That drumbeat is what we are all about.

(15:7) *Wherefore, accept one another, just as Christ also accepted us to the glory of God.*

"Accept..." (*proslambanesthe* from *proslambano*; see this same verb in some form with this meaning in Acts 28:2; Philem. 17).

The context makes it clear that the controversy behind these two chapters was primarily across ethnic lines, that is, a tension between Gentile and Jewish Christians. The latter still feeling bound in conscience to honor scruples formed under the conditioning of the old covenant. Their consciences could not let go of their qualms about these things, even if the ceremonial requirements of the old covenant had been abrogated with the establishment of the new covenant.

Tendency on the part of Gentile believers would be to look down on the Jews for this "silliness," to flaunt their liberty in the face of the Jews and to get tangled up in acrimonious and divisive quarrels with them about these issues. The Jews, on their part, would see Gentile liberty as religious laxity and would be prompt to condemn them for it. The end result would be two hostile camps slandering and rejecting each other as brethren disloyal to the Lord with, ironically, each seeking to glorify Him in their own way.

Paul has explained that this is not an issue of loyalty or laxity. It is an issue of a strong or weak conscience in matters indifferent to God. Each party is doing what they do in thanksgiving and as a tribute to God, even though they are doing opposite things. What they are doing is of no account to God. Why they are doing it... is. Each should recognize and respect what drives the brother on the other side of the conscience fence and agree to be united in the purpose of God to glorify the Father at any personal price.

The summary appeal, then, is for both sides of this tension to accept one another. The argument is from greater to the less. Surely if Christ has accepted us as brethren with all our deficits, how can we shun any fellow believer? The spiritual and moral gap between Christ and ourselves is far greater than between ourselves and any brother. We have no right ever to shun anyone who Christ accepts.

"To the glory of God." This can be connected either with the appeal to accept one another or with the example of Christ. It seems clear to me that the latter is the best construction since the next two verses emphasize not only the form the acceptance of Christ took in the cases of the Jews and Gentiles but also how it served in both instances to glorify God. It should be added, however, that in following His model, we are to include His motive.

(15:8) *For I say that Christ has become a servant to the circumcision on behalf of the truth of God to confirm the promises given to the fathers...*

"For..." Just what is the logic? Is Paul here about to 1) justify his statement that we should accept others, or less directly 2) explain just how Christ accepted Jews and Gentiles, or 3) amplify upon the phrase "to the glory of God"?

The content doesn't seem designed to confirm that Christ accepted us. In fact, that point has already been established. That effort, therefore, would be an exercise in redundancy. Moreover, the language is most circuitous, if, that is, the points and parts of it are even superfluous. Nor does it seem to be a straightforward explanation of how He accepted the Jews or the Gentiles. The information supplied goes well beyond that, in the case of the Jews, and seems to be getting at something else. In the case of the Gentiles, the content is only indirectly concerned with acceptance, but rather, it appears to address one outcome of His work as a servant of the circumcision.

It seems to me better to link verses 8–9 logically to "for the glory of God" and understood as amplifying how God's glory was advanced in Christ's acceptance. Commentators, it seems to me, have generally overlooked the prominence of this motif in this context and the importance Paul attaches to believers getting in alignment with Christ's passion and purpose for the glory of God as the fundamental basis of Christian harmony. That emphasis on glorifying God is there in 15:3 and verse 6 as well as here. It is the motive that drives renunciation of self-gratification in favor of my neighbor's spiritual interests and compels mutual acceptance.

The example of Christ lies not simply in the fact that He accepted us, but more importantly, it seems to me, in the fact that He was consumed by the desire to glorify God. "Zeal for Your house consumes Me" (Psa. 69:9) is the model to which we are directed.

In becoming a servant of the Jews (acceptance is implicit in that), He glorified God by confirming His faithfulness in fulfilling God's promises to their fathers. A second intention (if we rightly construe the grammar of verse 9) was to cause the Gentiles to glorify God for His mercy (acceptance implied again), again in faithful fulfillment of His ancient prophetic word.

Why does Paul bother to explain *how* Christ's acceptance of Jews and Gentiles glorified God? My guess is that in urging them to follow in His steps of obedience, he wishes to remind them 1) that God is always faithful to His Word (which reminder elevates hope), and 2) owing their relationship to God to mercy, the Gentiles are in no position to be arrogant toward the Jews (see 11:17–21 for a clear hint of this tendency he is combatting) and unaccepting. The message is oblique because he is sensitive about appearing too bold in upbraiding the Roman church, a church well-established and one which he personally did not found (cf. 15:14–15).

In the case of the "circumcision," that is, the Jews, Christ stooped to become their servant, not because they intrinsically merited this divine favor but for the sake of demonstrating His faithfulness in fulfilling the promises He graciously made to their fathers. Bottom line: the Jews owe their acceptance by Christ, not to their faithfulness to God but strictly to God's faithfulness to His word of promise. In short, His acceptance of the Jew is unconditional and has nothing to do with personal merit.

"The circumcision" is a metonymical code word for the Jews. Circumcision was a surgical procedure performed on Jewish male babies for religious purposes. It signified the covenant bond that existed between the Jews who walked in the faith of the patriarch Abraham. Those Jews who walked in the faith of Abraham were heirs of the promises embedded in that covenant. Among those promises was the pledge that through Abraham and his seed, the whole world would be blessed, an obvious anticipation of the extension of God's grace through the Jewish Messiah to the Gentile nations. "Circumcision" in this context is apposite because it, more than "Jew," evokes that association between the covenant promises and the blessing of the Gentiles.

"Christ has become the servant of the Jews for the sake of God's faithfulness, in order to establish the divine promises made to the fathers."[420]

"Has become..." (*gegenesthai* from *ginomai*). The perfect tense of the verb accentuates the fact that this standing is more than historical; it continues to this hour.

"Servant..." The humility of Christ is particularly apropos in this context because it is precisely the absence of that spirit that gets in the way of mutual acceptance among believers. The tendency of the strong is contempt toward the weak, and the proclivity of the weak is censoriousness and condemnation of the strong. What is missing is the willingness for the sake of the glory of God to stoop to be our brother's servant.

> He is the servant of the Jewish people, inasmuch as born a Jew, of the seed of David according to the flesh, living almost all His life within the confines of Palestine, limiting His ministry of teaching and healing... almost exclusively to the Jews, He both was in His earthly life and His atoning death, and also still is, as the exalted Lord, the Messiah of Israel. [421]

"On behalf of the truth of God to confirm..." Nearly always in the Scriptures, if not invariably, the idea of "faithfulness" to a standard is embedded in the biblical conception of truth. The benchmark of faithfulness is either the word or character of God. Anything that deviates from that criterion is false. Our idea of truth as conforming to reality is present in the sense that whatever behaviors, attitudes, or doctrines that are consistent with God's Word or character have in that conformity a basis in reality, and those that are incompatible rest on false assumptions about the way things are or the way they work.

"It was in order that God's faithfulness to His covenant promises might be honoured; it was in order that He (Christ) might fulfil the promises made by God to the patriarchs."[422]

> (15:9) *And for the Gentiles to glorify God for His mercy; as it is written, "Therefore I will give praise to You among the Gentiles, and I will sing to Your name."*

The overall thought of these two verses is, I take it, this: Christ's acceptance of them, for the glory of God, was demonstrated when the Son of God laid aside His heavenly dignity, appeared in the world as a man, and reduced Himself to a servant of the circumcision (i.e., he says "circumcision" instead of "Jews" because that seal of their covenant relation with God evokes the memory of God's promises to the fathers implicit in it) for the sake of God's faithfulness that 1) He might confirm the promises God made to the fathers and that 2) the Gentiles might glorify God for the sake of His mercy.

The original in verse 9 is grammatically difficult to link up with what precedes. None of the proposed resolutions is without problems. However, since stylistic objections are among the least secure objections (and I myself am far less certain that this construction in Greek would be the "stylistic horror" that Cranfield feels it is), I favor this way to construing the syntax, for it yields, it seems to me, by far, the best sense in context.

It demonstrates not only that Christ has indeed accepted both Jews and Gentiles but shows by implication how that acceptance is perfectly gratuitous, owing nothing to their merits or worthiness but aimed entirely at glorifying God. In the case of the Jews, he stooped to become their servant in order that God's faithfulness might be confirmed with respect to the promises he had made to their fathers and secondly (and consistent with those same promises) in order that the Gentiles might be saved, brought into the community of faith, and glorify God for His mercy.

Why go into all this complicated explanation of the roots and motives of His acceptance? I think to show the Gentiles that their acceptance hinged on His acceptance of the Jews and to stress to the Jews that embedded in His promises to the fathers was the anticipation that He would save the Gentiles.

We must not reject those who God accepts, disown those whom God owns, or dispraise those who, with them, worship the God and Father of our Lord Jesus Christ. Accept one another, then, and do it with the glory of God in view.

"As it is written..." In the early church, tension, as noted before, between Jews and Gentiles sometimes ran high. It was crucial that each learned to value the other in the sight of God as co-equals and co-heirs of the kingdom of God. The Apostle rings the changes because this issue was really a big deal at the time.

For the assurance of the Gentiles in the mercy of God and to help Jews accept them, Paul goes to some length to establish the fact that their salvation is linked to the same faithfulness for which the Jews themselves praise God. He cites a series of OT passages, where we find prophetic hints and anticipations of the inclusion of the Gentiles in the family of God. All of this is part and parcel of God's faithfulness to the patriarchs.

The citations below reflect mainly the Greek version of the OT, the Septuagint, which was the text with which the vast majority of the early church was familiar.

Here, David, speaking under the influence of the Spirit, uses language that anticipates the work of his descendant, the Messiah, who will conquer His enemies and (by implication) make the name of God known *among the nations*.

"Therefore I will give praise to You among the Gentiles, and I will sing to Your name" (Psa. 18:49; 2 Sam. 22:50).

(15:10) *And again he says, "Rejoice, O Gentiles, with His people"* (Deut. 32:43).

Moses, early on, used language in connection with His song praising God for His triumph over Pharoah that bespeaks redeemed Gentiles united with the Jews in celebrating the God of Abraham, Isaac, and Jacob.

(15:11) *And again, "Praise the Lord all you Gentiles, and let all the peoples praise Him"* (Psa. 117:1).

This brief call to praise implied the partnership of redeemed Gentiles with the Jews in the community of the people of God.

(15:12) *And again Isaiah says, "There comes the root of Jesse, And He who arises to rule over the Gentiles; In Him shall the Gentiles hope"* (Greek version of Isa. 11:10).

An explicit prediction that the Messiah will also embrace the Gentiles and will rule over them as Lord and King, and they will place their hope in Him. This series of verses emphasizes that the Gentiles are indeed acceptable to God, that He is pleased to acknowledge them and their worship.

If He has so mercifully accepted them, then they are obliged to accept the Jews through whom the Savior came to them.

All duties become less onerous when hope runs strong... when the prospect of glory stands before our eyes. Then all the aggravations and irritations of this present world diminish in proportion to our confidence in the glory of the next one.

(15:13) *Now may the God of hope fill you with all joy and peace in believing, that you may abound in hope by the power of the Holy Spirit.*

The apostle puts his desire in the form of prayer, for he knows that, ultimately, only God can provide the enablement to override the fleshly barriers to Christian harmony. Prayer in the Spirit, that is, prayer that is according to the will of God, is really a form of prophesy that will, in its time, in God's way, take effect. This is not an empty wish dressed up as prayer.

"The God of hope..." The God who gives hope, or the God in whom we hope? Both are true, but, here, the concern is enriching hope, and the first option best suits the context.

"Fill you with all joy and peace in believing...," that is, cause you to abound in every legitimate form of joy and peace while trusting in God as you await the outcome of your salvation.

Christian "joy" is that externally unaccountable gladness that the Spirit of God gives even in the presence of pain and the absence of temporal pleasures.

Christian "peace" is that externally unaccountable sense of security and well-being that the Spirit of God gives, also like joy in the presence of pain and disaster, and the absence of those protections that men usually require to sustain such feelings.

That you may abound in hope by the power of the Holy Spirit.

Elevated levels of joy and peace are part of the causal equation in intensifying Christian hope. The power of the Spirit of God is the key to that result. For the Spirit works in us to cause us to will and to do of God's good pleasure (Phil. 2:13). Paul calls for the exertion of His power in ways that will direct us into the paths that lead to heightened joy and peace.

"Abound in hope..." Hope is the expectation element of Christian faith. Without it, there is no faith. However, it is subject to elevation and intensification. It should grow in strength in the normal course of Christian living as the power of the Spirit exerts itself. So, he asks that God will, through the presence and power of the Holy Spirit, increase incrementally and intensify their "original equipment" (hope).

Now that God has extended the Christian hope to the Gentiles, Paul's prayer is that now He will enrich it in them.

(15:14) *And concerning you, my brethren, I myself also am convinced that you yourselves are full of goodness, filled with all knowledge, and able also to admonish one another...*

Since Paul did not personally found the church in Rome, and since it also was well-established by this time, with capable Christian leadership of its own and presumably well-grounded in the faith, Paul, ever sensitive to human nature and not wanting to seem condescending and paternalistic in his boldness to instruct a congregation he had never even visited, goes out of his way to reassure the Roman Christians that he acknowledged their competence by the grace of God to deal with the spiritual issues that confronted it. He is compelled not by any want of local competence or out-of-control crisis in their midst but strictly by the authority of His calling to share with them the benefit of the grace God had bestowed upon him as His special envoy to the Gentiles.

"Goodness..." Murray puts it nicely when he defines it in general terms as that which is opposed to "all that is mean and evil and includes uprightness, kindness and beneficence of heart and life." [423] In contextual terms he allows that we may see it as that combination of moral attributes which will "constrain the strong to refrain from what will injure the weak." Similarly, "knowledge" refers to their grasp of the nuances of Christian faith.

"To admonish..." (*nouthetein* from *noutheteo* = to admonish, warn, instruct.[424]

(15:15) *But I have written very boldly to you on some points, so as to remind you again, because of the grace that was given me from God... I have written to refresh your memory, and written somewhat boldly at times (NEB).*

"So as to remind you..." It is not as though he presumes ignorance of all these matters on their part but as a matter of divine calling and personal passion feels the need to remind (*epanamimneskon* = present participle) the saints repeatedly in those areas where the resistance of the flesh is mighty.

His boldness (some might call it presumption) to tell the Roman church how to deal with its internal frictions derives from his God-given office, derives not from any disrespect for the grace and gifts of God operative among them but from God's commission to the Gentiles and His priestly passion to present them to God as an offering acceptable to Him, that is, purified by the sanctifying activity of Holy Spirit indwelling them.

(15:16) *To be a minister of Christ Jesus to the Gentiles, ministering as a priest the gospel of God, that my offering of the*

Gentiles might become acceptable, sanctified by the Holy Spirit.

"A minister..." (*leitourgon* from *leitourgos* = servant, minister, but in the public rather than private sense with the regular connotation in biblical literature of priestly service, specifically.)

Paul sees his ministry in terms of a priestly office. A priest is one officially appointed to offer gifts and sacrifices acceptable to God. The offering Paul is obliged to offer in terms of his special commission is the Gentiles washed and purified in the sight of God. His admonition to the Romans is within the context of that commission and purpose, not with any presumption of ignorance or incompetence on their part. He is not intruding but simply, according to the grace and calling of God, boldly augmenting what God has already given them (cf. Isa. 66:20 for perhaps the source of his perspective on his work).

"Sanctified (*hagiasmene*) by the Holy Spirit." The ultimate cleansing agent and the only one acceptable to God. The aorist participle is used because the emphasis is not on the ongoing process but that positional set-apartness of the justified represented in the indwelling presence of the Holy Spirit. Some Jews may have questioned the acceptability or "cleanness" of Gentile converts, but the gift of the Holy Spirit has qualified them as an offering to God and verified their acceptability (cf. Acts 10:47; 15:8).

Barrett calls attention to the appearance of Trinitarian distinctions embedded here (of Christ Jesus... of God... in the Holy Spirit).[425]

(15:17) *Therefore in Christ Jesus I have found reason for boasting in things pertaining to God."*

Paul is always logical, but at times, his logic challenges because his thought is condensed or elliptic. This is another one of those spots. Amplified, the thought seems to be: "I recognize that I have taken it upon myself to instruct you with surprising boldness for someone who has never even visited you. My calling and office to you Gentiles constrains me. Please do not think that I presume to put myself forward as your minister on the authority of any personal accomplishments on my part.

"Because of the office and calling God has given me, I limit any boasting to the things of God, not the things of Paul. Whatever glorying I do is confined to whatever God has done through me; I do not presume to boast of anything that I have done for God. It is all the other way around. So, I don't come to you to tell you about the great things Paul had done for God; my glorying has to do strictly with what God has through me."

Barrett gives this sense: "Here then is the [basis of] glorying I have in Christ Jesus, in things relating to God."[426]

(15:18) *For I will not presume to speak of anything except what Christ has accomplished through me, resulting in obedience of the Gentiles by word and deed.*

What he glories in is not anything that belongs to him but the things that God has done by His grace through Him.

Barrett says, "The sentence is confused because Paul is trying to say two things at once."[427] He understands those intertwined thoughts thusly:

"I would not dare to speak of this if it were not Christ's work (rather than mine) and I would not dare to speak of this if it were not Christ's work through me (rather than anyone else)."

"Obedience of the Gentiles..." A phrase that refers to the obedience of faith, that is, that form of obedience to God which is faith. Compare John 6:29: "This is the work of God, that you believe in Him whom He has sent." Also, Romans 1:5, "to bring about the obedience of faith among all the Gentiles."

"By word and deed." Paul's ministry consisted in his serving through the Spirit as a conduit of both the words and works of Christ. The latter would include all his endeavors as well as his personal example. The next verse defines the milieu of his words and works, as well as the stage upon which (and the faithfulness with which) they were heard and performed.

(15:19) *In the power of signs and wonders, in the power of the Spirit; so that from Jerusalem and round about as far as Illyricum I have fully preached the gospel of Christ.*

The ministries of Jesus, of Paul, and the other apostles, in addition to others like Philip, were often attended by signs (*semeion-singular form*) and wonders (*tepaton-singular form*). They refer to the same phenomenon but in different ways. Wonders underscore the miraculous nature of them while signs emphasize the spiritual import or significance of those same events.

"In the power of signs and wonders..." that is, God's power manifested in strategic outpourings of signs and wonders.

"In the power of the Spirit..." Since it is mentioned separately, we are probably to understand by "the power of the Spirit," momentous spiritual effects (as in conversion) of the Spirit wrought through Paul other than miracles of the natural realm.

"Fully preached..." (*hoste me. . .peplerokenai to euaggelion*). He had discharged his apostolic commission, that is, covered the bases that the Spirit of God had directed him to.

"From Jerusalem and round about as far as Illyricum..." The accounts in Acts are compressed and do not record every missionary movement of Paul. Although his labors did not technically begin in Jerusalem but from Antioch, we can presume that on some occasion, he did preach there. Nor does Acts record any venture in Illyricum, but there is room for it in the record. In that geographical circle between the two points, he considered himself fully discharged. Now he is prepared to move on to new frontiers.

(15:20) *And thus I have aspired to preach the gospel, not where Christ was already named, that I might not build upon another man's foundation.*

His particular policy is to extend the gospel to those who have never heard it... to establish new foundations, not build upon existing ones. It is not that one is the right approach, and the other is wrong; it is simply a matter of personal calling. Paul's strategy is adapted to his commission.

(15:21) *But as it is written, "They who had no news of Him shall see, and they who have not heard shall understand."*

Compare Isaiah 52:15 LXX (or Septuagint) , where Paul quotes the Greek version of an OT text taken from a context which foresees the humiliation and suffering of God's Anointed One (the Messiah) and previews His eventual exaltation and the extension of His saving embrace to the nations that once did not know him, all to the great surprise and dismay of the astonished rulers of the earth. In that day, people will see something that had never been told them and will understand what they had never heard.

Paul sees his apostolic commission to carry the gospel to the Gentiles who have never heard the gospel, part and parcel of the fulfillment of that prophecy.

(15:22) *For this reason I have often been hindered from coming to you...*

"For this reason. . ." That is, because of his commitment to refrain from redundancy... from consuming valuable time in ministering to churches established by others. His divine mandate was to carry the gospel where Christ was not known.

"Hindered..." thwarted by divine mandate and personal principle or strategy rather than spiritual opposition. To fulfill his ministry and kick a dent in history, Paul had to forego some of the Christian fellowship that he longed for. He had to put limits around his life in order to find the liberty in his life to do God's work. Freedom to minister always involves some self-imposed fetters.

(15:23) *But now, with no further place for me in these regions, and since I have had for many years a longing to come to you.*

"With no further place for me in these regions..." Paul sees his missionary course in the area he described as completed. Now he anticipates the fulfillment of a long-standing desire to visit the capitol itself and minister and be ministered to en route to a new frontier.

"A longing..." (*epipothian* from *epipothia* = a longing, a desire, a yearning).

(15:24) *Whenever I go to Spain—for I hope to see you in passing, and to be helped on my way there by you, when I have first enjoyed your company for awhile...*

"Whenever I go to Spain..." We have no record that God ever allowed Paul to make it to Spain. Tradition has him executed under Nero in Rome. What we don't know for certain is whether he was released from his Roman imprisonment and then re-arrested and where he might have gone in the interim.

"To be helped..." Rome will be an ideal staging area for his venture into Spanish territory, a project in which he will ask their escort and material assistance. He entertains no doubt that they will be ready to support his endeavor there (the verb *propempo* = to accompany, escort or help on one journey, i.e., with food, money, arranging companions, means of travel).[428] His confidence in their sharing his agenda is remarkable. He clearly takes their support for granted. It was common for other churches to furnish escort service (cf. Acts 15:3; 1 Cor. 16:6; 2 Cor. 1:16).

"Enjoyed your company for awhile..." Even apostles need and covet the society of other Christians. John Wesley once said that "Christianity is a social religion; make it solitary and you kill it."[429] Something is amiss when Christians do not gravitate to the company of other Christians.

(15:25) *But now, I am going to Jerusalem serving the saints.*

Right now, he has another priority. The churches in Macedonia and Achaia had heard reports of impoverished saints in Jerusalem, owing perhaps in part to their ostracism from the mainstream of Jewish society and excommunication from the synagogue and partly to the purpose of God in targeting the poor and humble (James 2:5; 1 Cor. 1:26–27; Matt. 5:3) for saving grace. The poor in spirit (humble) most often correspond with the poor in substance.

Paul and his party were messengers to those churches entrusted with their gifts for the poverty-stricken believers in Jerusalem.

(15:26) *For Macedonia and Achaia have been pleased to make a contribution for the poor among the saints in Jerusalem.*

An appeal to the church in Achaia, citing the example of the brethren in Macedonia, regarding a collection for the saints in Jerusalem is found in 2 Corinthians 8–9. Both churches are highly commended for their readiness to contribute despite, in the case of the Macedonia churches, contending with poverty of their own.

"Poor..." (*ptochous* from *ptochos* = originally, begging, dependent on others for support, poor, miserable, beggarly.)[430]

"Have been pleased..." (*eudokeo* = be well pleased, consider good, resolve, determine, to take delight). This was not a grudging offering solicited by apostolic arm-twisting but one that the Macedonians in particular were begging (2 Cor. 8:4) to be allowed to do, and the Corinthian area churches had initiated the idea a year before (8:10).

(15:27) *Yes, they were pleased to do so, and they are indebted to them. For if the Gentiles have shared in their spiritual things, they are indebted to minister to them also in material things.*

The impulse for their generosity was a sense of indebtedness. The saints in Jerusalem shared with them their spiritual wealth; now they felt obligated in their physical need to share with the Jews in Jerusalem their physical means.

"To minister..." (*leitourgesai*). This gift Paul puts in the context of a priestly offering to God. Gifford observes that Paul applies to this ministry to the material needs of the body the same honorable title (*leitourgia*) that he used earlier with reference to the preaching of the gospel. [431]

(15:28) *Therefore, when I have finished this, and have put my seal on this fruit of theirs, I will go on by way of you to Spain.*

"Finished..." The verb *epiteleo* in conjunction with *leitourgeo* ("to minister") has the connotation in biblical literature of performing a priestly function. In this case, it is an offering of thanksgiving to God but received in His name by His needy people.

"Put my seal on this fruit of theirs..." The original is more literally, "sealed to them this fruit." I take it that Paul refers to securing their contribution in the official custody of the intended recipients or their representatives.

"Fruit..." that is, the alms represent a harvest of the work of God in their lives.

(15:29) *And I know that when I come to you, I will come in the fulness of the blessing of Christ.*

Only when Paul has completed Christ's will can he come to them in the full assurance of His blessing. He did come in the fullness of Christ's blessing, but the blessing took the form of a burden, which worked out to the strategic advantage of the gospel (cf. Phil. 1:12–14).

(15:30) *Now I urge you, brethren, by our Lord Jesus Christ and the love of the Spirit to strive together with me in your prayers to God for me...*

Concerted prayer is the best assurance of answered prayer simply because a shared burden of God's people is a supplication most likely to be prompted by the Spirit and, therefore, an expression of the will of God. Moreover, the more saints who own a prayer, the more glory God has at stake in that petition in terms of thanksgiving to be reaped and souls to be strengthened by the exhibition of His power and grace.

"By (*dia* = literally, through) our Lord Jesus Christ and (by = *dia* again) the love of the Spirit..." Christ and His interests represent the common purpose and passion that links their hearts, and the love of the Holy Spirit is fruit of the presence of the Holy Spirit in their lives and the bond that knits Christian hearts together even when they are strangers.

(15:31) *That I may be delivered from those who are disobedient in Judea, and that my service for Jerusalem may prove acceptable to the saints...*

Paul anticipates great hostility from the unbelieving Jews in Jerusalem. Only the power of God can frustrate their designs against him. Unbelief is properly a form of disobedience (cf. John 6:28–29; 1 John 3:23) to the word of God.

Knowing the Jewish prejudices against the Gentiles and the widespread resentment of his mission to them, he cannot help but be apprehensive about how alms from Gentiles might be received. Some might possibly consider this "offering" tainted because it has a Gentile source. Paul's prayer is for God to cause them to find it "acceptable" and the basis of a spiritual bonding between Jews and Gentiles.

(15:32) *So that I may come to you in joy by the will of God and find refreshing rest in your company.*

That prayer answered, Paul anticipates a release by the will of God to visit them with a joyful soul and much needed refreshment in their midst.

"By the will of God" is a reminder that his freedom to make such decisions has always been subject to God's will, not personal whim. He expects now that when his present duty is performed, he will enjoy the liberty to make a visit long postponed by divine priorities but also one that promises a much longed-for renewal.

(15:33) *Now the God of peace be with you all. Amen.*

A prayer that God would provide for their internal harmony and spiritual well-being in Christ. Again, his prayer in the will of God is, in function, though not in form, the apostolic equivalent of a prophetic word. It is a sacred blessing that he is confident will be affirmed by the Spirit of God. As such, it is more than a pious wish but a promise.

"Amen." So be it!

The Travel Plans of an Itinerant Preacher: Some Notes Worth Filing

Romans 15:22–33

I am by no means an amateur naturalist, but nature films like those shown on the cable *Discovery Channel* have always fascinated me.

One of the things that has always impressed me is what a wealth of flora and fauna one discovers in harsh and arid environments that one would think could never sustain life, much less exotic forms of exquisite beauty.

In a similar way, tide pools along the Oregon Coast have always enamored Olsie and me. Who would expect to find so much variety of life trapped in little pools in the rocks after the tide has gone out!

Those phenomena always come to mind in the form of analogies when, in the course of my teaching, I come to passages in the Scriptures that, on the face of it, seem to be dry holes. As a teacher of the Scriptures, some passages challenge me because the subject matter requires so much backgrounding that people have a tendency to jump off the train before I can pull it out of the station. Others scare me because on the face of it, the passage appears to be so barren of substance, so historically particular (i.e., rooted personal matters and in bygone historical circumstances) that they appear on the surface as irrelevant and a sure cure for insomnia. Nothing appears to be there that is capable of sustaining the life of the soul... nothing meaningful is there... it is a dry run... why bother?

Passages of this kind are the sort that prompted students in my preaching classes to ask me occasionally if I believed (I will use my words) that one could draw blood out of the turnips in Scriptures; that is, if all the Scripture was profitable for teaching, correction, reproof, and training in righteousness or just part of it? That is, was some Scripture intended to be nothing more than setup material for the teaching corpus or if, in fact, God had vested even the apparently dry and arid parts with living water.

Though I am inclined to the latter view, one thing I have learned in teaching the Scriptures, particularly this sort: one must learn how to ferret out the principles behind the particulars and see what is implicit in the explicit. That is why I back track here to share with you what I have found here.

Embedded in these ordinary travel notes are kernels of extraordinary lessons. Some are implicit; some are explicit. All are useful anchors to help us think straight when the shifting winds of human opinion threaten to blow us off course. They also act as a kind of *ballast* to keep us and keep our mental ship on keel in the storms of life.

The apostle's personal notes indirectly remind us, for example, that:

1. Freedom always involves fetters.

"For this reason (his strategic purpose to preach Christ to those who had never been reached for Him and thus to not [redundantly build on another's missionary foundation]), I have often been hindered (by this mission strategy) from coming to you (in Rome)" (verse 22).

The hindrance Paul refers to was the limitation his ministry mandate imposed upon his choices. His freedom to choose fellowship, support, and comfort that he longed for was restrained by the demands of God's calling and direction. The freedom to serve God means that we must throw fetters around self-gratification. Moses had to make this choice (Heb. 11:24–26).

This point brings into focus a broader life principle that applies across the board... a reality that is lost on libertarians who think of freedom as the liberty to do whatever I want to do anytime I want to do it. That sort of freedom is a myth. The paradox of Christian liberty is that it involves limitations. Think about this: freedom is purchased at the high price of fetters.

Think of any freedom you want. Whatever choice you make of necessity eliminates other choices. The key is to recognize this and make sure that we know what choices we are making and that we are not purchasing the freedom to do the wrong things at the expense of the right ones.

For example, in the political realm, without some legal restraints, there would be anarchy. However, as Martin Luther somewhere

476

pointed out, anarchy does not make the rebel freer of tyranny. It just replaces one with a hundred.

Freedom to serve Christ always involves some self-imposed fetters. To be free to minister, God calls some of His servants to withdraw from the marketplace... from the quest for financial and material security and to devote themselves full-time to advancing His kingdom. To do that, God has ordained that the Church undertake the support of His servants that they themselves have had to depend upon God to provide (1 Cor. 9:14).

This freedom to minister involves imposing upon oneself fetters that narrow one's options. I don't know of anything worthwhile and difficult to accomplish or perform well that does not involve narrowing the compass of one's life. The freedom to devote oneself to what is important...critical...meaningful, means that we must restrain ourselves and not try to do everything.

So, in exercising our freedom, spiritual, political, or personal, we always have to make choices that limit us in one way so we can have freedom in another way. It is rarely possible to have our cake and eat it too.

What are your priorities in life? Is your priority to be a disciple of Christ? You have all kinds of freedom, but there are limits as to the choices you can make. So, also, parents need to make some choices for themselves and their families about what fetters they are going to put around themselves and their kids. If you are determined to be out playing or visiting or whatever half the time, you are putting some fetters on your ability as a disciple to grow and serve and be a force and so on.

2. The more one is invested in the things of Christ, the more one appreciates being around other disciples of Christ.

"I have had for many years a longing to come to you whenever I go to Spain—for I hope to see you in passing, and to be helped on my way there by you, when I have first enjoyed your company for awhile..." (verse 23–24).

It is never a real good sign about where a person is if they do not gravitate first and foremost to the company of the saints. The absence of that law of attraction suggests that maybe one does not resonate as much with the people of God as with the people of the world. Flies go to a corpse, and bees go to honey.

3. Poverty is no stranger in God's family and may even be a servant to His purpose.

"But now (before I come to Rome) I am going to Jerusalem (the other direction) serving the saints. For Macedonia and Achaia have been pleased to make a contribution for *the poor* among the saints in Jerusalem" (v. 26, italics mine).

First, let's acknowledge, poverty or indigence or financial deficiency can be a self-inflicted wound. If we didn't know it from experience, the book of Proverbs would remind us redundantly. Sometimes people are flat imprudent with what God gives them. They spend more than they bring in. And when your outgo exceeds your income, then what you have is going to be less than you need. You're in trouble. People sometimes get in that fix through circumstances beyond their control and need the help of those who have means. Other folks are lazy, lack initiative, and pay the price that slugs usually pay. The chickens come home to roost, and they eat slugs.

But that is not the whole story. In God's providence, God allows believers sometimes to taste indigence, as were the saints back in Judea. They were being ostracized and discriminated against socially and economically. Their means were sorely challenged to say the least. The whole circumstance brings to mind 1) the lie of this prosperity theology currently pervasive on these religious cable channels, teaching that God promises abounding health and material wealth to those bold enough to believe God for it, and 2) temporal fiscal deficiency may be a testing from God (i.e., to test the faith of those in need in the goodness and faithfulness of God and to test Christian love of those who have means to see if we are the real deal or just a bag of pious gas).

So, poverty among God's people may even be a result of faith (so here and Heb. 11:37).

Poverty is an opportunity for growth. Remember the poor widow and her son who lacked means when Elisha came along (2 Kings

4:18).

Poverty represents an opportunity to serve (so here).

Let us remember this: Heaven is not on a gold standard. Wealth and poverty are not measured in heaven by the same criteria as they are measured on earth. Earth's paupers may be heaven's princes. Kings parading around us may be curs in the sight of God.

There is no discrepancy between temporal poverty and the blessing of God. The true measure of wealth is an inheritance in heaven, not a bankroll on earth.

Material prosperity is not a sin in itself, but it creates conditions inimical to faith and dangerous to the health of the soul.

4. By the way, as a general principle, we might say that until there is hip service, there is only lip service (verses 26–27).

"Saints in Macedonia and Achaia (Greece) have been pleased to make a contribution for the poor among the saints in Jerusalem. Yes [he emphasizes], they were pleased to do so."

Saints who are not pleased to be able to help those in need, most especially those of their own Christian family, may be suspected of being "aints."

There is no way that one can be a faithful servant of God who is unwilling to be good steward of God's benefits. The two go hand in hand. And no way can I be a good steward of the assets God has put in my trust if I am unwilling to share those resources with God's needy people (first) and help underwrite the cost of doing His work on earth.

Yes, there are people who will throw generous amounts of money at people and projects who are not good servants of Christ, but there are no good servants of Christ who will not rise up, as they are able and acquainted with the need, and do something for God's people and God's projects. If you were a pastor for very long, you would figure that out in a hurry.

Without hip service, there is only lip service.

5. Those who have material means are obliged to share with those who share with them in spiritual things.

Respecting the offering of the (largely) Gentile churches in Macedonia and Achaia and being sent to assist the (largely) poor saints in Jerusalem, Paul says this is more than a matter of Christian charity; it is a matter of obligation:

"For if the Gentiles have shared in their spiritual things (i.e., the Jewish believers in Jerusalem when the gospel of Christ went forth to the Gentile world), they (the Gentile believers) are indebted to minister to them also in material things" (15:27).

Nothing has changed about that. It says something pretty condemning about those churches who expect so much of their pastors, complain so much about them, and compensate them so poorly that they barely have a subsistence level of income, forcing them, oftentimes, to have to moonlight to exist. Shameful.

In the four ministries I have had, salary was never an issue. If there is any thing that makes me uneasy about a pastor, it is when money or salary is a big issue. The minute I hear that, a big red flag is planted in my mind.

However, there was one occasion when I was invited to be the pastor of a church of 1500 in Kansas (this was c. 1975, I would guess). They informed me that my salary would be $15,000, which was more than I was making teaching at the Bible college in Denver. I flat turned it down without another look. Why? That salary for a church of that size told me that that body lacked any sense of this principle Paul lays down. It told me that they did not really appreciate those who devoted their lives to sharing with them the most important things in the world—the spiritual food of the Word of God.

6. Only when we go forth and do Christ's bidding can we go forth and expect His blessing.

"Therefore, when I have finished this, and have put my seal on this fruit of their (their material gift he views as a fruit of godly love—a fruit of the Spirit), I will go on by way of you to Spain. And I know when I come to you, I shall come in the fulness of the blessing of Christ" (verses 28–29).

7. Concerted prayer is the best assurance of answered prayer.

"Now I urge you, brethren, by our Lord Jesus Christ and by the love of the Spirit to strive together with me in your prayers to God for me, that I may be delivered from those who are disobedient (i.e., unbelieving) in Judea, and that my service for Jerusalem (carrying back there this offering from the Gentile churches) may be acceptable (not insulting) to the saints; so that I may come to you in joy by the will of God and find refreshing rest in your company (v. 30–32).

- Concerted prayer is the best evidence of praying in the Spirit.

- Concerted prayer opens more windows for honoring God.

- In elevating the faith of God's people.

- In showcasing the provision of God.

- In multiplying prayers of thanksgiving.

8. God's blessing often wears the face of a heavy burden.

"That I may be delivered from those who are disobedient (i.e., unbelieving) in Judea..." (v. 31).

---

[410] Cranfield, *ICC: Romans, Vol. 2*, 731.

[411] Arndt & Gingrich, *Greek-English Lexicon of the New Testament*, 136-37.

[412] Hodge, *Epistle to the Romans*, 432.

[413] Arndt & Gingrich, *Greek-English Lexicon of the New Testament*, 105.

[414] Hodge, *Epistle to the Romans*, 432. Hodge cites an unidentified writer.

[415] Ibid, 432.

[416] Ibid, 432.

[417] Hodge, *Epistle to the Romans*, 433.

[418] Calvin, *The Epistles of Paul to the Romans and Thessalonians*, 304.

[419] Ibid, 304.

[420] Cranfield, *ICC: Romans Vol. 2*, 740.

[421] Ibid, 741.

[422] Ibid, 741-742.

423 Murray, *NICNT: The Epistle to the Romans, Vol. 2,* 209.
424 Arndt & Gingrich, *Greek-English Lexicon of the New Testament,* 546.
425 Barrett, *The Epistle to the Romans,* 275.
426 Ibid, 275.

427 Ibid, 276.
428 Arndt & Gingrich, *Greek-English Lexicon of the New Testament,* 716.
429 https://www.ccel.org/ccel/wesley/sermons.v.xxiv.html, accessed 10/21/2023
430 Arndt & Gingrich, *Greek-English Lexicon of the New Testament,* 735.
431 Gifford, *Romans,* 229.

Romans Chapter 16

The Bible is dry only for those who don't know how or where to look for its water. There are wells where one would least expect to find them. Any decent interpreter and gifted expositor *must have an eye for implications*, that is, be able to draw out 'new' knowledge from ' old' knowledge or, put another way, to see under the skin of the text. That aptitude, as I learned from my teaching experience, is far less common than one might think.

Way back in my seminary days (in my case, just before the Civil War), one of my professors, Howard Hendricks, a gifted teacher by all accounts, illustrated in one famous assignment, the "detective" mentality needed to be a good expository preacher.

As the end of one class approached, "Howie," as he was familiarly called by students, gave us an assignment for the next class.

"Gentlemen, your assignment. Take Acts 1:8 and scrutinize it carefully. Only Acts 1:8. Nothing outside those parameters. Next, class, bring back a list of twenty-five exegetical observations in this one verse."

My goodness, there were only (as I recall) a mere thirty-seven words, including articles and prepositions in that one text! A collective groan. We dispersed and came back next time with our respective lists of observations. Granted, some of them were a bit sketchy, a reach, one might say. We had exhausted ourselves with that assignment. Then Howie called on various of us to give the fruits of our labor.

"Good job, men!"

"Now for the next class, I want you to take the same verse and come back with twenty-five more observations."

Collective apoplexy. Mission impossible.

Yet, believe it or not, we dug, we scratched, we pulled and tugged on that text, and somehow, most of us managed to surface twenty-five more textual 'observations' that we had overlooked earlier. Most

DTS students never forgot that one assignment. It taught us that when we came to the Scriptures, put on laser eyes and look deeper.

I bring up that experience because before us is a chapter (16) that, on the face of it, probably strikes the average reader as a classic "dry hole," a dead ringer for boring people to death, somewhat like biblical genealogies or what Hendricks used to call "the pots and pans" chapters.

That would be a great mistake.

So, in winding up this exposition of Romans, I seize this opportunity to show you there is always more there than meets the eye. If the content of Romans 16 seems irrelevant for us believers and churches today, we just are not observing too well. As "detectives," we would fail miserably. There is in fact quite a bit of personal and contemporary relevance in this chapter.

Fishing for insight in the Scriptures sometimes reminds me a great deal of steelhead fishing in Oregon streams. One inexperienced might think that the chances of finding big fish in shallow waters (like creeks) are next to nil. Yet I, a real novice, once pulled out steelhead from such unpromising streams.

Let's unpack it and see what I mean.

> (16:1) *I commend to you our sister Phoebe, who is a servant of the church which is at Cenchrea...*

Mention of Phoebe occurs only here in the NT record.

"Commend..." (*sunisteme* = present, introduce or recommend someone to someone else) suggests that Phoebe, enroute to Rome on some business, personal or spiritual, personally delivered Paul's letter to the Roman church. She was a member of the church in Cenchrea, which was proximate to Corinth and, likely, closely connected with the church there.

Cenchrea was one of two seaports in the neighborhood of Corinth, one opening to the east and the other to the west. Cenchrea was located in the Saronic Gulf situated on the east side. This was the port from which Paul set sail when he was enroute to Jerusalem to deliver the alms collected from the saints in Macedonia and Achaia, to relieve the poor in Jerusalem.

Phoebe is a name associated with the Greek god Apollo, a passive vestige of her pagan heritage. As it was only a popular cultural name and bore no religious significance for her, there was no need to storm a deserted fortress by changing it. For similar pagan christenings, also note Narcissus and Hermes in verses 11 and 14, respectively.

Noting some of these pagan birth names in this roster of believers reminds me that we should devote our attention to attacking Satanic strongholds, not wasting our energies shadow boxing in deserted fortresses. Over my long years in the ministry, I have noted how some will get all hung up on ancient historical roots of some Christian tradition or practice, roots that are long forgotten in our day and bear no real significance in our time, yet they will make a federal case of something like the origins of a Christmas tree or such. It seems to me that we have too many serious fish to fry than looking for pagan ghosts in our attics (if I may mix a few metaphors).

We shouldn't whip people up into a frenzy to go out and smite dead horses or scorch the earth where a deceased monster used to stand.

NT precedent is warrant for not re-investing old customs or traditions with a pagan significance that they no longer contain.

"Who is a servant..." (*diakonon* = servant, minister). Regarding this word, S. F. Hunter remarks that:

> "Servant" is too vague and "deaconess" is too technical. In the later church there was an order of deaconesses for special work among women, owing to the peculiar circumstances of oriental life, but we have no reason to believe that there was such an order at this early period. If Phoebe voluntarily devoted herself "to minister unto the saints" by means of charity and hospitality, she would be called a *diakonos*. She was a servant in the sense that she made herself a minister to others in these respects. It is ambiguous where 1 Tim. 3:11 refers to the wives of deacons or a class of deaconesses, but most likely the former. [432]

(16:2) That you receive her in the Lord in a manner worthy of the saints, and that you help her in whatever matter she may have need of you; for she herself has also been a helper of many, and of myself as well.

"Receive her..." (*prosdechesthe* from *prosdechomai* = receive or welcome.) Hospitality to the saints is a Christian virtue as well as obligation. The "saints" are those set apart as the family of God.

We should receive such as though we are receiving the Lord Himself, for He identifies with them. If we honor the brethren, we honor the Lord. On the other hand, we cannot mistreat the children without mistreating their Father in heaven (cf. Matt. 25:31–46).

"In whatever matter..." Whether her mission in Rome was personal or ecclesiastical is not clear but more likely the former since Paul enlists the carte blanche assistance of the Rome church on her behalf.

"For she herself has also been a helper (*prostasis* = protectress, patron, helper) of many and of myself as well." The Greek noun refers to more than mundane assistance but connotes the kind of benefaction that we associate with a patron. Most likely, Phoebe was one of those more well-to-do people, like Lydia, whom God, in His providence, raised up in a church that was predominantly poor with a hospitable spirit and generous heart. She, too, may have opened her home as a meeting place for the church, accommodated the saints passing through with meals and lodging, and supported those in need out of her more liberal means. She had been a great friend of the saints and because of that one whom she has befriended goes to bat for her in a situation where she will need the same services she has so faithfully rendered to others.

(16:3) Greet Prisca and Aquila my fellow workers in Christ Jesus...

For other NT references to this couple, see 1 Corinthians 16:19, 2 Timothy 4:19; Acts 18:2, 18, 26. Four of the six times, Prisca (Priscilla is the diminutive version) is mentioned first, more likely because she was the dominant personality rather than because of their relative social standing.

On Paul's second missionary journey, in Corinth, he first met this couple, having recently immigrated from Rome when the Emperor Claudius (AD 41–54) issued an edict expelling all Jews from Rome c. AD 52–53. Like Paul, they sustained themselves through the tent making craft, and they got well acquainted working together there. When Paul departed from Cenchrea, Aquila and Priscilla accompanied him (Acts 18:18) on his trip to Jerusalem as far as Ephesus (verse 19). Since Claudius died in AD 54, we can assume that Aquila and Priscilla (as well as many other Jews of Rome) returned home after an interlude in Ephesus between that time and around AD 57 when this epistle was written.

"My fellow workers..." (*tous synergous mou*). It is noteworthy in these salutations that the credentials that gain the apostle's honorable mention have to do with service, not office. Paul salutes players, not pretenders. See this service motif verses 2, 6, 9, 12. We are called to be faithful performers, not distinguished achievers.

Contrast this with contemporary accent on platforming 'leaders.' Is there something wrong with this picture? I think so.

(16:4) *Who for my life risked their own necks, to whom not only do I give thanks, but also all the churches of the Gentiles...*

"Who for my life risked their own necks..." What events or incidents are referred to are not recorded in the book of Acts, which record is a selective, not exhaustive, account of the Acts of the Apostles. Depth of a friendship is often in direct proportion to our sacrifices for others. Friendships too easily won have shallow roots and are easily disturbed and detached.

(16:5) *Also greet the church that is in their house, greet Epaenetus my beloved, who is the first convert to Christ from Asia...*

Aquila and Priscilla opened their Roman home as a meeting place for the believers there. The language suggests that the Roman church was subdivided into house groups. At this time in church history, local houses of worship did not yet exist per se.

"...the church that is in their house. . ." That situation (a house church), note, is simply descriptive of a cultural circumstance, not, as some would make it, a prescriptive model for all time.

"...my beloved..." Someone who had earned the special affection of Paul, if for no other reason than the simple fact that he represented the first harvest of God's fruit in the western provinces of Asia Minor, referred to in ancient times as "Asia."

(16:6) *Greet Mary, who has worked hard for you...*

"Worked hard..." (*ekopiasen* from *kopiao* = to become weary, tired; to work hard, toil, strive, struggle) is a compliment sufficient to immortalize one in the courts of Heaven and the thoughts of the great apostle. The coin (values) of the kingdom of Christ and those of worldly kings and their kingdoms are very different.

(16:7) *Greet Andronicus and Junias, my kinsmen, and my fellow prisoners, who are outstanding among the apostles, who also were in Christ before me...*

"Andronicus and Junias..." Is it Junia or Junias? The Greek text is ambiguous. If a female, then this was doubtless a man and wife. It is quite a reach to put Junias, if female, forward as an official apostle. Feminists will hang their hats on the thinnest of evidence.

"My kinsmen" refers most likely to their mutual Jewishness rather than any blood relations.

"...my fellow prisoners..." We must assume that Paul means this literally, not metaphorically. However, the NT record provides no other information as to the circumstance in which they were imprisoned together for Christ. Sharing His sufferings was and is a badge of honor among the saints, although it is not the credential that commends a pastor to the average search committee for a modern church looking for a few good men.

As I survey this litany of friends and associates of the apostle who shared in various ways his labors and his passions, what comes to mind is that great friendships are usually purchased with great sacrifice (vv. 2, 4, 13). The people who lay it all on the line for others will find others who will lay it all on the line for them. A true friend like Paul never lacks friends.

"Outstanding among the apostles..." Grammatically, the syntax may mean 1) held in high esteem by the apostles or 2) creme de la creme, that is, exceptional apostles. If the second option is taken, then "apostles" is used in a nontechnical sense of those engaged in missionary activity, as today we might would speak of a husband-and-wife team as "missionaries." However, the term "apostle" is regularly used, it seems, in a technical sense, and this is against a generic usage here when another option is easily available. But some with a feminist agenda, like the mythical Sisyphus, will try to force any boulder up to the top of the mountain if it will service their bias.

(16:8) *Greet Ampliatus my beloved in the Lord.*

Bruce tells us that this name is repeatedly attested as a cognomen of the imperial household, specifically of the Aurelia family.[433] Among the people of God, there are not many noble, but in His mercy, some always appear. Wealth and power, so inimical to humble dependence on God, make it improbable for the rich and famous to enter the kingdom of God, but nothing is impossible with God (Matt. 19:23-24).

(16:9) *Greet Urbanus our fellow-worker in Christ, and Stachys my beloved.*

We know nothing of these saints except that they were sufficiently outstanding in service to merit mention. In the kingdom of God there is a way to be notable without being famous, a way of being outstanding without standing out.

(16:10) *Greet Apelles the approved in Christ. Greet those who are of the household of Aristobulus.*

"Approved" because Paul apparently knew of some circumstance in which Apelles's faith had been through the fire and tested out.

"Aristobulus..." This person most likely was dead since Paul salutes saints representing his household. Cranfield says that this Aristobulus is most likely the grandson of Herod the Great and the brother of Agrippa I, who lived in Rome as a private person and friend of the Emperor Claudius. [434] The reference is to Christians belonging to his household, not assimilated to that of the Emperor's.

(16:11) *Greet Herodion my kinsman. Greet those of the household of Narcissus, who are in the Lord.*

"Herodion" suggests someone with connections to the Herodian family, and "my kinsman" indicates a Jew, not a family member.
"Household of Narcissus" probably refers, Cranfield thinks, to Christian family members of "the notorious freedman of the Emperor Claudius, whose wealth was proverbial... and whose influence with Claudius had been practically unlimited, but who had been forced to commit suicide by Agrippina shortly after Nero's accession and only a year or two before Paul was writing." [435]

(16:12) *Greet Tryphaena and Tryphosa, workers in the Lord. Greet Persis the beloved, who has worked hard in the Lord.*

All three are female names, the first two possibly twins. Who said the apostle and the early church had a low view of women? At least ten women dear to Paul appear in this catalogue of special friends.
What we have in this space is a roll call of royal family members from all over, the Church in capsule. Herein is a good reminder that the Church Universal, not our natural family, not our ethnic tribe, or social or business or political circle, is the most significant and sacred family we believers have. All others are just ghosts and shadows. All others may break up, die off, or betray us. This one sacred family endures forever and most elevates our human dignity and shares a common purpose and singular universal Lord. Let us prize it and safeguard it above all others.

(16:13) *Greet Rufus, a choice man in the Lord, also his mother and mine.*

This Rufus, we assume, is the same one referred to in Mark 15:21 as one of the sons of Simon Cyrene, the civilian passerby who was impressed into service by the Roman soldiers to bear the cross under which Jesus faltered after His beatings and abuse at the hands of the soldiery.

God used that brief and disagreeable providential detour in his plans to change the life of him and his family forever and to inscribe his name not only in history but, more importantly, to write it down in heaven. Initially, Simon bore the cross of Jesus by force of the Roman will but soon by force of Christian conviction.

"His mother and mine." Rufus's mother was as good a mother to the apostle, I take it.

(16:14) *Greet Asyncritus, Phlegon, Hermes, Patrobas, Hermes and the brethren with them.*

We know nothing of these five men except that they stood out for mention in the apostle's mind. That passing mention for Christian posterity is as good as an Olympic medal in the race of faith.

(16:15) *Greet Philologus and Junia, Nereus and his sister, and Olympas, and all the saints who are with them.*

The same goes for these individuals. Their enrollment here is their resume, however, where distinction is concerned. More godly women noted with apostolic admiration.

(16:16) *Greet one another with a holy kiss. All the churches of Christ greet you.*

We learn from Justin, the Apostolic Father, that "after prayers we salute one another with a kiss." [436] Others like Tertullian and Origen refer to the same practice; a custom, I imagine, a bit like a friendly handshake in Western culture.

The fact that Paul had so many dear friends in a church that he didn't found and had never visited is eloquent testimony to the confluence of people moving to and from Rome during this era. It also bears witness to the swelling impact of his missionary enterprise as well as to the providential reward of his many sufferings and sacrifices with a host of great friends and soul mates in the work of Christ. He always went about his labors with the assurance that many were with him in spirit if not in presence. That reminds us of our Lord's promise to His disciples in Matthew 19:29.

(16:17) *Now I urge you, brethren, keep your eye on those who cause dissensions and hindrances contrary to the teaching which you learned, and turn away from them.*

Ever conscious of the devil's devices, the apostle warns the Roman church against tares, which the enemy might sow among the wheat.

"Keep your eye on..." (*skopein* = to note, watch, keep an eye on). Vigilance is the watch word. To keep one's eye peeled for persons and teachings inimical to the spiritual health of God's people is not an exercise in paranoia, negativity, or lack of charity but a show of pastoral responsibility and care.

Of course, there is always the ill-motivated or unbalanced person who makes a vice of virtue, finds a worm in every apple, and carries vigilance to paranoid extremes. Reaction to such would be an extremity in the opposite direction if we stopped taking our ills to the doctor because of our fear of being labeled a hypochondriac or if a scientist ceased to warn the public of environmental hazards for fear of being dismissed as a jeremiad. The church has a mandate not only to proclaim the truth but to expose those who pervert the truth, import enervating error, which masquerades as the truth.

"On those who cause dissensions (*dichostasias*)..." At the root of the original word is the notion of "standing apart" and then comes to mean dissensions.

"Hindrances" (*ta skandala*) referred originally to the bait stick of a trap, hence a snare or what a snare causes, namely, an obstacle or hindrance.

"Contrary to the teaching which you have learned..." (*para ten didachen hen hymeis emathete*). Those who are to be noted and shunned are those whose doctrines violate the apostolic traditions. To contradict apostolic teaching is to fly in the face of prophetic revelation and, therefore, in the face of reality. That renders these doctrines not only false (by definition) but destructive in effect, for whatever God has made known to us is for our welfare (Deut. 10:12–13).

Bad theology is the spiritual equivalent of bad medicine. And those who promulgate it are the spiritual equivalents of quack doctors.

What the apostle insists upon is unity in the truth, not unity at the expense of the truth. Nowhere do the apostles or prophets place any premium on unity at any cost. Those who stand theologically in the apostolic (orthodox) tradition always represent the unifying center; those who leave that center are the dividers, even when their kind so multiplies that they become the majority and are thereby able to usurp influential positions and take over the institutional structures that do not rightly belong to them. These abominable Ahabs, not the churches' faithful Elijahs, are the real troublers of Israel.

"Teaching you have learned" is a phrase that reminds the church that to recognize error, one first must have an acquaintance with the truth. It has been said that bank tellers learn to recognize counterfeit bills better by familiarity with real currency than from analyzing phony money.

"Turn away from them" (_ekklinete ap auton_). The best way to prevent the spread of the equivalent of a spiritual parasite is to avoid it, not serve as its broadminded host. We ought always to be open to ideas where the truth is not clearly established and, in the case of leaders, seek to understand error, like a medical scientist seeks to understand disease. However, where the truth is clear and the believing Church has spoken, entertainment of contrary ideas is no more of an intellectual virtue than hospitality to the notions that the earth is square, that the sun rotates around the earth, and that the law of gravity is a myth. All those ideas represent regress, not progress, in human understanding. To persist in pushing such notions is not an exercise in free thinking, but non-thinking... in irrationality. For the Christian who believes in divine revelation and takes the position that what the Bible teaches, God teaches, to deviate from those givens, to question those absolutes, is to guarantee that the best man can do is discover pieces of the puzzle but never put the picture together. That is a sure recipe for knowledge without understanding.

(16:18) *For such men are slaves not of our Lord Christ but of their own appetites; and by their smooth and flattering speech they deceive the hearts of the unsuspecting.*

"Such men..." We cannot be sure what specific teaching or teachers the apostle had in mind. Most likely, this warning included any and all of the false doctrines and unsound teachers, Jewish and Gentiles, that, like termites, invaded and fed on the Church from the inside.

Their noxious errors can take different forms, but the common denominators were these:

"Slaves not of our Lord Christ but of their own appetites..." These people are not devoted to Christ, not dedicated to promoting his Lordship but advancing their own self-serving interests. The Church should always understand that religious mercenaries masquerade as Christian ministers and that Satan disguises himself as an angel of light and his servants as servants of righteousness (2 Cor. 11:13–15). See in this connection 1 Timothy 6:3–5.

"By their smooth (*chrestologias* = fair speaking) and flattering speech (*eulogias*)... They talk well... are able, as one Greek writer put it, to make the worse sound like the better reason and aim to please men rather than God (2 Tim. 4:2–3).

Satan crafts his instruments and fits them to stalk and seduce their prey. Satan, whose slaves they are, adapts his teachers to "pitch" the unsuspecting (*ton akakon*). By their self-serving, smooth-talking, crowd-pleasing ways, they seduce spiritual "suckers." Those who get deceived by their clever blandishments are not those who have their guard up but those whose guard is down because they aren't theologically equipped to recognize error when they meet it or because they are not intellectually capable of distinguishing such things or because they are of that naive disposition that tends to take the sincerity of every teacher of granted.

(16:19) *For the report of your obedience has reached to all; therefore I am rejoicing over you, but I want you to be wise in what is good, and innocent in what is evil...*

"For" is logically connected with the appeal for vigilance. His appeal is based on his confidence in their spiritual integrity and the desire to maintain their noble reputation in the cause of Christ. The Roman church cannot take itself for granted. Satan is always reconnoitering the walls, looking for weak defenses and a way to insinuate his errors into the mix to the detriment of Christ and His church.

It is noteworthy that good reputations as well as bad ones have a tendency to follow us. Better the former than the latter. Eventually, a lackadaisical stewardship of the truth would give error a point of entry, and the once good reputation of the Roman church gave way to a bad one that led at last to the necessity of the Protestant Reformation.

"I am rejoicing over you..." Paul is encouraged, not alarmed at all, by what he knows of the church in Rome. His concern is they will maintain their good order and watchfulness so that they will remain wise (_sophous_) with respect to what is good—able to differentiate between good and evil and not susceptible to being taken in when smooth talkers, who make the worse appear the better reason, attempt to change the labels, dismissing good as evil and passing off evil as good (Isa. 5:20). "Wise in what is good" would comprehend, in addition to the ability to discern good and evil, understanding the rightness and outcomes of good as opposed to the wrongness and detrimental effects of evil. On the other hand, he would have them to be guileless (_akeraious_) or simple (in the sense of harmless) when it comes to evil. In short, he wants them to be shrewd in doing good and clueless and unpracticed in performing evil.

> (16:20) *And the God of peace will soon crush Satan under your feet. The grace of our Lord Jesus be with you.*

As an added incentive to keep rank and maintain their obedience, the apostle reminds them that their faith is not in vain. They are on the victory side of the equation. Their adversary and accuser, Satan, will be laid low under their feet.

"The God of peace..." Whenever these functional appellations are added, they always underscore attributes pertinent to the subject matter. In God, we have the source and guarantor of our spiritual safety and welfare. He is called the God of peace because it lies within His power, His purpose, and His promises to deliver us from the power of sin and the malignant designs of the Evil One.

"Will soon crush (*syntripsei en tachei*)..." If Paul were here referring to some specific dissension instigated by instruments of Satan, he would be predicting that God would shortly decisively rebuff Satan. The context doesn't lend much weight to this.

Paul appears to be speaking of the eschatological (end times) victory of the saints and defeat of Satan. Does "soon" imply that he mistakenly believed that the return of Christ was at hand in his own time or that, in God's own time, Satan's defeat would be swift and decisive? The latter. In other words, any 'delay' in the return of the Lord has to do with God's plan, not His powerlessness. This is not a desperate struggle for the upper hand. Whenever the cup is full, God will intervene and crush our adversary at our feet. Most likely, we find an echo of the prophecy of Genesis 3:15 here.

"The grace of the Lord Jesus be with you." A prayer for sustaining grace to stand against the wiles of the devil until such time as God's purposes are served and He brings down the curtain on Satan's evil activities.

(16:21) *Timothy my fellow worker greets you and so do Lucious and Jason and Sosipater, my kinsman.*

Paul's co-workers present with him in Corinth chime in with greetings of their own to the saints in Rome. Timothy is Paul's familiar young protege to whom he addressed two epistles. Lucious is possibly Luke, whom internal evidence in Acts implies was with Paul at this time. Jason, we believe, was the same Jason mentioned in Acts 17:5–9. He was from Thessalonica and became at least temporarily part of Paul's Christian escort service. Likewise, Sosipater is probably a variant of Sosipater, a Jew of Berea.

(16:22) *I Tertius, who writes this letter, greet you in the Lord.*

"Who writes..." Not as the author, but as the amanuensis or secretary to whom Paul dictated. Tertius adds his own greeting but transcends mere formality by adding "in the Lord." His greeting is not a matter of form but real solidarity of purpose and feeling in union with Christ.

That little phrase goes beyond "me too" and says, "I am with you in the calling and purpose of Jesus Christ." Behind his pen, there is passion and purpose.

(16:23) *Gaius, host to me and to the whole church, greets you. Erastus, the city treasurer greets you, and Quartus, the brother.*

(16:24) *[The grace of our Lord Jesus Christ be with you all. Amen.]*

This text does not appear in the most authoritative Greek texts nor in the body of the NIV. After verse 20, it seems redundant. That may explain the rationale for some copyist considering it an accidental repetition of the so-called prayer wish of verse 20 and, therefore, discarding it as the error of a previous copyist.

On the other hand, perhaps a copyist accidentally inserted the formula in verse 20, caught his error, and covered it by dispensing with it at verse 24 since it did not really violate the flow of thought. Who knows. In any event, no precious thought is lost in the textual confusion.

(16:25) *Now to Him who is able to establish you according to my gospel and the preaching of Jesus Christ, according to the revelation of the mystery which has been kept secret for long ages past...*

A doxology is a fitting climax in praise of God, who, having chosen them for salvation, will surely, in accordance with the gospel message and the proclamation concerning the Person and work of Jesus Christ, keep them (i.e., establish them).

"According to the revelation of the mystery..." That good news proclaims our security in Christ is further explicated by this phrase. The gospel is a divine secret once hidden but now fully disclosed in the progress of revelation.

What does this explication add? Simply that the good news was in the old revelation concealed. Let no one stumble over the fact that

God has broken a new seal on the book of His revelation of the plan of redemption.

(16:26) *But now is manifested, and by the Scriptures of the prophets, according to the commandment of the eternal God, has been made known to all the nations, leading to the obedience of faith...*

"By the Scriptures of the prophets..." The good news, in a germinal way, was there in the prophets all along. Only now, in retrospect, do we see the adumbrations of the gospel embedded in the prophetic writings.

The remaining thought, though grammatically tangled, seems to be that the gospel, by divine commandment, no less, has been extended now to the Gentiles *also* with the result that they, too, are yielding obedience to the living God in that form that He requires of us, namely, faith.

(16:27) *To the only wise God, through Jesus Christ, to whom be glory forever. Amen.*

Paul salutes the unfathomable wisdom of God and prays that His glory may redound forever through Jesus Christ. It is in Christ that the Father is most especially glorified, for it is in Him and His work that His goodness is most expansively magnified.

In closing this section, a few accents come to mind in light of it and bells that need to be rung lest our ears are dull.

Whatever we sacrifice on the altar of God's service has a way of coming back to us with interest in a more enduring form.

Nobody ever outgives God. If by coming to Christ, Paul acquired a lot of enemies who were dying to take his life, he also acquired a lot of friends who were willing to give their lives for him. If he was disowned by any kinsmen, he was owned by far more than ever disowned him. If he lost the love of some, he gained a greater love of far more than he ever lost.

In that purer stage of the young Church, we observe that the standing of a person in the ranks is measured (at least by the

Apostles) by their relationship to Christ, not rank in the world, by service rendered to Him, not by office in the Church.

In the kingdom we should measure people differently than the world. Not by their pedigree, or by their wealth or worldly social standing.

People in the early church were more esteemed by service, not office; by performance, not position. That is why women as well as slaves were so highly honored.

The dignity and standing of women were based not on their platform or being in the public eye, but on simple, sacred service.

And I cannot help but notice that Christ's Church is the greatest social leveler on earth. All do not have the same responsibility nor the same function, but every single member shares the same worth, the same dignity, the same sacred purpose without which none of us is anything.

---

[432] *International Standard Bible Encyclopedia, Vol. IV,* 2386.
[433] Bruce, *The Epistle of Paul to the Romans,* 272.
[434] Cranfield, *ICC: Romans Vol. 2,* 791.
[435] Ibid, 792-93.
[436] Justin, *The First Apology of Justin Martyr,* 65.

Epilogue

There you have it. The unvarnished truth, the pure gospel of our Lord Jesus, mediated through the authoritative pen of the great apostle Paul to the first-century church in Rome, the capital of the Roman world.

In its broadest sense, the "Good News" encompasses the redemptive provision of God in Christ Jesus for us sinners. That is its core. However, never forget, the gospel includes what the faithful believer in joyful thanksgiving ought to do for Him. Not, of course, in order to be justified but because we have been saved by God's grace through faith in Jesus the Christ alone.

The latter part is what some contemporary Christians often overlook to the detriment of the gospel and of any credible witness to the world. And that's a huge problem.

Truth matters—big time, all the time.

In my exposition of this cornerstone epistle, I have been at pains to drill down beneath the historical particularity (i.e., the cultural and historical veneers) of the text to expose the bedrock of the author's timeless message. There, gleaming out in the fog, is the core truth for yesterday, today and forever.

My definition of sound expository preaching is to bring the truth of God's Word into collision with the issues of life. There, to use the old cliché, is where the rubber meets the road, and when, as they used to say, the pastor comforts the afflicted and afflicts the too comfortable.

Truth matters, and like true prophets, sooner or later, its proclaimers still get punished, just like those of old.

I would hope that in this commentary, the truth of the gospel in both dimensions has broken through like sunlight at dawn.

Love it, cherish it, and proclaim it in all its timeless promises, principles, precepts, and practices for the good of the Church and the glory of Christ. Don't trim it or add to it. Fearlessly teach it and confidently trumpet it. Forget the timid critics hung up on political correctness, postmodern relativism, or self-preservation. Take the Word and run with it. Never apologize for sticking with it. Be bold in the face of inevitable backlash from the pusillanimous parishioners or from this truth-despising culture.

In the end, we win, and we win big. Meanwhile, we have God's help to stand tall in the face of ignorant opposition. Truth matters. Public approval doesn't.

Bibliography

Abbott-Smith, G. 1921. *A Manual Greek Lexicon of the New Testament.* 3rd. Edinburgh: T. & T. Clark.

Arndt, William F., and Gingrich, F. Wilbur. 1952. *A Greek-English Lexicon of the New Testament and Other Early Christian Literature.* Chicago: The University of Chicago Press.

Bainton, Roland H. 1955. *Here I Stand: A Life of Martin Luther.* New York: New American Library.

Barrett, C.K. 1957. *Harper's New Testament Commentaries: The Epistle to the Romans.* Edited by Henry Chadwick. New York: Harper & Row.

Brown, F., Driver, S., Briggs, F. 1906. *Hebrew and English Lexicon.* Peabody, Massachusetts: Hendrickson Publisher's Marketing, LLC.

Bruce, F.F. 1963. *Tyndale New Testament Commentaries: The Epistle of Paul to the Romans.* Edited by R.V.G. Tasker. Grand Rapids: Wm. B. Eerdmans Publishing Company.

Calvin, John. 1973. *Calvin's New Testament Commentaries: The Epistles of Paul to the Romans and Thessalonians.* Edited by David W., and Torrance, Thomas F. Torrance. Translated by Ross Mackenzie. Grand Rapids: Wm. B. Eerdmans Publishing Company.

Cranfield, Charles E.B. 1975. *The International Critical Commentary.* Edited by J.A. Emerton and C.E.B. Cranfield. Vol. II. Edinburgh: T. & T. Clark.

—. 1975. *The International Critical Commentary: Romans.* Edited by J.A. Emerton and C.E.B. Cranfield. Vol. I. Edinburgh: T. & T. Clark.

DeYoung, James B. 1988. "The Meaning of "Nature" in Romans 1 and its Implications for Biblical Proscriptions of Homosexual Behavior." *Journal of the Evangelical Theological Society,* December: 429.

Epstein, Joseph. 1989. *Ambition: The Secret Passion.* United States: Elephant Paperbacks.

Gifford, E.H. 1886. *Romans.* London: John Murray.

Godet, Frederic. 1883. *Commentary on St. Paul's Epistle to the Romans.* Translated by A Cusin. New York: Funk & Wagnalls.

Harrison, Everett F. 1976. *The Expositor's Bible Commentary: Romans.* Edited by Frank E. Gaebelein. Vol. 10. Grand Rapids: Zondervan.

Hodge, Charles. 1886. *Commentary on the Epistle to the Romans.* Grand Rapids: Wm. B. Eerdmans Publishing Complany.

Lewis, C.S. 1962. *The Problem of Pain.* New York: MacMillan Publishing Co.

Liddon, H.P. 1961. *Explanatory Analysis of St. Paul's Epistle to the Romans.* Grand Rapids: Zondervan Publishing House.

Lloyd-Jones, Martin. 1973. *Romans: The Law: Its Functions and Limits.* Grand Rapids: Zondervan.

Martyr, Justin. 1912. *The First Apology of Justin Martyr.* Translated by John Kaye. Edinburgh: John Grant.

Moulton, James, and George Milligan. 1960. *The Vocabulary of the Greek New Testament.* Grand Rapids: Wm. B. Eerdmans Publishing Company.

Murray, John. 1959. *The New International Commentary on the New Testament: The Epistle to the Romans.* Edited by F.F. Bruce. Vol. 1. 2 vols. Grand Rapids: Wm. B. Eerdmans Publishing Company.

—. 1965. *The New International Commentary on the New Testament: The Epistle to the Romans.* Edited by F.F. Bruce. Vol. 2. 2 vols. Grand Rapids: Wm. B. Eerdmans Publishing Company.

Nygren, Andrew. 1949. *Commentary on Romans.* Phildelphia: Fortress Press.

Ridderbos, Herman. 1975. *Paul: An Outline of His Theology.* Translated by John Richard De Witt. Grand Rapids: Eerdman's.

Robertson, Archibald, and Plummer, Alfred. 1911. *The International Critical Commentary: 1 Corinthians.* 2nd. Edited by Samuel Driver, Alfred Plummer and Charles Briggs. Edinburth: T. & T. Clark.

Sanday, William, and Headlam, Arthur. 1895. *The International Critical Commentary: The Epistle to the Romans.* 5th. Edited by Samuel Driver, Alfred Plummer and Charles Briggs. Edinburgh: T. & T. Clark.

Smyth, Herbert Weird. 1956. *Greek Grammar.* Cambridge, Massachusetts: Harvard University Press.

Stifler, James M. 1960. *The Epistle for the Romans.* Chicago: Moody Press.

1992. *The Apocrypha, New Revised Standard Version.* Cambridge: Cambridge University Press.

Trench, Richard. 1960. *Synonyms of the New Testament.* 9th. Grand Rapids: Wm. B. Eerdmans Publishing Company.

Various. 1984. *Evangelical Dictionary of Theology.* Edited by Walter Elwell. Grand Rapids: Baker House.

Vine, W.E. 1966. *Expository Dictionary of the New Testament.* Westwood, N.J.: Fleming H. Revell Company.

Von Logau, Friedrich, quotation. 1959. *The Oxford Dictionary of Quotations.* 2nd. Translated by Henry Longfellow. Oxford: Oxford University Press.

Wesley, John. n.d. *ccel.org.* Accessed October 21, 2023. https://www.ccel.org/ccel/wesley/sermons.v.xxiv.html.

.